The Elections of 2016

The Elections of 2016

Michael Nelson

EDITOR

Rhodes College

Los Angeles | London | New Delhi
Singapore | Washington DC | Melbourne

FOR INFORMATION:

CQ Press
An Imprint of SAGE Publications, Inc.
2455 Teller Road
Thousand Oaks, California 91320
E-mail: order@sagepub.com

SAGE Publications Ltd.
1 Oliver's Yard
55 City Road
London, EC1Y 1SP
United Kingdom

SAGE Publications India Pvt. Ltd.
B 1/I 1 Mohan Cooperative Industrial Area
Mathura Road, New Delhi 110 044
India

SAGE Publications Asia-Pacific Pte. Ltd.
3 Church Street
#10-04 Samsung Hub
Singapore 049483

Printed in the United States of America

ISBN 978-1-5063-7808-4 (pbk)

This book is printed on acid-free paper.

17 18 19 20 21 10 9 8 7 6 5 4 3 2 1

Acquisitions Editor: Matthew Byrnie
Editorial Assistant: Zachary Hoskins
Production Editor: Tracy Buyan
Copy Editor: Amy Marks
Typesetter: Hurix Systems Pvt. Ltd.
Proofreader: Annette Van Deusen
Cover Designer: Rose Storey
Marketing Manager: Jennifer Jones

Contents

Preface

"A massive landslide victory, as you know, in the Electoral College"? Despite Donald Trump's postelection claim to have won one, not really. From 1788 to 2016, forty-five of fifty-eight presidential elections were decided by a larger electoral vote majority than Trump's 306–232 victory over Hillary Clinton (304–227 after seven "faithless electors" voted for a different candidate than the one to whom they were pledged). In only four other elections did the winner not also secure more votes from the people than did his opponent.

But a surprise? Absolutely. At every turn of the election calendar, from June 16, 2015, when Trump announced his candidacy, until well into the evening of election day—November 8, 2016—political analysts of every stripe were confident that Donald Trump would not be the forty-fifth president of the United States. His candidacy wouldn't last long enough even to contest the Iowa caucuses and New Hampshire primary, they—we—all said. When it did, we agreed, he certainly wouldn't be the nominee of the Republican Party. And, once nominated, he was sure to lose the general election. The Princeton Election Consortium's forecast model gave Clinton a 99 percent chance of winning; the *Huffington Post* forecast gave her a 98 percent chance.

The luster of Trump's victory was undermined to some degree by his loss of the national popular vote to Clinton by a margin of nearly three million votes. But as in baseball, where games are decided not by how many hits a team has but by how many runs, Trump won a clear (if not massive) victory in the Electoral College.

The presidential election was not the only one whose outcome surprised the experts. Most observers forecast that the results of the Senate elections, in which the Republicans were forced to defend more than twice as many seats as the Democrats, would turn control of that chamber from the Republican to the Democratic Party. Wrong again. The Democrats gained but two seats, not the five they needed to secure a majority. Predictions for the House elections generally were that the Democrats would gain about fifteen or twenty seats, bringing them within striking distance of a majority, perhaps in 2018. That didn't happen, either. They gained a paltry six seats, leaving the GOP in control of a united party government: the White House and both houses of Congress.

The Elections of 2016 is the ninth in a series of postelection books by eminent scholars that began in 1984. Understanding why the elections turned out as they did is an important enterprise. Thus, in Chapter 1 Michael Nelson considers the broadening of the presidential talent pool that guaranteed that on election day the nation would choose either its first woman president or its first career businessman. In Chapter 2 William G. Mayer recounts the presidential nominating process that in 2016 generated the candidacies of the Republican Trump and the Democrat Clinton. In Chapter 3 Marc J. Hetherington carries forward the narrative and analysis through the general election campaign that ended on November 8, 2016. Nicole E. Mellow assays the regional, demographic, and other bases of voter behavior in Chapter 4. Marjorie Randon Hershey chronicles the rapidly changing role of the media in Chapter 5, and Marian Currinder examines the equally transformed campaign funding landscape in Chapter 6.

Understanding the consequences of the elections for politics and government is also an important task. Gary C. Jacobson in Chapter 7 and Paul J. Quirk in Chapter 8 write revealingly about the election campaign and results. But their main concerns are for how in coming years the elections will affect Congress and the presidency, respectively. The same is true of the book's final chapter, in which Andrew Rudalevige assesses the additional challenges confronting Trump, Congress, and the nation.

On behalf of myself and the other contributors, I offer much-deserved thanks to the outstanding editorial, production, and marketing teams at CQ Press for the assurance, skill, warmth, enthusiasm, and helpfulness with which they worked on this book. We especially thank executive editorial director Charisse Kiino, production editor Tracy Buyan, copy editor Amy Marks, and editorial assistant Zachary Hoskins. As editor of the book, I am also grateful for the reviews of previous works in this series by Andrew Battista (East Tennessee State University), Jeffrey Crouch (American University), John Dinan (Wake Forest University), Dorothy B. James (Connecticut College), and Kevan M. Yenerall (Clarion University).

Michael Nelson
January 2017

About the Editor

Michael Nelson is the Fulmer Professor of Political Science at Rhodes College and a senior fellow of the University of Virginia's Miller Center. In 2015, the American Political Science Association gave Nelson the Richard E. Neustadt Award for the Outstanding Book on the Presidency and Executive Politics published during the previous year for *Resilient America: Electing Nixon in 1968, Channeling Dissent, and Dividing Government*. He and coauthor John Lyman Mason, won the Southern Political Science Association's 2009 V.O. Key Award for Outstanding Book on Southern Politics for *How the South Joined the Gambling Nation: The Politics of State Policy Innovation*. Nelson's coedited and coauthored volume, *42: Inside the Bill Clinton Presidency,* was a featured selection of the History Book Club. He has published articles in multiple political science journals, including the *Journal of Politics*, *Presidential Studies Quarterly*, and *Journal of Policy History*, as well as writing on a range of topics, including sports, music, and religion, for periodicals such as the *Weekly Standard* and *Claremont Review of Books*.

The Elections of 2016 is the ninth in a series of postelection books that Nelson has edited beginning in 1984. His other books for CQ Press include *The Presidency and the Political System,* tenth edition; *The American Presidency: Origins and Development, 1776–2014,* seventh edition, with Sidney M. Milkis; *The Evolving Presidency,* fifth edition; *Guide to the Presidency and Executive Branch,* fifth edition; *Debating the Presidency: Conflicting Perspectives on the American Executive,* with Richard J. Ellis, fourth edition; and *Debating Reform: Conflicting Perspectives on How to Fix the American Political System,* third edition, with Richard J. Ellis.

About the Contributors

Marian Currinder is policy director for U.S. government accountability at Transparency International USA. Previously she was senior fellow and curriculum director at the Government Affairs Institute at Georgetown University. She was an assistant professor of American politics at the College of Charleston from 2003 to 2006, and an American Political Science Association Congressional Fellow from 2003 to 2004. She has published several journal articles and book chapters on congressional politics and campaign finance and is the author of *Money in the House: Campaign Funds and Congressional Party Politics* and coauthor of *Congress in Context.*

Marjorie Randon Hershey researches and writes about political parties and campaigns in the United States. Her most recent book is *Party Politics in America*, 17th ed. She also examines media coverage of campaigns and election results. She has published scholarly articles in *American Journal of Political Science*, *Journal of Politics*, *Political Communication*, and other professional journals and has received several teaching awards.

Marc J. Hetherington is professor of political science at Vanderbilt University. He specializes in the study of political trust and party polarization in the electorate. He has published three books: *Why Washington Won't Work: Polarization, Political Trust, and the Governing Crisis* (with Thomas J. Rudolph); *Authoritarianism and Polarization in American Politics* (with Jonathan D. Weiler); and *Why Trust Matters: Declining Political Trust and the Demise of American Liberalism.* He has also published numerous articles in a variety of political science journals, including the *American Political Science Review, American Journal of Political Science,* and *Journal of Politics.* He received the Emerging Scholar Award from the Elections, Public Opinion, and Voting Behavior Section of the American Political Science Association in 2004 and has won numerous teaching awards.

Gary C. Jacobson is Distinguished Professor of Political Science, Emeritus, at the University of California, San Diego, where he taught from 1979 until 2016. He specializes in the study of U.S. elections, parties, interest groups, public opinion, and Congress. He is the author of *Money in Congressional Elections, The Politics of Congressional Elections,* and *The Electoral Origins of Divided Government;* the coauthor of *Strategy and Choice in*

Congressional Elections and *The Logic of American Politics;* and the author of more than 100 research articles. His most recent book is *A Divider, Not a Uniter: George W. Bush and the American People.*

William G. Mayer is professor of political science at Northeastern University in Boston. He is the author or coauthor of ten books, including *The Front-Loading Problem in Presidential Nominations*, *The Making of the Presidential Candidates 2016*, and *The Swing Voter in American Politics*. He has also written numerous articles on such topics as voting, public opinion, and media and politics.

Nicole E. Mellow is professor of political science at Williams College, where she teaches classes on American political development, the presidency, political parties, American state-building, and political geography. In addition to articles on parties, political geography, and political leadership, she is the author of the books *The State of Disunion: Regional Sources of Modern American Partisanship,* and with Jeffrey K. Tulis, *Legacies of Losing in American Politics* (forthcoming). She is currently working on a book about eugenics and Progressive Era state-building.

Paul J. Quirk holds the Phil Lind Chair in U.S. Politics and Representation at the University of British Columbia. He has published widely on the presidency, Congress, public opinion, and public policymaking and has received the Aaron Wildavsky Enduring Contribution Award of the Public Policy Section of the American Political Science Association and the Brownlow Book Award of the National Academy of Public Administration. He is coauthor of the book chapter "Reconsidering the Rational Public: Cognition, Heuristics, and Mass Opinion" in *The Elements of Reason*, edited by Lupia, McCubbins, and Popkin. His chapter on presidential competence appears in the 10th edition of *The Presidency and the Political System*, edited by Michael Nelson.

Andrew Rudalevige is Thomas Brackett Reed Professor of Government at Bowdoin College and chair of the Presidents and Executive Politics Section of the American Political Science Association. His books include *Managing the President's Program: Presidential Leadership and Legislative Policy Formulation,* which won the Richard E. Neustadt prize; *The New Imperial Presidency: Renewing Presidential Power after Watergate;* as well as the coauthored textbook *The Politics of the Presidency* and a series of edited volumes on the Bush and Obama presidencies. Rudalevige writes frequently on executive power and national politics as a contributor to the *Washington Post*'s "The Monkey Cage" blog; he is also the creator of *Founding Principles,* a series of videos on American government and civics available on the Bowdoin College website and as a PBS LearningMedia resource. Before entering academe, he was a city councilor and state senate staffer in his native Massachusetts.

1

The Setting

Broadening the Presidential Talent Pool—for Better and Worse

Michael Nelson

Every four years, candidates, consultants, commentators, and, yes, political scientists proclaim the historic nature of the current presidential election. America stands at a crossroads, we solemnly intone, and our nation is at a critical turning point. Usually we are wrong. Most elections are ordinary affairs. But not the election of 2016.

From the beginning, 2016 promised to be one of the most wide-open contests for president in all of American history. For only the second time since George Washington was chosen unanimously as the first president in 1788, it was clear from the outset that neither the incumbent president nor the incumbent vice president would be on the ballot. Barack Obama, like George W. Bush in 2008, was barred from seeking a third term by the Twenty-second Amendment's two-term limit, which was added to the Constitution in 1951. Most recent vice presidents have made a run for the presidency, but Vice President Joe Biden announced more than a year before the election that he would not be a candidate.

The 2016 election was also wide open in a different, more significant way. Never before had a major political party nominated a woman, a Jewish American, or a candidate older than seventy-three. Yet the two leading Democratic contenders were former New York senator and secretary of state Hillary Clinton, a woman (not to mention a recent first lady), and Sen. Bernie Sanders of Vermont, a Jew who was seventy-four years old. The field of Republican contenders was equally unprecedented for that party: it included three candidates with no experience in government (physician Ben Carson and business leaders Donald J. Trump and Carly Fiorina), an African American (Carson), two Latino Americans (Sen. Marco Rubio of Florida and Sen. Ted Cruz of Texas), and an Indian American (Gov. Bobby Jindal of Louisiana). By late summer, after the parties held their nominating conventions, the general election ballot guaranteed that the United States would elect either its first woman president (Clinton) or its first lifelong businessman (Trump). The sum of the two major-party nominees' ages was the largest in history: 139 (Trump was seventy and Clinton was sixty-nine). This guaranteed that on January 20, 2017, the United States would inaugurate either its oldest or second-oldest newly elected president.

To demonstrate just how remarkable the 2016 election was in the breadth and variety of its pool of candidates, I review the record of the previous two and one quarter centuries of presidential elections to see what answers history long provided to the question of who can be president—that is, what kinds of people have any realistic chance of being elected to the office. I also describe and analyze how that record was transformed by the events of several recent elections, including the elections of 2016. Finally, I briefly assess the ways in which the broadening of the presidential talent pool contributes to and detracts from the presidential selection process.

Who Can Be President? The Constitutional Answer

The first answer to the question of who can be president is in the Constitution, which was written in 1787, ratified in 1788, and implemented in 1789. Article II, section 1, paragraph 5 states:

> No person except a natural born Citizen, or a Citizen of the United States, at the time of the Adoption of this Constitution, shall be eligible to the Office of President; neither shall any Person be eligible to that Office who shall not have attained to the Age of thirty five Years, and been fourteen Years a Resident within the United States.

Why the Framers chose to include this list of qualifications—thirty-five years or older, natural-born citizen, and fourteen years a resident—is hard to explain.[1] The recorded debates on presidential qualifications at the Constitutional Convention of 1787 are meager. The delegates labored through the first three months of the convention without any apparent interest in establishing qualifications for president. Then, on August 20, Elbridge Gerry of Massachusetts moved that the convention's Committee of Detail recommend such qualifications. Two days later, it did: the president "shall be of the age of thirty five years, and a Citizen of the United States, and shall have been an Inhabitant thereof for Twenty one years."[2] On September 4, the newly formed Committee on Postponed Matters offered a revised recommendation, changing "Citizen of the United States" to "natural born Citizen" and "Twenty one years" to "fourteen years a resident." Although no debate or explanation accompanied Gerry's motion or either committee's recommendations, the convention unanimously approved the Committee on Postponed Matters version on September 7.

Why did the delegates decide, late in the game, to insert qualifications for the presidency into the Constitution? Although they never said as much, their actions throughout the convention manifested a consistent principle: a constitution that states qualifications for those who fill an office need not state qualifications for the office itself, but a constitution that states no qualifications for the electors must do so for the elected. In the case of Congress, the need for a qualifications clause for members was agreed on from the beginning. Conversely, in the case of judges, ambassadors, consuls, ministers, heads of departments, "inferior officers," and other public officials mentioned in the Constitution, no qualifications ever were stated or even proposed. None were needed, the delegates seemed to assume, because these individuals would be selected by constitutional officials for whom qualifications had been established.

The presidency received more varied but no less principled treatment from the delegates. During most of the convention they remained wedded to the idea that the chief executive should be chosen by the legislature. Because age (twenty-five for representatives, thirty for senators), citizenship (at least seven years for a representative, and at least nine years for a senator), and residency (in their state, in either case) requirements were included for members of Congress, the delegates saw no need to establish any for the president. They believed that constitutionally qualified legislators could be counted on not to select an unqualified president.

By midsummer, however, the tide of opinion in the convention clearly had turned against election of the president by Congress. Although it took until September for the Framers to agree that presidents would be chosen by the Electoral College, one thing was certain: however the president was chosen, it would not be by an electorate for which the Constitution stated qualifications. Hence, the logic behind Gerry's motion on August 20 to establish qualifications for the presidency, the two committees' prompt responses, and the convention's willingness to adopt a presidential qualifications clause without controversy.

Such qualifications would have to be high, in the delegates' minds, because of a second principle they deemed relevant: the greater the powers of an office, the higher the qualifications for holding that office must be. Just as senators had to satisfy stiffer eligibility requirements than House members, so would the president have to be more qualified than senators: five years older and five years longer a resident of the United States. As for the requirement that the president be a natural-born citizen, it was not only steeper than the unadorned citizenship requirement for legislators, but it also helped to solve a political problem that the delegates anticipated as they considered how to get the Constitution ratified by the states.

The Framers realized that the presidency they were creating was the closest thing in the new constitution to a king. During the summer, rumors spread across the country that the delegates were plotting to import a foreign prince—perhaps even Frederick, Duke of York, the second son of King George III—to rule the United States. So vexatious did the situation become that the delegates momentarily lifted the convention's veil of secrecy with a leak to the *Pennsylvania Journal*:

> [August 22] We are informed that many letters have been written to the members of the Federal Convention from different quarters, respecting the reports idly circulating that it is intended to establish a monarchical government, to send for [Frederick] &c. &c.—to which

> it has been uniformly answered, "though we cannot, affirmatively, tell you what we are doing, we can, negatively, tell you what we are not doing—we never once thought of a king."[3]

However effective the delegates' squelching of this rumor may have been, they knew that the mere presence of an independent executive in the Constitution would prompt further attacks on its latent monarchical tendencies. If nothing else, they could defuse the foreign-king issue by requiring that the president be a natural-born citizen.

The final reason for setting a special citizenship requirement for the president was the office's power as commander in chief. With troops at his disposal, it was feared that a foreign subversive serving as president could seize tyrannical power or lay down American arms before an invading army. John Jay of New York sent a letter to this effect to George Washington, the president of the convention, on July 25:

> Permit me to hint, whether it would not be wise and reasonable to provide a strong check on the admission of foreigners into the administration of our National Government, and to declare expressly that the commander in chief of the American Army shall not be given to, nor devolve upon, any but a natural born citizen.[4]

One cannot be certain when Washington read Jay's letter or what effect it had. The record shows, however, that on September 2 Washington replied to Jay, "I thank you for the hints contained in your letter."[5] Two days later, the Committee on Postponed Matters recommended that the president be "a natural born citizen or a citizen of the U.S. at the time of the adoption of this Constitution," a sharp departure from the Committee of Detail's recommendation, made on August 22, that the president merely be "a Citizen of the U.S."

How does the Constitution's presidential qualifications clause affect the nation's choice of its president? Chiefly by eliminating (in the 2010s) about 60 percent of the population from eligibility: the 146 million who are younger than thirty-five, the 11 million who are undocumented immigrants, and the 29 million who are either naturalized citizens or legal immigrants eligible for citizenship.[6] Partly, too, by muddying the waters of presidential eligibility. "Natural-born citizen" is an especially murky term. At the time the Constitution was written, two meanings could be found in the English common law from which the term was borrowed: *jus sanguinis*, which held that anyone whose parents were citizens was a natural-born citizen, and *jus soli*, which held that one had to be born on a nation's soil to gain this status. American law is more helpful. The Naturalization Act of 1790, for example, provided that "the children of the United States that may be born beyond the sea, or out of the limits of the United States, shall be considered as natural-born citizens."

The effects of the qualifications clause were felt in 2016. Trump had risen to national political notoriety in 2011 by challenging Obama's bona fides as a natural-born citizen and demanding to see his birth certificate, fueling the so-called birther controversy. In an interview with Bill O'Reilly of Fox News, Trump said that even if Obama had an American birth certificate, "maybe it says he's a Muslim," mistakenly implying that this would make him constitutionally ineligible if it was true.[7] (It wasn't.) A year after the president released the document in April 2011, Trump tweeted that "an 'extremely credible source' has called my office and told me that @BarackObama's birth certificate is a fraud."[8] Trump claimed he had dropped the issue by 2016, but when asked in January by CNN's Wolf Blitzer where he thought Obama was born, he said, "Who knows?"[9] In a YouGov poll released that month, 53 percent of Republicans answered "not" when asked if "Obama was born in the United States, or not?"[10] By suggesting that Obama, an African American, was also a foreigner and a Muslim by birth, Trump arguably was stirring three dark strains in American political culture: racism, xenophobia, and Islamophobia.

Trump also raised questions about Senator Cruz's eligibility to be president. Although anyone born to a U.S. citizen is automatically a citizen by birth, Trump argued that because Cruz was born in Canada and only his mother was a U.S. citizen, Cruz's eligibility was "very precarious."[11] "Ted Cruz is an anchor baby in Canada," Trump added, using a crude term to suggest that Cruz's mother wanted him to be born with Canadian citizenship.[12] Legal scholars found this argument to be "specious," the term used by former solicitors general Neal Katyal and Paul Clement in a *Harvard Law Review* article on the subject.[13]

Who Can Be President? Career Background

The answer the Constitution provides to the question of who can be president is not very useful. About 140 million Americans were constitutionally qualified to be president during the 2010s, according to the most recent census. Far more important historically was an unwritten requirement of experience that included recent, prominent service in government. Nearly everyone elected or even nominated by a major political party for president since the founding has been a current or former senator, governor, vice president, general, or cabinet member.[14] Unlike the constitutional qualifications, this requirement was never debated at the convention, much less codified in law. Instead, it emerged from the habits and preferences of the American people. These habits and preferences were challenged in 2016, especially among Republican voters.

The relative value of each of the traditional career background credentials to would-be presidents has varied over the years in response to changing public expectations. In the early nineteenth century, secretary of state was the leading stepping stone to the Executive Mansion. Starting with Thomas Jefferson, four consecutive presidents held this office between 1801 and 1829. From then until 2012, however, only three secretaries of state were even nominated by a major party, none of whom were serving at the time and none at all since 1884.[15] Indeed, the only cabinet members of any kind to be nominated for president in the twentieth century were chosen about a century ago: Secretary of War William Howard Taft in 1908 and Secretary of Commerce Herbert Hoover in 1928. Hillary Clinton's experience as Obama's first-term secretary of state ended shortly after the 2012 election and, like that of Jefferson and the other early occupants of the position, was preceded by several years in elective office, in her case as a twice-elected senator from New York.

Military general was another much-valued credential for candidates seeking the presidency prior to the twentieth century. Washington, Andrew Jackson, William Henry Harrison, Zachary Taylor, and Ulysses S. Grant all became famous throughout the country as generals. After that, only World War II Supreme Allied Commander Dwight D. Eisenhower was able to use his army service as a presidential springboard. Gen. Wesley Clark sought the Democratic nomination in 2004 and Gen. David Petraeus was a much-discussed potential Republican candidate in 2016. But Clark's bid foundered in the primaries and Petraeus's prospects were undone by scandal.

What modern cabinet members and generals have in common is that they are unelected officials, most of them inexperienced and often uninterested in political campaigning. This was no barrier in the eighteenth and nineteenth centuries, when party leaders controlled the presidential nominating process and nominees did not campaign publicly to get elected. Subsequently, the rise of primaries, joined to new public expectations that candidates run rather than stand for office, placed cabinet members and generals at a disadvantage. Even former general Colin Powell, who was enormously popular in 1996, chose not to undergo the ordeal of a modern presidential campaign. "I never woke up a single morning saying, 'Gee, I want to go to Iowa'," Powell told an interviewer.[16] Hillary Clinton, in contrast, was an experienced vote seeker, having campaigned for Bill Clinton, her husband, in more than a half-dozen elections in Arkansas and two for president of the United States, as well as for herself in two successful Senate elections and a nearly successful campaign for the Democratic presidential nomination in 2008. Many of Clinton's political problems as a candidate in 2016 actually stemmed from her service as secretary of state, notably her improper use of a private email server and her hesitancy in responding to a mob's fatal attack on the American diplomatic compound in Benghazi, Libya.

Except for Taft, Hoover, and Eisenhower, every president elected from 1876 to 2012 was a current or former senator, governor, or vice president. Each of these offices allows candidates to make a distinctive claim about their qualifications for the presidency. Governors, like presidents, have been chief executives. Senators, like presidents, have dealt with national and international issues. Vice presidents, although lacking independent responsibilities, have stood first in the line of presidential succession and, in most cases, were senators or governors before they became vice president. Even the Libertarian Party, which since its formation in 1972 had frequently nominated candidates with little or no prominent political experience, acknowledged the electoral appeal of traditional credentials by choosing two former governors to head its ticket in 2016: Gary Johnson of New Mexico and Bill Weld of Massachusetts. The added credibility they brought to the party helped to raise the Libertarian vote from its usual 1 percent or less in presidential elections to 3 percent.

Over the years, the persuasiveness of the competing claims by senators, governors, and vice presidents waxed and waned. Governors dominated presidential elections in two periods: 1900–1932, when four of seven presidents were governors, and 1976–2004, when four of five presidents were. Compared to state governments, the government in Washington was relatively unimportant during the first period, which preceded the federal government's rise to prominence after the New Deal, and was unpopular during the second, in the aftermath of the Vietnam War and Watergate crisis. Senators, in contrast, dominated the post–New Deal, post–World War II era. In the twelve-year stretch from 1960 to 1972, all eight major-party nominees for president were either senators or vice presidents who had served in the Senate. In 2008, both major parties nominated senators for president: Democrat Barack Obama of Illinois and Republican John McCain of Arizona. Both candidates, however, stressed their independence from congressional "politics as usual."

The vice presidency became a leading stepping stone to a presidential nomination when the Twenty-second Amendment was added to the Constitution. By imposing a two-term limit on presidents, the amendment freed second-term vice presidents to campaign actively for president themselves. Richard Nixon in 1960, George H. W. Bush in 1988, and Al Gore in 2000 each won his party's presidential nomination at the end of his second term as vice president. That pattern was interrupted when George W. Bush and Barack Obama chose vice presidents whose presidential ambitions were thought to be in the past and who therefore could serve them free from political distraction. "When you're getting advice from somebody . . . ," said Bush, explaining his choice of Vice President Dick Cheney, "if you think deep down part of the advice is to advance a personal agenda, . . . you discount that advice."[17]

In preparation for the 2016 election, having sought the Democratic nomination twice before without ever exceeding 2 percent of the vote in any primary or caucus, Vice President Biden considered running again for president. But he badly trailed Clinton and Sen. Bernie Sanders of Vermont in fall 2015 polls and was actively discouraged from entering the race by most party leaders and by President Obama. When Biden was slow to take the hint (his son Beau's dying wish was that he run one more time), Obama sent campaign aide David Plouffe to tell the vice president he did not want to see his career "end in some hotel room in Iowa with you finishing third behind Bernie Sanders."[18] Soon after, Biden announced that he would not run. Restoring the previous pattern of vice presidential selection, both Clinton and Trump chose running mates—Sen. Tim Kaine of Virginia and Gov. Mike Pence of Indiana, respectively—who were young enough (Kaine, age fifty-eight, and Pence, age fifty-seven) that a future presidential candidacy was entirely possible for either or both of them.

Historically, presidential candidates from outside government made only an occasional appearance on the national scene. In 1940, seeking to thwart Franklin D. Roosevelt's quest for a third term, the Republicans nominated business executive Wendell Willkie. In both 1984 and 1988, civil rights leader and ordained minister Jesse Jackson made a determined run for the Democratic nomination. In 1992 and 1996, another well-known business leader, Ross Perot, ran strongly as an independent candidate. None were elected, but a certain *Mr. Smith Goes to Washington*–style romance seemed attached to the idea of finding a president outside the usual political channels. The October 1967 issue of *Esquire* magazine, for example, featured a large photograph of industrialist J. Irwin Miller under the heading "This Man Ought to Be the Next President of the United States." The accompanying article offered a long list of university, corporation, and foundation leaders who were said to have the "honesty, high purpose, and intelligence to be elected president of the United States."[19]

In 2016, the Democrats followed the traditional pattern, limiting their choice to two high-ranking government officials—Clinton and Sanders. Even the announced candidates whose campaigns failed to ignite fit the traditional profile: former governor Martin O'Malley of Maryland, former senator Jim Webb of Virginia, and former governor and senator Lincoln Chafee of Rhode Island. "Make a virtue of her longevity," urged the Clinton campaign's communications director in an internal memo. "Embrace all the Clinton-ness—the forty years in politics, the decades on the national stage."[20]

The GOP went in an entirely different direction. None of the nine former or current governors in the race—including those who held the position in major states such as Texas, Florida, New York, Ohio, New Jersey, Virginia, and Wisconsin—gained much traction for their candidacies. Of the five current or former senators who ran, only Cruz remained in the contest as late as March 16. None of these high-ranking officials led in polls of Republican voters at any point during the twelve months preceding the GOP convention.[21] In fact, the only candidates who ever did hold the lead in this period were retired pediatric neurosurgeon Ben Carson (briefly) in the summer of 2015 and businessman Donald Trump from that point on.

Trump's candidacy was initially regarded as a "sideshow" by mainstream media outlets. On the morning of his announcement, "anchors on CNN and elsewhere openly doubted that he would actually run."[22] The *Huffington Post* refused for months to "report on Trump's campaign as part of [our] political coverage. Instead we will cover his campaign as part of our entertainment section."[23] Yet Trump's attractiveness as a candidate in 2016 stood squarely at the confluence of two roaring political rivers: the mood at his party's grassroots and his iconoclastic, celebrity-based personal appeal. The ascendant Tea Party movement within the Republican Party that had helped the GOP win control of the House of Representatives in 2010 and the Senate in 2014 was not just anti-Washington, the national sentiment that had elevated governors above senators in most presidential elections since 1976. It was anti-government in all its forms. As someone who had never held public office, Trump could appeal to primary voters as a complete outsider committed to clean up "the mess in Washington" or, in his more vivid phrase, to "drain the swamp." Trump was already well known as a best-selling author of braggadocious business books, a frequent talk show guest, the host of the popular NBC television series *The Apprentice* and *Celebrity Apprentice,* and an occasional character in blustery World Wrestling Entertainment (WWE) staged confrontations. Former Florida governor Jeb Bush and Hillary Clinton are "controlled by those people," declared Trump, referring to wealthy individuals and interest groups. "Trump has none of those people. I'm not controlled. I do what's right for the people."[24] On the eve of the campaign, in a September 2015 *Washington Post*/ABC News poll, 58 percent of Republicans said they would prefer "someone from outside the existing political establishment" to "someone with experience in how the political system works."[25] "Do you want someone who gets to be president and that's literally the highest-paying job he's ever had?" asked Trump, whose Secret Service codename was "Mogul."[26]

Trump's freewheeling comments on a whole range of issues and rival candidates impressed many voters as evidence of "authenticity," undiluted by normal political constraints. Exceeding the bounds of previously accepted political rhetoric, Trump dismissed Republican opponents Cruz as "Lyin' Ted," Rubio as "Little Marco," and Bush as "low-energy," and labeled Democrats Clinton and Sanders as "Crooked Hillary" and "Crazy Bernie"—all of which delighted his massive crowds and the hordes of blue-collar Republicans who supported him in the primaries. So did Trump's promises to halt illegal immigration from Mexico, which he said "is sending people that have lots of problems. . . . [T]hey're bringing drugs, they're bringing crime. They're rapists."[27] In addition to promising to "build a great, great wall on our southern border" and "have Mexico pay for that wall," Trump demanded repeal of the North American Free Trade Agreement and a "total and complete shutdown of Muslims entering the United States."[28] Of the "at least 11 million people that came in this country illegally," he said, "They will go out."[29] In the global war on terror, Trump declared, "Torture works. . . . Water boarding is fine, but it's not nearly tough enough."[30]

To the white working-class voters who had gradually been moving from the Democratic Party to the GOP since Richard Nixon was elected president in 1968, the Republican leadership's longstanding support for entitlement reform, restrictions on abortion, an assertive foreign policy, and free trade was tolerable at best, objectionable at worst. These voters had supported nominees such as McCain, Romney, and the Bushes despite, not because of, the party orthodoxy on these issues. They cheered when Trump said that Social Security and Medicare "are here to stay" and "I'm not going to cut [them] like every other Republican," declared that "millions of women are helped by Planned Parenthood," claimed that former Republican president George W. Bush "lied" about weapons of mass destruction as a pretext for waging war against Iraq in 2003, and favored protectionist trade policies.[31] With their income, security, and social status in gradual decline, blue-collar whites applauded Trump's attacks on the "political correctness" that they saw as conferring privileged status on racial and ethnic minorities. As for Trump's wealth and professed willingness to pay for his own campaign, these were widely interpreted by grassroots Republicans as evidence that he could not be bought.[32]

Trump's inexperience as a candidate who had not been vetted in previous campaigns was tested in the general election when the electorate included Democrats and independents as well as Republicans. Only 23 percent of Democratic voters and 40 percent of independent voters said they preferred "outside" status to political "experience." When Trump attacked Clinton in their third debate by saying, "The one thing you have over me is experience, but it's bad experience, because what you've done has turned out badly," Clinton rejoined, "He raised my thirty years of experience. . . . On the day when I was in the Situation Room, monitoring the raid that brought Osama bin Laden to justice, he was hosting 'Celebrity Apprentice.' So I'm happy to compare."[33] As Trump's performance demonstrated in all three fall debates, during which he had to hold the floor for a combined two hours as compared with the relatively few and scattered minutes that were his share of the multicandidate Republican primary debates, his knowledge of public policy appeared skin deep at best. Indeed, the one aspect of the presidency Trump seemed to look forward to—the one most closely related to his business career—was negotiating deals with foreign leaders.[34]

None of these limitations prevented Trump from being elected president. Many voters cut him the kind of slack concerning language and behavior that they more readily accord to celebrities from the entertainment world (not to mention the world of professional wrestling) than to career politicians. "I could stand in the middle of Fifth Avenue and shoot somebody and I wouldn't lose voters," he claimed, an exaggeration that contained a grain of truth.[35] To be sure, election day exit polls showed that among voters who regarded having "the right experience" for the office as "the most important candidate quality" in making their choice, 90 percent supported Clinton. By contrast, only 8 percent of those voters supported Trump. But among the roughly twice as many people who placed the highest value on electing the candidate who would bring "needed change" in government, 83 percent voted for Trump, compared to the 14 percent who voted for Clinton.

Remarkably, 20 percent of those who said Trump lacks "the temperament to serve effectively as president" voted for him, along with 21 percent of those who said he is not "honest and trustworthy" and 18 percent of those who said he is not "qualified to be president."[36]

Who Can Be President? Social Background

Even among those potential presidential candidates with the requisite career background to be taken seriously, a further set of criteria long defined the field of eligible contenders: the social background characteristics traditionally associated with presidents.

From the first presidential election in 1788 to the fifty-fifth presidential election in 2004, every president—indeed, every major-party nominee for president—was white. In addition, all were men and at least nominally Christian. All were older than forty and younger than seventy at the time of their inauguration. Taken together, barriers of race, gender, religion, and age prevented more than half of the adult population and a large share of its political leaders from being seriously considered for the presidency.

Not every lesson from this long history was discouraging even at the time, however. Starting in the latter half of the twentieth century, a host of other longstanding social barriers to the presidency fell. In a book published on the eve of the 1960 presidential campaign, the distinguished political scientist Clinton Rossiter offered a catalog of historically grounded "oughts" and "almost certainly musts" for would-be presidents that included: "northerner or westerner," "lawyer," "more than forty-five years old," "less than sixty-five years old," "Protestant," "a small-town boy," and "a self-made man."[37]

None of these barriers remained standing by year's end. In November 1960, forty-three (not forty-five) year-old John F. Kennedy, a rich (not self-made), urban (not small-town), Roman Catholic (not Protestant) candidate with no law degree, was elected president. Subsequently, from 1964 to 2012, southerners Lyndon B. Johnson, Jimmy Carter, George H. W. Bush, Bill Clinton, and George W. Bush won seven of thirteen presidential elections. Five of the nine presidents in this era—Johnson, Carter, Reagan, and both Bushes—were not lawyers. Reagan was divorced ("an ought not to be" on Rossiter's list of the country's unwritten rules). The class backgrounds of these presidents could not have been more varied. The Bushes were born into wealth; Johnson, Carter, and Gerald R. Ford grew up in middle-class families; and Nixon, Reagan, Clinton, and Obama were sons of the working class. Obama was African American. Two women, Democratic representative Geraldine Ferraro of New York in 1984 and Republican governor Sarah Palin of Alaska in 2008, were nominated by their party for vice president in this period and one, Hillary Clinton, nearly won the Democratic presidential nomination in 2008. In 2016, Ted Cruz said that if he secured the GOP nomination, his running mate would be Carly Fiorina.[38]

Barriers typically fell during the half-century beginning in 1960 in one of four ways, most of which were relevant to the 2016 election: vice presidential succession, changing social tolerance, facing the issue, and positive bias.

Vice Presidential Succession

Vice presidential succession to the presidency was one means of toppling social barriers to the presidency. After Whig Party nominee Zachary Taylor of Louisiana was elected in 1848, no southerner was nominated for president by a major party for more than a century. Intense opposition among southern whites to the nationally popular civil rights movement of the 1950s and early 1960s made it seem even less likely that either the Republicans or Democrats would nominate a southerner any time soon. The vice presidency, however, was a different matter. Kennedy of Massachusetts added Johnson of Texas to the ticket in 1960 to help carry the South. Three years later, Johnson succeeded to the presidency when Kennedy was assassinated. Defying regional stereotype, the new president became an ardent champion of civil rights. By the time Johnson ran for a full term in 1964, anti-southern prejudice had nearly vanished from the electorate. Jimmy Carter of Georgia, Bill Clinton of Arkansas, and the two Bushes of Texas won six of the eight presidential elections between 1976 and 2004.

Since Johnson, no vice president has succeeded to the presidency as the result of a presidential death—a remarkable record considering that from 1841 to 1963 presidents died in office an average of once every fifteen years. On October 28, 2015, the previous record for the longest period in American history without a presidential death—fifty-one years, eleven months, and five days, set during the founding era—was broken.[39] What accounts for the current era of presidential longevity? Regarding natural death, the marathon nature of the modern election process all but guarantees that whoever wins is in good health, despite a Trump campaign ad's farfetched claim that "Hillary Clinton doesn't have the fortitude, strength or stamina to lead in our world."[40] And if the strains of office wear down the president, the best medical care is always at hand. As for assassination, the security that surrounds the presidency has gotten tighter and tighter, shattering the old axiom that anyone willing to die in the effort could get close enough to the president to fire a fatal shot.

Changing Social Tolerance

The second way social barriers have fallen is through growing social tolerance. Like being a southerner, being divorced was long considered a disqualifier for the presidency. As recently as a half-century ago, when Democratic nominee Illinois governor Adlai Stevenson was defeated in 1952 and 1956, and Gov. Nelson Rockefeller of New York unsuccessfully sought the Republican nomination in 1964 and 1968, divorce proved an insuperable obstacle to presidential candidates. In 1980, however, Reagan was elected president with scarcely a hint that his divorce from actress Jane Wyman should be held against him. Society's tolerance for divorce had grown so great during the late 1960s and 1970s that it was no longer a barrier by the time Reagan ran.

Trump's path to the White House in 2016 was unobstructed by his two divorces. He paid a greater price in the general election for his many degrading comments about and behavior toward women—conduct about which Americans had grown *less* tolerant in recent years. Before entering politics, Trump had a long history of making dismissive remarks about women in public forums such as shock-jock Howard Stern's national radio show. (He even agreed with Stern's characterization of daughter Ivanka as "a piece of ass.")[41] In September 2016, a Clinton campaign ad showed young girls looking in the mirror over audio recordings of Trump making remarks such as "she's a slob," "she ate like a pig," and "a person who is flat-chested, it's very hard to be a 10." The ad concluded: "Is this the president we want for our daughters?"[42] Most astonishing, in a video-recorded 2005 conversation with *Access Hollywood* host Billy Bush that became public in October 2016, Trump bragged that when he saw beautiful women, "I just start kissing them. . . . And when you're a star, they let you do it. They let you do it. . . . Grab 'em by the pussy. You can do anything."[43]

Concerning religion as a social barrier, in 2000, Democratic presidential candidate Al Gore chose Sen. Joseph Lieberman of Connecticut as the first non-Christian nominee for vice president. In election day exit polls, 72 percent of voters said they thought Lieberman's Jewish religion would make him neither a better nor a worse vice president, and of the remaining 28 percent, twice as many thought it would make him a better one.[44] In February 2007, only 7 percent of respondents to a Gallup poll said that they would not vote for "a generally well-qualified person for president who happened to be Jewish." But more than half—53 percent—said they would not vote for an atheist.[45] Eight years later, the resistance to a Jewish president remained at 7 percent and the share opposed to voting for an atheist fell to 40 percent, with 76 percent of younger voters and 64 percent of Democrats (but only 45 percent of Republicans) willing to support a nonbeliever.[46]

In 2016, Bernie Sanders became the first Jewish candidate to win a presidential primary or caucus by sweeping to victory in New Hampshire and going on to win twenty-two more contests, finishing a strong second in the battle for the Democratic nomination. Sanders's Jewishness proved no obstacle. Nor, at least among Democrats, did his expressed decision to be "not actively involved in organized religion" as an adult or his answer to late-night television host Jimmy Kimmel's question about whether he believed in God: "What my spirituality is about is that we're all in this together and it's not a good thing to believe that as human beings we can turn our backs on the suffering of other people. This is not Judaism."[47] In a general election, however, Sanders's self-identification as a strongly secular person might have cost him substantially more votes than his Jewish upbringing.

Looking ahead, additional historical barriers to a major-party nomination for the presidency may be cracking in the face of changing social attitudes. In 2015, 74 percent of Americans said they would be willing to vote for a "gay or lesbian" candidate for president, up from 67 percent in 2011. Among younger voters and Democrats, the proportion was even higher: 85 percent and 84 percent, respectively; among Republicans, it was 61 percent. As a result of the 2016 election, one openly lesbian, gay, bisexual, or transgender (LGBT) senator and six LGBT representatives were serving in Congress—all of them Democrats. Oregon elected the nation's first bisexual governor, Democrat Kate Brown.

In the same 2015 poll, 60 percent of respondents said they would be willing to vote for a Muslim for president. Again, the numbers for young voters (76 percent) and Democrats (73 percent) were considerably higher than for other groups, and that still left 38 percent of all voters (and 55 percent of Republicans) whose views were consistent with Republican contender Ben Carson's statement that "I would not advocate that we put a Muslim in charge of this nation."[48] Three Muslims, all of them House Democrats, were elected to the 115th Congress. One might reasonably forecast that if present trends continue (always a dangerous assumption), at some point in the future, as younger cohorts replace older ones in the electorate and more members of these historically disfavored groups win prominent elective office, the nation will regard without prejudice its first atheist, LGBT, and Muslim candidates for president.

Facing the Issue

Facing public prejudices squarely was the strategy John F. Kennedy employed to overcome widespread prejudice against a different religious group, Roman Catholics, in 1960. Although adherence to Protestant Christianity was a requirement for office in several states at the time of the nation's founding, the Constitutional Convention voted unanimously that "no religious Test shall ever be required as a Qualification to any Office or public Trust under the United States." In practice, however, all thirty-four presidents from Washington to Eisenhower had been Protestants, at least in name.

Kennedy's strategy, unusual in an era when entering presidential primaries was generally regarded as a sign of political weakness, was to enter several in order to convince the leaders of his party (many of them Catholic themselves) that a Catholic could win. In the midst of his crucial primary campaign in overwhelmingly Protestant West Virginia, Kennedy told a television audience in May 1960: "When any man stands on the steps of the

Capitol and takes the oath of office as President, he is swearing to support the separation of church and state."[49] In September, again with cameras rolling, he addressed the Greater Houston Ministerial Association, declaring: "I do not speak for my church on public matters; and the church does not speak for me."[50] In 1958, 24 percent of Americans said they would not vote for any presidential candidate "who happened to be Catholic." Soon after Kennedy was elected, that number fell to 13 percent and, by 1969, to 8 percent. By 2011, it was a negligible 7 percent.[51]

The candidate who faced the most difficult religious challenge after Kennedy was former Republican governor Mitt Romney of Massachusetts, who first sought his party's nomination in 2008 and won it in 2012. In a 2007 Gallup poll, 24 percent said they would not vote for a Mormon. Kennedy's mission as a Catholic in 1960 had been to convince voters that his religion did not matter. Romney's challenge was different: to persuade white evangelical Christians, who expect candidates to speak freely about their faith and constitute a large share of the Republican primary electorate, that he was one of them. In a much-publicized speech in December 2007, Romney declared, "I believe that Jesus Christ is the Son of God and the Savior of mankind."[52]

Age was another unwritten barrier to the presidency, less so for younger candidates than for older ones. The Constitution includes a minimum age requirement for the presidency but places no limit on how old a president can be. The voters had a different take on the matter. An August 2007 Gallup poll offered a national sample of Americans a long and varied list of social and career characteristics of potential presidential candidates and asked if each "would be a desirable characteristic for the next president to have, an undesirable characteristic, or if it wouldn't matter much to you either way?" Of the twenty characteristics on the list, a majority of voters identified only two as undesirable. One was employment as a "government lobbyist." The other was being "70 years of age or older." Although an identical 52 percent of voters found both characteristics to be undesirable, 19 percent said lobbying experience was desirable, compared with only 5 percent who said this about age.[53]

Unlike other social background characteristics, commentators felt comfortable raising doubts about John McCain's age when he sought the presidency in 2008. (McCain was seventy-two). "McCain's Age Is a Legitimate Issue" was the headline of one typical article; another was titled "Is McCain Too Old to Be President?"[54] Pundits trotted out actuarial tables attempting to prove that men of McCain's age and medical history were likely to deteriorate or die during the four to eight years that he would serve as president.[55] Comedians added to McCain's woes. David Letterman, for example, said, "He's the kind of guy who picks up his TV remote when the phone rings."[56]

McCain worked hard to overcome, through words and actions, the political stigma of age. He chose to hang a lantern on his problem with humor, joking that he was "older than dirt" and leaving "the old soldiers' home for one last charge."[57] More seriously, his campaign days were long and vigorous, and he asked voters to regard age as a proxy for experience. "My friends, I'm not the youngest candidate," he told a Wisconsin primary crowd, "but I am the most experienced."[58] In the end, McCain overcame enough of the concerns about his age to win the Republican nomination.

Concerning race, after two centuries of being closed to African Americans, the doors of the White House at last were ready to be opened when Obama announced his candidacy for president in February 2007. Americans had grown accustomed, at least notionally, to the idea of an African American president. "Colin Powell's flirtation with a presidential run was a critical turning point in this shift in white attitude," noted sociologist Orlando Patterson, "effectively priming the nation for the possibility of a black candidate."[59] Steeply increasing numbers of constituencies with white majorities had elected African Americans to office, including Illinois, which sent Obama to the Senate with 70 percent of the vote in 2004.[60] In a February 2007 Gallup poll, 94 percent of voters said they were willing to support a "generally well-qualified" African American for president, a number that had risen sharply since 1937, when only 33 percent said they would.[61]

Most political experts assumed that Obama's main challenge in seeking the Democratic nomination would be to win votes from whites. Yet his candidacy initially was greeted with greatest skepticism in the African American community. "You can't take black people for granted just 'cause you're black," warned activist philosopher Cornel West.[62] The forty-two-member Congressional Black Caucus initially split down the middle between Obama and Hillary Clinton, with older members from the civil rights era, most of them representing majority black districts, supporting Clinton.[63] African American voters initially favored Clinton as well, by 46 to 37 percent in a November 2007 *Wall Street Journal*/NBC News poll.[64] Like the older black leaders, they doubted that Obama could receive enough white votes to be elected.[65] Consequently, Obama approached the January 2008 Iowa caucuses knowing that he needed to win the overwhelmingly white state to demonstrate that whites would vote for a black man for president. He succeeded, finishing first by a healthy margin. Right after Iowa, both candidates' internal polls showed Obama garnering support from 75 to 80 percent of African American voters.[66] In the crucial January 26 South Carolina primary, Obama won nearly 80 percent of the black vote.

If Obama rallied black voters by first winning the votes of whites, he won these white votes with a three-pronged strategy that was part substantive, part rhetorical, and part symbolic. Substantively, Obama based his campaign on issues that transcended race, such as tax cuts for the middle class, expanded health care, and his early opposition to the war in Iraq. He downplayed issues that white voters tended to associate with black political leaders, such as poverty, urban blight, and affirmative action. Rhetorically, Obama emphasized the value of national unity. In his keynote address to the 2004 Democratic National Convention, which introduced him to the American people, his theme had been: "There's not a black America and white America and Latino America and Asian America; there's the United States of America." Symbolically, Obama featured images of the white mother and grandparents who had raised him in his commercials, and never spoke, as Clinton sometimes did when referring to her gender, about the historic importance of electing the nation's first black president.

Obama's efforts to transcend race in his own campaign met their sternest challenge on March 13, 2008, when video recordings of some of his Chicago pastor's incendiary sermons were aired. Rev. Jeremiah Wright's declaration on the Sunday after September 11, 2001, that "America's chickens are coming home to roost. . . . God damn America" was shown endlessly on broadcast and cable news programs and on the Internet.[67] Overriding his campaign advisers' judgment, Obama chose the path Kennedy had taken in 1960 to address voters' concerns about his religion: he faced the issue directly in a speech. On March 18, Obama declared that Wright had "expressed a profoundly distorted view of this country—a view that sees white racism as endemic."[68]

Both candidates in the fall 2008 general election campaign between Obama and McCain worked to tamp down age and race as issues. Obama stopped referring to McCain's "half-century" of public service, a thinly veiled reference to his advanced years. McCain consistently rejected his supporters' advice to run attack ads linking Obama to Reverend Wright and publicly corrected a voter at a town hall meeting who said she "can't trust Obama . . . he's an Arab." "No, ma'am," McCain repeated four times. "He's a decent family man, citizen, that I just happen to have disagreements with on fundamental issues."[69]

McCain's age was a political burden on election day. In exit polls, 39 percent of voters said that age was a factor in their decision, and 66 percent of them voted for Obama. In contrast, race proved no obstacle to Obama's election. From 1968 to 2004, an average 39 percent of white voters had supported Democratic candidates for president.[70] In 2008, Obama won 44 percent of the white vote.[71] He did especially well among whites younger than age thirty, earning 54 percent of their support.

Remarkably, Donald Trump, who was more than a year older than Hillary Clinton in 2016, implicitly raised the age issue by questioning his rival's "stamina." He repeated the charge that "She doesn't have stamina" in four consecutive sentences during their first televised debate and then, days prior to the third debate, insisted that both candidates "take a drug test," the implication being that Clinton was relying on performance-enhancing drugs to overcome her supposed lack of endurance.[72] Trump, who tweeted that stamina is "one of my greatest assets" and claimed in an interview that he saw "a person who is thirty-five years old" when he looked in the mirror, persisted in charging that Clinton was too frail to be president and implying that she was too old.[73]

Positive Bias

A fourth historical barrier-buster in presidential elections has been positive bias. Although Kennedy's religion cost him some votes among anti-Catholics, it also won him support among Catholics proud to see one of their own contending for the presidency. In general, anti-Catholic voting hurt Kennedy in the South, and pro-Catholic voting helped him in the much larger and more populous North.[74] Similarly, Romney benefited in some ways from his Mormonism: he won strong support from the 2 percent of Republican voters who are Mormon, as well as raising substantial contributions from Mormon donors, especially in Utah.

As the first African American major-party nominee for president in 2008, Obama secured 95 percent of the black vote, up from Sen. John Kerry's 88 percent share in 2004. This prize turned out to be all the more valuable because black turnout surged from 11 percent of the electorate in 2004 to 13 percent in 2008. Obama also won 66 percent of Latino votes, a thirteen-point improvement over Kerry's 53 percent showing. The pattern was repeated when Obama sought reelection in 2012 and won 93 percent of the black vote and 71 percent of Latino votes.

Hillary Clinton's campaigns for her party's presidential nomination—nearly successful in 2008 and entirely successful in 2016—were distinctive because she is a woman. In surveys taken from 1937 to 2007, the Gallup poll found that Americans had become increasingly willing to vote for a "generally well-qualified" woman for president. In 1937 and 1945, only 33 percent said they would consider doing so, but that number rose to 52 percent in 1955, 66 percent in 1971, 73 percent in 1975, 80 percent in 1983, and 88 percent in 2007.[75] About 8 percent of voters in 2015 still said they would not vote for a woman, but their numbers were offset by the many women and some men who were eager to elect the first woman president. In part, this was because the ranks of women meeting the public's career background criteria for president had grown. As recently as 1976, no women served in the Senate and only one was a governor. By 2008, there were nine woman governors and sixteen woman senators, including Clinton, whom New Yorkers elected to the Senate in 2000 and reelected in 2006. By 2015, twenty-seven states had been led by a woman governor and twenty senators were women.[76]

Feminists, however, argued that Clinton faced unfairly high hurdles when seeking her party's nomination in 2008 because of her gender. Facebook had a group with tens of thousands of members called "Hillary Clinton: Stop Running for President and Make Me a Sandwich."[77] "Gender is probably the most restricting force in American life, whether the question is who must be in the kitchen or who could be in the White House," argued Gloria Steinem in a much-quoted article.[78] Clinton herself protested against "the incredible vitriol that has been engendered" against her "by people who are nothing but misogynists."[79]

Clinton handled the gender dimensions of her campaign for the 2008 Democratic nomination in two basic ways. One was to embrace her identity as the first woman with a serious chance to be selected. Calling on voters to break "the highest and hardest glass ceiling in America" by choosing her, Clinton said in campaign speeches: "As I go by, shaking hands and meeting people, I often hear a dad or mom lean over to a little girl and say, 'See, honey, you can be anything you want to be.'"[80] But Clinton's other gender-inspired strategy was to claim leadership qualities traditionally associated with men, especially strength. For fear of appearing weak, she refused to join other candidates who had voted in Congress to authorize the war in Iraq in 2002 by saying that she had made a mistake. "Apologizing would have been especially difficult for a female candidate," said one top Clinton campaign aide. "It would have made her look weak and vacillating."[81] In the end, Clinton lost the nomination to Obama but came very close. She ran strongly among older white women, but younger women and African American women mostly supported Obama. Just as Clinton was not the candidate of all women, however, neither was she just a woman's candidate. Indeed, every group of Democratic primary voters preferred her to any of the white male candidates in the race.

In 2016, Clinton again faced overt displays of gender bias. Some attendees at Trump rallies sported "Trump That Bitch" T-shirts and Trump himself, after his second debate with Clinton, sneered, "she walked in front of me [and], believe me, I wasn't impressed."[82] In her second bid for the presidency, Clinton decided to emphasize rather than downplay her gender, telling *Time* magazine, "This really comes down to whether I can encourage and mobilize women to vote for the first woman president."[83] In campaign speeches, she argued, "One of my merits is I'm a woman, and I think that makes a big difference in today's world."[84] Clinton wove women's issues into most elements of her policy agenda, including paid leave for new mothers, equal pay for women, and incorporating women's rights into the nation's foreign policy agenda. "If fighting for women's health care and paid family leave is playing the 'woman card,' then deal me in," she said.[85] Clinton's website featured merchandise such as a "Make Herstory" T-shirt and "A Woman's Place Is in the White House" throw pillows.[86]

Clinton faced obstacles related to her gender in both the nomination contest and the general election. As in 2008, her main rival for the 2016 Democratic nomination ran more strongly among younger women than Clinton did, once again frustrating older feminists such as Steinem, who charged that young women were supporting Sanders because "the boys are with Bernie," and former secretary of state Madeleine Albright, who said, "There's a special place in hell for women who don't help each other."[87] Younger women, wrote *Washington Post* digital producer Molly Roberts, "see it as inevitable that one day a woman will occupy the [office] that is oval-shaped. So the necessity of having that occupant be Hillary Clinton, or of having that moment occur in 2017, feels less urgent."[88] To them Clinton was flawed by not having risen to national prominence on her own but rather on the basis of her service as first lady in her husband's administration, as well as by her status as a wealthy white woman, which in newer theories of "intersectional" feminism made her gender less meaningful politically because of her privileged race and class.[89] "It's not good enough for someone to say, 'I'm a woman. Vote for me,'" said Sanders soon after the election. "What we need is a woman who has the guts to stand up to Wall Street, to the insurance companies, to the drug companies, to the fossil fuel industry."[90] Others suggested that Clinton's "I'm With Her" campaign slogan was too much about her ambition to be the first woman president and too little about the concerns on voters' minds, thereby opening the door for Trump's counter appeal: "I'm With You: The American People."[91] Nevertheless, older women solidly supported Clinton in the primaries, enabling her to run more strongly overall among women than men against Sanders in every primary by an average of 11 percentage points.[92]

Many younger women rallied to Clinton in the general election, in large part because of Trump's over-the-top rhetoric and behavior. To be sure, Trump raised legitimate questions about Clinton's efforts—as "one of the all time great enablers!"—to discredit women who had affairs with her husband during the 1980s and 1990s.[93] (She called Monica Lewinsky a "narcissistic looney tune," for example.)[94] But Trump had been all too prone over the years to refer to women as "fat pigs, dogs, slobs, and disgusting animals" and, after Fox News anchor Megyn Kelly called him out on this in an early primary debate, said that Kelly had "blood coming out of her eyes, blood coming out of her wherever."[95] "Look at that face!" Trump said of Republican rival Carly Fiorina. "Would anyone vote for that?"[96] In the aftermath of his first debate with Clinton, Trump launched a barrage of tweets attacking a former Miss Universe about her weight. Concerning Clinton, he said she was "too disgusting" for taking a bathroom break during a Democratic primary debate, claimed "she got schlonged" by Obama in the 2008 election, and sniffed, "I just don't think she has a presidential look."[97] "If Hillary Clinton were a man,' he added, "I don't think she'd get 5 percent of the vote."[98] "Donald thinks belittling women makes him bigger," Clinton said in their final debate. "He goes after their dignity, their self-worth, and I don't think there is a woman anywhere who doesn't know what that feels like." "Such a nasty woman," Trump replied.[99]

In the end, exit polls showed that 54 percent of women voted for Clinton, even as 53 percent of men voted for Trump. Her margin over Trump among all women was 12 percentage points. This was about the same margin that Obama secured in 2008 (13 points) and 2012 (11 points), which led some observers to argue that Clinton did not benefit "much—if at all—from group solidarity among women."[100] This interpretation provoked angry reactions from some feminists. "What leads a woman to vote for a man who has made it very clear that he believes she is subhuman?" wrote *Slate* associate editor L. V. Anderson. "Self-loathing. Hypocrisy. And, of course, a racist view of the world that privileges white supremacy over every other issue."[101]

In truth, Clinton's 48 percent share of the overall popular vote—3 points below Obama's share in 2012 and 5 points below his share in 2008—meant that in relative terms she outperformed Obama among women voters. She did especially well among African American women (94 percent) and Latina women (68 percent). College-educated white women gave her 51 percent of their votes, compared with the 46 percent they cast for Obama in 2012. And despite her defeat in the general election, Clinton benefited enormously from Democratic women's support in breaking the "glass ceiling" that had prevented all previous women from securing a major-party nomination for president.

Conclusion

The nomination of the first woman candidate for president by a major party in 2016—like the election of the first Catholic president in 1960, the first African American president in 2008, and the first southern president in more than a century in 1964—represents an altogether sensible broadening of the talent pool from which the United States draws its chief executives. So does growing public receptivity, as measured by public opinion polls and by nominations and elections to other prominent political offices, to the possibility of choosing future presidents without regard to their religion, age (as opposed to health), ethnicity, and sexual orientation. Historically, these and other artificial barriers have excluded large numbers of potentially excellent presidents from consideration on the basis of social characteristics unrelated to their ability to do the job. Vice presidential succession, changing social attitudes, positive bias, and facing the issue—sometimes in combination—seem likely to be the vehicles of change in the future, just as they have in the past.

To be sure, Hillary Clinton's nomination did not represent unalloyed progress. Many voters were rightly uncomfortable with the dynastic implications of her candidacy. If Clinton had been elected in 2016 and reelected in 2020, it would have meant that by the end of her second term, the United States would have been governed by a Clinton or a Bush—four people from two families—for twenty-eight of the previous thirty-six years. (The same would have been true if Jeb Bush was nominated, elected, and reelected.) Few if any mature democracies have been led for such a long period of time by so small a number of families. But many less stable ones than the United States are familiar with the pattern of spouses or children of rulers succeeding them in power, constituting the functional equivalent of a ruling family—the Bhuttos in Pakistan, the Peróns in Argentina, the Bandaranaikes in Sri Lanka, the Arroyos in the Philippines, and so on.

The presidency was created in 1787 as a republican office, not a monarchy. But old habits die hard; in a sense, Americans have always been closet royalists. Almost certainly, more Americans can name the sons of Prince Charles than their own senators. In this sense, the United States may have dodged a bullet in the form of de facto royal families when four of the first five presidents, including George Washington, had no sons. The one exception was John Adams, whose son John Quincy did become president—a cautionary event if one fears that political dynasties could all too easily have formed at the outset of the republic. Since then, the Harrison, Roosevelt, and Bush families have produced more than one president, and the Clintons came close. Looking ahead from the vantage point of 2016, however, most of the prominent women on the American political stage are, like British prime minister Theresa May and German chancellor Angela Merkel, leaders who have risen to eminence without family connections, including Sen. Elizabeth Warren of Massachusetts and Gov. Nikki Haley of South Carolina, whom Trump appointed as ambassador to the United Nations. As a result of the 2016 elections, four additional women entered the ranks of Democratic senators, raising their number to sixteen and, when added to the five Republican female senators, to a record high of twenty-one women in that chamber.

The recent broadening of the presidential talent pool to include candidates lacking in governing experience is a more worrisome matter. Virtually without precedent in American history, the public's growing openness to political novices in the presidency originated in the late twentieth century, when frustration with government led many voters first to devalue service in Washington and then (especially among Republicans) to look askance at any experience in governing at all. Reforms of the political parties that devolved control of nominations from party leaders to primary and caucus voters, as well as the court-ordered easing of ballot access laws that made it easier for independent candidates to file for election, accelerated this process.

Trump's presidential candidacy came less than a quarter-century after the independent campaigns launched in the 1990s by another celebrity business leader, Ross Perot. Perot, like Trump, led in the polls for a period of time. Like Trump, Perot caught fire with his appealing performances in a debate setting. But like Trump, too, once Perot's snappy one-liners were exhausted in his first televised encounter with general election opponents Bill Clinton and George H. W. Bush in 1992, the shallowness of his understanding of the challenges a president must address became all too apparent.

Despite Trump's claim that "I can be as presidential as anybody who's ever lived. I can be so presidential if I want," president of the United States is not an entry-level job.[102] A candidacy based on appeals such as "I'm not part of that mess," "My success in business (or academe or the media or some other realm) proves that I can lead the government," "I'll pay for my own campaign," or (Trump's own words), "Nobody knows the system better than me, which is why I alone can fix it" may sound good but are ungrounded in reality. Presidents need a distinctive array of skills if they are to lead effectively.[103] Skills of political rhetoric and bargaining seem to be developed best by running for office and serving in government for a period of years. The same can be said of the subtle but vital capacity to sense the public's willingness to be led in different directions at different paces at different times. The challenges of administrative management are different in government than in the corporate or academic world. Success in the private sector may speak well of a person and usually requires some of these skills. But only politics and government require all of them.[104]

Notes

1. A fuller account of the argument that follows may be found in Michael Nelson, "Constitutional Qualifications for President," in *Inventing the Presidency*, ed. Thomas E. Cronin (Lawrence: University Press of Kansas, 1989), 1–32.
2. Nearly all of the quotations from the Constitutional Convention in this section are from James Madison's notes of the debates, which are included in *The Records of the Constitutional Convention*, 4 vols., edited by Max Farrand (New Haven, Conn.: Yale University Press, 1911).
3. Quoted in Cyril C. Means Jr., "Is Presidency Barred to Americans Born Abroad?" *U.S. News & World Report*, December 23, 1955, 26–30.
4. Quoted in Charles C. Thach Jr., *The Creation of the Presidency* (Baltimore: Johns Hopkins University Press, 1969), 137.
5. Quoted in Means, "Is Presidency Barred to Americans Born Abroad?"
6. U.S. Census Bureau, *Statistical Abstract of the United States 2012* (Lanham, Md.: Rowman & Littlefield, 2011, 11; and Jens Manuel Krogstead, Jeffrey S. Passel, and D'Vera Cohn, "Five Facts about Illegal Immigration in the U.S.," Pew Research Center, September 20, 2016, www.pewresearch.org/fact-tank/2016/09/20/5-facts-about-illegal-immigration-in-the-u-s/.
7. Michael D'Antonio, *Trump Revealed: Donald Trump and the Pursuit of Success* (New York: St. Martin's Press, 2015), 287.
8. "Trump's Reversal on Obama Birthplace Conspiracy Stokes More Controversy," *Chicago Tribune*, September 16, 2016.
9. Nick Gass, "Trump Concedes Obama Was Born in the US," *Politico*, September 15, 2016, www.politico.com/story/2016/09/donald-trump-birtherism-campaign-statement-228261.
10. Charles M. Blow, "Trump: Grand Wizard of Birtherism," *New York Times*, September 19, 2016.
11. Robert Costa and Philip Rucker, "Trump Says Cruz's Canadian Birth Could Be 'Very Precarious' for GOP," *Washington Post*, January 5, 2015.
12. Jeremy Diamond, "Donald Trump: Ted Cruz Is an 'Anchor Baby,'" *CNN Politics,* January 29, 2016, www.cnn.com/2016/01/29/politics/donald-trump-ted-cruz-gop-debate-pummeled/.
13. Neal Katyal and Paul Clement, "On the Meaning of 'Natural Born Citizen,'" *Harvard Law Review Forum*, March 11, 2015, cdn.harvardlawreview.org/wp-content/uploads/2015/03/vol128_ClementKatyal.pdf.
14. The exception was Abraham Lincoln, whose previous political experience consisted of several terms in the Illinois legislature and one term in Congress.
15. They were Martin Van Buren, James Buchanan, and James Blaine.
16. Quoted in David Remnick, "The Joshua Generation," *New Yorker*, November 17, 2008.
17. Stephen F. Hayes, *Cheney: The Untold Story of America's Most Powerful and Controversial Vice President* (New York: HarperCollins, 2007), 307.

18. Janet Hook and Colleen McCain Nelson, "WSJ Poll: Hillary Clinton Widens Lead in Primary Race," *Wall Street Journal*, October 20, 2015; and Glenn Thrush, "Party of Two," *Politico Magazine* (July/August 2016), www.politico.com/magazine/story/2016/07/2016-barack-obama-hillary-clinton-democratic-establishment-campaign-primary-joe-biden-elizabeth-warren-214023.
19. Steven V. Roberts, "Is It Too Late for a Man of Honesty, High Purpose, and Intelligence to Be Elected President of the United States?" *Esquire* (October 1967), 89ff.
20. Annie Karni, "Clinton Aides Blame Loss on Everything but Themselves," *Politico*, November 10, 2016, www.politico.com/story/2016/11/hillary-clinton-aides-loss-blame-231215.
21. "2016 Republican Presidential Nomination," www.realclearpolitics.com/epolls/2016/president/us/2016_republican_presidential_nomination-3823.html.
22. Brian Stelter, "A Media-Savvy TV Star, an Anti-media Campaign," in Thomas Lake, *Unprecedented: The Election That Changed Everything* (New York: Melcher Media, 2016), 165.
23. Ryan Grim and Danny Shea, "A Note about Our Coverage of Donald Trump's 'Campaign,'" *Huffington Post*, July 17, 2015, www.huffingtonpost.com/entry/a-note-about-our-coverage-of-donald-trumps-campaign_us_55a8fc9ce4b0896514d0fd66.
24. Thomas B. Edsall, "Hurricane Trump," *New York Times*, September 23, 2015.
25. "Rise of the Anti-establishment Presidential Candidates," *Washington Post*, September 14, 2015, www.washingtonpost.com/apps/g/page/national/rise-of-the-anti-establishment-presidential-candidates/1822/.
26. Quoted in Maureen Dowd, *The Year of Voting Dangerously: The Derangement of American Politics* (New York: Hachette, 2016), 47, 67.
27. Rebecca Kaplan, "Trump's Immigration Comments Open Rift in GOP," *CBS News*, July 5, 2015, www.cbsnews.com/news/trump-immigration-comments-open-rift-gop/.
28. Miriam Valverde, "How Trump Plans to Build, and Pay for, a Wall along the U.S.-Mexico Border," *PolitiFact*, July 26, 2016, www.politifact.com/truth-o-meter/article/2016/jul/26/how-trump-plans-build-wall-along-us-mexico-border/; and Jenna Johnson, "Trump Calls for 'Total and Complete Shutdown of Muslims Entering the United States,'" *Washington Post*, December 7, 2015.
29. "The CNN-Telemundo Debate Transcript, Annotated," *Washington Post*, February 25, 2016, www.washingtonpost.com/news/the-fix/wp/2016/02/25/the-cnntelemundo-republican-debate-transcript-annotated/.
30. Ali Vitali, "Donald Trump: 'Torture Works,'" *NBC News*, February 17, 2016, www.nbcnews.com/politics/2016-election/donald-trump-torture-works-n520086.
31. Noam M. Levey and Noah Bierman, "Trump Pledged to Protect Medicare," *Los Angeles Times*, November 29, 2016; Gregory Krieg, "Donald Trump Stands by Softer Tone on Planned Parenthood," *CNN Politics*, March 2, 2016, www.cnn.com/2016/03/02/politics/donald-trump-planned-parenthood-good-work/; and Eugene Kiely, "Yes, Trump Said Bush 'Lied,'" *FactCheck*, March 17, 2016, www.factcheck.org/2016/03/yes-trump-said-bush-lied/.
32. In the end, Trump spent $65 million of his own money, raising the rest of the $322 million his campaign spent from others. Jeremy Peters and Rachel Shorey, "Trump Spent Far Less Than Clinton, but Paid His Companies Well," *New York Times*, December 9, 2016.
33. "Full Transcript: Third 2016 Presidential Debate," *Politico*, October 20, 2016, www.politico.com/story/2016/10/full-transcript-third-2016-presidential-debate-230063.

34. Robert Draper, "Trump in April: 'If I Lose, I'll Let It All Out,'" *New York Times Magazine*, October 23, 2016.
35. Jeremy Diamond, "Trump: I Could 'Shoot Somebody and I Wouldn't Lose Voters,'" *CNN*, January 24, 2016, www.cnn.com/2016/01/23/politics/donald-trump-shoot-somebody-support/.
36. "Exit Polls," *CNN*, edition.cnn.com/election/results/exit-polls/national/president.
37. Clinton Rossiter, *The American Presidency*, rev. ed. (New York: New American Library, 1960), 193–194.
38. Tal Kopan, John Berman, and Sunlen Serfaty, "Ted Cruz Names Carly Fiorina as VP Pick," *CNN Politics*, April 27, 2016, www.cnn.com/2016/04/27/politics/ted-cruz-carly-fiorina-vice-president/.
39. Michael Nelson, "A New Record for Presidential Longevity," *Cook Political Report*, October 22, 2016, cookpolitical.com/story/8954.
40. Chris Cillizza, "Donald Trump's New Attack Ad on Clinton's Health Is Brutal. It Will Also Fail," *Washington Post*, October 11, 2016.
41. Louis Nelson, "Trump Told Howard Stern It's OK to Call Ivanka a 'Piece of A–,'" *Politico*, October 8, 2016, www.politico.com/story/2016/10/trump-ivanka-piece-of-ass-howard-stern-229376.
42. "Clinton Ad Asks about Impact of Trump on Our Daughters," *CNN Politics*, September 23, 2016, www.cnn.com/videos/politics/2016/09/23/hillary-clinton-trump-attack-ad-women-newday.cnn.
43. David A. Farenthold, "Trump Recorded Having Extremely Lewd Conversation about Women in 2005," *Washington Post*, October 8, 2016.
44. Michael Nelson, "The Election: Ordinary Politics, Extraordinary Outcome," in *The Elections of 2000*, ed. Michael Nelson (Washington, D.C.: CQ Press, 2001), 75.
45. Jeffrey M. Jones, "Some Americans Reluctant to Vote for Mormon, 72-Year-Old Presidential Candidates," *Gallup*, February 20, 2007, www.gallup.com/poll/26611/some-americans-reluctant-vote-mormon-72yearold-presidential-candidates.aspx.
46. Justin McCarthy, "In U.S., Socialist Presidential Candidates Least Appealing," *Gallup*, June 22, 2015, www.gallup.com/poll/183713/socialist-presidential-candidates-least-appealing.aspx.
47. Aaron Blake, "Bernie Sanders: Our First Non-religious President?" *Washington Post*, January 27, 2016.
48. Adam Edelman, "Carson 'Would Not Advocate We Put Muslim in' White House," *New York Daily News*, September 21, 2015.
49. Quoted in Theodore H. White, *The Making of the President 1960* (New York: Pocket Books, 1961), 128–129.
50. John F. Kennedy, "Address to the Greater Houston Ministerial Association," www.americanrhetoric.com/speeches/jfkhoustonministers.html.
51. George H. Gallup, *The Gallup Poll: Public Opinion, 1935–1971*, vol. 3 (New York: Random House, 1971), 1605, 1735, and 2190; Jones, "Some Americans Reluctant to Vote for Mormon, 72-Year-Old Presidential Candidates"; and Lydia Saad, "In U.S., 22% Are Hesitant to Support a Mormon in 2012," *Gallup*, June 20, 2011, www.gallup.com/poll/148100/hesitant-support-mormon-2012.aspx.
52. "Transcript: Mitt Romney's Faith Speech," *National Public Radio*, December 6, 2007, www.npr.org/templates/story/story.php?storyId=16969460.
53. Joseph Carroll, "Which Characteristics Are Most Desirable in the Next President," *Gallup*, September 17, 2007, www.gallup.com/poll/28693/Which-Characteristics-Most-Desirable-Next-President.aspx.

54. Bud Jackson, "McCain's Age Is a Legitimate Issue," *Politico*, May 22, 2008; and Steve Chapman, "Is McCain Too Old to Be President?" *RealClearPolitics*, September 9, 2007, www.realclearpolitics.com/articles/2007/09/is_mccain_too_old_to_be_presid.html.
55. Alexander Burns, "McCain and the Politics of Mortality," *Politico*, September 4, 2008.
56. Julie Bosman, "So a Senior Citizen Walks into a Bar . . . ," *New York Times*, March 9, 2008; and Dick Polman, "The Age Factor," *Philadelphia Inquirer*, May 25, 2008.
57. Holly Bailey, "An Answer for Every 'Little Jerk,'" *Newsweek*, June 2, 2008, 27.
58. Ibid.
59. Orlando Patterson, "An Eternal Revolution," *New York Times*, November 7, 2008.
60. Rachel L. Swarns, "Quiet Political Shifts as More Blacks Are Elected," *New York Times*, October 14, 2008.
61. Jones, "Some Americans Reluctant to Vote for Mormon, 72-Year-Old Presidential Candidates"; and Linda Feldman, "In 2008, Many Presidential 'Firsts' Are Possible," *Christian Science Monitor*, February 16, 2007.
62. Richard Wolffe and Daren Briscoe, "Across the Divide," *Newsweek*, July 16, 2007, 24.
63. Matt Bai, "Is Obama the End of Black Politics?" *New York Times Magazine*, August 10, 2008.
64. Jonathan Kaufman, "Whites' Great Hope?" *Wall Street Journal*, November 10, 2007.
65. See, for example, Perry Bacon Jr., "Can Obama Count on the Black Vote?" *Time*, January 23, 2007.
66. Ibid.
67. Brian Ross and Rehab El-Buri, "Obama's Pastor: God Damn America, U.S. to Blame for 9/11," *ABC News*, March 13, 2008 abcnews.go.com/Blotter/DemocraticDebate/story?id=4443788
68. "Barack Obama's Speech on Race," *New York Times*, March 18, 2008.
69. Monica Langley, "As Economic Crisis Peaked, Tide Turned against McCain," *Wall Street Journal*, November 5, 2008; and Evan Thomas, "How He Did It," *Newsweek*, November 17, 2008, 108.
70. John Harwood, "Level of White Support for Obama a Surprise," *New York Times*, November 3, 2008.
71. All exit poll results are from "President: National Exit Poll," *CNN*, www.cnn.com/ELECTION/2008/results/polls/#USP00p1.
72. "The First Trump-Clinton Presidential Debate Transcript, Annotated," *Washington Post*, September 26, 2016, www.washingtonpost.com/news/the-fix/wp/2016/09/26/the-first-trump-clinton-presidential-debate-transcript-annotated/; and Nick Corasaniti, "'We Should Take a Drug Test' before Debate, Donald Trump Says," *New York Times*, October 15, 2016.
73. Adam Edelman, "Donald Trump, 70, Tells Dr. Oz He Feels 'the Same Age' as 39-year-old QB Tom Brady," *New York Daily News*, September 15, 2016; and "First Trump-Clinton Presidential Debate Transcript."
74. Philip E. Converse et al., "Stability and Change in 1960: A Reinstating Election," in *Elections and the Political Order*, eds. Angus Campbell et al. (New York: Wiley, 1966).
75. Jones, "Some Americans Reluctant to Vote for Mormon, 72-Year-Old Presidential Candidates."
76. Kate Zernike, "Both Sides Seeking to Be What Women Want," *New York Times*, September 15, 2008.

77. Marie Cocco, "Clinton Campaign Brought Sexism out of Hiding," *RealClearPolitics*, May 13, 2008, www.realclearpolitics.com/articles/2008/05/clinton_campaign_brought_sexis.html; and Amanda Fortini, "The Feminist Reawakening," *New York Magazine*, April 13, 2008.
78. Gloria Steinem, "Women Are Never Front-Runners," *New York Times*, January 8, 2008.
79. Lois Romano, "Clinton Puts Up a New Fight," *Washington Post*, May 20, 2008.
80. Anne E. Kornblut, "Encouraged by Women's Response, Clinton Stresses Female Side," *Washington Post*, October 14, 2007.
81. Roger Simon, "Lost in Hillaryland," *Politico*, August 25, 2008.
82. Nolan D. McCaskill, "Trump: Clinton Walked in Front of Me, and 'I Wasn't Impressed,'" *Politico*, October 14, 2016, www.politico.com/story/2016/10/trump-clinton-debate-walk-not-impressed-229810.
83. Nicholas Kristof, "Clinton, Trump and Sexism," *New York Times*, January 23, 2016.
84. Peter Nicholas, "Clinton Steps Up Efforts to Woo Women Voters," *Wall Street Journal*, September 11, 2015.
85. Amy Chozick and Ashley Parker, "Donald Trump's Gender-Based Attacks on Hillary Clinton Have Calculated Risk," *New York Times*, April 28, 2016.
86. Dowd, *The Year of Living Dangerously*, 38.
87. Alan Rappeport, "Gloria Steinem and Madeleine Albright Rebuke Young Women Backing Bernie Sanders," *New York Times*, February 7, 2016.
88. Molly Roberts, "Why Millennials Are Yawning at the Likely First Female Major-Party Nominee for President," *Washington Post*, June 7, 2016. See also Gloria Borger, "A Woman President? Millennials Can Wait," in Thomas Lake, *Unprecedented*, 113.
89. Janell Ross, "Hillary Clinton: A Woman and Candidate with Seriously Complicated Woman Issues," *Washington Post*, May 11, 2016.
90. Brent Griffiths, "Sanders Slams Identity Politics as Democrats Figure Out Their Future," *Politico*, November 21, 2016, www.politico.com/story/2016/11/bernie-sanders-democrats-identity-politics-231710.
91. Ian Schwartz, "Trump: Clinton's Slogan Is 'I'm with Her'"; My Response Is, 'I'm with You: The American People,'" *Real Clear Politics*, June 22, 2016, www.realclearpolitics.com/video/2016/06/22/trump_clinton_believes_she_is_entitled_to_the_presidency_im_with_you_the_american_people.html.
92. Barbara Norrander, "Women Vote at Higher Rates Than Men. That Might Help Clinton in November," *Washington Post*, June 27, 2016.
93. Gabby Morrongiello, "Tweeting Trump: Clinton Is One of the 'All Time Great Enablers,'" *Washington Examiner*, April 29, 2016.
94. Frances Stead Sellers, "Clinton, Feminists and the Politics of Voting for 'the Old White Guy,'" *Washington Post*, February 11, 2016.
95. Holly Yan, "Donald Trump's 'Blood' Comment about Megyn Kelly Draws Outrage," *CNN Politics*, August 8, 2015, www.cnn.com/2015/08/08/politics/donald-trump-cnn-megyn-kelly-comment/.
96. Paul Solotaroff, "Trump Seriously: On the Trail with the GOP's Tough Guy," *Rolling Stone*, September 9, 2015.
97. "'She Got Schlonged': Trump's Vulgar New Attack on Hillary Clinton," *New York Post*, December 22, 2015; and Ashley Parker, "Donald Trump Says Hillary Clinton Doesn't Have 'a Presidential Look,'" *New York Times*, September 6, 2016.
98. Chozick and Parker, "Donald Trump's Gender-Based Attacks."
99. "Full Transcript: Third 2016 Presidential Debate," *Politico*, October 20, 2016, www.politico.com/story/2016/10/full-transcript-third-2016-presidential-debate-230063.

100. Michael Tesler, "Monkey Cage: Why the Gender Gap Doomed Hillary Clinton," *Washington Post*, November 9, 2016, www.emailnewsletterstand.com/e/monkey-cage-why-the-gender-gap-doomed-hillary-clinton.
101. L.V. Anderson, "White Women Sold Out the Sisterhood and the World by Voting for Trump," *Slate*, November 9, 2016, www.slate.com/blogs/xx_factor/2016/11/09/white_women_sold_out_the_sisterhood_and_the_world_by_voting_for_trump.html.
102. Quoted in Dowd, *The Year of Living Dangerously*, 36.
103. Erwin C. Hargrove and Michael Nelson, *Presidents, Politics, and Policy* (Baltimore, Md.: Johns Hopkins University Press, 1984), ch. 4. For the Trump quote, see Lake, *Unprecedented*, 189.
104. Michael Nelson, "Who Vies for President?" in *Presidential Selection*, eds. Alexander Heard and Michael Nelson (Durham, N.C.: Duke University Press, 1987), 120–154.

2

The Nominations

The Road to a Much-Disliked General Election

William G. Mayer

At the end of a remarkably unpredictable election, I can, I believe, make one prediction with some assurance: Political scientists and historians will be studying and puzzling over the 2016 election for many years to come. Although many different questions will be asked about this election, some of the most intriguing concern the presidential nominations. How and why did the two major American parties choose Hillary Clinton and Donald Trump to be their presidential standard-bearers? Given the issues and powers at stake, given the significance that is invariably ascribed to the office of the presidency, how could the Democrats and Republicans have conferred their nominations upon perhaps the two most widely disliked figures in American politics?

As other chapters in this volume will amply demonstrate, a large number of Americans wanted nothing to do with either of these candidates. Though about 94 percent of the voters ultimately cast their ballots for one of the two major-party nominees, that should not be interpreted to mean that they were satisfied with the choices. In the exit polls taken in conjunction with the general election, only 43 percent of the voters had a favorable opinion of Clinton; 55 percent viewed her unfavorably. Trump's numbers were even worse: 38 percent favorable, 60 percent unfavorable. According to another question, only 41 percent of voters said they strongly favored the person they voted for. Thirty-two percent admitted to having "reservations" about their vote choice, and 25 percent could only say that they disliked his or her opponent even more.[1]

So how did we wind up with these two presidential nominees?

The Race Takes Shape: Democrats

Well before Hillary Clinton formally resigned her position as secretary of state on February 1, 2013, it was widely anticipated that she would be a candidate for the Democratic presidential nomination in 2016. The more open question concerned who—if anyone—would take the field against her. In the end, four other candidates entered the race: Vermont senator Bernie Sanders, former Maryland governor Martin O'Malley, former Rhode

Island senator and governor Lincoln Chafee, and former Virginia senator Jim Webb. (For their announcement dates, see Table 2.1.) Of these, it's fair to say, Chafee and Webb were regarded as extreme longshots; Sanders had some significant strengths but also some major weaknesses; and O'Malley might best be described as solid but not very exciting.

In light of Clinton's weakness as a general election candidate, it is impossible not to wonder why the 2016 Democratic race attracted so few strong entrants. One widely touted explanation for the small field of Democratic presidential candidates was the claim that the party had a "weak bench."[2] Prior to Trump's victory, it was widely assumed that the pool of plausible presidential candidates was limited to a party's senators, governors, and vice presidents. But the Republican tsunami in the 2010 and 2014 midterm elections had wiped out a substantial swath of these presidential possibilities, reducing the number of Democratic senators from fifty-nine to forty-six and the number of Democratic governors from twenty-nine to eighteen.

So the Democrats did have a comparatively small pool of presidential prospects to draw upon in 2016. But it would be a gross exaggeration to suggest that the five people who finally entered the race were the only ones available. Writing in 2014 and early 2015, political columnists and pundits who looked over the Democratic field were able to compile a long list of potential presidential candidates who were said to be considering a race or were being urged to consider one or who might have jumped in under the right circumstances. Among the names that appeared on most such lists were senators Elizabeth Warren (Massachusetts), Mark Warner (Virginia), Cory Booker (New Jersey), and Amy Klobuchar (Minnesota); governors Andrew Cuomo (New York), John Hickenlooper (Colorado), and Steve Bullock (Montana); and former governor Deval Patrick (Massachusetts).[3]

The most conspicuous non-entrant into the 2016 Democratic race was incumbent vice president Joe Biden. Since 1960, it has been an axiom of American politics that the vice presidency, whatever its other limitations, is an unrivaled launching pad for winning a presidential nomination, although the position also seems to be a net liability in the general election.[4] Richard Nixon, Hubert Humphrey, Walter Mondale, George H. W. Bush, and Al Gore all used the vice presidency as a stepping stone to a presidential nomination. By some measures, moreover, Biden was among the more popular figures in the Obama administration. In early October 2015, Biden's favorability numbers were 46 percent favorable, 39 percent unfavorable, as compared to 47–47 for Obama and 42–51 for Hillary Clinton.[5]

Yet there also seems to have been a widespread perception, even among Democrats, that Biden just wasn't presidential material: too old (he would have been seventy-four when sworn into office), too gaffe-prone. As one participant at a 2014 liberal gathering told a reporter, "I love Joe Biden, but I can't imagine him running for president."[6] History offered ample support for this person's skepticism: Biden had run for the Democratic presidential

Table 2.1 Announcement and Withdrawal Dates for 2016 Presidential Candidates

Candidate	*Formal Announcement*	*Statement of Candidacy*	*Statement of Organization*	*Withdrawal Date*
Democrats				
Hillary Clinton	April 12, 2015	April 13, 2015	April 13, 2015	none
Bernie Sanders	April 30, 2015	April 30, 2015	April 30, 2015	July 12, 2016
Martin O'Malley	May 30, 2015	May 29, 2015	May 29, 2015	February 1, 2016
Lincoln Chafee	June 3, 2015	June 16, 2015	June 19, 2015	October 23, 2015
Jim Webb	July 2, 2015	July 14, 2015	July 14, 2015	October 20, 2015
Republicans				
Ted Cruz	March 23, 2015	March 23, 2015	March 23, 2015	May 3, 2016
Rand Paul	April 7, 2015	April 8, 2015	April 7, 2015	February 3, 2016
Marco Rubio	April 13, 2015	April 13, 2015	April 13, 2015	March 15, 2016
Carly Fiorina	May 4, 2015	May 4, 2015	May 4, 2015	February 10, 2016
Ben Carson	May 4, 2015	May 4, 2015	March 2, 2015	March 2, 2016
Mike Huckabee	May 5, 2015	May 2, 2015	May 8, 2015	February 1, 2016
Rick Santorum	May 27, 2015	May 27, 2015	May 27, 2015	February 3, 2016
George Pataki	May 28, 2015	June 1, 2015	May 19, 2015	December 29, 2015
Lindsey Graham	June 1, 2015	June 1, 2015	June 1, 2015	December 21, 2015
Rick Perry	June 4, 2015	June 19, 2015	June 14, 2015	September 11, 2015
Jeb Bush	June 15, 2015	June 15, 2015	June 15, 2015	February 20, 2016
Donald Trump	June 16, 2015	June 22, 2015	June 29, 2015	none
Bobby Jindal	June 24, 2015	June 29, 2015	June 29, 2015	November 17, 2015
Chris Christie	June 30, 2015	July 1, 2015	July 1, 2015	February 10, 2016
Scott Walker	July 13, 2015	August 5, 2015	July 2, 2015	September 21, 2015
John Kasich	July 21, 2015	July 23, 2015	July 23, 2015	May 4, 2016
Jim Gilmore	July 30, 2015	July 29, 2015	August 4, 2015	February 12, 2016

Source: Formal announcement and withdrawal dates are based on contemporary news coverage. Statements of candidacy and organization are taken from the official candidate filings with the Federal Election Commission, available at fec.gov.

nomination on two previous occasions—in 1988 and 2008—and both times had fared very poorly. In presidential primaries, vice presidents typically benefit from their close association with the incumbent president, who is almost always very popular among his own party's adherents.[7] In 2016, however, Hillary Clinton had as good a claim to the pro-Obama vote as Biden. After sending conflicting signals through much of Obama's second term, Biden finally announced on October 21, 2015, that he would not be a candidate for president in 2016.[8]

Biden may have been unwilling to undertake the rigors and stresses of a presidential campaign in part because he and his family were still grieving over the death of his oldest son from cancer in May 2015. But why did all the other Democrats listed earlier finally decide not to throw their hats in the ring?

One factor that scared off many potential opponents was all the obvious assets that made Clinton not just a likely candidate, not just a strong early front-runner, but also (or so most pundits informed us) an almost prohibitive favorite. She had universal name recognition, a depth and variety of governmental experience that none of her opponents could match, extensive support among other Democratic officials and party leaders, an unrivaled fundraising machine, and an experienced, battle-tested team of advisers and consultants. In polls of the potential Democratic primary electorate conducted in 2013 and 2014, Clinton absolutely dominated the field. About 60 percent of the nation's Democrats regularly said they wanted Clinton to be their party's 2016 presidential nominee. In second place was either Joe Biden or Elizabeth Warren, with only about 10 percent support. These sorts of numbers led one pundit to call Clinton the strongest nonincumbent presidential candidate ever.[9]

Had they paid more attention to history, however, Democrats might have been less impressed by Clinton's apparent advantages. In the Republican Party, early front-runners generally tend to win the presidential nomination. Among the more fractious, disorderly Democrats, by contrast, early front-runners have a much rockier track record.[10] That was what Edward Kennedy learned in 1980, what Gary Hart learned in 1988, and what Howard Dean found out in 2004. Walter Mondale only narrowly escaped the same fate in 1984. An even more relevant precedent, of course, was Clinton's own experience in 2008. That year, too, she had been a strong early favorite with a sizable lead in the polls (though not as large as the lead she enjoyed in 2013 and 2014). Once the actual primary and caucus season began, however, Clinton was quickly overtaken by a charismatic but relatively inexperienced Illinois senator named Barack Obama. In retrospect, it is surprising that more Democrats were unwilling to put her to the test again in 2016.

Another important factor working to Clinton's advantage was timing. The contemporary presidential nomination process generally requires prospective candidates to begin their planning years before the primary and caucus season commences—but many of Clinton's weaknesses were not so obvious until relatively late in the election. As Clinton occasionally lamented during the general election campaign, during her tenure as secretary of state she had been quite popular. According to one polling aggregation website, on February 4, 2013, three days after Clinton left that office, she was viewed favorably by 56 percent of the American public, while just 35 percent had an unfavorable opinion of her. Yet the Democrats cannot claim that they had no advance warning as to what lay ahead. Clinton's popularity started to decline almost immediately after leaving office. By November 10, 2014, less than a week after the midterm elections, Clinton's ratings were just barely positive: 48 percent favorable, 44 percent unfavorable. And by June 1, 2015, when there was still ample time for other candidates to enter the race, her numbers were "under water": 44 percent favorable, 48 percent unfavorable.[11]

All of which suggests a final important reason for the small Democratic candidate field: The party had learned the wrong lesson from the last major Clinton scandal. In Bill Clinton's second term as president, he had been hit with accusations that he had had an affair with a White House intern and then lied about it during a civil deposition. When those charges were first aired, lots of people—Republicans, Democrats, and members of the press alike—predicted that if the accusations were proven true, as they eventually were, there would be widespread public outrage and Clinton would be forced to resign. In fact, the American public was surprisingly unmoved by the whole controversy. Clinton's approval ratings remained high, and when the House of Representatives nevertheless brought impeachment charges against him, polls regularly showed that a substantial majority of the public did not want the Senate to convict him.

When Republicans charged Hillary Clinton with maintaining a private email server in apparent violation of both State Department policy and federal law and thereby endangering classified information, lots of Democrats were inclined to dismiss the whole thing as a tempest in a teapot: as one more attempt by the Republicans to manufacture a scandal where none really existed. But this time, there was solid evidence that the public took the email scandal seriously. The general election exit polls, for example, included a question asking respondents how much Clinton's use of a private email server bothered them. Fully 45 percent of the voters said it bothered them a lot; only 19 percent said it didn't bother them at all.

In addition to the small number of declared candidates, one other prominent feature of the 2016 Democratic nomination race had become clearly visible by the summer of 2015: the emergence of Bernie Sanders as the main rival—indeed, the only real rival—to Hillary Clinton. In March 2015, as shown in Table 2.2, just 4 percent of the nation's Democrats said they intended to vote for Sanders in the upcoming primaries and caucuses. But something in the Sanders candidacy caught on. His support jumped to 8 percent in April, to 15 percent in May, and to around 20 percent in August.

Table 2.2 Presidential Nomination Preferences of National Democrats, January 1, 2015–February 1, 2016 (percent)

	Clinton	*Sanders*	*Biden*	*O'Malley*	*Webb*	*Chafee*	*Warren*
March 26–29, 2015	66	4	11	1	2		11
May 28–31, 2015	63	9	14	2	2	1	
July 16–19, 2015	62	14	14	1	2	1	
September 7–10, 2015	46	20	21	2	1	1	
October 15–18, 2015	54	23	16	1	1	*	
November 16–19, 2015	60	34		3			
December 10–13, 2015	59	28		5			
January 21–24, 2016	55	36		4			
Quinnipiac							
February 26–March 2, 2015	56	4	10	0	1		14
April 16–21, 2015	60	8	10	3	1	*	
May 19–26, 2015	57	15	9	1	1	1	
July 23–28, 2015	55	17	13	1	1	*	
August 20–25, 2015	45	22	18	1	1	*	
September 17–21, 2015	43	25	18	0	0	0	
October 29–November 2, 2015	53	35		0			
November 23–30, 2015	60	30		2			
December 16–20, 2015	61	30		2			

Source: All polls were conducted by ABC News and the *Washington Post.*

Note: Blank spaces indicate that that person's name was not included in the list of candidates read to survey respondents; asterisks indicate values less than 1 percent.

Meanwhile, the only other candidate besides Clinton who scored above the low single digits was Joe Biden, and even he lagged behind Sanders in most polls. In October, both Jim Webb and Lincoln Chafee acknowledged the obvious and withdrew from the race; on October 21, Biden ended any speculation that he would be a candidate. Polls conducted after these events showed quite starkly that the Democratic contest had become a two-person race, and that although Clinton was still the clear front-runner, her lead was considerably smaller than one might have anticipated from the polls conducted just a year or two earlier. In late November, for example, a Quinnipiac University Poll gave Clinton 60 percent of the vote, 30 percent to Sanders, and just 2 percent to Martin O'Malley.

Polls in the crucial early states of Iowa and New Hampshire showed an even closer race. In Iowa, two early September 2015 polls found Sanders leading Clinton, though she would regain the lead later that month. In the Granite State, where Sanders had the substantial benefit of living in neighboring Vermont, Sanders led the polls almost continuously from August 2015 to the primary in early February 2016.[12]

The rise of Bernie Sanders was a mixed blessing for the Clinton campaign. Obviously, she and her supporters hoped that none of her opponents would catch on and that she would thus have an essentially uncontested path to the nomination. Yet, if she was going to have a single major opponent, she could have done worse than Sanders. Sanders's message of economic inequality and how the system was rigged against ordinary Americans undoubtedly resonated with many voters, especially younger voters. But as we will see later, Sanders's appeal also had some decided limitations. In particular, lots of Democrats proved unwilling to give their presidential nomination to a man who had spent his entire political career running as an independent.

Her poll numbers aside, Clinton had one other advantage that became increasingly controversial as the 2016 primary season approached: her huge lead among the so-called superdelegates. Superdelegates—in party rules they are formally known as unpledged party leaders and elected officials—are a special class of delegates to the Democratic National Convention. When the Democrats redesigned their delegate selection rules in the early 1970s, one conspicuous consequence was a sharp decline in the number of major Democratic elected officials, including senators and governors, who served as convention delegates. So in 1982, the party decided to give automatic delegate status to certain types of elected officials and party leaders. Superdelegates, that is to say, are not chosen in the primaries and caucuses, nor are they bound by the results in their home state or district. They become national convention delegates because of the party or governmental positions they hold and can vote for whichever candidate they want. Though the rules have been tweaked a bit over time, since 1996 all members of the Democratic National Committee, all Democratic members of the U.S. House and Senate, all Democratic governors, and a few other "distinguished party leaders" have been awarded automatic delegate seats at the national convention.[13] In 2016, that meant there were 712 superdelegates, or about 15 percent of the convention total.

Not surprisingly, given Clinton's and Sanders's very different past relationships with the Democratic Party, it soon became clear that the superdelegates had given Clinton a large lead in the delegate count before a single caucus or primary had taken place. As of November 2015, according to a count by the Associated Press, 359 superdelegates were publicly committed to Clinton; just 8 said they would vote for Sanders.[14]

The Race Takes Shape: Republicans

Until June 2015, the 2016 Republican nomination race looked to be a fairly conventional affair. There was by then a sizable contingent of declared candidates, with a number of others clearly planning to join the race. But large candidate fields are actually the norm in nomination races for the party that does not control the White House. By some counts, the Democrats had fourteen announced candidates in 1972, seventeen in 1976. The full roster of 2016 Republican candidates, along with their announcement dates, is in Table 2.1.

What was unusual, at least for Republicans, was the absence of an early front-runner. In polls of the nation's Republicans conducted throughout 2014 and the first few months of 2015 (see Table 2.3), no candidate was ever supported by more than about 20 percent of the potential party electorate. Putting aside Paul Ryan and Mitt Romney, both of whom ultimately decided not to enter the race, most early polls showed Jeb Bush, Mike Huckabee, and Rand Paul competing for the top slot, but none of them established anything like the clear lead that Ronald Reagan had over every other Republican in 1978 and 1979, that George H. W. Bush enjoyed in 1986 and 1987, or that Bob Dole had in 1994 and 1995.[15]

One other lesson from the data in Table 2.3 is the severe beating the Bush name had sustained from the presidency of George W. When Republicans wanted a candidate to regain the White House in 2000, they had, to a remarkable extent, rallied around the candidacy of the then-governor of Texas. By March 1999, more than 50 percent of the nation's Republicans said they wanted Bush to be their next nominee. By the time George W. Bush left office, however, most Republicans apparently wanted nothing more to do with the Bushes. Even with his substantial advantage in early name recognition, Jeb Bush never exceeded 20 percent support in the polls shown in Table 2.3.

And then, on June 16, in the atrium of his own skyscraper, Donald Trump announced that he too would be a candidate for the 2016 Republican nomination. The race—and, it may turn out, the country—were never the same after that.

Table 2.3 Presidential Nomination Preferences of National Republicans, January 1, 2014–February 1, 2016 (percent)

	January 2014	*April 2014*	*October 2014*	*December 2014*	*March 2015*	*May 2015*
Jeb Bush	18	12	10	10	20	13
Ben Carson			6	7	7	7
Chris Christie	13	9	8	6	6	5
Ted Cruz	12	7	3	6	13	7
Carly Fiorina					1	2
Lindsey Graham					1	1
Mike Huckabee		14	10	6	8	9
Bobby Jindal		2	1	2	1	1
John Kasich		1	1	2	1	3
George Pataki						1
Rand Paul	11	15	9	9	9	11
Rick Perry		5	5	4	2	2
Mitt Romney			21	21		
Paul Ryan	20	12	5	8		
Marco Rubio	10	6	6	4	7	9
Rick Santorum			4	3	2	3
Donald Trump						5
Scott Walker		5	1	5	12	11
	July 2015	*September 2015*	*October 2015*	*November 2015*	*December 2015*	*January 2016*
Jeb Bush	13	10	7	6	5	5
Ben Carson	6	18	22	22	12	7
Chris Christie	4	1	3	2	4	4
Ted Cruz	4	7	6	8	15	21
Carly Fiorina	*	2	5	4	1	3
Lindsey Graham	*	*	1	1	1	
Mike Huckabee	7	3	3	3	1	2

(Continued)

Table 2.3 (Continued)

	July 2015	*September 2015*	*October 2015*	*November 2015*	*December 2015*	*January 2016*
Bobby Jindal	2	1				
John Kasich	2	3	2	3	2	2
George Pataki	2	*	1	*	0	
Rand Paul	6	4	2	3	2	1
Rick Perry	3	1				
Marco Rubio	9	6	10	11	12	11
Rick Santorum	1	1	*	1	*	*
Donald Trump	23	34	32	32	38	37
Scott Walker	11	2				

Source: All polls were conducted by ABC News and the *Washington Post*.

Note: Blank spaces indicate that that person's name was not included in the list of candidates read to survey respondents; asterisks indicate values less than 1 percent.

It was no great shock that Trump declared his candidacy. He had publicly toyed with the idea in several previous elections. He undoubtedly loved being in the public spotlight, and running for president offered him a new opportunity to speak in front of large crowds, give interviews, and appear on national television. What was surprising was what happened after his announcement: Trump's poll numbers immediately started on a long and sustained increase. By late July 2015, he was clearly the Republican front-runner—and save for a three-day period in early November, he never surrendered that position.[16] By early December, he had a 15-percentage-point lead over the rest of the GOP field. The final poll in Table 2.3, taken just a week before the Iowa caucuses, showed Trump with the support of 37 percent of the country's Republicans. The only two candidates within shouting distance were Ted Cruz, at 21 percent, and Marco Rubio, at 11 percent.

Why Trump, a political novice with a highly negative public image, was able to win the Republican nomination is a knotty question that will receive a more extended examination later in this chapter. But three points should be mentioned here, as they go far toward explaining his rise in the pre-primary polls. First, though he spent relatively little on paid advertising, Trump received an extraordinary amount of free publicity—what is sometimes called "earned media"—on television and radio, in newspapers and magazines, and in online sources. Throughout his campaign, Trump complained about his treatment by most major media organizations. But no matter how much reporters and editors may have disliked Trump and impugned his policies and abilities, they couldn't resist covering him. As CBS president

Les Moonves said in a moment of candor, "It may not be good for America, but it's damn good for CBS. . . . The money's rolling in and this is fun. I've never seen anything like this, and this [is] going to be a very good year for us. Sorry. It's a terrible thing to say. But bring it on, Donald. Keep going."[17] At the end of February 2016, a firm called mediaQuant estimated that Trump had received the equivalent of $1.898 billion in free media coverage. The next-most-favored candidate, Hillary Clinton, had received just $746 million. The second-most-covered Republican candidate, Ted Cruz, had received $313 million worth of coverage, less than one-sixth of what Trump had been given.[18] In an election in which no other Republican candidate except perhaps Jeb Bush was well-known, the media probably helped Trump far more than they hurt him.

Second, though much of what Trump said was highly controversial and helped give him a decisively negative public image, he was clearly saying things that some people—especially Republican people—wanted to hear. A particularly good example is the immigration issue, the most publicized subject in Trump's announcement speech, the issue that probably best explains his initial rise in the polls. As is true of many policy issues, public opinion about immigration is complicated. Depending on what is asked about and how the question is worded, support can be found for a variety of different postures and policy options. But there is a good deal of evidence to show that lots of Americans—in many cases, a clear majority—do not believe that our borders are secure and think that illegal immigration imposes a variety of significant costs on the country. Yet the two most recent presidents, Bush and Obama, were almost entirely unwilling to recognize the problem, much less work to solve it. So when Trump accused illegal immigrants of bringing crime and drugs to America, many of his listeners thought he was only telling a much-needed truth.

Finally, Trump became the Republican front-runner because most of his opponents refused to take him seriously. Until far too late in the campaign, his opponents assumed that Trump was a flash in the pan, a passing fad whose campaign would collapse once the voters got a good look at him. Most of Trump's rivals accordingly designed their campaigns on the premise that their proximate task was to emerge as Trump's principal rival. Then, facing Trump in a one-on-one contest, they thought they could easily put him to rout and wrap up the nomination. Well after Trump had assumed the lead in all the polls, the other Republican candidates spent far more time and money attacking each other than going after Trump.

Perhaps the best example of this tendency was Right to Rise, the well-funded Super PAC that was organized to boost the campaign of Jeb Bush. In August 2015, Mike Murphy, the chief strategist of Right to Rise, openly described his organization's battle plan: "If other campaigns wish that we're going to uncork money on Donald Trump, they'll be disappointed. Trump is, frankly, other people's problem. We'd be happy to have a two-way race with Trump in the end, and we have every confidence that Governor Bush would beat him."[19] Murphy was true to his word. As of mid-February 2016, according to a study by ProPublica, Right to Rise had spent just 4 percent of its funds attacking Trump, less than a quarter of the money they spent attacking John Kasich, one seventh of the money they used to attack Marco Rubio.[20] Said one conservative commentator, "Right to Rise, like an all-pro right guard, helped clear a path for Trump by blocking several of his would-be tacklers, in particular Marco Rubio."[21]

The Delegate Selection Season: Democrats

The Democratic primary and caucus season, which ran from February 1 through June 14, was not, on the whole, a particularly suspenseful affair. It began on an auspicious note for the Sanders campaign. The Vermont senator came within an eyelash of beating Clinton in the Iowa caucuses, clobbered her in the New Hampshire primary, and then finished a close second in the Nevada caucuses. Hovering over these results was Clinton's experience in the 2008 Democratic nomination race, when she had entered the primary season with a large lead in the national polls, only to lose most of the primaries and caucuses—and thus the nomination—to Barack Obama. Would something similar, many observers wondered, happen in 2016?

Any such apprehensions were decisively put to rest by the results of the South Carolina primary on February 27. In 2008, it was South Carolina that had first shown just how formidable Obama's candidacy would be. Largely because of his appeal to black voters, Obama trounced Clinton in the Palmetto State by a two-to-one margin. In 2016, South Carolina sent a very different message. This time it was Sanders who had trouble appealing to black voters. Sixty-one percent of the South Carolina Democratic primary electorate was black, and 86 percent of them voted for Clinton. Add in a small majority of the white vote, and Clinton won an overwhelming victory, 73 percent to 26 percent. Three days later, she won seven of the nine primaries held on March 1 (one of the exceptions was Sanders's home state of Vermont), then won all but one of the nine remaining Democratic primaries held in March. (As we will see later, it was Sanders's success in the caucuses that made his campaign appear more competitive than it really was.) According to most media delegate counts, Clinton clinched the Democratic nomination on June 6, with six primaries still to take place.

In light of the controversy over the role of the superdelegates, it is important to emphasize that Clinton did *not* win the 2016 Democratic nomination because of them. Had there been no superdelegate provision in the Democratic Party rules, Clinton would still have won a solid majority of the convention delegates, 2,205 (54 percent) to 1,846 for Sanders (46 percent).[22] Clinton's advantage among superdelegates undoubtedly padded her lead: With the superdelegates added in, she received 60 percent of the votes in the actual convention balloting.[23] It may also have helped reassure some of her more nervous supporters in the weeks before South Carolina. But the bottom line is that Clinton won in 2016 because most Democrats wanted her to be their party's nominee and expressed that preference in the primaries and caucuses.

Clinton's popularity among her party's ordinary, rank-and-file voters emerged with special clarity in the primaries, the complete results of which are shown in Table 2.4. Of the thirty-nine Democratic presidential primaries held in 2016, Clinton won twenty-nine, receiving 55 percent of the total vote to just 43 percent for Sanders. In most other subfields of American political science, an election in which the winner bests his or her closest competitor by 13 percentage points would not be considered close. As indicated in Table 2.5, Sanders fared far better in the caucuses, winning twelve of fourteen. Thus, one could say, Clinton won thirty-one of fifty-three contests. But this way of summarizing the results significantly understates the extent of Clinton's dominance. Caucuses tend to be held in small states; large states almost always select their delegates via primary. Of the twenty most populous states in America in 2016, only one (Washington) held a Democratic caucus. Clinton's thirty-one victories thus included wins in the nine most-populous states, whereas many of Sanders's victories came in states with comparatively small populations.

Caucuses, moreover, have often been criticized for doing a poor job of representing the concerns and preferences of ordinary voters. Caucuses are almost always characterized by very small turnout rates—usually no more than about 2 or 3 percent of the party electorate—and are thus susceptible to domination by a small number of zealous candidate and issue activists.[24] Nebraska's experience in 2016 provides an instructive example. On March 5, Nebraska held precinct caucuses, the results of which were used to select twenty-five delegates to the Democratic National Convention. On May 10, Nebraska also held a presidential primary, but the primary was purely advisory—it had no effect on the selection or binding of any convention delegates. Whereas just 33,460 participated in the delegate-selecting caucuses, 80,436 people voted in the nonbinding primary. And although Sanders won the Nebraska caucuses 57 percent to 43 percent, Clinton won the more participatory primary 53 percent to 47 percent.

In sum, whatever criticisms Sanders and his supporters may have about the 2016 presidential nomination process, they cannot reasonably complain that Hillary Clinton won even though the voters really preferred him. The primary results, in particular, speak loudly to the contrary. As for Sanders's disproportionate success in the caucuses, this may only reflect the fact that caucuses have such a small and unrepresentative voter turnout. A more broadly based delegate selection device, such as a primary, would probably have awarded even more delegates to Clinton.

To get a better sense of why Clinton prevailed, Table 2.6 combines the results of twenty-five separate exit polls, which were conducted after almost every Democratic primary held between February 9 and May 10. Sanders had

Table 2.4 Democratic Presidential Primary Results

Date	*State*	*Clinton*	*Sanders*
February 9	New Hampshire	37.7%	60.1%
February 27	South Carolina	73.4	26.0
March 1	Alabama	77.8	19.2
March 1	Arkansas	66.1	30.0
March 1	Georgia	71.3	28.2
March 1	Massachusetts	49.7	48.3
March 1	Oklahoma	41.5	51.9
March 1	Tennessee	66.1	32.5
March 1	Texas	65.2	33.2
March 1	Vermont	13.6	85.7
March 1	Virginia	64.3	35.2
March 5	Louisiana	71.1	23.2
March 8	Michigan	48.3	49.7
March 8	Mississippi	82.5	16.6
March 15	Florida	64.4	33.3
March 15	Illinois	50.6	48.6
March 15	Missouri	49.6	49.4
March 15	North Carolina	54.5	40.9
March 15	Ohio	56.1	43.1
March 22	Arizona	56.3	41.4
April 5	Wisconsin	43.0	56.6
April 19	New York	57.5	41.6
April 26	Connecticut	51.8	46.4
April 26	Delaware	59.8	39.2
April 26	Maryland	62.5	33.8
April 26	Pennsylvania	55.6	43.5
April 26	Rhode Island	42.2	53.6
May 3	Indiana	47.5	52.5
May 10	Nebraska	53.1	46.9
May 10	West Virginia	35.8	51.4
May 17	Kentucky	46.8	46.3
May 17	Oregon	42.1	56.2
May 24	Washington	52.4	47.6

Date	State	Clinton	Sanders
June 7	California	53.1	46.0
June 7	Montana	44.2	51.6
June 7	New Jersey	63.3	36.7
June 7	New Mexico	51.5	48.5
June 7	South Dakota	51.0	49.0
June 14	District of Columbia	78.0	20.7
Summary Statistics	Total vote	17,121,442	13,210,249
	Percent	55.5	42.8
	Number of primaries won	29	10

Source: In most cases, primary results are based on the actual data reported by the state boards of elections, with occasional supplementary information from *The Green Papers* (thegreenpapers.com).

Table 2.5 Democratic Caucus Results

Date	State	Clinton	Sanders
February 1	Iowa[a]	49.8%	49.6%
February 20	Nevada[a]	52.6	47.3
March 1	Colorado	40.3	59.0
March 1	Minnesota	38.1	61.2
March 5	Kansas	32.3	67.7
March 5	Nebraska	42.9	57.1
March 6	Maine[a]	35.5	64.3
March 22	Idaho	21.2	78.0
March 22	Utah	19.8	77.2
March 26	Alaska	20.2	79.6
March 26	Hawaii	30.0	69.7
March 26	Washington[a]	27.1	72.7
April 9	Wyoming[a]	44.3	55.7
June 7	North Dakota[a]	25.6	64.2
Summary Statistics	Average percentage	34.3	64.5
	Number of caucuses won	2	12

[a] Entries are the percentage of delegates each candidate won to the next round of delegate selection meetings (usually a state convention). In all other states, entries are the percentage of actual votes cast at the caucuses.

Table 2.6 Who Voted for Whom in the 2016 Democratic Primaries: Cumulative Results from New Hampshire through West Virginia

Variable	*Percent of the Primary Electorate*	*Percent Voting for Clinton*	*Percent Voting for Sanders*
All 25 Primaries		56	42
Gender			
Men	42	52	47
Women	58	64	35
Age			
18–29	16	30	69
30–44	23	52	47
45–64	40	67	32
65 or older	20	72	25
Race/ethnicity			
White	60	49	49
Black	27	79	20
Latino	9	NA	NA
Asian	2	NA	NA
Other	3	NA	NA
Education			
High school or less	16	66	32
Some college	31	55	44
College graduate	30	55	43
Postgraduate	23	61	38
Income			
Less than $30,000	20	62	37
$30,000–$50,000	22	56	43
$50,000–$100,000	31	55	43
$100,000 or more	27	60	38
Party Identification			
Democrat	75	66	33
Independent	22	36	62
Republican	3	NA	NA
Ideology			
Very liberal	25	51	48
Somewhat liberal	36	58	42

Variable	*Percent of the Primary Electorate*	*Percent Voting for Clinton*	*Percent Voting for Sanders*
Moderate	32	65	34
Conservative	7	NA	NA
Most Important Issue			
Health care	21	63	36
Economy/jobs	40	61	37
Terrorism	11	69	28
Income inequality	25	45	54
Top Candidate Quality			
Electability	13	82	17
Cares	28	45	54
Honest	26	28	71
Experience	31	88	11
Next President Should			
Continue Obama policies	54	74	26
Be more liberal	29	33	67
Be less liberal	12	41	49

Source: Results for individual state exit polls were taken from CNN.com. State turnout figures were taken from *The Green Papers* (thegreenpapers.com).

Note: Entries represent the percentage of the primary vote received in twenty-five Democratic primaries (New Hampshire through West Virginia), weighted by state turnout. "NA" indicates that there were so few respondents in the given category that the results were not reported in most exit polls.

great appeal for younger primary voters: He won 69 percent of the votes cast by those aged eighteen to twenty-nine. He also won a majority of the votes cast by independents, those whose most important issue was income inequality, and the 29 percent of Democratic primary voters who thought that the next president should be more liberal than Obama.

As suggested earlier, however, the exit polls also show some major limitations on the Sanders vote. The first such limitation involved *partisanship*. Not everyone who votes in a Democratic primary thinks of themselves as Democrats: 22 percent of Democratic primary voters identified as independents; 3 percent said they were Republicans. But 75 percent *were* Democrats, and most Democrats were understandably reluctant to vote for a man who had joined the party only when he decided to seek its presidential nomination. Among Democrats, 66 percent voted for Clinton, just 33 percent for Sanders.

A second important limitation on the Sanders vote was *race*. As was often noted during the campaign, Sanders had trouble talking about the special concerns of minority voters. Part of the problem may have been that all of his previous elections had taken place in Vermont, a state that has only the smallest trace of black or Hispanic residents. As a self-declared socialist, moreover, Sanders tended to see most problems as economic in nature. One political scientist commented, "That's kind of the fundamental problem between some blacks and white progressives, this notion that white progressives talk about class so much, that they forget that there's class diversity within African-American communities. And that there are ways that racism affects blacks regardless of their class status."[25] The result was that whereas white voters split their ballots evenly between Clinton and Sanders, Clinton won 79 percent of the black vote to just 20 percent for Sanders. The candidate preferences of Hispanic voters were reported for only four states—Texas, Florida, Illinois, and New York—but in these states, Clinton out-polled Sanders 67 percent to 33 percent among Hispanics.

There are also indications in Table 2.6 that at least some Democrats thought Sanders's views were too extreme. Although voters who said they were "very liberal" divided about equally between Clinton and Sanders, Clinton won 65 percent of the votes cast by self-described moderates. Only 13 percent of Democrats said that electability was the "top candidate quality" they were looking for—but 82 percent of them voted for Clinton.

Lest it seem that Clinton won only because of Sanders's weaknesses, there is also evidence in Table 2.6 of the many positive reasons that Democrats were attracted to her candidacy. She won 64 percent of the votes cast by women, while also winning a small majority of the men's vote. Almost a third of Democratic primary voters said that "experience" was the quality they valued most in a presidential candidate—and 88 percent of them voted for Clinton. Those who were most concerned with the terrorism issue also saw Clinton as a better choice than Sanders.

Finally, a word should be said about the charge that the Democratic National Committee had rigged the nomination process in Clinton's favor. Though the Sanders campaign had been complaining about the DNC's role throughout the nomination campaign, these protests received special attention in the days immediately before the Democratic convention, when Wikileaks released the text of some 20,000 emails that had been sent by a small number of top DNC officials. Over the next few days, the Internet was filled with stories headlined "Leaked DNC Emails Confirm Democrats Rigged Primary" and "DNC Undermined Democracy."[26] The most notable result of the furor was to compel the resignation of DNC chair Debbie Wasserman Schultz.

The Wikileaks emails do show that many top DNC officials disliked Sanders and wished his campaign would end. Some of what the party did probably violated the Democratic Party charter, which requires that "national officers and staff of the Democratic National Committee maintain impartiality and evenhandedness during the Democratic Party Presidential nominating process."[27] In general, however, what the emails really show is how little the national party organization can do to aid a candidate it favors.

In one of the offending emails, a DNC officer raised the possibility of accusing Sanders of being an atheist, in order to reduce his vote in the upcoming Kentucky and West Virginia primaries. The suggestion was never acted upon, however—and, if it had been a good idea, could easily have been implemented by the Clinton campaign itself or by one of its surrogates. The DNC's press secretary also suggested trying to "push a narrative" that the Sanders campaign "was a mess." Again, not a particularly devastating accusation—and there does not seem to have been any follow-up. Several DNC officials, including Wasserman Schultz, said a variety of uncomplimentary or dismissive things about Sanders, but none of these statements was ever made public until the Wikileaks release. Many of the alleged "smoking gun" emails were purely defensive in character. The DNC consulted with a Clinton campaign lawyer—but only because the Sanders campaign had attacked the two organizations for improperly conducting a joint fundraising operation. When the Rhode Island state government decided to open up a relatively limited number of polling places for its April 26 primary, the DNC worried that if Clinton fared better than she was doing in the polls, the "Bernie camp will go nuts and allege misconduct." Although the decision of the Rhode Island government may have been wrong, the DNC's reaction was neither improper nor surprising. And since Sanders won the primary anyway, the DNC's fears never materialized.

The one thing the DNC did that may have had a significant effect on the outcome of the Democratic race was the way it chose to organize and structure the candidate debates. Unlike past nomination contests, when the national party organizations had generally left the debates to whichever groups and news outlets cared to organize them, in the 2016 election both the Democratic and Republican National Committees attempted to impose their own debate calendar on the candidates, apparently on the assumption that there had been too many debates in past years, to the detriment of the party in the general election. As a result, on May 5, 2015, the DNC announced that this time there would be only six debates among the Democratic presidential candidates, as compared to more than twenty in 2008.[28] When the schedule was announced, it was widely interpreted as an attempt by the DNC to shield Clinton, the clear early front-runner, from the exposure and attacks she was likely to receive during an extended series of debates. As if to confirm this criticism, the number of debates was later increased to nine—but only because the Clinton campaign requested the addition. Widespread criticisms of the truncated debate calendar from other Democrats, including former DNC chair Howard Dean and House minority leader Nancy Pelosi, were simply ignored.

Several other features of the debates were also said to work in Clinton's favor. An unusual number of them were scheduled for the weekend or other times when the viewing audience was likely to be comparatively small. The rules were also set so that Clinton received a disproportionate amount of the speaking time.

It is difficult to say what would have happened if the DNC had not set up the debates this way. No doubt a larger number of debates and a more even division of speaking time would have given the second-tier candidates a chance to make their case to a wider audience. But would any of them actually have taken advantage of the opportunity? It is always difficult to predict just which candidates will "catch on" with the voters. Based on their performances in the debates in which they did participate, however, O'Malley, Webb, and Chafee seem unlikely to have lit up the nation's television screens. Moreover, the DNC's worries notwithstanding, Hillary Clinton was herself a formidable debater.

The Delegate Selection Season: Republicans

The Republicans' invisible primary ended, as we have seen, with Donald Trump holding a significant lead in the polls over a large field of declared candidates. The emergence of a clear front-runner is a fairly common occurrence in contemporary presidential nomination races. Much the same thing had occurred in the Democratic nomination race of 1984 and the Republican contests of 1980, 1988, 1996, and 2000. Typically, this sets up a competition among the non-front-runners to see who will emerge as the principal rival to the early leader, with the first two events on the delegate selection calendar—the Iowa caucuses and the New Hampshire primary—generally playing a major role in thinning out the field and establishing at least some sort of "pecking order" among those who make it through the first hurdles.

If Ted Cruz was to score an early win in 2016, few venues could have provided a better opportunity than the Iowa caucuses. As in past years, attendance at the Iowa caucuses was top heavy with two groups that the Cruz campaign had long targeted: 40 percent of the 2016 Iowa Republican caucus attendees described their ideology as "very conservative," and 64 percent said they were born-again or evangelical Christians. Cruz won 44 percent of the votes cast by the former group, 34 percent from the latter, and thus eked out a narrow win over Trump, 28 percent to 24 percent.[29] Marco Rubio came in a respectable third, with 23 percent.

Cruz would soon learn a lesson, however, that had also been taught to past Iowa winners such as Mike Huckabee and Rick Santorum: The profile of the New Hampshire primary electorate is very different from that of the Iowa caucusers, which means that success in the first event frequently doesn't transfer to success in the second. Though 71 percent of New Hampshire Republicans said they were conservative, only 26 percent were "very conservative." More important, Granite State conservatives are of the traditional limited-government variety, not the social and cultural conservatives who dominate Republican politics in the Iowa caucuses and many Sunbelt states. Just 25 percent of New Hampshire Republican voters said they were born-again Christians, the second smallest percentage of the twenty-four Republican primary electorates for which 2016 exit poll data exist.

On January 31, the day before Iowa, Cruz stood at 11 percent in the New Hampshire polls—almost exactly where he finished eight days later. The Iowa win, in other words, brought him not a bit of additional support in New Hampshire.

The candidate who did seem to be riding a wave of momentum in the first few days after Iowa was third-place finisher Marco Rubio. His numbers in the *Real Clear Politics* polling average in New Hampshire jumped from 10 percent on January 31 to 16 percent on February 6. And then came one of the critical moments in the 2016 campaign.

On the Saturday before the primary, the major candidates took part in a debate. In a by-now familiar pattern, New Jersey governor Chris Christie, who was lagging badly in the polls, trained his fire not on front-runner Trump, but on Rubio. The key exchange began when Rubio was asked about Christie's warning against "voting for another first-term senator as America did with Barack Obama in 2008." Rubio responded by offering a quick, nonspecific list of his accomplishments, then said, "And let's dispel once and for all with this fiction that Barack Obama doesn't know what he's doing. He knows exactly what he's doing. Barack Obama is undertaking a systematic effort to change this country, to make America more like the rest of the world."

The debate moderator then turned to Governor Christie, who said of Rubio, "You have not been involved in a consequential decision where you had to be held accountable. You just simply haven't. . . . The fact is it does matter when you have to make decisions and be held accountable for them." Rubio offered a brief criticism of Christie's gubernatorial record, then repeated the claim he had made a minute earlier: "Let's dispel with this fiction that Barack Obama doesn't know what he's doing. He knows exactly what he's doing. He is trying to change this country." And now Christie pounced: "You see, everybody, I want the people at home to think about this. That's what Washington, D.C. does. The drive-by shot at the beginning with incorrect and incomplete information and then the memorized 25-second speech that is exactly what his advisors gave him." In response, Rubio offered another criticism of Christie's record and then, as if to confirm everything Christie said, repeated his main rebuttal line a third time: "This notion that Barack Obama doesn't know what he's doing is just not true. He knows exactly what he's doing." "There it is," Christie said exultantly. "There it is. The memorized 25-second speech. There it is, everybody."[30]

Rubio's inability to offer a more plausible defense of his capacity to be president, endlessly replayed on television, was immediately recognized as one of "the gravest debate lapses of modern presidential campaign history."[31] Never again would Rubio be a serious threat to win the Republican nomination.

Three days later, when New Hampshire voters went to the polls, the results could not have been better for Donald Trump. On the one hand, the New York businessman won a thumping victory, beating his nearest competitor by almost 20 percentage points. At the same time, New Hampshire put a significant damper on whatever momentum both Cruz and Rubio had acquired in Iowa. Cruz finished third, with just under 12 percent of the vote. Rubio fell to fifth place, with 11 percent. In one final bit of good fortune for Trump, a fourth candidate, John Kasich, did just well enough to keep him in the race. Having spent an enormous amount of time campaigning personally in New Hampshire, Kasich finished second—a distant second—to Trump. Kasich, who had a solid conservative record both in Congress and as governor of Ohio, had decided to present himself to the Republican electorate in 2016 as a moderate and unifier. As subsequent primaries would prove, such a stance would bring Kasich some support in a handful of northeastern states, but gave him little chance of winning the nomination. His continued presence in the Republican race, however, meant that the anti-Trump vote remained even more finely divided. Kasich would also prove to be a disruptive presence in future debates. Whenever Cruz and Rubio would attack Trump, Kasich, who refused to criticize any of his opponents, could usually be counted on to change the subject when it was his turn to speak.

With three significant opponents still in the race, none of whom had yet clearly emerged as the main rival to Trump, and with Trump himself still dominating the media, the real estate mogul won sixteen of the next nineteen primaries. Particularly noteworthy was his March 15 victory in the Florida primary, Rubio's home state, which finally convinced the Florida senator to drop out of the race. As can be seen in Table 2.7, not once during this time period did Trump win a majority of the primary vote. In more than half of his early victories, he was held under 40 percent.

Trump did stumble in Wisconsin, where the combination of a united party establishment, heavy Super PAC spending, and strong opposition from some local talk radio hosts gave Cruz a significant victory. Unfortunately for Cruz, the next primary on the Republican calendar was in New York, Trump's home state. Never a great venue for the Texas senator, Cruz had further diminished his chances in the Empire State by saying back in January that Trump embodied "New York values," with the clear implication that such values were viewed unfavorably by the rest of the country. The result, on April 19, was a blowout win for Trump, in which he garnered 60 percent of the vote to 25 percent for Kasich and just 15 percent for Cruz. Trump followed that up with five more impressive victories in northeastern states, in each case winning a solid majority of the vote.

That set up the Indiana primary on May 3 as the final showdown between Trump and his two last rivals. Cruz threw all of his remaining resources into Indiana, a conservative state that might in other circumstances have been a favorable locale for the Texas senator. But the Trump juggernaut proved impossible to stop. Trump won 53 percent of the vote in the Hoosier State, and by the next day both Cruz and Kasich had withdrawn.

Table 2.7 Republican Presidential Primary Results

Date	*State*	*Trump*	*Cruz*	*Kasich*	*Rubio*
February 9	New Hampshire	35.2%	11.6%	15.7%	10.5%
February 20	South Carolina	32.5	22.3	7.6	22.5
March 1	Alabama	43.4	21.1	4.4	18.7
March 1	Arkansas	32.8	30.5	3.7	24.8
March 1	Georgia	38.8	23.6	5.6	24.4
March 1	Massachusetts	49.0	9.5	17.9	17.7
March 1	Oklahoma	28.3	34.4	3.6	26.0
March 1	Tennessee	38.9	24.7	5.3	21.2
March 1	Texas	26.8	43.8	4.2	17.7
March 1	Vermont	32.3	9.6	30.0	19.1
March 1	Virginia	34.8	16.7	9.5	32.0
March 5	Louisiana	41.4	37.8	6.4	11.2
March 8	Idaho	28.1	45.4	7.4	15.9
March 8	Michigan	36.5	24.7	24.3	9.3
March 8	Mississippi	47.2	36.1	8.8	5.3
March 15	Florida	45.7	17.1	6.8	27.0
March 15	Illinois	38.8	30.2	19.7	8.7
March 15	Missouri	40.8	40.6	10.1	6.1
March 15	North Carolina	40.2	36.8	12.7	7.7
March 15	Ohio	35.9	13.3	47.0	2.3
March 22	Arizona	45.8	27.5	10.5	11.6
April 5	Wisconsin	35.0	48.2	14.1	1.0
April 19	New York	60.2	14.8	25.1	0.0
April 26	Connecticut	57.9	11.7	28.3	0.0
April 26	Delaware	60.8	15.9	20.4	0.9
April 26	Maryland	54.1	19.0	23.2	0.7
April 26	Pennsylvania	56.6	21.7	19.4	0.7
April 26	Rhode Island	62.9	10.3	24.0	0.6
May 3	Indiana	53.3	36.6	7.6	0.5
May 10	Nebraska	61.5	18.4	11.4	3.6
May 10	West Virginia	77.1	9.0	6.7	1.4
May 17	Oregon	64.2	16.6	15.8	0.0
May 24	Washington	75.5	10.8	9.8	0.0

(Continued)

Table 2.7 (Continued)

Date	*State*	*Trump*	*Cruz*	*Kasich*	*Rubio*
June 7	California	74.8	9.5	11.3	0.0
June 7	Montana	73.7	9.4	6.9	3.3
June 7	New Jersey	80.4	6.2	13.4	0.0
June 7	New Mexico	70.6	13.3	7.6	0.0
June 7	South Dakota	67.1	17.0	15.9	0.0
Summary Statistics	Total vote	13,757,244	7,452,060	4,197,460	3,324,927
	Percent	45.6	24.7	13.9	11.0
	Number of primaries won	33	4	1	0

Source: In most cases, primary results are based on the actual data reported by the state boards of elections, with occasional supplementary information from *The Green Papers* (thegreenpapers.com).

In all, as can be seen in Table 2.7, Trump won thirty-three of the thirty-eight Republican presidential primaries held in 2016, to just four for Cruz. John Kasich's lone victory came in his home state of Ohio. On the other hand, Trump finished with just 45 percent of the total primary vote, the lowest percentage for a Republican presidential nominee since the delegate selection rules were rewritten in the early 1970s. Like Bernie Sanders, Trump's opponents fared far better in the caucuses (see Table 2.8). Trump won just three of the eleven 2016 Republican caucuses.

Table 2.9 combines the results of twenty-four exit polls conducted after all of the major Republican primaries that took place before Cruz and Kasich withdrew. In strictly demographic terms, there is nothing terribly striking about the Trump vote: He succeeded in assembling a diverse cross-section of the Republican primary electorate. Many of the variables that might have been expected to matter had little effect on the vote. Gender offers a good example. His many crude comments about women notwithstanding, Trump ran only slightly worse among women than among men, and he won a clear plurality of the vote from both groups. As the least obviously religious Republican candidate in memory, Trump nevertheless won 39 percent of the votes cast by born-again and evangelical Christians, compared with 44 percent of non-evangelicals. The only demographic trait that significantly distinguished Trump voters from those who supported one of the other Republican candidates was education. Trump won 50 percent of the votes cast by those with a high school education but only 30 percent from voters with a postgraduate degree. Yet even in the latter category, Trump won a larger percentage of the vote than any of his competitors.

Ideology and partisanship also seem to have had little effect on the Trump vote. Unlike Democrats, most of whom were unwilling to vote for an

Table 2.8 Republican Caucus Results

Date	*State*	*Trump*	*Cruz*	*Kasich*	*Rubio*
February 1	Iowa	24.3	27.6	1.9	23.1
February 23	Nevada	45.9	21.4	3.6	23.8
March 1	Alaska	33.6	36.4	4.0	15.2
March 1	Minnesota	21.4	29.0	5.8	36.2
March 5	Kansas	23.4	47.5	11.1	16.8
March 5	Kentucky	35.9	31.6	14.4	16.4
March 5	Maine	32.6	45.9	12.2	8.0
March 8	Hawaii	43.4	32.3	10.0	13.2
March 12	District of Columbia	13.8	12.4	35.5	37.3
March 12	Wyoming	7.4	65.4	0.0	20.0
March 22	Utah	13.8	69.5	16.7	0.0
Summary Statistics	Average percentage	26.9	38.1	10.5	19.1
	Number of caucuses won	3	6	0	2

Note: Entries are the percentage of preference votes cast for each candidate in the caucuses. Results for the North Dakota and Colorado caucuses are unavailable.

election-year convert like Bernie Sanders, Republicans showed little reluctance to embrace a candidate who had joined their party in 2012. Indeed, Trump actually fared somewhat better among Republican identifiers than among independents. Similarly with ideology: Though Trump had once espoused the liberal position on many issues, including abortion, gun control, and single-payer health care, he ran about equally well among very conservative, conservative, and moderate voters. A question that asked primary voters to name their "most important issue" indicates, not surprisingly, that Trump ran best among those who were concerned about immigration. But only 10 percent of the Republican primary electorate named immigration as their top issue; terrorism, government spending, and the economy all ranked far higher in the voters' scale of priorities.

Why Trump?

Why did Trump, widely dismissed as a nonserious candidate when he entered the race, win the Republican nomination? One factor was his complete domination of the news coverage. This also helps explain why none of the demographic variables in Table 2.9 seemed to matter very much. As Larry Bartels showed almost thirty years ago, political substance matters only when the voters have learned enough about the candidates to draw meaningful distinctions.[32] Given the media's obsession with Trump and the outcomes in Iowa

Table 2.9 Who Voted for Whom in the 2016 Republican Primaries: Cumulative Results from New Hampshire through Indiana

Variable	*Percent of the Primary Electorate*	*Percent Voting for . . .*			
		Cruz	*Kasich*	*Rubio*	*Trump*
All 24 Primaries		27	15	13	41
Gender					
Men	51	26	14	11	45
Women	49	27	15	15	37
Age					
18–29	11	29	15	17	33
30–44	19	29	13	14	38
45–64	44	27	14	12	43
65 or older	25	24	16	12	43
Born-Again or Evangelical Christian					
Yes	55	34	10	12	39
No	45	19	20	13	44
Education					
High school or less	17	27	9	9	50
Some college	32	28	11	11	46
College graduate	32	27	17	14	38
Postgraduate	19	26	22	17	30
Income					
Under $50,000	29	25	12	11	46
$50,000–$100,000	35	32	13	12	40
$100,000 or more	37	23	19	16	39
Party Identification					
Republican	69	29	12	13	42
Independent	26	24	18	13	38
Democrat	5	NA	NA	NA	NA
Ideology					
Very conservative	33	42	7	10	37
Somewhat conservative	42	23	14	15	44
Moderate	22	14	25	14	41
Liberal	3	NA	NA	NA	NA

Variable	*Percent of the Primary Electorate*	*Percent Voting for . . .*			
		Cruz	*Kasich*	*Rubio*	*Trump*
Most Important Issue					
Immigration	10	25	6	7	59
Economy/jobs	36	22	18	14	40
Terrorism	23	27	13	15	41
Government spending	28	33	15	13	35
Top Candidate Quality					
Electability	12	24	12	24	33
Shares my values	35	42	22	16	14
Tells it like it is	20	8	6	4	80
Can bring change	32	22	13	10	50
When Did You Decide?					
Within last week	33	29	21	16	29
Last month	24	30	16	15	33
Before that	43	24	8	8	55

Source: Results for individual state exit polls were taken from CNN.com. Actual results and state turnout data are, in most cases, taken from the official election returns, with occasional assistance from *The Green Papers* (thegreenpapers.com).

Note: Entries represent the percentage of the primary vote received in the twenty-four Republican primaries held between February 9 and May 3 (New Hampshire through Indiana) for which an exit poll was conducted, weighted by state turnout. "NA" indicates that there were so few respondents in the given category that the results were not reported in most exit polls.

and New Hampshire, most voters probably never did learn enough about many of Trump's rivals to consider them as real alternatives.

Second, many Republicans liked what Trump was selling. This is shown most clearly by the penultimate item in Table 2.9, which asked voters about the top quality they were looking for in a candidate. Relatively few Republican voters felt that Trump "share[d] their values." Those who were most concerned with values—about a third of the Republican primary electorate—voted disproportionately for Ted Cruz. Nor did Trump fare especially well among those concerned about electability. Trump scored big, however, among two groups. The first was those who wanted a candidate who could "bring change." After eight years of George W. Bush's big government, pro-immigration conservatism, followed by eight years of Barack Obama's unabashed liberalism, many Republicans wanted someone who would approach the federal government not with a surgical scalpel but with a sledgehammer. Trump convinced such voters that he was the person most likely to do this. Trump ran even better among voters who sought a candidate who would "tell it like it is." At a time when many voters think that far too much has been surrendered to the forces of political correctness, Trump's unguarded, often abrasive rhetoric, for all the criticism it received, clearly impressed many voters as just what the country needed.

Third, Trump won because, for a substantial part of the American electorate, none of his critics had the legitimacy necessary to make their criticisms stick. It is a well-established principle of public opinion research that the persuasive effect of a given communication depends to a great extent on the credibility of the source. If I think a particular person is unreliable or biased or has bad judgment, I am unlikely to be persuaded by anything that person says. In an extreme case, where the communicator is actively disliked by the audience, a criticism may actually work to the advantage of the person being criticized. Marco Rubio, for example, often boasted about the fact that he was the Republican candidate singled out for special attack by the Clinton campaign.

Though there is little indication that they have recognized the full dimensions of the problem, most so-called mainstream media organizations face a real crisis of credibility with Republicans and conservatives. Far from being seen as neutral arbiters and purveyors of fact, most media are viewed as (to quote one blogger) Democratic partisans with a by-line. A good illustration comes from a question that the Gallup Poll asked in 2010: "In general, do you think the news media are too liberal, just about right, or too conservative?" Republicans had no doubts about the answer: 76 percent said the media were too liberal, just 6 percent said the media were too conservative. Lest one dismiss these results on the grounds that the media are required by their job to be skeptical and critical and that everybody therefore views the media as an antagonist, Democrats had a quite different view. Just 26 percent of Democrats said the media were too conservative, whereas an almost equal number, 22 percent, actually thought the media were too liberal. The most popular answer among Democrats, chosen by 48 percent, was that the news media got things "just about right." Small wonder, against this background, that Trump paid so little apparent price for all the editorials and commentary that denounced him. Many Republicans probably reacted by deciding that, if so many in the media disliked Trump, he must be doing something right.

Finally, Trump won because none of his major opponents ran a very good campaign. For all the early talk that 2016 featured one of the strongest Republican candidate fields ever assembled, all of Trump's major opponents except Jeb Bush were relatively new to the national stage and, either for that reason or because they hired bad consultants, made lots of glaring mistakes. A number of these errors have already been mentioned: Kasich's strange decision to present himself as a moderate; Rubio's fumbling performance in the pre–New Hampshire debate; and the all-but-universal failure to take Trump seriously as a candidate until it was too late.

Perhaps the worst single mistake by a Republican candidate occurred before the campaign began. As of late 2012, no candidate seemed better positioned to win the 2016 Republican presidential nomination than Marco Rubio. A senator from one of the two most important swing states in the nation, of Cuban ethnicity, and with a compelling personal story, Rubio had also been a Tea Party favorite when first elected to the Senate in 2010. And then, in one move, he went a long way toward neutralizing all of these advantages. Though Rubio had opposed amnesty when running for the Senate in 2010, in early 2013 he became one of the "Gang of Eight" that coauthored a "comprehensive immigration reform" bill that was spectacularly unpopular among conservative Republicans. Though a few Republicans supported the bill, most viewed it as a horrendous piece of legislation that granted the Democrats everything they wanted—increased levels of immigration, amnesty for illegals that were already here—and got almost nothing in return by way of stricter enforcement or increased border security. Well before Rubio's stumble in New Hampshire, this was the principal issue that his opponents used against him.

Denouement and Conclusion

The rest is anticlimax. On July 15, Trump picked Indiana governor Mike Pence to be his running mate. Perhaps the most noteworthy feature of the Republican National Convention, which was held in Cleveland July 18–21, was the substantial number of Republican Party leaders who declined to attend, including home-state governor Kasich and all of the party's living presidential nominees except Bob Dole. The most memorable moment was Ted Cruz's speech to the delegates, in which he had been expected to endorse Trump but instead only recommended that voters "stand, and speak, and vote your conscience, vote for candidates up and down the ticket who you trust to defend our freedom and be faithful to the Constitution."

The day after the GOP convention ended, Hillary Clinton announced that her vice presidential candidate would be Virginia senator Tim Kaine. The Democratic National Convention took place in Philadelphia July 25–28 and showed a party that seemed to be a good deal more united than the Republicans.

I began this chapter by asking how the two major parties could have nominated two such generally unpopular presidential candidates as Hillary Clinton and Donald Trump. Having reviewed both parties' nomination races in some detail, I wish at the end to pose a slightly different question: Was there an alternative set of rules that might have produced a different outcome?

The analysis presented in this chapter provides little reason to think that any plausible change in the rules would have yielded a different nominee, in either party. The Democratic superdelegate rule may or may not be a good idea, but in 2016 it had no effect on the final result. Hillary Clinton won her party's nomination because she won a clear majority of the votes cast in the Democratic primaries and thus won a majority of the ordinary, non-superdelegates who were selected in the primaries and caucuses. A strong case can be made that the Democrats significantly overestimated Clinton's appeal to the general electorate and underestimated the importance of all her many negatives, but there is nothing the rules could have done to alter such beliefs. The only rules change that might have given Bernie Sanders a reasonable chance of winning the nomination would have been a switch by a very large number of states from primaries to caucuses—but such a change would have helped Sanders only because caucuses are generally characterized by a low and unrepresentative turnout and therefore might have allowed a less popular candidate to win a majority of the delegates. Precisely for that reason, it is difficult to imagine a large-scale national movement to increase the use of caucuses.

A good case can be made that the Democratic National Committee, and especially DNC chairperson Debbie Wasserman Schultz, violated the party rule requiring that organization to be impartial and evenhanded during the presidential nomination process. But ever since the delegate selection rules were rewritten in the early 1970s, there has been little that the formal party organization can do to help a favored candidate. For all the controversy the Wikileaks emails generated, when evaluated dispassionately they actually show how few real powers and resources the DNC has. The one exception—the one intervention by the DNC that might have made a difference—was its decision to hold a very limited number of debates and to schedule them at times when the viewing audience was likely to be relatively small. But it is far from clear that a larger number of debates would have transformed one of the second-tier candidates into a serious contender or significantly increased the electoral appeal of Bernie Sanders.

But suppose that Sanders had been nominated. Would he really have fared better in the general election than Clinton did? Sanders's partisans are fond of citing their candidate's favorability ratings, which were consistently higher than Clinton's throughout the election year—higher, indeed, than those of any other major presidential aspirant in either party. On January 30, 2016, on the eve of the Iowa caucuses, Sanders's average rating was 47 percent favorable, 38 percent unfavorable; Clinton's numbers were 39 percent favorable, 55 percent unfavorable. Similarly, on November 5, 2016, three days before the general election, Sanders was viewed favorably by 54 percent of the American public, unfavorably by 35 percent. Clinton's average ratings on the same day were 42 percent favorable, 56 percent unfavorable. Trial-heat polls also showed Sanders running far better against Trump than Clinton did.

As a guide to what would have happened if Sanders had actually been the Democratic nominee, however, these numbers are highly misleading. Sanders was popular throughout the 2016 election campaign because no one made any serious, prolonged effort to attack him. No one had any reason to. Clinton offered a few mild criticisms of his record and policy proposals but was reluctant to go full bore after a candidate who was unlikely to win the nomination and whose supporters she would need in the general election. Nor did the Republicans make any effort to reduce Sanders's popularity. From their perspective, the longer his nomination campaign lasted and the more blood he drew from Clinton, the better for the Republican nominee in November. Had Sanders actually won the nomination, however, the Republicans would have delightedly launched an all-out assault on the Vermont senator. And they would have had a lot to work with: his socialism, his alleged atheism, his promise to increase taxes on the middle class, his perceived weakness on terrorism, his fondness for Castro and many other Third World radicals. Though we cannot, of course, say how many of these attacks would have struck a responsive chord with the voters—2016 was a notoriously bad year for predictions—we can at least say that Sanders's high favorability numbers are an inadequate guide to his likely fortunes as the Democratic presidential nominee.

The general verdict I have just pronounced with respect to the Democrats also applies to the Republicans: There is little reason to think that a different set of rules would have produced a different nominee. Trump's nomination was the product of a variety of special circumstances: the unusually large number of declared candidates in the race, the media's decision to cover Trump's doings so intensively, the failure of the other candidates to take him seriously, the unwillingness of so many prominent Republican leaders to recognize just how unpopular their stance on immigration was. But it is hard to imagine how any of these factors would have been altered by a different rules regime.

Like his Democratic counterpart, Republican National Committee chair Reince Priebus made a concerted effort to reduce the number of Republican presidential debates, in the belief that the large number of debates in 2012 had hurt Mitt Romney's chances in the general election. But the premise underlying this effort is mistaken. Romney lost the presidential election because he ran a very poor campaign, not because he was severely damaged by the Republican debates.[33] An expanded number of debates, where the other candidates had something like equal airtime with Trump, would undoubtedly have given them a better chance to slow the Trump steamroller. But would they have used the opportunity to cut Trump down to size, or would they simply have continued to attack each other in a mad scramble for second place? Based on their behavior in the debates that were held, the latter seems more likely.

Ever since the late 1960s, parties that have just lost a presidential election have often reacted by blaming the process. If only we had had a different set of rules and procedures, the losers lament, we would have selected a better candidate—or at least put the candidate we did nominate in a better position to win the general election. But no process is foolproof. Even the best-designed process must be operated by humans, who are inevitably subject to error, bias, and misjudgment. For the last several decades, the Clintons have occupied a unique position in the Democratic Party, which goes a long way toward explaining why they so greatly overestimated Hillary's appeal as a general election candidate. In the aftermath of the 2016 election, most Republicans were convinced that their process worked just fine—that the mistakes were all on the other side. But whether they will still think this in 2020 or 2024 is an open question.

Notes

1. All exit poll results cited in this paragraph are taken from www.cnn.com/election/result/exit-polls. These results are slightly different from those that CNN reported earlier, apparently because an updated weight variable has been applied to the data.
2. See, for example, Nicholas Confessore, Jonathan Martin, and Maggie Haberman, "Democrats See a Field of One Heading to '16," *New York Times*, March 12, 2015, A1.
3. The names given in the text are a "consensus list" drawn from the following sources: Jason Linkins, "The Brutalist Guide to 2016's Democratic-Contenders (Not Named Hillary Clinton)," *Huffington Post,* July 13, 2014, www.huffingtonpost.com/2014/07/13/2016-democratic-contenders_n_5579531.html; Bob Cusack, "The 65 People Who Might Run for President in 2016," *The Hill*, August 20, 2014, thehill.com/homenews/campaign/215523-the-65-people-who-may-run-for-president-in-2016; Ginger Gibson, "Election 2016: Hillary Clinton Isn't the Democrats' Only Candidate," *International Business Times*, January 21, 2015, www.ibtimes.com/election-2016-hillary-clinton-isnt-democrats-only-candidate-1786932; Jonathan Bernstein, "Democrats Have No Bench? Be Serious," *Bloomberg,* March 12, 2015, www.bloomberg.com/view/articles/2015-03-12/democrats-have-no-bench-be-serious-; and Tim Cavanaugh, "21 Democrats Who Could (Maybe) Take Hillary Clinton's Place in 2016," *Washington Examiner*, March 14, 2015, www.washingtonexaminer.com/21-democrats-who-could-maybe-take-hillary-clintons-place-in-2016/article/2561521.
4. On the emergence of the vice presidency as a stepping stone to higher office, see William G. Mayer, "A Brief History of Vice Presidential Selection," in *In Pursuit of the White House 2000: How We Choose Our Presidential Nominees*, ed. William G. Mayer (New York: Chatham House, 2000), 341–345.
5. All numbers cited here are based on the October 4, 2015, averages reported at elections.huffingtonpost.com/pollster#favorability-ratings.
6. As quoted in David Catanese, "What If Hillary Clinton Doesn't Run?" *U.S. News & World Report,* July 22, 2014, www.usnews.com/news/blogs/run-2016/2014/07/22/if-not-hillary-clinton-then-who-will-the-democrats-pick.
7. This is perhaps the major reason why vice presidents do so well in presidential nomination races. See William G. Mayer, "Retrospective Voting in Presidential Primaries," *Presidential Studies Quarterly* 40 (December 2010): 660–685.
8. Peter Baker and Maggie Haberman, "Biden Concludes There's No Time for a 2016 Run," *New York Times*, October 22, 2015, A1.
9. Nate Silver, as quoted in Garance Franke-Ruta, "Nate Silver: Hillary Is the Strongest Non-incumbent Ever," *The Atlantic,* June 28, 2013, www.theatlantic.com/politics/archive/2013/06/nate-silver-hillary-is-the-strongest-non-incumbent-ever/277337/.
10. See, in particular, the discussion of how candidates emerge as front-runners in contemporary nomination races in William G. Mayer, "The Basic Dynamics

of the Contemporary Nomination Process: An Expanded View," in *The Making of the Presidential Candidates 2004*, ed. William G. Mayer (Lanham, Md.: Rowman & Littlefield, 2004), 82–132.

11. All Clinton favorability numbers reported here are taken from elections.huffingtonpost.com/pollster/hillary-clinton-favorable-rating.
12. Based on the compilation of polling data at www.realclearpolitics.com/epolls/2016/president/Iowa_New_Hampshire_Nevada_South_Carolina_Dem_Contests.html.
13. For further details about the hows and whys of superdelegates, see William G. Mayer, "Superdelegates: Reforming the Reforms Revisited," in *Reforming the Presidential Nomination Process*, ed. Steven S. Smith and Melanie J. Springer (Washington, D.C.: Brookings Institution Press, 2009), 85–108.
14. The AP survey is discussed in Domenico Montanaro, "Clinton Has a 45-to-1 'Superdelegate' Advantage over Sanders," *NPR,* November 13, 2015, www.npr.org/2015/11/13/455812702/clinton-had-45-to-1-superdelegate-advantage-over-sanders.
15. The tendency of past Republican nomination races to produce a clear early front-runner is discussed in Mayer, "Basic Dynamics." The appendix to that chapter contains survey data on the 1980, 1988, and 1996 GOP contests.
16. This conclusion is based on data at www.realclearpolitics.com/epolls/2016/president/us/2016_republican_presidential_nomination-3823.html.
17. As quoted in Paul Bond, "Leslie Moonves on Donald Trump: 'It May Not Be Good for America, but It's Damn Good for CBS,'" *Hollywood Reporter,* February 29, 2016, www.hollywoodreporter.com/news/leslie-moonves-donald-trump-may-871464.
18. The mediaQuant results are discussed in Nicholas Confessore and Karen Yourish, "Measuring Trump's Big Advantage in Free Media," *New York Times*, March 17, 2016, A3.
19. As quoted in Robert Costa and Philip Rucker, "GOP Field Wrestles a Trump Tornado," *Washington Post*, August 21, 2015, A2.
20. See Philip Bump, "The Giant Super PAC Backing Jeb Bush Has Spent Very Little Fighting Donald Trump," *Washington Post,* February 20, 2016, www.washingtonpost.com/news/the-fix/wp/2016/02/20/the-giant-super-pac-backing-jeb-bush-has-spent-very-little-fighting-donald-trump/.
21. Stephen F. Hayes, "How Jeb Cleared the Way for Trump," *Weekly Standard,* January 23, 2016, www.weeklystandard.com/how-jeb-cleared-the-way-for-trump/article/2000726.
22. This is the count for non-superdelegates provided at both www.thegreenpapers.com/P16/ and www.bloomberg.com/politics/graphics/2016-delegate-tracker.
23. The final roll call totals at the Democratic convention were 2,842 for Clinton and 1,865 for Sanders, with 56 abstentions.
24. For a detailed discussion of all these points, see William G. Mayer, "Caucuses: How They Work, What Difference They Make," in *In Pursuit of the White House: How We Choose Our Presidential Nominees*, ed. William G. Mayer (Chatham, N.J.: Chatham House, 1996), 105–157.
25. Andra Gillespie, as quoted in Sam Sanders, "On Race, Sanders and Clinton Stumble but Engage," *NPR,* March 3, 2016, www.npr.org/2016/03/07/469554117/on-race-sanders-and-clinton-stumble-but-dont-shy-away.
26. See Tyler Durden, "Leaked DNC Emails Confirm Democrats Rigged Primary, Reveal Extensive Media Collusion," *ZeroHedge,* July 23, 2016, www.zerohedge.com/news/2016-07-23/leaked-dnc-emails-confirm-democrats-rigged-primary-reveal-extensive-media-collusion; and Michael Sainato, "Wikileaks Proves Primary Was Rigged: DNC Undermined Democracy," *Observer,* July 22, 2016, observer.com/2016/07/wikileaks-proves-primary-was-rigged-dnc-undermined-democracy.

27. See "The Charter of the Democratic Party of the United States," Article V, sec. 4, at www.demrulz.org/wp-content/files/DNC_Charter_Bylaws_9.11.2009.pdf.
28. An exact count on the number of debates in 2008 is difficult to find, in part because it is not always clear what constitutes a "debate."
29. All poll numbers cited here are taken from www.cnn.com/election/primaries/polls/IA/Rep.
30. All quotations from the debate are based on "Transcript of the New Hampshire GOP Debate, Annotated," *Washington Post,* February 6, 2016, www.washingtonpost.com/news/the-fix/wp/2016/02/06/transcript-of-the-feb-6-gop-debate-annotated/.
31. The quoted assessment is from Jeremy W. Peters and Jonathan Martin, "Rubio Is Tested as Rivals Sense Vulnerabilities," *New York Times*, February 8, 2016, A1.
32. See Larry M. Bartels, *Presidential Primaries and the Dynamics of Public Choice* (Princeton, N.J.: Princeton University Press, 1988).
33. See William G. Mayer, "How the Romney Campaign Blew It," *The Forum* 13 (December 2015).

3

The Election

The Allure of the Outsider

Marc J. Hetherington

Just as Cassius Clay did in 1964 when he won the heavyweight boxing title from the supposedly unbeatable Sonny Liston, Donald Trump shook up the world in 2016. Not only was his general election victory over Hillary Clinton completely unanticipated by political commentators and scholars, but his ability to dispatch more than a dozen Republicans—many of them very highly credentialed—in the battle for the Republican party's nomination was similarly stunning. At the beginning of 2015, Trump seemed the darkest of dark horses. No one other than perhaps the New York real estate mogul himself foresaw that he would run for president. Even midway through that year, when he announced his bid after gliding down the golden escalators into the lobby of the Trump Tower, only 7 percent of likely Republican voters favored him.[1] Most serious political watchers viewed Trump as a sideshow, a carnival barker, a joke, or worse. He shocked them all.

Trump's path to triumph in both the Republican primaries and the general election was, to say the least, unconventional. He did not do much of anything the way other presidential hopefuls had done them. He did not have much of a formal campaign organization. While his opponents spent hundreds of millions of dollars on campaign offices, armies of staffers, expensive consultants, and myriad thirty-second television ads, Trump hosted big rallies, went on morning television talk shows, and took to Twitter. His campaign organization featured people with short or nonexistent political résumés. His press secretary, Hope Hicks, had never been involved in a political campaign, much less one for president. Trump went through a few campaign managers. One, Corey Lewandowski, had to be let go after he tried to throw a female reporter to the ground by her arm. Another, Paul Manafort, had enjoyed his most recent political successes managing the campaigns of autocratic leaders in Ukraine. These were not the people established Republicans were trying to recruit to run their campaigns.

Not only was his campaign organization unusual, but Trump also said and did things that would have sunk any conventional candidate. This started on day one in June 2015, when Trump kicked off his campaign with a speech in which he referred to Mexican immigrants as "rapists." He later promised repeatedly to build a wall between the United States and Mexico that would stretch roughly two thousand miles to keep illegal immigrants out of the country, and he promised that he would make Mexico pay for its construction. These seemed like particularly self-damaging steps because Republicans, after Mitt Romney lost the 2012 election, had conducted an "autopsy" of what went wrong that year in which they concluded that a key problem was the party's failure to attract Latino voters, by far the fastest growing ethnic group in the country. Trump took a different tack. He realized that, because there are few Latino Republicans, he could curry favor with working-class whites who were concerned about the quality of their jobs and free trade with Mexico and worry about Latinos later.

Trump's assault on the Republican establishment was brutal and, with each attack, longtime political watchers expected his candidacy to sink as a result. Yet it never did. A full account of his broadsides would require a full chapter all by itself, but detailing one example illustrates the point. Trump derided Sen. John McCain, the 2008 Republican presidential candidate and a party leader of the highest order, for having been a prisoner of war in Vietnam. No one derides a former POW and gets away with it. Indeed the respect and admiration that Americans have for McCain because of the years of abuse he absorbed at the hands of his captors has never been in question. Regardless, Trump said about McCain, "I like people who weren't captured."[2] Pundits immediately forecast the Trump campaign's imminent demise, which never came.

An incident nearly a year later during the Democratic National Convention was similar. At the convention, the parents of Humayun Kahn, a Muslim American army captain who was killed by a suicide bomber in Iraq in 2004, criticized Trump for his proposed ban on Muslims entering the United States. Their Muslim son, they argued, had served his country heroically, and it was dangerous to paint a whole religious group with such a broad brush. Trump responded via Twitter by attacking Captain Kahn's parents.[3] No politician attacks a Gold Star family—a family whose child has made the ultimate sacrifice for his country—and survives. Although Trump's poll numbers sagged a bit, his victory in November makes clear that he survived just fine.

Neither of these examples was even the most egregious of Trump's missteps. The most compelling evidence that Donald Trump had at least nine political lives occurred just before the second presidential debate in early October. A decade-old *Access Hollywood* video was leaked to the *Washington Post*.[4] In it, Trump was seen and heard bantering with host Billy Bush about women. "I'm automatically attracted to beautiful [women]—I just start kissing them. It's like a magnet. Just kiss. I don't even wait. And when you're a star they let you do it. You can do anything. . . . Grab them by the pussy. You can do anything."

One month later, Trump was president-elect. Perhaps he was right when he said in January 2016, "I could stand in the middle of 5th Avenue and shoot somebody and I wouldn't lose voters."[5] This chapter explores this most unusual, indeed unprecedented, of presidential elections, one that set Washington, specifically, and the country as a whole, on its ear.

The Road to the Nomination

Those who work in politics often criticize those who study politics for developing theories that are irrelevant to what goes on in the real world. One clear exception is a book called *The Party Decides*, which was published in 2007. It served as something of a bible for political commentators who wanted to make predictions about presidential nominations. In the book, Marty Cohen and his coauthors argue that, even though nominations are no longer controlled by political kingmakers in smoke-filled rooms at political conventions, party elites still dominate the nomination process. Governors, senators, and other party leaders effect their desired outcome by endorsing their favored candidate and directing campaign contributions that way in the months leading up to the primary and caucus season. Between 1980 and 2004, party leaders almost always got their man, even though voters, not party bosses, cast the actual primary and caucus votes. That man was the one deemed most electable by the party establishment; he (always he) was usually the front-runner at the beginning of the battle for the nomination.

Cracks in *The Party Decides* thesis began to show in 2008, at least on the Democratic side.[6] Party insiders overwhelmingly favored Hillary Clinton in the year leading up to the first primaries and caucuses. She far outstripped Barack Obama when it came to endorsements and large contributions from major-party donors. Yet Obama overcame Clinton's advantages and won a very tight race for the Democratic nomination. Mitt Romney's nomination in 2012 was a more typical case, suggesting once again that the party establishment could decide. Romney, the front-runner and top choice among Republican insiders, secured the GOP nomination. *The Party Decides* would have predicted that Hillary Clinton would breeze to the Democratic nomination and that one of several high-quality establishment Republicans—someone like Jeb Bush, John Kasich, Scott Walker, or Marco Rubio—would emerge from the crowded GOP field to oppose her. It turned out that 2016 was more like 2008 than 2012.

The Democrats

Although most of the action in 2016 occurred on the Republican side, what happened among Democrats was important in its own right. Hillary Clinton's difficulty dispatching Bernie Sanders's insurgent candidacy despite the overwhelming support she received from party insiders was telling. Clinton not only shared the last name of the popular former president, Bill Clinton, but she also enjoyed many other advantages in her pursuit of the Democratic nomination. The party's establishment was foursquare behind her, with almost all of the endorsements from Democratic leaders going her way. Clinton raised more money than Sanders, even though Sanders raised money from more people. Clinton secured the support of the big-money, establishment donors. As the front-runner with more resources, she was able to stock her campaign organization with the most sought-after professionals. Experts think that having excellent campaign talent can make a significant difference in getting people to the polls and winning their votes.

Not only that, Bernie Sanders did not, on paper, look like much of a threat. He hailed from tiny Vermont, a state that rarely launches national political careers. The seventy-four year old had a personality that many considered akin to a crotchety grandfather. Although he had served in either the House or Senate for twenty-five years, he was not popular among his congressional peers. Moreover, Sanders's time in the U.S. Senate was not particularly distinguished. In his nine years as a member of "The World's Greatest Deliberative Body," only one bill that he sponsored passed the Senate.[7] Undermining Sanders's prospects further was the fact that he did not even call himself a Democrat. Although he caucused with the Democrats during his time in both the House and Senate, he appeared on the ballot as an independent when he ran for office in Vermont. He referred to himself as a democratic socialist, the latter a word that all but disqualified him in the eyes of a significant number of Americans.

Despite his liabilities, Sanders hung tough against Clinton's campaign machine until the very end of the primary process. Although commentators often attributed this to Sanders's folksy style and tell-it-like-it-is approach, it is probably more the case that Hillary Clinton was an unusually weak candidate. Her ties to Wall Street put her out of step with many Democrats. Her honesty and integrity had been a source for concern since her earliest days as first lady. Perhaps most fundamentally, the perception that Clinton was the ultimate insider fueled Sanders's support. With the possible exception of George H. W. Bush in 1988, Clinton had the most complete résumé of any presidential candidate in recent memory. Experience as first lady, U.S. senator from New York, and secretary of state might have, in a different time, been viewed as a virtue. Instead, Clinton's public service seemed a liability in 2016. She was old news, someone who had been in Washington forever. Many Democrats perceived her as part of the problem rather than as a solution. This weakness would manifest itself again in the general election campaign. Trump pilloried Clinton for her insider status. One of his most effective campaign appeals urged voters to judge the effectiveness of someone who had been around Washington as long as Clinton had while so many problems persisted in the country.

Long, protracted nomination struggles are the exception in presidential politics, not the rule. Usually a candidate has locked up the party's nomination by April. Clinton, in contrast, struggled with Sanders until June. The beginning of the caucus and primary season was surprisingly competitive. Sanders nearly won the important Iowa caucuses (a mere 0.2 percent of caucus-goers separated his share of the vote from Clinton's). He romped in the first primary state, New Hampshire, winning Vermont's neighbor by more than 20 percentage points. What saved Clinton from another ignominious nomination defeat like the one she absorbed from Barack Obama in 2008 was the overwhelming support she received from racial and ethnic minorities. When the primary race turned to the South, with its high concentration of African American Democrats, and to the Southwest, with its high concentration of Hispanic American voters, Clinton steadied herself.

Ultimately Clinton slugged out a close victory for the nomination, but it took until June 7 to secure enough pledged delegates to assure her the nomination. Her defeats in several upper midwestern states, however, including Wisconsin and Michigan, were a harbinger of things to come in the general election. The Rust Belt features a larger than average number of older white voters with less than a college degree, so-called working-class whites. These two states, along with Ohio and Pennsylvania, proved crucial to Clinton's undoing against Donald Trump. Three of them (Wisconsin, Michigan, and Pennsylvania) had voted for the Democratic presidential candidate in each of the last six elections, and most pollsters thought it impossible that they would go for Trump. But they did. Perhaps Clinton's Rust Belt struggles—she also lost Indiana to Sanders—during the nomination phase should have alerted pundits and scholars to the big surprise ahead.

The Republicans

Many Americans were in a sour mood in 2016. When people are unhappy, they turn to political outsiders. This is what happened in 1992. In that year's election, another business mogul, Ross Perot, won nearly 20 percent of the national popular vote running as an independent candidate. His was the most successful independent candidacy since Theodore Roosevelt's Bull Moose campaign in 1912. Another outsider, Barack Obama, a half-term Senator and erstwhile law school professor and community organizer, shocked the political class by knocking off Hillary Clinton for the Democratic nomination in 2008, in the midst of one of the most unpopular wars in the nation's history, a war that Clinton had supported. It would be hard to be more of an outsider than Donald Trump, a person who never even sought political office before his run for the White House.

In the unusual world of 2016, however, Trump was not alone in this regard. Ben Carson, a retired pediatric neurosurgeon with no political experience, also sought the Republican nomination, as did Carly Fiorina, the former CEO of Hewlett-Packard. Although Fiorina had once run for a Senate seat in California, she lost that race and had never held political office. Another outsider, Ted Cruz, was a U.S. senator but had served less than a term when he ran for president. Moreover, Cruz's best-known acts as senator were shutting down the government in 2015 and reading *Green Eggs and Ham* during a filibuster. No one was more anti-Washington than Cruz.

Outsider candidates like these can be the perfect antidote for Americans who are dissatisfied with the political class.

Later in this chapter, I will detail the sharp increase in negative feelings that partisans have about the other political party. Worth noting here, however, is that in late 2015 Republicans were also expressing much less positive feelings than usual toward their own side. In late 2015, the NBC News polling unit asked Americans to rate how they felt toward each of the major parties. In years past, Republicans and Democrats have been similarly favorable toward their own party. In the NBC survey, Republicans were much less positive than Democrats in response to a "feeling thermometer" question, in which people were asked to rate their feeling about the parties on a scale from 0 to 10.[8] Partisans who gave their own party a score of 8 or more on the question are scored as "loving their own party." Those who gave the other party a score of 2 or less are classified as "hating the other party." As has been true in the past, about the same percentage of Democrats gave scores about the two parties that suggested love of their own and hate of the other.

The Republicans were different. The results in Figure 3.1 tell the story. To be sure, they hated the Democratic Party at the same 58 percent rate that Democrats hated the Republican Party. But less than 40 percent expressed love for their own party. More important, these attitudes structured Republican voters' preference for a nominee. Specifically, those with particularly negative feelings about the Democrats *and* lacking particularly positive feelings about their own party were especially attracted to the outsider candidates for the Republican nomination. Among those Republicans supporting Marco Rubio, the top establishment candidate at the time of the poll, about as many loved their own party as hated the other. In contrast, Carson, Trump, and Cruz supporters had love versus hate gaps of 15, 23, and 45 points, respectively. By these margins, they hated the Democratic Party but did not love the GOP.

These apparently angry voters were those who supported the outsider, anti-politics candidates for the Republican nomination. Had Republicans remained positive about their own party, it would almost certainly have benefited candidates like former Florida governor Jeb Bush, Ohio governor John Kasich, Wisconsin governor Scott Walker, and Florida senator Rubio. Republican voters' mood instead favored the four antiestablishment contenders. Indeed, starting in late 2015, Trump, Cruz, Carson, and Fiorina, who between them had fewer than six years of experience in elected public office, commanded about 60 percent support among prospective Republican primary voters in poll after poll. The other dozen or so Republican hopefuls, most of whom had enjoyed long careers in public office, duked it out for the remaining 40 percent. With these data in mind, it is perhaps not surprising that Trump and Cruz were the only two viable candidates left standing through the primary and caucus season. Trump ended up with a sizable delegate advantage going into the convention, where he closed the door on Cruz for good.

Figure 3.1 Candidate Support by Percentage of Republicans Who Report "Loving" and "Hating" the Parties, Likely Republican Voters, 2015

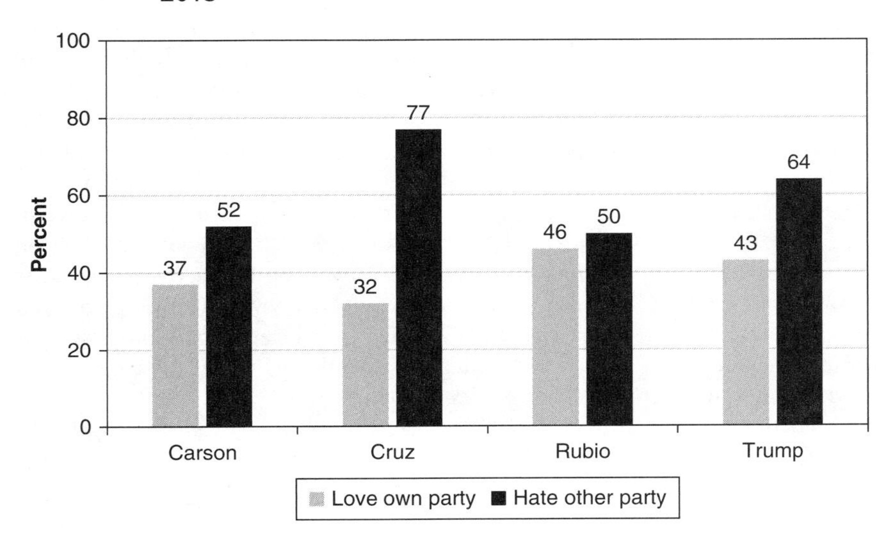

Source: NBC News poll.

The Polls

The preelection polls taken after the parties' national conventions showed much more volatility in Americans' preferences than was the case in 2012. The Obama-Romney contest featured a few twists and turns in response to major political events, such as a sag in Obama's numbers after his lackluster performance in the first debate and a similar drop in support for Romney after he was caught on video suggesting that 47 percent of Americans were living off the government. But the margin between the two remained relatively steady for months. The lead for either candidate in the average of preelection polls never exceeded a couple percentage points. The final tally was nearly as close.

In 2016, the preelection swings were much larger. Clinton emerged from the Democratic convention well ahead, fueled by Trump's misguided dustup with the Kahn family and Clinton's embrace by Michelle and Barack Obama, who both gave remarkable speeches on her behalf. Trump's numbers began to surge when the news turned to matters involving Hillary Clinton's improper use of a private email server when she was secretary of state; potential conflicts of interest involving donors to the Clinton Foundation, a nonprofit organization devoted to global health initiatives; and concerns about the robustness of Clinton's health. Indeed, when all three issues came together in September, punctuated by Clinton's nearly fainting because of dehydration at a 9/11 memorial event, Trump nosed into a slight lead in some polls. After the *Access Hollywood* video and Trump's disastrous performance in the first two debates, however, Clinton found herself well ahead, in some polls by double-digit margins. Maintaining a lead that large is impossible, especially in this age of partisan polarization, but Clinton maintained a 5- to 7-point lead into late October. With election day little more than a week away, it did not appear the election would be close.

That calculus changed in response to an October surprise delivered by the FBI director, James Comey. Although the Justice Department had announced in the summer that it would not pursue criminal charges against Secretary Clinton for the misuse of her private email server, Comey, in a letter released on October 28, alerted Congress that he was reopening the investigation to examine thousands of new emails discovered on one of Clinton's top aide's computers. Comey's decision was stunning to most observers because he presented no evidence in the letter to Congress that these emails contained classified material. Indeed they might have been copies of emails that had already been examined.

Within a week, FBI investigators found that there was nothing problematic in the emails. Even so, publicizing the new investigation damaged Clinton, whose lead in the polls dropped below 5 points. The reason is found in a social science theory called *priming*. Voters can evaluate candidates based on any number of different criteria. These could include, for example, their competence, experience, debate performance, or trustworthiness. Clinton's weakness had long been her trustworthiness. Indeed, on the specific matter of the private email server, she had prevaricated, misled, and outright lied about it in the year leading up to the election. Simply reminding voters of this controversy caused them to evaluate her on an area where she was especially weak. Clinton's comfortable lead before the Comey letter was halved to a handful of points in most of the final polls before election day.

Even though the race had become tighter, Clinton campaign operatives remained confident of victory. Forty of the fifty states had voted for same party's candidate in every election since 1992, and Democrats had won four of these six elections. The 2016 election was taking place during a Democratic era at the presidential level. Moreover, most observers viewed Trump as a much weaker candidate than any of the other recent Republican nominees. They believed that surely Clinton would do at least as well with white voters as Barack Obama had, given that Clinton is white and Obama is not. And, minority voters whose racial groups had been attacked vigorously by Trump for months would surely be as resolute in support of Clinton as they had been for Obama. And, yet, that is not what happened.

After the results were in, commentators and pundits derided the pre-election polls. Yet even though they predicted the wrong winner, the national polls were actually not far off. With most high-quality polls showing either a 3- to 4-point Clinton advantage on election eve, they missed the marked by less than most remember: Trump lost the national popular vote by just over 2 percentage points. No candidate since Rutherford B. Hayes in 1876 has lost the popular vote by this large a margin and still won in the Electoral College.[9] The key was Trump's unexpected, razor-thin victories in the Rust Belt states that offset Clinton's huge margins in states like California and New York.

The General Election Map

How did Trump win the election with a minority of the national popular vote? In one sense, the 2016 Electoral College map ought to look somewhat familiar to people who have been following American politics for the past twenty-five years. Democrats dominated the Pacific Coast and the Atlantic Coast from Maine to Virginia. The Republicans dominated most of the areas in between. Figure 3.2 illustrates the state-by-state outcomes.

A closer look reveals important differences in 2016, which account for Trump's 306–232 electoral vote victory, which a handful of "faithless electors" changed to 304–227. The Democrats' traditional blue wall of states stretching across the Rust Belt from Pennsylvania to Minnesota crumbled. In every election since Michael Dukakis lost in a landslide in 1988, Pennsylvania, Michigan, Illinois, Wisconsin, and Minnesota had voted for the Democratic presidential candidate. Ohio voted Democratic four times out of six in this period, and Iowa did so five times out of six. This part of the map looked very different in 2016, with Pennsylvania, Ohio, Michigan, Wisconsin, and Iowa all turning Republican red.

Only six states changed sides between 2012 and 2016, so it is important not to ignore the general continuity, with fully forty-four states voting for

Figure 3.2 2016 Electoral Map

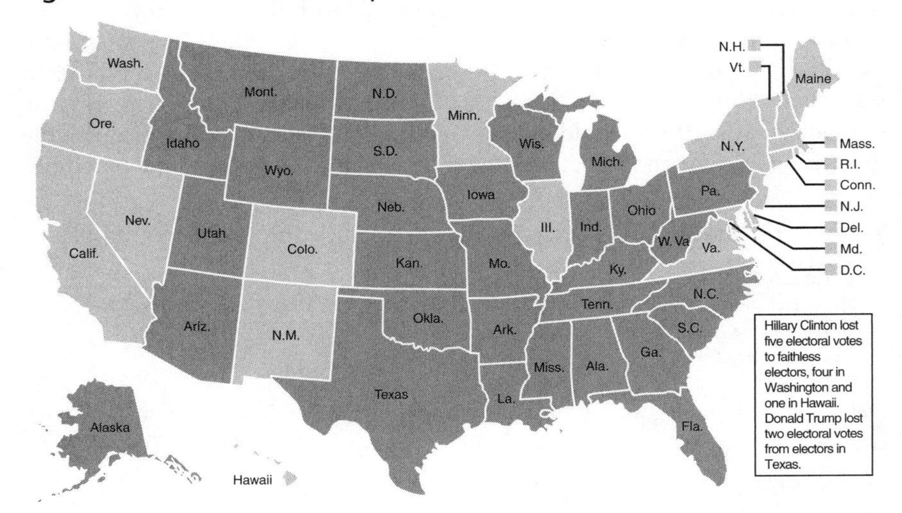

Source: Compiled by the author.

the same party in both elections. The six that changed, however, all flipped from Democrat to Republican. Table 3.1 lists these states, along with the margins that Obama won them by in 2012 and that Trump won them by in 2016. Four (Florida, Michigan, Pennsylvania, and Wisconsin) of the six favored the GOP nominee by 1.2 percentage points or less, and together they accounted for seventy-five electoral votes. Had Clinton won any three of them, or Florida (twenty-nine electoral votes) plus any one of the other three, she would have been elected president. As Edward McClellan observed on Twitter, the number of people who would have needed to change their votes in Michigan, Pennsylvania, and Wisconsin combined was so small that the sum total of people would have fit in the Big House, the University of Michigan's football stadium.

Although Florida and Ohio went to Obama by less than 5 points in 2012, none of the other four states were that close. In every recent election, Republicans believed they had a shot at Pennsylvania and Michigan, but their candidate never won and rarely came close. But this time was different. If one examines the map more broadly to include the thirteen swing states in which either or both of the campaigns concentrated resources, it becomes clear that Trump's message simply resonated better than Clinton's. David Wasserman of the *Cook Political Report* noted on Twitter that, in these swing states, where the campaign actually took place, Trump improved over Romney by an average of 5.4 percentage points. In the thirty-seven states not targeted by either of the campaigns, Trump underperformed Romney by 0.1 point.

In the next several sections, I attempt to identify the most promising explanations behind the subtle changes that brought Donald Trump to power. In truth, the race was so close that analysts can safely argue that almost anything was decisive. Had Jill Stein and Gary Johnson not run, had the Russians not hacked the Democratic Party's computers and leaked embarrassing documents to the news media throughout the fall, had Clinton's campaign allocated more resources to the Rust Belt states they needed to win and fewer to states like North Carolina, Georgia, and Arizona that they hoped to win, the outcome almost surely would have been different. Instead, I try to evaluate the more fundamental and structural forces that might help explain the outcome.

Table 3.1 States That Flipped from Democratic in 2012 to Republican in 2016

State	*Electoral Votes*	*Obama Margin*	*Trump Margin*
Florida	29	0.9%	1.2%
Iowa	6	5.8	9.4
Michigan	16	9.5	0.2
Ohio	16	3.0	8.1
Pennsylvania	20	5.4	0.7
Wisconsin	10	6.9	0.8

Source: Compiled from official sources by David Wasserman @Redistrict, Cook Political Report @CookPolitical.

Is It Still the Economy, Stupid?

When Bill Clinton announced his candidacy for president in 1992 against the incumbent president, George H. W. Bush, it appeared that he would have no chance of winning. In early 1991, Bush enjoyed 90 percent approval in the afterglow of the U.S. victory in the first Gulf War and the collapse of the Soviet Union. But the economy was entering a recession. As it grew worse and became a bigger news story, Bush's approval numbers sagged. By July 1992, his approval rating had dropped below 30 percent.[10] James Carville, Clinton's campaign manager, coined the phrase "It's the economy, stupid" to remind his troops to emphasize its weakness. If people based their vote on Bush's record on foreign policy, Carville realized, Clinton would lose. But if people decided whom to support based on the state of the economy, Clinton would win. Most commentators credit Clinton's laser-like focus on the economy's softness for his victory.

Scholars have long identified the economy as perhaps the most important factor in determining who wins a presidential election. In fact, both economists and political scientists have developed "forecasting models" that rely heavily on economic performance data gathered well before the general election campaign even starts to predict the winner. These models usually get the outcome right. Things like real income growth, growth in gross domestic product, changes in inflation, and similar factors measured months before election day have an uncanny ability to distinguish winners from losers. The success of these models suggests that listening to James Carville has traditionally been smart, at least if you are running against an incumbent during soft economic times. It really is the economy, stupid!

A quarter-century has passed since Bill Clinton won his first term, and a lot has changed since then. Among the most consequential changes is how differently people living in the same country have come to perceive its economy's health and vitality. The assumption of the economic forecasting models is that all voters perceive conditions identically and correctly. If the economy is bad, they punish the incumbent party, but if it is good, they reward it. Evidence is building that this assumption may no longer be accurate, however. People instead perceive the economy as being how they want it to be rather than how it actually is because of a psychological process called *partisan-motivated reasoning*.[11] This process is quite similar to the reaction of fans watching a sporting event. When there is a close play (or maybe even not such a close play), fans tend to see their side as in the right and the other side as in the wrong. Partisans act the same way.

Partisans, whether Republicans or Democrats, want to see the world in the best possible light when their party is in power. Seeing the economy as good makes them feel better about their party and, consequently, better about themselves. But if their party is not in power, their motivation is to perceive the very same economy as poor. They do not want to give the other side credit for a job well done when they think their side could do better. Partisan-motivated reasoning is nothing new. Indeed, since at least the 1980s and probably for a lot longer, there has been a slight tendency for Republicans to perceive the economy as better than the Democrats do when a Republican is president and vice versa when a Democrat is in the White House.[12] What has changed is that partisans' motivation to see the world as they wish it would be, rather than how it is, seems to have taken a cycle of steroids.

The degree of partisan-motivated reasoning in 2016 was so strong that it makes one question whether Republicans and Democrats live in the same country. In early 2016, the American National Election Study asked a cross-section of Americans the same retrospective economic evaluation questions it has been asking since 1980. The question reads, "Would you say over the past year the nation's economy has gotten better, stayed the same, or gotten worse?" Although room exists for a bit of subjective interpretation on the part of the survey respondents, it is still the case that there is an objectively right answer to the question. In 2015, for example, real income growth improved markedly for the first time in nearly a decade, inflation held steady, and unemployment was on a steep decline. The economy had, in an objective sense, improved markedly compared with the previous year.

Americans' survey responses were not so cut and dried. Their perceptions broken down by party appear in Figure 3.3. Democrats in the electorate saw economic improvement over the past year, with 52 percent answering that the economy had gotten better, 34 percent answering it was about the same, and only 14 percent saying it had gotten worse. Republican responses were the opposite. A mere 8 percent said conditions were better, 38 percent said they were the same, and 54 percent said the economy had gotten worse. Republicans were not lying about what they perceived. It is just that what they perceived was divorced from reality.

Some commentators suggested that, for working-class voters, things weren't actually better even if the overall national picture had improved. This group is particularly significant because, as is detailed below, white working-class Americans—people who have a high school degree or less—voted overwhelmingly for Trump. Their *personal* experiences with the economy may have caused them to believe the *national* economy was worse. Perhaps this is true, but it is more likely that people's partisan leanings are the cause of their differing economic perceptions. Working-class Democrats and working-class Republicans perceived things exactly as the non-working-class members of their parties did, not like each other. Among working-class Democrats, 51 percent thought the economy had gotten better, whereas only 7 percent of working-class Republicans did. Again, it is important to remember that all Americans live with the same national economy. These results ought to cause scholars to wonder how important the actual economy is now that people perceive how it is doing through such partisan lenses.

For those who clung to the belief that Republicans and Democrats were simply experiencing the same economy in different ways, this view became

Figure 3.3 Evaluations of the National Economy over the Past Year, by Party, 2016

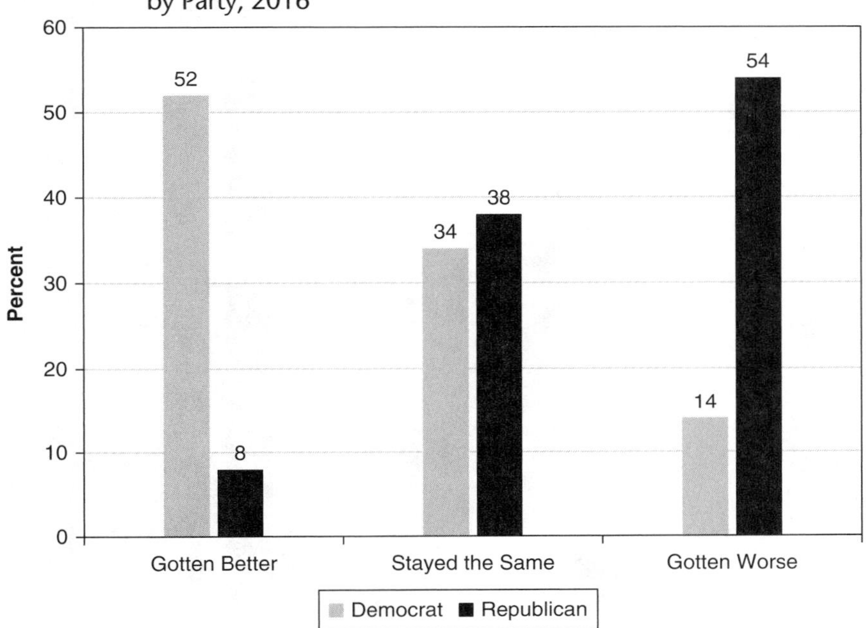

Source: American National Election Study, 2016 Pilot Study.

harder to maintain a week after the election. The Gallup organization asked Americans whether they thought the economy was "getting better" or "getting worse" in its poll the week before election day. The survey was taken November 1–7. Then Gallup asked the same question during the week after the election in a poll fielded November 9–13. The results of these two polls, broken down by party appear in Figure 3.4. Although the economy couldn't possibly have changed very much in the space of a week, the percentage of Republicans who said the economy was getting better more than tripled, from 16 percent to 49 percent. Democrats suddenly grew more pessimistic, with the percentage thinking the economy was getting better plummeting from 61 to 46—all this in the space of a week.[13]

Is it the economy, stupid? Is that why Donald Trump defeated Hillary Clinton? That question used to be easy to answer. Now it is hard to know what Americans are thinking about when they consider the economy. It no longer seems to be the actual economy. Instead, it seems to be which party they belong to combined with whether the president is of the same party. American politics is all about partisanship in this deeply polarized political world. Combined with the allure of an anti-elite outsider like Donald Trump, the power of partisanship—the subject of the next section—is central to understanding what happened in the 2016 general election.

Figure 3.4 Change in Economic Outlook before versus after the Election

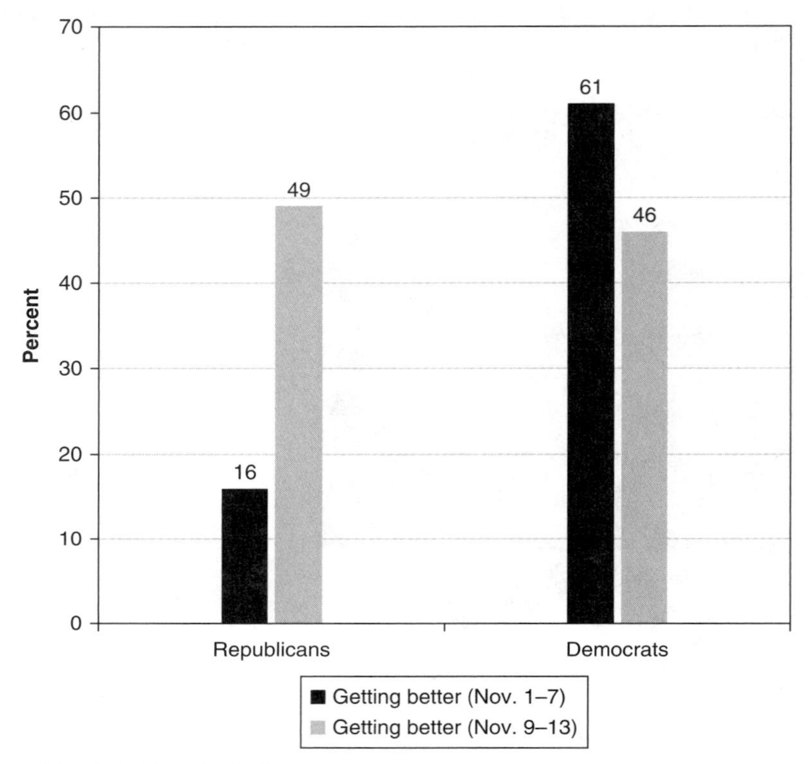

Source: Gallup Polls, November 2016.

Partisan Voting in a Deeply Polarized Time

Whether a person thinks of himself or herself as a Republican or a Democrat—wears a red or a blue uniform—has never more central to presidential voting decisions since perhaps the 1870s.[14] In other words, the only period in American history that is close to comparable in the centrality of partisanship occurred before the introduction of the secret ballot. Although definitive data are not yet available, it appears that 2016 was among the most partisan elections in the history of the country. One way to consider the effect of partisanship on people's votes is to measure the amount of split-ticket voting that occurs. Split-ticket voting involves casting a ballot for a presidential candidate from one party and a congressional candidate from the other.

Little splitting of tickets happened in 2016. For the first time in American history, every state that had a U.S. Senate race (about one-third of them) elected a senator of the same party as the party of the presidential candidate for which it voted. Trump won every state that elected a Republican senator, and Clinton won every state that elected a Democratic senator. It also appears that the 2016 election set a record for the fewest split votes between House candidates and the president. Only 25 of the 435 House districts elected a member of one party and cast a plurality of their presidential votes for the other party.[15] This is the lowest number since 1920, the first year such data were kept. According to the exit poll, only 6 percent of voters reported having voted for a presidential candidate from one party and a House candidate from the other.

What has driven the increased importance of partisanship is also noteworthy as it relates to 2016. As mentioned earlier, partisans' negative feelings about the other political party have increased steeply. The trend over time appears in Figure 3.5, which is based on answers to the American National Election Study (ANES) feeling thermometers. People are asked, on a scale ranging from 0 (most negative) to 100 (most positive) how they feel about a wide range of political and social groups. Survey interviewers tell respondents to answer 50 degrees if their feelings about each group are neutral. Among the groups the interviewers ask about are the Republican Party and the Democratic Party. The figure traces the average score that Democrats have given to the Republican Party and Republicans have given to the Democratic Party since 1980.

During the last twenty years of the twentieth century, partisans' feelings about the other party remained relatively constant. In 1980, when Jimmy Carter was president, both sides scored the other close to the neutral point. In fact, the averages were always above 40 degrees for both parties until 2000, when Democrats' feelings about Republicans fell into the high 30s for the first time. Since then, partisans' feelings toward the other side have grown much more bitter. In fact, in the 2016 ANES Pilot Study, administered during the nomination process, Republicans' rating of the Democratic Party and Democrats' rating

Figure 3.5 Deteriorating Feelings about the Other Political Party, 1980–2016

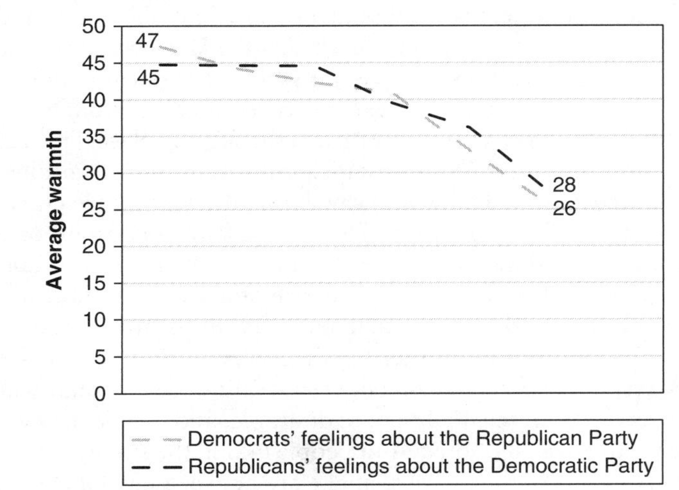

Source: American National Election Studies, 1980–2016.

of the Republican Party dropped below 20 degrees. That sounds cold, and it is compared to how people felt about all the other people and groups that the ANES asks about. In fact, those who identify as Republicans have more positive feelings toward "Atheists" than they have toward the Democratic Party. Similarly, those who identify as Democrats have more positive feelings toward "Christian Fundamentalists" than toward the Republican Party.

These negative feelings about the other party manifest themselves in many different ways. Partisans on both sides are more likely than ever to see the other party as a grave threat to the future of America.[16] Negative feelings run so deep that a substantial percentage of partisans even express dismay at the prospect that their child might marry a member of the other political party.[17] One study reveals that attributing a party identity to a person in a picture causes partisans to evaluate his or her physical attractiveness differently. Republicans judge the person as less attractive if she is labeled a Democrat, and vice versa for Democrats.[18] In fact, recent studies suggest that partisans' automatic prejudices toward the other party are stronger than people's prejudices about those of other races.[19] All this suggests that negative feelings about the other party are powerful and run deep.

Research has not demonstrated conclusively the precise causes of the rising negativity toward the other party. A number of things probably have contributed. Among the most promising explanations is one that centers on what divides Republicans from Democrats these days. Because of the issues that have been highlighted by conservative and liberal politicians—racial issues; feminism; issues related to the lesbian, gay, bisexual, and transgender (LGBT) community; immigration; the best way to deal with terrorist threats—a deeply felt new fault line has developed in the American electorate: *worldview*.[20] A worldview is a general sense of the best way for society to be organized.

The Republican Party is now dominated by those with a *fixed* worldview. They are tradition-minded; hierarchical in their thinking; resistant to change; concerned about racial, ethnic, and sexual-orientation differences; and highly attuned to threats to safety that may exist. On the Democratic side are those with a *fluid* worldview. These people are skeptical about tradition, inclined to question authority, open to new experience, embracing of differences of all sorts, and less likely to perceive the world as a threatening place. Fixed and fluid voters are wired differently both physiologically and psychologically. As the parties have become sorted by worldview during the past couple decades—the fixed into the GOP, the fluid into the Democratic Party—partisans of different stripes have found it difficult to understand each other. It is also during this period that partisans have come to dislike each other so much more intensely.

Revealing of worldview's fundamental nature is how social scientists measure it. To estimate how fixed or fluid a person's worldview is, they ask survey respondents to choose between qualities they would want their children to have. All of the qualities are desirable, and people may well want their children to have all of them. But people taking the surveys are required to choose. The choices they have to make are between having children who (1) are independent or respect their elders, (2) are obedient or self-reliant,

(3) have curiosity or good manners, (4) are considerate or well-behaved. Those who answer "respect their elders," "obedient," "good manners," and "well-behaved" reveal themselves as having the most fixed worldview. Those who answer "independent," "self-reliant," "curiosity," and "considerate" have the most fluid worldview. People can score anywhere between these extremes depending on their mix of fixed and fluid answers.

Hard as it may be to believe, the answers to these four questions about raising children are increasingly predictive of people's partisanship and, in turn, how they vote.[21] According to the 2016 Cooperative Campaign Analysis Project study,[22] only one-quarter of whites with the most fluid worldview voted for Trump. Fully three-quarters of those with the most fixed worldview did. It is also interesting to note that these answers are also related to (1) where people prefer to live—the fixed prefer suburban and rural areas and the fluid like the cities, (2) what people watch on television—the fixed like reality shows and the fluid like shows with weird, quirky characters, (3) what people eat—the fixed like traditional American food and the fluid like ethnic cuisine, and (4) what music people like—the fixed like country music and classic rock and the fluid like hip hop and alternative music.[23] Put another way, the fixed and fluid do not live together, eat together, watch TV together, or listen to music together. Perhaps this is why Republicans and Democrats have come to view each other with such suspicion—they disagree about almost everything.

Worldview-fueled strong partisan bonds are central to understanding why about 90 percent of Republicans stayed loyal to Trump and about 90 percent of Democrats stayed loyal to Clinton in the 2016 election. These percentages are quite high by historical standards. But the percentages are even more remarkable given how unpopular both candidates were. Indeed, Americans expressed a less favorable impression of both Clinton and Trump than any two presidential candidates in the history of political surveys. In fact, both candidates were seen more unfavorably than favorably in the polls taken right before the election, which was unprecedented. Regardless, Republicans who said during the primaries that they would never vote for Trump held their nose and did it. Disaffected Sanders supporters had the same type of misgivings about Hillary Clinton, yet they reluctantly cast ballots for her. Partisans followed this path because the idea of the other party occupying the White House was too painful to consider.

The Exit Polls: Anger toward Washington and a Desire for Change

The economy and partisanship are big, systemic explanations for election outcomes that can be applied to every election over time. But all elections also include factors that are unique to a particular moment in time. For example, the fallout from the Watergate scandal cost Gerald Ford the presidency in 1976, and Al Gore's seeming unwillingness to embrace Bill Clinton's legacy probably allowed George W. Bush to win in 2000. Exit polls allow us to explore explanations such as these. Voters' answers to several of the questions asked by pollsters as people were voting appear in Table 3.2.

Table 3.2 Exit Poll Data, 2016

	Percent of Electorate	*Clinton*	*Trump*
Race			
White	71	37%	57%
Black	12	89	8
Latino	11	66	28
Asian	4	65	27
Other race	3	56	36
Population Density			
Urban	34	60	34
Suburban	49	45	49
Rural	17	34	61
Gender			
Women	53	54	41
Men	47	41	52
Illegal Immigrants Working in U.S. Should Be			
Offered legal status	70	61	33
Deported to home country	25	14	83
Mexican Border Wall			
Support	41	10	85
Oppose	54	76	16
Feelings about the Federal Government			
Enthusiastic/satisfied	29	76	19
Dissatisfied/angry	69	36	57
Right Direction/Wrong Track			
Right direction	33	89	7
Wrong track	62	26	68
Which Candidate Quality Mattered Most			
Cares about me	15	57	34
Can bring change	39	14	82
Right experience	22	90	7
Good judgment	20	65	25

Source: National exit poll data from CNN.com.

The exit poll makes clear that the biggest fault lines underlying the stark partisan divide in American politics today are race and geography. When we think about "race," the tendency is to think about racial minorities. And it is true that minorities voted overwhelmingly for Clinton. Her advantage over Trump among African Americans, Latino Americans, and Asian Americans was 81, 38, and 38 points, respectively. Taken together, nonwhites voted 72–21 in favor of Clinton. Nonwhites also made up a larger than ever chunk of the electorate in 2016 at 29 percent of all voters. Democrats expected that they would cruise to victory if that percentage exceeded or even equaled nonwhites' 28 percent share of voters in 2012, when Obama was reelected.

That didn't happen because whites favored Trump over Clinton by 20 percentage points, up from 17 points for the Republican nominee in the Romney-Obama race. Although 3 points might not seem like much, it translates into a lot of votes when 71 percent of the electorate belongs to that group. Most postelection analyses focused on working-class whites, those with a high school education or less, and it is true that Trump did particularly well among this group. But he dominated among whites of almost all kinds. He won among white men (by 31 points), white women (by 9 points), whites under thirty (by 4 points), whites over sixty-five (by 19 points), and all white age groups in between. White college graduates favored Trump (by 3 points) as did whites with no college degree (by 37 points). America is almost certainly more racially polarized in its voting behavior than at any time in its history.

The division between the parties reflected in population density also has become incredibly stark. Commentators often talk about red states and blue states, but those labels are misleading. Pennsylvania, for example, has two major cities—Philadelphia and Pittsburgh—that vote overwhelmingly Democratic, but it also has vast swaths of rural counties between them that vote overwhelmingly Republican. The reason that regions of the country like the South and the Great Plains are so Republican is that the states in these regions are more rural than urban. Recall the earlier discussion of worldview, fixed or fluid. It turns out that those with the most fixed worldviews favor the predictability and traditions that exist outside the big cities, while those with a fluid worldview prefer the diversity and new experiences that are available in urban centers. With that in mind, it should not be surprising to find that Clinton won by 26 points among voters living in urban areas while Trump won by 27 points among those in rural areas.[24]

With the first woman major-party presidential candidate on the ballot, pundits expected a swell of support among women for the Democratic nominee. Although women did favor Clinton over Trump by a lot, the margin was not much different than it was for Obama in 2012. Specifically, women favored Clinton by 13 points after favoring Obama by 11 points. This is arguably the most surprising aspect of the 2016 election. Not only was Clinton a woman, but Trump's treatment of women was, to many, troubling at best. The *Access Hollywood* clip aside, news of his alleged misbehavior toward women was a constant drumbeat during the entire election.

In late October, National Public Radio catalogued allegations of untoward sexual behavior made by twenty different women against Trump since the 1980s.[25] These included an allegation of rape by his first wife as part of their divorce settlement, concerns expressed by several beauty pageant contestants of Trump walking into their changing rooms while they were partially or completely naked, and other allegations (from Jessica Leeds, Kristin Anderson, Jill Harth, and Natasha Stoynoff, among others) that Trump had kissed and/or groped them during unwanted advances. Yet Trump's showing with women was not statistically different from Romney's, and he won a majority of votes among white women.

Some observers have suggested that Trump's stances on key issues, especially immigration, won him the election. The data do not provide much evidence of this. For example, the exit poll asked voters whether they thought illegal immigrants working in the United States should be "offered legal status" or "deported to their home country." Trump had repeatedly endorsed the latter course during the Republican primaries. Although he won the 25 percent of voters who favored deportation by a margin of 83–14, an overwhelming majority of Americans (70 percent) rejected that policy course. In addition, a solid majority (54 percent) opposed building a wall along the Mexican border, with only 41 percent supporting Trump's signature proposal.

Instead the evidence suggests that Americans were simply dissatisfied with government in general. For example, the exit poll asked voters about their feelings about the federal government. Only 29 percent said they were either enthusiastic or satisfied, with Clinton dominating 76 percent to 19 percent among this sliver of Americans. A large majority (69 percent) said that they were either dissatisfied or angry, with Trump winning 57–36 among those in this group. Similarly only one-third of voters said that they thought the country was going in the right direction, whereas nearly two-thirds believed it was on the wrong track. Although Clinton romped (89–7) among those in the former group, Trump won big (68–26) among those in the more numerous latter group.

Trump was uniquely positioned to take advantage of this dissatisfaction, which helped him overcome his many self-inflicted political wounds. The exit poll asked which of the following four candidate qualities mattered most to them: "cares about me," "can bring change," "has the right experience," and "has good judgment." Clinton won a majority of voters who said cares about me, has the right experience, and has good judgment. But the quality that mattered most to a plurality of voters was which candidate could bring change. Trump won by a margin of 82–14 among the 39 percent of Americans who valued change most. Trump, the ultimate outsider, was in precisely the right place at the right time, which allowed him to overcome his many liabilities. Clinton, the ultimate insider, was in precisely the wrong place at the wrong time, which only spotlighted hers.

Conclusion

The effort to make sense of the 2016 presidential election will keep pundits, strategists, and scholars busy for many years to come. First, it calls into question how much, or even whether, campaign spending and organization matters. Although scholars have traditionally been dubious about how much campaigns matter, Washington insiders tend to think they make a big difference. The practitioners' side of the argument seemed to gain the upper hand over the scholars' with Barack Obama's two victories, in which his campaign's voter mobilization efforts helped him to victory. It is nearly impossible to get voters to abandon their party ties because of polarization, but it is possible to persuade people who are already sympathetic to one side but who might otherwise stay home to come out to vote.[26] Even if a campaign cannot change minds, it can change the universe of voters through mobilization.

If this type of voter mobilization always worked, as it seemed to for Obama, then Clinton should have won easily. She outspent Trump by several hundred million dollars during the fall. As a consequence, she had more advertisements in more places. She had field offices in every state and dozens of them in battleground states. She had the best analytics team that money could buy—one that used big data to micro-target resources to places where it thought they needed to go. Trump's campaign not only lagged Clinton's in these areas, but it also lagged Romney's efforts in 2012. In the weeks leading up to the election in November, campaign professionals thought it likely that Clinton would over-perform her poll numbers, by turning unlikely voters into actual voters on election day while Trump lacked the organization to get his voters to the polls. That the opposite happened has left many wondering what campaigns actually buy.

Second, the election of 2016 will cause the political class to explore whether the Democratic Party is in trouble or whether its message only requires fine-tuning. That such postelection navel gazing will occur among Democrats is surprising to say the least, because most commentary in the months leading up to Trump's victory focused on the degree to which the GOP was broken. Not only did the Democrats lose the presidency to an opponent whom many consider the most crass, least prepared major-party candidate of all time, but they failed to win a majority of seats in the House and fell short of winning enough seats in the Senate to take the majority. At the state level, the Democrats' problems are even more obvious. Republicans haven't held more legislative seats or governor's chairs since the 1920s. All this looks to some observers as if the Democrats are a party in crisis.

Some Democrats see the situation differently. They argue that Hillary Clinton, a weak candidate who ran an awful campaign, still won the popular vote by about three million votes. Had the Comey letter not been released at the end of October, she would have won comfortably in the Electoral College, too. And had she won, the focus would be on all the demographic advantages that Democrats enjoy. Specifically, Democrats do much better among minorities, young people, and the well educated, and the country is becoming more diverse, younger, and better educated with time. Whether or not the Democrats decide to make big changes in how they appeal to voters in the future will be worth watching.

What is clear is that the election of 2016 will live on in Americans' memories for quite some time. It is not every year that a real estate tycoon turned reality television star is elected president. Similarly, it is not every year that the intelligence community believes that a hostile foreign power has successfully intervened in the campaign to advantage a candidate, as the Russians did for Trump. And it is not every year that party polarization is so intense that most partisans on the side benefiting from Moscow's meddling seem completely untroubled by it.

In fact, Republicans appear increasingly positively disposed toward the apparent mastermind of the Russian hacking plot, Vladimir Putin, whose intent was to elect his favored candidate. Consider the results of two surveys taken four months apart.[27] A late summer YouGov/*Economist* poll revealed that, among Republicans, 50 percentage points more had an unfavorable impression of Russia's leader than had a favorable impression of him. When YouGov/*Economist* asked about Putin again in early December, after Donald Trump had been elected, the percentage of Republicans with an unfavorable impression of Putin outnumbered those with a favorable impression by only 10 points. To put those numbers into some context, Republicans' unfavorable impressions of Barack Obama—the president of the United States—outnumbered their favorable impressions by 64 points. As Obama suggested, Ronald Reagan, Republicans' favorite Republican of the past hundred years, would be stunned by this development.[28]

What these data suggest is how deeply polarized Americans are. Democrats will certainly take umbrage at this kind of "the enemy of my enemy is my friend" thinking that Republicans are engaging in relative to Vladimir Putin. But there is little to suggest that Democrats wouldn't have welcomed a push from one of the world's worst dictators, too, if it meant victory for their candidate. It is a troubling set of circumstances. During the previous eight years, it appeared to many political observers that a significant chunk of Republicans was rooting for Barack Obama to fail. Democrats already appear to be hoping for Donald Trump's failure. Partisanship can play many useful roles in helping organize political conflict, but it ceases to be useful when it causes half the country to root against the president and, hence, the country's success.

Notes

1. See, for example, HuffPost Pollster, "2016 National Republican Primary," *Huffington Post,* elections.huffingtonpost.com/pollster/2016-national-gop-primary.
2. See, for example, Ben Schreckinger, "Trump Attacks McCain: 'I Like People Who Weren't Captured,'" *Politico,* July 18, 2015, www.politico.com/story/2015/07/trump-attacks-mccain-i-like-people-who-werent-captured-120317.

3. See, for example, Eric Bradner, "Did Trump Go Too Far?" *CNN.com,* August 1, 2016, www.cnn.com/2016/07/31/politics/donald-trump-khizr-khan-family-controversy/.
4. For the original story on the recording, see David A. Fahrenthold, "Trump Recorded Having Extremely Lewd Conversation about Women in 2005," *Washington Post,* October 8, 2016, www.washingtonpost.com/politics/trump-recorded-having-extremely-lewd-conversation-about-women-in-2005/2016/10/07/3b9ce776-8cb4-11e6-bf8a-3d26847eeed4_story.html.
5. See, for example, Jeremy Diamond, "Trump: I Could 'Shoot Somebody and I Wouldn't Lose Voters,'" *CNN.com,* January 23, 2016, www.cnn.com/2016/01/23/politics/donald-trump-shoot-somebody-support/.
6. Marty Cohen, David Karol, Hans Noel, and John Zaller, *The Party Decides: Presidential Nominations before and after Reform* (Chicago: University of Chicago, 2008).
7. For a comparison of Sanders's and Clinton's legislative records, see Jeffrey Lazarus, "Hillary Clinton Was a More Effective Lawmaker Than Bernie Sanders," *Washington Post,* April 7, 2016, www.washingtonpost.com/news/monkey-cage/wp/2016/04/07/hillary-clinton-was-a-more-effective-lawmaker-than-bernie-sanders/.
8. Thanks to Carrie Roush for making these data available. See Josh Clinton, John Lapinski, and Carrie Roush, "How Republicans and Democrats Feel about Their Opponents," NBC News, January 5, 2016, www.nbcnews.com/storyline/data-points/how-republicans-democrats-feel-about-their-opponents-n490391.
9. MSNBC host Rachel Maddow noted this. See Steve Benen, "The Size of Donald Trump's Popular-Vote Loss Keeps Growing," *MSNBC.com,* November 22, 2016, www.msnbc.com/rachel-maddow-show/the-size-donald-trumps-popular-vote-loss-keeps-growing.
10. For details, see the Gallup Organization's high- and low-water marks for each president: "Presidential Approval Ratings—Gallup Historical Statistics and Trends," www.gallup.com/poll/116677/presidential-approval-ratings-gallup-historical-statistics-trends.aspx.
11. Milton Lodge and Charles S. Taber, *The Rationalizing Voter* (New York: Cambridge University Press, 2013).
12. Larry M. Bartels, "Beyond the Running Tally: Partisan Bias in Political Perceptions," *Political Behavior* 24 (2002): 117–150.
13. See Andrew Soergel, "Many Americans Now More Confident in Trump, the Economy," *U.S. News & World Report,* November 16, 2016, www.usnews.com/news/articles/2016-11-16/many-americans-more-confident-in-economy-trump-after-the-election.
14. Julia Azari and Marc J. Hetherington, "Back to the Future? What the Politics of the Late-Nineteenth Century Can Tell Us about the 2016 Election," *Annals of the American Academy of Political and Social Science* 667 (2016): 92–109.
15. Thanks to Bruce Oppenheimer for calculating these numbers for me.
16. Marc J. Hetherington and Thomas J. Rudolph, *Why Washington Won't Work: Polarization, Political Trust and the Governing Crisis* (Chicago: University of Chicago Press, 2015).
17. Shanto Iyengar, Gaurav Sood, and Yphtach Lelkes, "Affect, Not Ideology: A Social Identity Perspective on Polarization," *Public Opinion Quarterly* (2012).
18. Stephen P. Nicholson, Chelsea M. Coe, Jason Emory, and Anna V. Song, "The Politics of Beauty: The Effect of Partisan Bias on Physical Attractiveness," *Political Behavior* 38 (2016): 883–898.
19. Shanto Iyengar and Sean J. Westwood, "Fear and Loathing across Party Lines: New Evidence on Group Polarization," *American Political Science* 59 (2015): 690–707.

20. Marc J. Hetherington and Jonathan D. Weiler, *Authoritarianism and Polarization in American Politics* (New York: Cambridge University Press, 2009).
21. Marc J. Hetherington and Jonathan D. Weiler, "Authoritarianism and Polarization in American Politics, Still?," in *American Gridlock: The Sources, Character, and Impact of Political Polarization,* ed. James A. Thurber (New York: Cambridge University Press, 2016).
22. The Cooperative Campaign Analysis Project (CCAP) is carried out by YouGov in cooperation with academics who buy time on the survey. The post-election wave of the survey was carried out in the week after election day.
23. Marc J. Hetherington and Jonathan D. Weiler, *Fixed or Fluid* (Boston: Houghton, Mifflin, Harcourt, forthcoming).
24. John Judis and Ruy Teixeira were first to note this trend in *The Emerging Democratic Majority* (New York: Simon & Schuster, 2002).
25. Danielle Kurtzleben, "1 More Woman Accuses Trump of Inappropriate Sexual Conduct. Here's the Full List," *NPR.com,* October 20, 2016, www.npr.org/2016/10/13/497799354/a-list-of-donald-trumps-accusers-of-inappropriate-sexual-conduct.
26. Steven J. Rosenstone and John Mark Hansen, *Mobilization, Participation and Democracy in America* (New York: Macmillan, 1993).
27. See Matthew Nussbaum and Benjamin Oreskes, "More Republicans Viewing Putin Favorably," *Politico,* December 16, 2016, www.politico.com/story/2016/12/gop-russia-putin-support-232714.
28. Obama offered these comments at his final meeting of 2016 with the White House press corps in December 2016.

4

Voting Behavior

Continuity and Confusion in the Electorate

Nicole E. Mellow

On August 6, 2015, Fox News hosted the first Republican presidential primary debate of the 2016 election season in Cleveland, Ohio. The ten leading candidates stood on the stage. Among them was Donald Trump, a real estate mogul and reality television star. Lacking political experience and polish, he was not taken seriously by any mainstream institution, including the establishment of his own (nominal) party. Yet sixteen months later when electors met to cast their ballots, he was elected to the presidency, winning 304 electoral votes to his Democratic opponent Hillary Clinton's 227, marking the first time in the nation's history that a candidate with no record of public or military service had been elected. The victory was no mandate, though, because Trump lost the popular vote by close to three million votes.[1] The abnormality of Trump's candidacy and widespread fears about his suitability for office even led to a popular effort after election day to defeat him in the Electoral College. Ultimately, seven electors voted "faithlessly," or "conscientiously," as it was named by the bipartisan movement in support of them.[2] Along with the election of 2000, 2016 marks the second in five elections that the presidency was *not* awarded to the popular vote winner. In both instances, and indeed in six of the last seven elections (all but 2004), the Democratic candidate won the popular vote.

The election, itself, was surely the most unusual in modern American history. Trump was the ultimate "outsider" candidate. Clinton was arguably the ultimate "insider." She had held the positions of first lady, senator, and secretary of state; she was on track to the Democratic nomination in 2008 before being derailed by the insurgent campaign of Barack Obama; and President Obama himself called Clinton the most qualified candidate ever to seek the presidency while stumping for her in 2016.[3] As testament to what was perceived to be the lopsided nature of the contest, Clinton received fifty-seven major newspaper endorsements, including many from traditionally pro-Republican editorial boards, to Trump's two. Trump received fewer such endorsements than any major-party candidate in history.[4] Notably, the ultimate insider candidate was also a true outsider in an important regard. She was the first female candidate to head a major-party ticket. Despite the vast differences in their experiences and backgrounds, as well as in what they represented for the electorate, both major-party candidates received unprecedentedly high levels of "unfavorable" ratings from the public. Never had two more different and yet similarly unpopular candidates vied for the office.

This chapter looks at a culminating event in this highly unusual and historic election—what voters did at the polls on November 8. In the immediate aftermath of the election (in fact, even as votes were being counted on election night), an army of analysts and prognosticators began to post online their interpretations of how and why voters acted as they did. The imperative to make sense of the election was all the more urgent because the preelection polls had made a Clinton victory seem a near certainty.

Did 2016 represent the revolt of a neglected white working class? Was it an indication that white voters generally are beginning to act politically on their shared racial identity? Did black and Latino voters, traditional Democratic Party constituents and crucial to Obama's 2008 and 2012 victories, stay at home and reject Clinton? Had the Clinton campaign miscalculated her midwestern support, wrongly assuming a "blue wall" in that region? Where was the support of women voters for the first female candidate? Most important, perhaps, was Trump's success a harbinger of future party alignments? Efforts to make sense of the election will continue for months and years ahead, especially as new factors come under scrutiny. For example, the Clinton campaign has claimed that FBI director James Comey's unprecedentedly public (and ultimately unwarranted) renewed investigation, days before the election, into Clinton's use of a private email server while secretary of state cost her the election.[5] And growing evidence of Russian-sponsored cyberattacks aimed at influencing the election has led a Republican Congress to declare that it will undertake an investigation and President Obama to indicate that there will be retaliation from the U.S. government.[6] Given how close election outcomes were in a small number of key states that broke for Donald Trump, it may eventually be determined that these factors were decisive, but that is beyond the scope of this analysis. Instead, I describe the ways that voters departed from past patterns of party support and the ways that they did not.

For all of its unusualness, there was much that stayed the same in the voting behavior of key demographic groups. Yet because Trump was not a normal candidate but was largely normalized through the processes surrounding the election, interpreting voter behavior requires special caution. Tentative assessments of the factors behind Trump's victory and their implications for party politics suggest that the 2016 election is likely to be remembered as one in which voters split sharply over the merits of globalization, neoliberalism, and related questions of national identity, or what it means to be American. Nonetheless, this schism was enacted largely within the confines of the traditional two-party system. With new and submerged issues brought to the fore, the election featured elements of party polarization but also indications of party rebranding that may lead to future party fractures. Whether these dynamics are sufficient to yield a realignment of the party system remains to be seen. Thus this election is a story of continuity, and considerable confusion.

A Partisan Affair

One popular narrative of the 2016 election was that the outcome turned on issues of character and the fitness for office of the two major-party nominees. Investigations into Clinton's use of a private email server while secretary of state; claims that she was responsible for an attack on the American diplomatic compound in Benghazi, Libya; and her relationship to foreign donors to the Clinton Foundation led Trump to label her "Crooked Hillary" while campaigning. Meanwhile, Trump's refusal to release his tax records; multiple pending lawsuits related to his business ventures; his denials and reversals on policy positions; evidence of his lack of knowledge about basic constitutional and governance issues; his demagogic rhetoric targeting racial, ethnic, and religious minority groups and women; a video-recorded admission of his sexual assault of women; and his busting of most norms of political life led to a "Never Trump" movement among Republican elites as well as accusations by Clinton surrogates that the country was at risk of electing a demagogue at best, a fascist with ties to the Russian government at worst. Even the three highly watched presidential debates were woefully short on policy and long on spectacle, more than is now typical for debates. All of this was relentlessly covered in mainstream and social media, leading to a campaign season saturated with incivilities, accusations, and conspiracy theories.

Reflecting the tenor of the campaign, voters consistently gave both candidates extremely high "unfavorable" ratings.[7] This was in line with the description voters ultimately offered for their vote choice in exit polls.[8] A majority of voters either expressed reservations about their preferred candidate or indicated that their vote reflected their dislike of the other candidates. Only 41 percent agreed with the statement "I strongly favor my candidate." Among this minority, a bare majority were Clinton supporters (53 percent) while 42 percent chose Trump.

Despite their general dislike of the candidates, major-party voters nonetheless overwhelmingly stuck by their party's nominee. Of the many ways to assess voter behavior, party affiliation is, far and away, the best predictor of vote choice. In 2016, 89 percent of Democrats supported Clinton, and 90 percent of Republicans supported Trump. Those claiming to be "independents or something else" split fairly evenly, with 42 percent supporting Clinton and 48 percent supporting Trump. As in other recent elections, roughly one-third of voters identified as Democrat, a third as Republican, and a third as independent or other, although studies find that independents typically lean toward one party or the other.[9]

The evidence of voters' party loyalties is consistent with recent elections. In 2016, voters were only slightly less loyal than in 2012, a year that represented a high-water mark for both parties in recent decades (see Figure 4.1).

Figure 4.1 Party Loyalty in Presidential Elections, 1976–2016

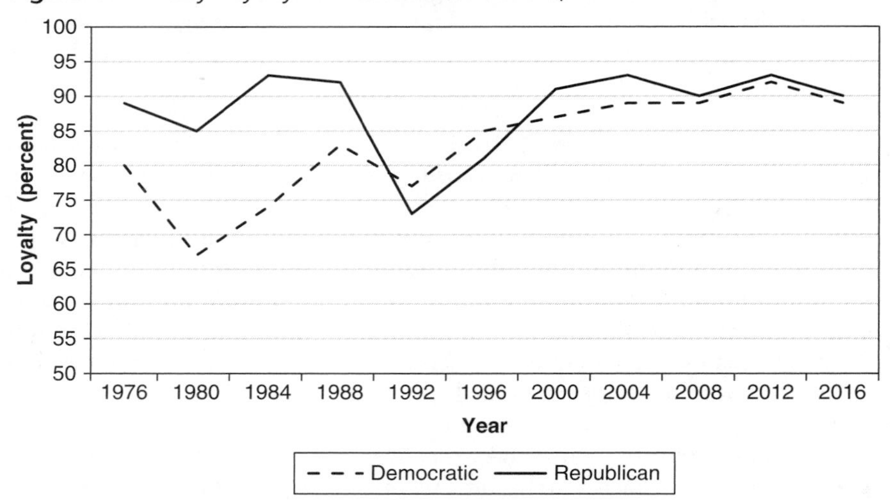

Sources: Roper Center National Election Pool (NEP) data (1976–2004); *New York Times* NEP data (2008–2016).

With the exception of 1992, when billionaire Ross Perot was on the ballot as an independent, Republican voters have been consistently loyal supporters of their party's presidential candidate. More interesting is the steady increase, since 1980, in Democratic loyalty. In large part, this development reflects the ideological realignment of voters in the two-party system in response to the clearer divisions among party elites. Democrats and Republicans in Washington, especially in Congress, have been clearly divided over economic, social justice, and foreign policy issues since the 1980s, but the process by which voters have sorted themselves into the party that best corresponds to their beliefs has taken longer to unfold. Conservative Democratic voters, who often voted for the Republican presidential candidate in the 1970s and 1980s, have slowly migrated out of the Democratic Party. To a lesser extent, liberal Republicans have shifted to the Democratic Party. The result, by the 2000s, is greater partisanship in both parties and across all levels of the party system.[10]

Many observers lament partisanship and its more severe cousin polarization, claiming that the extreme views of party elites do not represent the views of the American electorate.[11] It would be hard to argue that the electorate looks favorably on the effects of the elite polarization that has been on display in recent years in Washington—obstruction and stalemate (including on basic governing responsibilities such as filling vacancies on the Supreme Court), budget impasses, and government shutdowns. Public evaluations of Congress have sunk as polarization has intensified. In 2014, public approval of Congress dipped as low as 9 percent. Just before the 2016 election, approval of Congress was at 18 percent.[12]

Yet even if the public finds features of polarization regrettable, scholars find that clear party differences are useful for engaging voters and for helping them make sense of electoral choices by functioning as information shortcuts.[13] Clarified choices, and stakes that are made more evident by the closeness of the electoral division of the parties, have increased voter participation in most recent elections. After years of declining turnout, voters since 1996 have participated in increasing numbers. In 2008, 61.6 percent of the eligible electorate voted for president, the highest level of participation since the 1960s. This proportion dropped to 58 percent in 2012 but then climbed slightly, to 58.9 percent, in 2016.[14]

Voter loyalty to distinct and equally competitive national parties is a useful description of the political order that developed out of the 1960s and 1970s. Prior to that, from the 1930s to the 1960s, America was described as having a politics of consensus, with nonideological parties and frequent demonstrations of bipartisanship among lawmakers. This was the height of the New Deal era, when the ideas of the Democratic Party about national government activism defined the terms of normal politics. National institutions reflected the Democrats' commitments. Keynesian fiscal policy, the welfare state, a social contract between labor and capital, and containment of Soviet communism were regularly reauthorized by a broad majority of Americans from all regions of the country. Simply put, Democrats prevailed by using government activism to promote security at home and abroad, and Republicans were hard-pressed to compete. As E. J. Dionne has written, "To many in the late 1940s, it appeared that conservatives were doomed . . . to crankiness, incoherence, and irrelevance."[15] The one Republican president of the era, Dwight D. Eisenhower, was a moderate whose governance was more in step with the New Deal than with the conservatives in his own party. The similarities between Democrats and Republicans at the time led observers to lament the tweedle-dee and tweedle-dum nature of the parties.[16]

By the 1970s, Democratic dominance was gone and bipartisanship was soon to follow. The social disruptions of the 1960s from the civil rights and feminist movements, dissension over the war in Vietnam, and economic uncertainty upended the political order. To many people, Democratic solutions appeared obsolete or wrong-headed. Richard Nixon was the first Republican to capitalize on this weakness, and by 1980, with Ronald Reagan's election, the country seemed poised to embrace a new governing philosophy. Reagan summed up this new philosophy in his 1981 inaugural address, saying, "[G]overnment is not the solution to our problem; government is the problem."

Although skepticism of national government power has existed since the founding, Reagan's victory in 1980 restored the idea to public prominence. Republican philosophy combined military strength with limited government, stressing the benefits that would accrue from tax cuts, deregulation, and privatization. When the effects of this approach appeared volatile, conservative social values became the Republicans' new ballast.

Churning economic and social change, they argued, was best answered with the stability and security of traditional values.[17] In the new Republican agenda, neoliberal economic policies and devolution of power to the states were joined with an emphasis on race-neutral individual rights, a resurrection of traditional "family" values, and support for law and order. When Reagan's election was followed by a resounding reelection in 1984 and then the election, in 1988, of his vice president, George H. W. Bush, the string of Republican presidential victories seemed, at last, to be a repudiation of the New Deal. Indeed, recent works of political history tend to characterize the late twentieth century as a conservative, Republican era that began with Reagan, or possibly Nixon.[18]

But unlike the New Deal and earlier party eras, voters reacted with ambivalence to the new Republican regime. With the exception of the Senate from 1981 to 1987, Congress stayed under Democratic control throughout the 1970s and 1980s. Even after Republicans finally won control of both the House and the Senate in 1994, Democrat Bill Clinton remained in the White House and was reelected two years later. Indeed, divided party control has become the norm in Washington, with the same party ruling both houses of Congress and the presidency for just twelve of the past forty-eight years. This is not merely an artifact of the difficulty of dislodging congressional incumbents. No recent president has been able to secure a significant electoral mandate. Pluralities prevailed in the elections won by Clinton in 1992 and 1996, and George W. Bush was elected in 2000 with a minority of the popular vote. When recent presidents have won a majority of the popular vote, it has typically been by a slim margin. President Bush's reelection in 2004 was earned with just 51 percent, similar to President Obama's reelection showing in 2012, after winning "big" with 53 percent in 2008. In 2016, Trump was elected with just 46 percent of the vote, a popular vote loss even greater than Bush's in 2000. Additional evidence of the closeness of electoral division can be seen in Figure 4.2, which shows the margin of the popular vote victory since 1980.

Since Reagan's landslide reelection in 1984, when he won the popular vote by a whopping 18-percentage-point margin, presidential victories have become increasingly razor-thin. While the smallest margins were in 2000 and 2016, years when the popular vote victor lost the Electoral College vote, no president since Reagan has achieved a popular vote victory margin greater than 10 points. In short, with pluralities (or less) and small popular vote majorities deciding presidential contests and with divided government the norm, the evidence suggests that although the New Deal order faltered in the 1970s, the Republican order that replaced it has not achieved the same kind of electoral validation. Rather, the two parties have regularly battled for control of government, each backed by its own army of partisan voters.

In the days and weeks surrounding the 2016 election, scholars marveled at the consistency and stability of the electorate's party support despite the unusual campaign. Writing two days after the election, one scholar even

Figure 4.2 Margin of Victory in the Popular Vote for President, 1980–2016

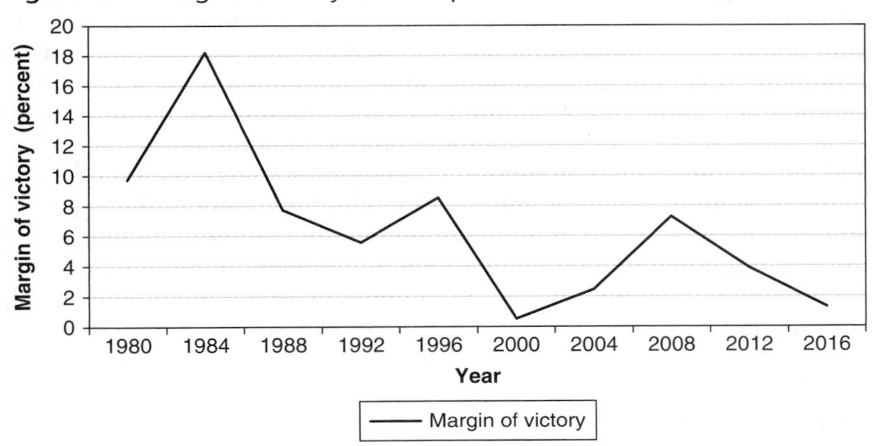

Source: Data from *David Leip's Atlas of U.S. Presidential Elections,* uselectionatlas.org.

claimed that 2016 was just "an ordinary election" with the outcome nothing more than a "coin toss."[19] The data presented here on party loyalty and electoral division support that conclusion: remarkable continuity.

Yet the data may tell only part of the story. The premise of the analysis thus far, consistent with research on party sorting and partisanship dynamics that have unfolded since the 1930s, is that voters' party identification and vote choice provide information about their ideological commitments, just as party elites' do. The Democratic Party is liberal, the Republican Party conservative. Yet what was abundantly evident in the 2016 campaign, especially if one includes the primaries, was that the candidates, to varying degrees, were disrupting the ideological premises of their parties. To begin with the smaller of the disruptions: Hillary Clinton's candidacy embodied a unique mixture of progressivism and centrism. After facing an unexpectedly robust challenge in the primaries from Bernie Sanders, a self-proclaimed "socialist democrat" who is not even formally part of the Democratic Party, Clinton tacked left in ways that were a significant departure—indeed, on issues such as trade, a repudiation—from her, and the party's, "New Democrat" centrism. Clinton was also the first woman nominee. Despite the party's longstanding commitment to gender equity, her candidacy as a woman with a strong pro-choice position and a campaign promise to appoint women to 50 percent of her cabinet positions, was new in American politics. These attributes suggest that caution is needed when interpreting Democratic loyalty in 2016 as evidence of just another "normal" party vote.

Far more significantly, Donald Trump's campaign defied traditional ideological definition and was in many respects a repudiation of mainstream

Republican ideology. His economic promises were a mixture of standard Republicanism, including tax cuts and deregulation, and populist, typically liberal, positions, such as infrastructure spending and trade protectionism. He even promised to defend popular entitlement programs that Republicans have long sought to reduce. Trump stayed true to Republican orthodoxy on some important cultural issues, notably abortion, while staying silent about and even occasionally endorsing progressive causes such as lesbian, gay, bisexual, and transgender (LGBT) rights. On foreign policy, he appeared less interventionist and hawkish than Clinton. And yet on issues of national identity—especially Latino and Muslim immigration—Trump was far to the right of the mainstream Republican Party. What "Republicanism" did Republican voters endorse with their support of Trump?

For these reasons, it is exceedingly difficult to rest with the assertion that 2016 was a normal election in which voters, in lockstep, turned out to support their party's candidate because that candidate represented the latest manifestation of a recognizable party ideology. In a recent experiment, scholars demonstrated that voters' partisan identities are now stronger than their racial identities.[20] If this is true, it may be that voters in 2016 simply succumbed to this dominant feature of their political orientation. Yet a full examination of the dynamics of the 2016 election suggests that voters are not fully comfortable with what that party identification has come to mean. In the sections that follow, I turn to different patterns of voter behavior, looking at the 2016 outcome in light of patterns of geographic and demographic support for the two major-party candidates. By doing so, it is possible to enrich the standard story of the partisan era to see that voters, in contrast to the parties' establishment elites, may be furthering polarization and even redefining the parties' core commitments.

A Red and Blue Nation?

Given his loss in the popular election, Donald Trump cannot legitimately claim to have a governing mandate. It is not simply that he failed to capture majority support, however. Neither party in recent elections has been able to claim a mandate of the sort that scholars have observed in past eras, in part because neither party has been able to secure a majority that is truly national in strength. In 1980, Ronald Reagan won the electoral votes of all but five states, and the forty-five states he carried were distributed throughout the country. In 1984, he won every state but Minnesota. In 1972, Richard Nixon won every state but Massachusetts. Presidential victories that were national in scope were the norm for much of the twentieth century. But since the 1990s, the Republican and Democratic parties have represented different regions of the country. The difference in their geographic strengths explains why, no matter how big the win in recent elections, a substantial partisan opposition has remained in government.

The geographic division of the parties first became apparent to the media in the 2000 election and was quickly labeled the "red state/blue state" divide. The red, or Republican, states captured in 2000 by George W. Bush were largely in the South and interior West, while the blue, or Democratic, states captured by Al Gore were concentrated in the Northeast, the Midwest, and the Pacific Coast. This basic division of red and blue states has been sustained in every election since then, including, with some important departures, the 2016 election. In fact, as the two maps in Figure 4.3 suggest, over the course of the past six presidential elections, the vast majority of states have consistently voted for one party or the other.

The first map in Figure 4.3 shows, by state, the number of presidential elections between 1996 and 2012 that Democrats won. In those years, the party consistently carried states in the Northeast, in the Midwest, and on the Pacific Coast. States in these regions chose the Democratic presidential nominee in at least four of those five elections. Conversely, states in the South and interior West chose the Democratic nominee either once or not at all. This stability accounted for the voting outcomes of the vast majority of the country: forty-five of the country's fifty states. Only five states—Florida, Ohio, Nevada, Virginia, and Colorado—had a "mixed" record, voting Democratic two or three times in the five elections prior to 2016. All five of these "swing" states went to Obama in 2008 and 2012.

Comparing this map to the 2016 results shown in the second map in Figure 4.3 reveals continuity as well as change. States on the Pacific Coast and in the Northeast continued their pattern of Democratic support by voting for Clinton. States in the interior West and the South continued their pattern of Republican support. Three of the five states that had a mixed record of Democratic support between 1996 and 2012—Nevada, Colorado, and Virginia—stayed blue in 2016, whereas the other two—Florida and Ohio—joined the Republican column.

Most notable, though, are the several states in the Midwest and the Northeast that had been consistently Democratic until 2016 but then flipped to Trump: Michigan, Iowa, Wisconsin, and Pennsylvania. These states became the subject of intense scrutiny after the election, because they were predicted to stay blue and because of the closeness of Trump's victories.[21] His margins of victory in Michigan, Pennsylvania, and Wisconsin—0.22 percent, 1.13 percent, and 0.81 percent, respectively—were among the closest in the nation (only Florida and New Hampshire were as close). Victory in these three states gave Trump the Electoral College votes he needed.

Although the margins of victory in these states were especially small—amounting to a difference of roughly 104,000 votes—the 2016 election, generally, saw an increase in competitive states from previous elections (see Figure 4.4).

With the exception of Reagan's landslide victory in 1984, presidential elections have become increasingly noncompetitive within states. In 2012, only three states had margins of victory of less than 3 percentage points and only one additional state had a margin of less than 5 points. This means that forty-six states were not competitive. One has to go back to 1984 to find a similarly noncompetitive election, with this crucial difference: in 1984, the

Figure 4.3 Geography of Presidential Election Results, 1996–2012 and 2016

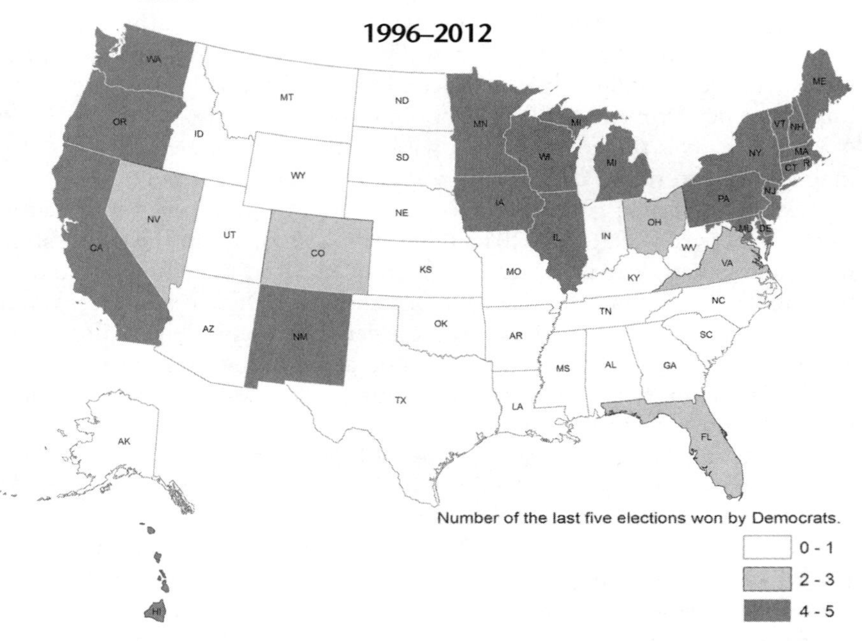

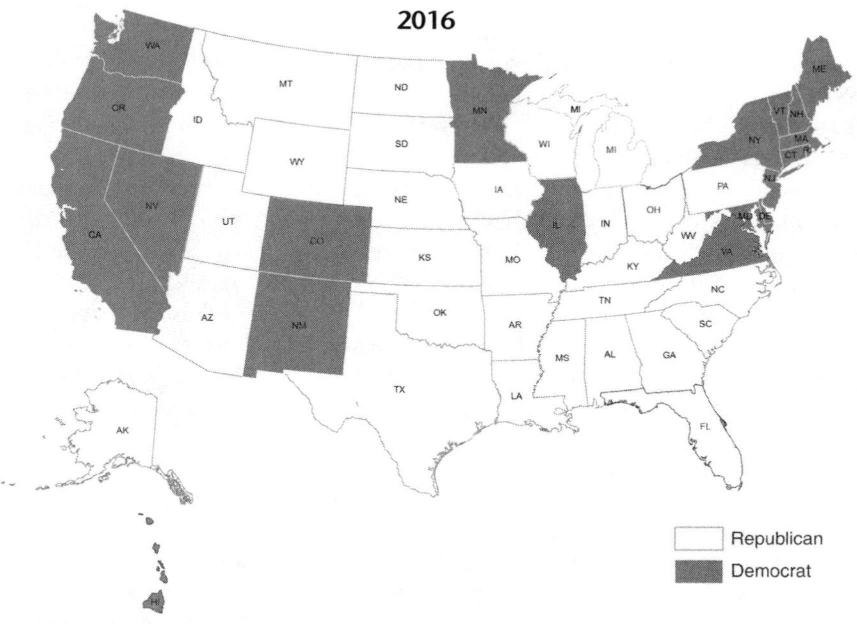

Source: Compiled by the author.

Figure 4.4 Number of Competitive States, 1980–2016

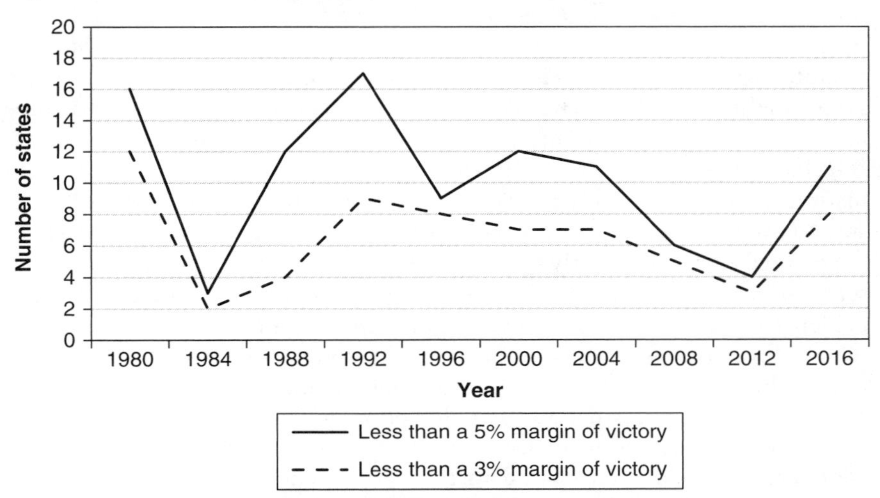

Source: Data from *David Leip's Atlas of U.S. Presidential Elections*, uselectionatlas.org.

Figure 4.5 Percentage of Major-Party Voters Selecting the Democratic Presidential Candidate, 1960–2016, by Region

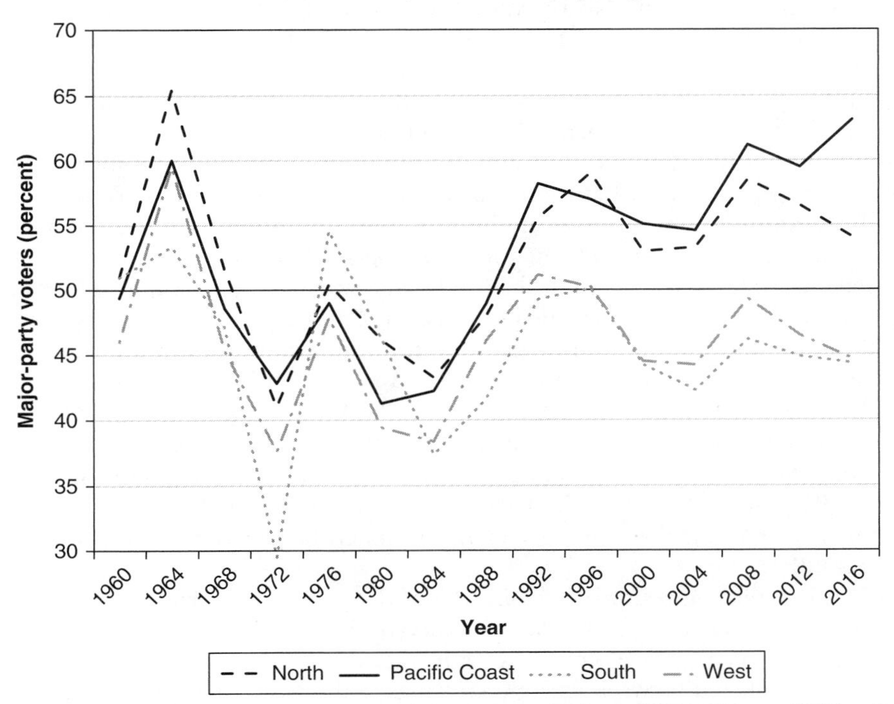

Sources: Presidential Elections, 1789–2000 (Washington, D.C.: CQ Press, 2002); CNN.com (2004 and 2016 data); and *David Leip's Atlas of U.S. Presidential Elections* (2008 and 2012 data), uselectionatlas.org. Regional calculations are the author's.

forty-seven noncompetitive states all went for Reagan, whereas in 2012, the forty-six noncompetitive states were split between Barack Obama and Mitt Romney. The 2016 contest saw an uptick in competitiveness: the number of states with competitive elections jumped from four in 2012 to eleven in 2016. Eight states had margins of victory of less than 3 points, and three additional states had margins of victory of less than 5 points.

Part of the stark division in the red state/blue state map derives from institutional contrivances; simple pluralities of voters dictate how nearly all states cast their electoral votes. The fact that most voters in one set of states have voted in a consistently different fashion from most voters in the other set of states, as evidenced in Figure 4.3, is by itself compelling. Yet further evidence of these longstanding geographic trends can be seen in Figure 4.5, which shows the percentage of major-party voters in each region who supported the Democratic presidential candidate from 1960 to 2016.[22]

In every election since 1960, major-party voters in the North (including the Northeast and the Midwest) and the Pacific Coast have supported the Democratic presidential candidate to a greater degree than voters in the South and the West. The exception is 1976, when Georgia's Jimmy Carter headed the Democratic ticket and, in an expression of regional pride, carried all but one southern state. Although the general trend since 1984 has been toward greater Democratic support in all regions, the partisan gap between voters in the North and the Pacific Coast and those in the South and the West has become increasingly wide in that time. In the five elections of the 2000s, majorities of voters in the North and the Pacific Coast states have supported the Democratic candidate whereas majorities in the South and the West have supported the Republican candidate.

This regional split was similar in 2016, demonstrating some continuity with recent elections. But there was more variation between the regions in this election. In previous elections, the levels of support for the winning candidate within regions tended to move together, likely reflecting the idiosyncrasies of the election and the candidate's appeal. For example, in 2012, Obama's total support declined by between 2 and 3 percentage points from the levels of 2008 in each of the four regions, but the gap in the support he received between the regions remained roughly the same. This was not the case in 2016. In both the North and the West, support for the Democratic candidate, Clinton, declined by 2.5 and 2 percentage points, respectively. Southern support dropped by only 0.5 percent, staying more similar to 2012 levels. Voters in the Pacific Coast states departed from these patterns, increasing their support of the Democratic nominee by 3.5 points from 2012.

The existing regional organization of the party system has its origins in the 1960s, when the New Deal Democratic Party still dominated national elections. The party's electoral strength since the 1930s had derived from an accord brokered between its regional wings in the North and the South. The basis of this accord was that national policy would be tailored to accommodate the dominant interests in each region: organized labor and manufacturers in the North, and agriculture and labor-intensive industry in the all-white electorate that still prevailed in the South. Issues that defied regional tailoring, such as civil rights for African Americans, were suppressed by the party. By the late 1960s and early 1970s, this accord was in jeopardy. Republican leaders were quick to exploit the emerging fissures in the New Deal coalition—most obviously, but not entirely, in the area of civil rights. The Republicans gained an advantage at this time by appealing to white southern Democrats, not just on racial issues but also on other social issues (for example, abortion), economic issues (such as welfare policies), and foreign affairs (including Vietnam).

The regional discord that marked the late New Deal era led to a dramatic reorganization of the geographic basis of the party system. The most obvious outcome of Republican efforts to destabilize the Democrats' geographic base was an acceleration of the GOP's capture of the South. But Republican leaders concentrated their attention on the West as well, a region that, like the South, contained states with fast-growing economies and populations. Also, as in the South, the farming, ranching, and mining states of the West had a political history of antagonism toward their perceived domination by northern financial and political elites. These economic, social, and symbolic resentments were fodder for a growing Republican Party.[23]

With the regional crackup of the Democratic Party, the New Deal coalition was revealed to be an ultimately unstable sectional fusion. Two new versions of the Republican and Democratic parties replaced the New Deal party system in the 1970s. One was an "emerging Republican majority" that was centered in the fast-growing suburbs and small towns of the South and the West.[24] The other was a refashioned Democratic Party, with enhanced electoral muscle in the historically urbanized, densely populated, and commercially developed states of the North and the Pacific Coast. Just as Republicans displaced Democrats in some regions, such as the South, Democrats, in turn, displaced Republicans in other regions, such as New England, where the GOP had historically reigned.

As the demands made by the South and the West on the national government began to clash with those of the North and the Pacific Coast, the parties responded. For example, in the 1970s, as northern lawmakers came to dominate the Democratic Party, they abandoned that party's long-held commitment to free trade in the face of the deindustrialization of their strongest region. As Republicans simultaneously shifted south and westward into the trade-dependent regions of the rising Sunbelt, the two parties came into increasing conflict with one another over trade policy.[25] On trade, as on a range of foreign and domestic policy measures, "red versus blue" partisan conflict intensified as the parties' geographic bases shifted. Less than a national realignment that elevated one or the other party to majority status, the current party system has been one of partisan stalemate between two regionally centered parties. This helps to explain why the number of competitive states has tended to decline in recent decades: the footprints of the parties are, by and large, in different areas of the country and each party has backed the dominant interests of its respective regions.

In 2008 and 2012, Obama appeared to partially disrupt this geographic pattern. He won the traditionally blue states in the Pacific Coast and the North and also picked up a number of red states, notably Virginia, Colorado, and Nevada. In 2016, these three states, along with New Mexico, stayed blue for Clinton, meaning that their support for the Democratic Party is more than simply a reflection of the "Obama phenomenon."

Despite the solidification of the Democrats' hold on several traditionally red states, the most arresting geographic change of this election was the collapse of the so-called blue wall in the Midwest that occurred when Wisconsin, Michigan, and Ohio, along with Pennsylvania, turned red. These states had voted twice for Obama, and Wisconsin, Michigan, and Pennsylvania had voted Democratic in every election since 1992.

As Figure 4.6 makes clear, the departure so evident and consequential in 2016 has roots in a pattern of voting behavior that extends back to the 1990s, when the northern bloc of states began to break apart. Along with the traditionally red midwestern state of Indiana, voters in Wisconsin, Michigan, Ohio, and Pennsylvania—vital wins for Trump in 2016—have

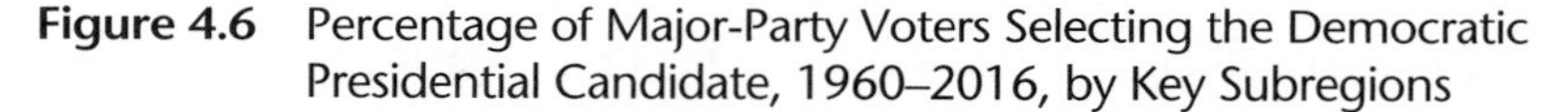

Figure 4.6 Percentage of Major-Party Voters Selecting the Democratic Presidential Candidate, 1960–2016, by Key Subregions

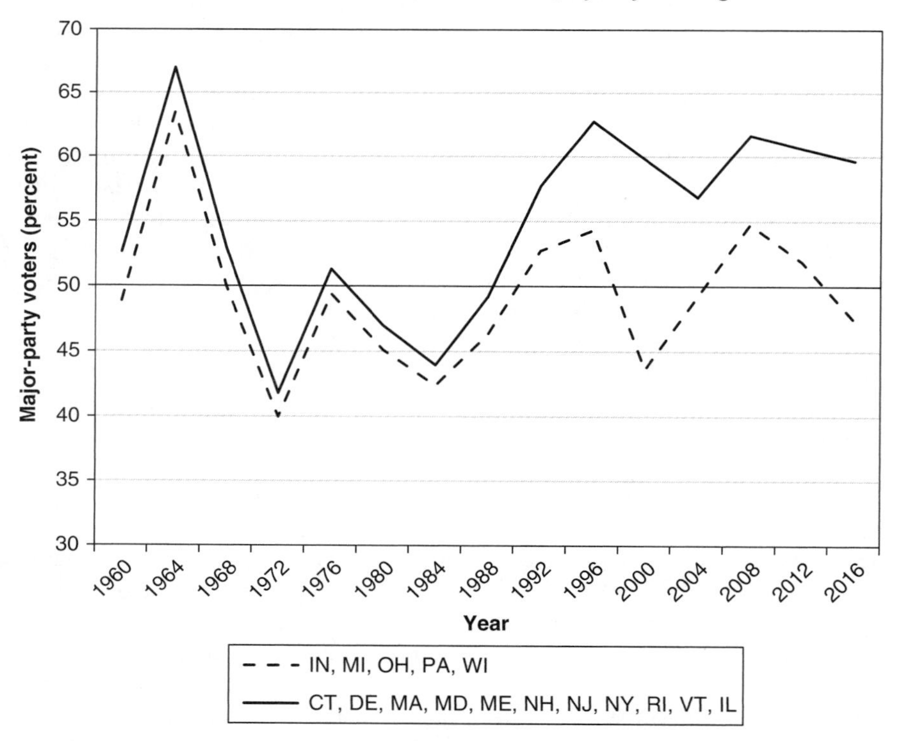

Sources: Presidential Elections, 1789–2000 (Washington, D.C.: CQ Press, 2002); CNN.com (2004 and 2016 data); and *David Leip's Atlas of U.S. Presidential Elections* (2008 and 2012 data), uselectionatlas.org.

been much less supportive of the Democratic candidate since 1992. This subregion of the Midwest (excluding Illinois) was closely aligned with the rest of the states in the North from 1960 until 1992. But in every election since Bill Clinton's 1992 victory, the difference in Democratic support between voters in these five midwestern states and voters in the rest of the North has been greater than 5 percentage points. In the elections of 2000 and 2016, when the popular vote winner lost the Electoral College, the differences between the two subregions were 16 and 12 percentage points, respectively.

Debating Globalization and the Neoliberal Economic Order

> *This TPP [Trans-Pacific Partnership] sets the gold standard in trade agreements to open free, transparent, fair trade, the kind of environment that has the rule of law and a level playing field. And when negotiated, this agreement will cover 40 percent of the world's total trade and build in strong protections for workers and the environment.*
>
> —Secretary of State Hillary Clinton, November 15, 2012[26]

> *I did say . . . three years ago, that I hoped it would be the gold standard . . . [but] in looking at it, it didn't meet my standards. My standards for more new, good jobs for Americans, for raising wages for Americans. And I want to make sure that I can look into the eyes of any middle-class American and say, "this will help raise your wages." And I concluded I could not.*
>
> —Democratic presidential candidate Hillary Clinton, October 13, 2015[27]

To the dismay of voters and the delight of the producers of negative campaign ads, politicians appear to reverse their positions on issues with some frequency. Sometimes this can be consequential, as when President George H. W. Bush raised taxes after famously pledging during his campaign that he would not, with the line, "Read my lips: no new taxes." The consequences of Hillary Clinton's reversal on the Trans-Pacific Partnership (TPP) trade deal may fall closer to those for Bush than those for the typical politician's reversal.

In 2012, as secretary of state, Clinton promoted the TPP, in line with the free-trade agenda of President Obama's Democratic administration. There was nothing unusual about this: presidents, regardless of party, have sought freer trade since the 1930s. Yet for congressional Democrats the story is different. By the 1970s, the dominant voices in the Democratic Party in Congress, northern Democrats, were routinely rejecting free trade in the face of the deindustrialization of the manufacturing belt, which had been accompanied by factory closings and job losses in their region. Democratic president Bill Clinton's promotion of the North American Free Trade Agreement (NAFTA), although in line with the business and financial interests that he was courting to help rebuild the party's national competitiveness, was met with resistance from most northern Democrats in Congress. They were even more strongly opposed to the Central American Free Trade Agreement (CAFTA) in 2005. One rustbelt Democratic governor, Jennifer Granholm of Michigan, had a campaign slogan that sums up northern resistance: "Let's give NAFTA and CAFTA the shafta!"[28] Given this history, it is unsurprising that Obama's proposed TPP, the "biggest free trade deal in history," was rejected by Democrats in Congress.[29] What is perhaps surprising is the strength of the issue in the 2016 election.

The resurrection of trade policy and Clinton's significant reversal had outsized implications for the parties' geographic support in 2016. During the Democratic nominating campaign, Bernie Sanders's populist economic agenda included a forceful rebuttal of the TPP, and he tended to do best in the northern states, where Democratic voters have typically prevailed in general elections. (Clinton fared better in the primaries in southern and southwestern states, where Democrats rarely succeed in the general election.) At the same time, Donald Trump, in a more direct contradiction of the standard Republican position on trade, railed against the TPP, promised to impose trade sanctions against China, and claimed he would bring manufacturing jobs back to the country. Squeezed on both the left and the right by a new populist anti-trade message, Clinton had no choice but to change her position. Regardless of how authentic Clinton's shift on trade, her earlier endorsement of the TPP, her long support for free trade as part of the New Democratic centrism, and her historically close ties to financial interests that benefit from trade and globalization ultimately made her pivot unconvincing to many voters. In exit polls, 42 percent of voters agreed that trade "takes away U.S. jobs." Of those voters, only 31 percent supported Clinton, compared with Trump's 65 percent.

To some extent, trade may have taken on an outsized role in the 2016 election, more reminiscent of the 1980s and 1990s battles between the parties, because it served symbolically as a benchmark for the candidates' attitudes toward the global neoliberal economic order that has prevailed since the 1980s.[30] As the United States shifted toward economic policies of deregulation, tax cuts, and privatization, income inequality grew. At the same time, national public policy outcomes have tended to reflect the preferences of affluent voters far more than they have low- and middle-income voters.[31] The relationship between any one policy and economic outcomes is complicated, but from a political standpoint, this may not matter. More than in any recent election, 2016 witnessed populist rejection of the economic precepts of neoliberalism and globalization, ideas that have been broadly endorsed by mainstream elements of both the Republican and Democratic parties even though there are important differences between the parties concerning the government's role in economic management. For these reasons, Clinton's long record as a centrist Democrat likely hurt her with certain Democratic constituents, and Trump's lack of a public record may have made his populist message more plausible.

Low-income and working-class voters have played a foundational role in Democratic victories since Franklin D. Roosevelt put together the New Deal coalition. This is unsurprising given the programmatic commitments of the party, especially initiatives, like Social Security and the G.I. Bill, that helped working-class voters move into the middle class during the middle decades of the twentieth century. Despite the challenges that the Democrats have faced in recent years in persuading voters that their party can effectively manage the economy, the party's relationship to low-income voters remained fairly strong as recently as Obama's reelection in 2012, when he won 60 percent of voters with family incomes of less than $50,000. In 2016, voters in this income bracket comprised a smaller percentage of the electorate (36 percent in 2016, compared to 41 percent in 2012), and although a small majority of those voters still voted Democratic, they were less supportive of Clinton than they had been of Obama, giving her only 53 percent of their vote. In other income brackets, support for Trump and Clinton was split fairly evenly, with Trump performing slightly better among the 54 percent of the middle- and upper-middle-income-earning electorate, those with annual family incomes between $50,000 and $200,000. So although Clinton did better among low-income voters, it was not at the levels that Democrats have traditionally enjoyed.

In 2016, the economic stances of the major-party candidates were different from in other elections. Not only were both Clinton and Trump different on key positions from past Democratic and Republican candidates, respectively, on at least a superficial level there were moments of agreement between the two: rejecting free trade, sustaining some entitlement programs, spending more on infrastructure. But the devil is in the details, and the 2016 campaign seemed less about actual policy and more about rhetoric. Nearly two-thirds of voters answered "no" when asked if they found Clinton or Trump, separately, to be "honest or trustworthy." It is not clear, then, that voters expected either candidate to deliver on a specific economic agenda even though demand for a new agenda was high in both parties.

If, rather, many voters punished Clinton because of her ties to a prevailing economic order with which they were dissatisfied, it is also not because, in the aggregate, they were feeling especially aggrieved about the state of the economy. In fact, although 52 percent of voters said the economy was the most important issue facing the nation, only 21 percent described the condition of the nation's economy as poor. This may have reflected voters' recognition of the general improvement of the economy since Obama took office in 2008, just after the start of the "Great Recession." Turning from the national economy to voters' pocketbooks, only a slightly higher proportion, 27 percent, said that their family financial situation is worse today. Among both groups—those saying the economy is poor and those saying their financial situation is worse (and there is likely overlap between the two)—the vast majority chose Trump. So even though a large majority of voters said the economy and their position in it is somewhere between fair and excellent, those who did not were ready for a real change. More interesting, when asked about the "most important candidate quality," 39 percent of voters answered "can bring needed change," and of those voters, 83 percent endorsed Trump. If the economy is one part of the change voters wanted, the candidates' positions on an ancillary feature of globalization—who belongs in the nation and what the nation stands for—may help to explain another part of the story of 2016.

"Make America Great Again": The Stakes in American National Identity

To just be grossly generalistic, you could put half of Trump's supporters into what I call the basket of deplorables. Right? The racist, sexist, homophobic, xenophobic, Islamaphobic—you name it. And unfortunately there are people like that. And he has lifted them up . . . . Now, some of those folks—they are irredeemable, but thankfully they are not America.

—Democratic presidential candidate Hillary Clinton, September 9, 2016[32]

In the aftermath of President Obama's historic 2008 election as the first black president, pundits wondered whether the country was entering a "post-racial" era. That notion was quickly put to rest by evidence of continued racism and racial bias, what scholars have termed "color-blind racism."[33] Nonetheless, Obama's election and his reelection in 2012 seemed to confirm that there was an "emerging Democratic majority" that was nurtured by the social commitments of the party as much as by its economic agenda.[34] Social and political changes in the 1960s, along with the changing demographics of the country, have led the Democratic Party to deemphasize its traditional appeals to working-class voters in favor of appeals to ethnic and racial minorities; women; LGBT individuals; and young, educated professionals of all races, ethnicities, and orientations. In 2008 and 2012, the winning Democratic coalition relied heavily on these voters. Not only have they increased their presence in the electorate, but their support for the Democratic Party has also helped to offset the loss of support from many white male voters.

During Obama's two terms, a host of policies and issues became flashpoints of debate about the country's social commitments. Police treatment of people of color, protections for undocumented immigrants, funding for Planned Parenthood and abortion access, the legalization of gay marriage, protections for transgender citizens, the scope of religious freedom, and even the propriety of statues and symbols of venerated Americans on college campuses are just some of the wide-ranging cultural and social issues that sparked controversy, including protests and counter-protests, in that eight-year period.

In the 2016 campaign, many of these strands of conflict seemed to converge and combust, leading to a backlash against socially progressive aims. Under the slogan "Make America Great Again," Donald Trump conducted a demagogic campaign that roused social divisions greater than any since the campaign of George Wallace in 1968. Two widely reported remarks exemplify Trump's rhetoric. In speaking about immigration at the kick-off of his presidential campaign, Trump said, "When Mexico sends its people, they're not sending their best. . . . They're sending people that have lots of problems, and they're bringing those problems with us. They're bringing drugs. They're bringing crime. They're rapists. And some, I assume, are good people."[35] In response, Trump proposed to build a wall between the United States and Mexico. And in calling for a new approach to combatting terrorism, he promoted "a total and complete shutdown of Muslims entering the United States until our country's representatives can figure out what is going on."[36] Comments like these—in which a specific group is targeted, sweeping generalizations made, and policies of dubious constitutionality suggested—typified Trump's campaign rhetoric. His supporters responded in kind. Campaign rallies included chants of "build the wall," and endorsements for Trump came from white supremacist groups who claimed that his presidency would be a "real opportunity" for white nationalists.[37]

On the Democratic side, Hillary Clinton forcefully repudiated Trump's rhetoric and policy ideas, instead calling for protections of targeted groups and promoting, and extending, traditional socially progressive aims. Her campaign slogan, "Stronger Together," was offered as a rebuttal to the divisiveness of Trump's candidacy. But the starkest terms of the divide were evident when, speaking at the LGBT for Hillary Gala in New York City on September 9, 2016, she described "half of Trump's supporters" as a "basket of deplorables" because of what she claimed was their commitment to racial, religious, gender, and sexual orientation hierarchies. In concluding that "they are irredeemable, but thankfully they are not America," Clinton effectively made the 2016 contest a referendum on American national identity.

American national identity—what it means to be an American and who belongs—has long been contested terrain. Most people recognize the liberal creed, the commitment to fundamental values of liberty, equality, and the rule of law, as the core of American identity. Yet throughout history, groups asserting an explicitly white and often Christian national identity have regularly gained influence. Battles between nativist conceptions of American identity and a more inclusive liberal nationalism (or civic pluralism) raged in the early part of the twentieth century, for example, as Americans debated how to respond to the large waves of immigration that the country was experiencing.[38] Similarly, a tradition of asserting status hierarchies among citizens, with white Protestant men on top, has been shown to exist simultaneously with liberalism, leading some observers to argue this is as much a part of American political culture as are liberal ideals.[39]

Much of the tenor of the 2016 campaign, both in candidate rhetoric and as expressed by supporters on social media and public commentary, is arguably a reflection of a debate over national identity. At some level, these themes are always at play in elections because the parties' platforms reflect different visions of America as much as they articulate policy positions. Since the 1960s, Democrats have offered a vision that is more explicitly inclusive whereas Republicans have tended to offer policies with a more exclusionary cast and ones that uphold traditional civic hierarchies.[40] But with globalization eroding national boundaries and increasing the racial, ethnic, and religious diversity of the nation, and with the championing of multiculturalism and cosmopolitanism by mainstream educational and professional institutions, the intensification of the argument is to be expected. Scholars have noted the rise of right-wing populism in a range of countries in recent years, rooted in a mixture of economic anxiety and racial resentment that is typically directed at immigrants.[41] In this context, the different visions signaled by Clinton and Trump, more explicit and polarized than in any recent election, may be part of a broader, global trend.

But to what extent were voters responding to this with their vote choices? This is difficult to determine because, unlike the questions on trade, surveys did not query voters about their views on American identity, and even if they did, it is likely that the results would be unreliable indicators of respondents' actual beliefs. However, two exit poll questions may shed some light on voter sentiments with regard to national identity and belonging. When asked about the most important issue facing the nation, only 13 percent of voters said immigration, yet 64 percent of those voters supported Trump, more than supported him on any other "most important" issue (the economy, foreign policy, terrorism). Similarly, 41 percent of voters supported Trump's idea of building a wall along the border with Mexico, and unsurprisingly, 86 percent of those voters chose Trump. Although not a direct commentary on national identity because respondents may have been concerned about what they believe to be the economic ramifications of immigration, these results are nonetheless consistent with a theme raised by Samuel Huntington in his book *Who Are We?* Huntington argued that Latin American immigration and the rise of multiculturalism were two factors eroding American national identity, which was, he contended, at its core Anglo-Protestant.[42]

Examining the voting behavior of key social groups is another way to gain some sense, suggestive at best, of what voters were saying with their ballots in the 2016 election. One of the largest and most consistent divisions in party support in recent decades has been along lines of race and ethnicity. And 2016 was no different. As Figure 4.7 makes clear, since the 1960s, no Democratic candidate has received a majority of white voter support, which has been declining since 2008. In 2016, Clinton earned only 37 percent of white votes. Importantly, after a campaign in which Trump repeatedly made derogatory remarks about women and was captured on video admitting to sexual assault, a majority of white women (52 percent) still supported him for president.

In contrast, black voters have consistently given strong support, above 80 percent, to Democratic candidates. In 2016, 88 percent of black voters supported Clinton. The 51-point gap between black and white voter support of Democrats is a continuation of the pattern of recent years. And just as white men and women alike gave majority support to Trump, so too did black men and women support Clinton. In fact, black women were the most cohesive group in favor of Hillary Clinton, giving her 94 percent of their votes.

Latinos, like blacks, have historically given majority support to the Democratic candidate, although their support has been more variable. After hitting a low of 53 percent in 2004, Latino support for the Democratic candidate climbed to 71 percent in 2012 before dropping down to 65 percent

Figure 4.7 Support for the Democratic Candidate among Black, Latino, and White Voters, 1972–2016

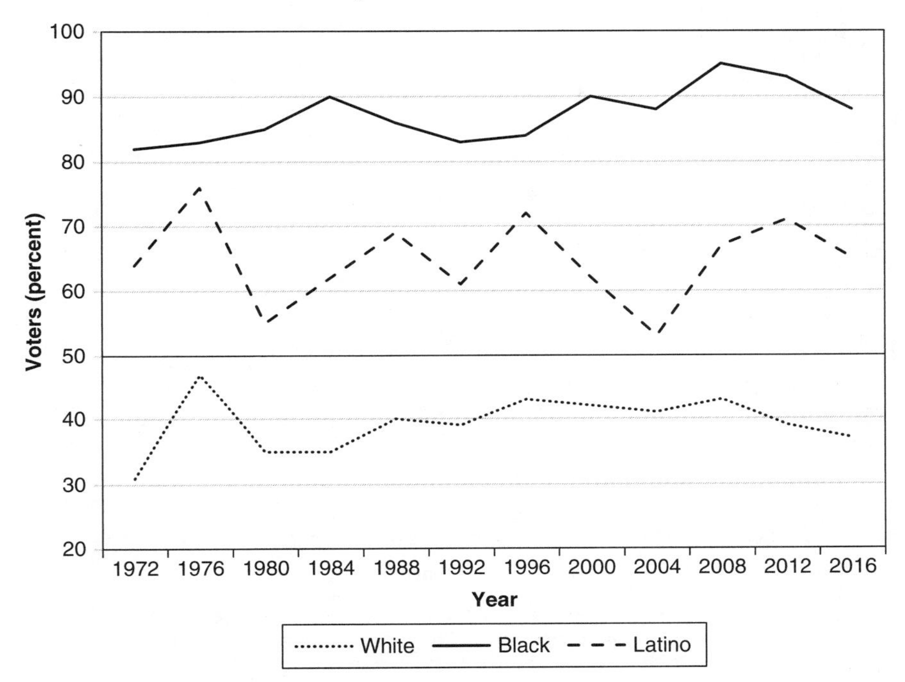

Sources: New York Times NEP data.

for Clinton in 2016. It is important to note that other polling, including that by Latino Decisions, found considerably stronger support for Clinton among Latinos, at 79 percent, a proportion more consistent with what might be expected given Trump's regular demonization of Latinos.[43]

The enduring strength of the racial and ethnic divisions in vote choice is largely a continuation of past patterns. Yet what makes 2016 different from past elections is the accelerated movement of large subgroups of white voters out of the Democratic Party. Whites without a college degree make up about one-third of all voters, and in elections since 1996, they have increasingly diverged in their support for the Democratic candidate from white voters with college degrees (also about one-third of voters). Support for the Democratic candidate among whites without a college degree dropped by 16 percentage points from 1996 to 2016, from 44 percent to just 28 percent. Meanwhile, support from white voters with a college degree has remained relatively stable, in the mid-40s, and increased slightly from 42 percent in 2012 to 45 percent in 2016.

As Figure 4.8 makes clear, this divergence in behavior between college-educated and non-college-educated whites accelerated dramatically between 2012 and 2016.

The spread between the two groups of whites jumped from 6 percentage points in 2012 to a high of 17 percentage points in 2016. This acceleration

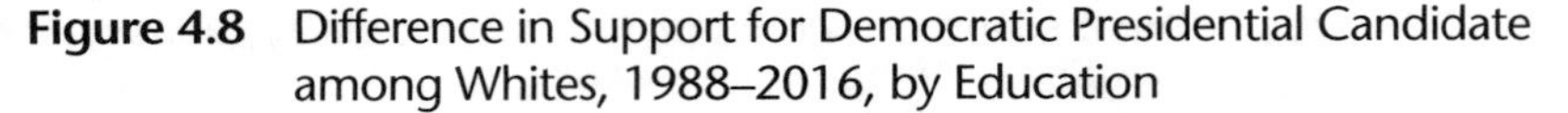

Figure 4.8 Difference in Support for Democratic Presidential Candidate among Whites, 1988–2016, by Education

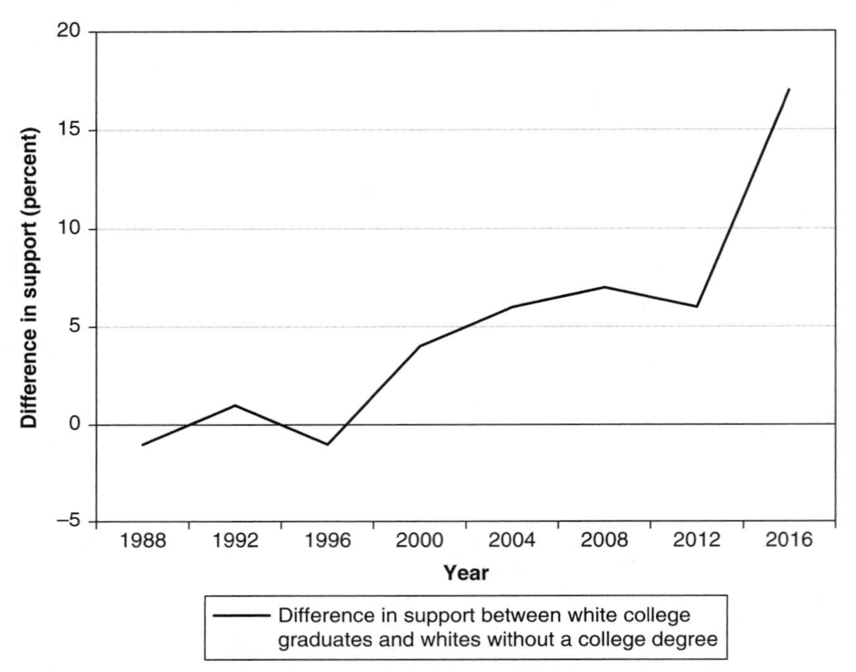

Source: New York Times NEP data.

from previous years likely reflects the potency of Trump's economic appeals (education and income are closely correlated) but also the ideas about belonging and status that his rhetoric invoked. Lending credence to this latter explanation, the gap between nonwhite voters with a college degree and nonwhite voters without a college degree is only 4 percentage points, about one-fourth the size of the gap among whites. In other words, the education gap mattered far more for whites than for nonwhites.

Also possibly significant in assessing the growing divide over national identity is that support for the Democratic candidate from those, of all races, with postgraduate study (18 percent of voters) climbed from 48 percent in 1988 to 58 percent in 2016. In their argument about an "emerging Democratic majority," John Judis and Ruy Teixeira saw the Democratic Party's post-1960s emphasis on post-material concerns as important in attracting highly educated, often high-income-earning, professionals who were unlikely to be swayed by the Democrats' traditional economic message.[44] It is these voters who were more likely to be influenced by the values of multiculturalism in higher education and who are more likely to live and work in areas where cosmopolitan values are applauded.[45] For these voters, Trump's proposals as well as his rhetorical tone and style were likely seen as a repudiation of their values and identities.

Shifting Grounds of Party Coalitions?

In the 1930s, Franklin D. Roosevelt established Democratic Party dominance with the principle that the national government should intervene actively in the economy to protect the welfare of its citizens. Beginning in the 1960s, the Democratic Party combined economic with social justice appeals in an attempt to build a broader, multiracial, and multiethnic base. This helped the party gain the support of minority voters and women, both of which are disproportionately represented among the poor, and it attracted new support from educated, often more affluent, voters, especially in the North and the Pacific Coast states. The cost was a loss of support in the white South, as well as among white middle-class voters more broadly. The Republican gains that resulted have led to several decades of rough electoral parity between the parties and an increasing partisan standoff on economic, social, and foreign policy issues.

In several respects, the 2016 election represented an intensification of trends already present in the electorate. Party loyalties remained high, as did the partisan character of most of the country's geographic regions. Divisions among voters along lines of race and ethnicity, education, and to a lesser extent income also remained as they were. But there were important departures from earlier voting patterns as well. More states were competitive in 2016 than in the past, including a band of states in the greater Midwest that flipped by consistent, if small, margins from Democratic to Republican. Also notable, declining support for the Democratic Party among lesser educated whites accelerated sharply. But perhaps the most significant departure is that, in electing Trump, voters bucked all mainstream, bipartisan elite opinion on the suitability, even the safety, of a candidate for the presidency.

Against the backdrop of an election different in tenor, substance, and candidate attributes from any in history, the continuities and changes in voting behavior prompt questions about future scenarios in the party system. Will the voter dissatisfaction with the neoliberal economic order that was evident in both parties in 2016 lead to shifts in the policy positions of the party establishments, dependent as they both are on business and financial interests that benefit from that order? The evidence of voter anger is already creating friction among Democratic Party elites as centrist Democrats, including House minority leader Nancy Pelosi, battle with progressives such as Bernie Sanders. If Trump pursues the economic populist policies of his campaign, the Republican Party is likely to either fracture or else redefine its core commitments. In a different vein, how will the vitriolic intensification of battles over socially progressive ends and cosmopolitan values intersect with the economic reorganization of the parties? Will Republicans abandon their effort to court minority voters, especially Latinos? Can the Democratic Party reinvigorate the coalition of economic progressives and social progressives that put Obama in office in 2008 and 2012? Perhaps here, more than anywhere, especially given the reach of executive unilateral action, what Trump chooses to do while in office—and who he relies on to advise him—will be telling.

The country is facing more squarely now than in a long time the question of what it means to be an American. To what rights and privileges are

Americans entitled, and who counts as an American in a world where ideas, goods, and people move easily and speedily across borders? The answers are not yet clear, but these are the stakes over which Americans, like citizens of nations throughout the world, will wrestle in the coming years. The vitriolic campaign of 2016 may represent the first salvos in this new battle.

Notes

1. David Wasserman, "2016 National Popular Vote Tracker," *Cook Political Report,* December 14, 2016, cookpolitical.com/story/10174. In addition, third-party candidates, notably Gary Johnson, of the Libertarian Party, and Jill Stein, of the Green Party, received over 5 percent of the popular vote. This article focuses on the major-party candidates and voters.
2. Michael Signer, "Make the Electoral College Great Again: Let 'Conscientious Electors' Do Their Jobs," *Vox*, December 18, 2016, www.vox.com/the-big-idea/2016/11/29/13771920/electoral-college-faithless-electors-independent-trump.
3. "Obama Says Clinton Is the Most Qualified Presidential Candidate Ever," *Politico*, July 5, 2016, www.politico.com/video/2016/07/obama-says-clinton-is-the-most-qualified-presidential-candidate-ever-059832.
4. Reid Wilson, "Final Newspaper Endorsement Count: Clinton 57, Trump 2," *The Hill*, November 6, 2016, thehill.com/blogs/ballot-box/presidential-races/304606-final-newspaper-endorsement-count-clinton-57-trump-2.
5. Amy Chozick, "Hillary Clinton Blames FBI Director for Election Loss," *New York Times*, November 12, 2016, www.nytimes.com/2016/11/13/us/politics/hillary-clinton-james-comey.html.
6. Adam Entous and Ellen Nakashima, "FBI in Agreement with CIA That Russia Aimed to Help Trump Win White House," *Washington Post,* December 16, 2016, www.washingtonpost.com/politics/clinton-blames-putins-personal-grudge-against-her-for-election-interference/2016/12/16/12f36250-c3be-11e6-8422-eac61c0ef74d_story.html.
7. Aaron Blake, "A Record Number of Americans Now Dislike Hillary Clinton," *Washington Post,* August 31, 2016, www.washingtonpost.com/news/the-fix/wp/2016/08/31/a-record-number-of-americans-now-dislike-hillary-clinton/.
8. Exit poll data were collected by Edison Research for the National Election Pool, a consortium of media outlets, and made available on member websites.
9. Pew Research Center, "Partisan Identification Trends: 1992–2016," June 13, 2016, www.people-press.org/2016/09/13/party-identification-trends-1992-2016/; and Bruce Keith, David Magleby, Candice Nelson, Elizabeth Orr, and Mark Westlye, *The Myth of the Independent Voter* (Berkeley: University of California Press, 1992).
10. Matthew Levendusky, *The Partisan Sort: How Liberals Became Democrats and Conservatives Became Republicans* (Chicago: University of Chicago Press, 2009).
11. Morris Fiorina (with Samuel J. Abrams and Jeremy Pope), *Culture War? The Myth of a Polarized America* (New York: Pearson Longman, 2005).
12. Justin McCarthy, "Ahead of Elections, US Approval of Congress at 18%," *Gallup*, October 12, 2016, www.gallup.com/poll/196268/ahead-elections-congress-approval.aspx.
13. Alan Abramowitz, *The Disappearing Center: Engaged Citizens, Polarization, and American Democracy* (New Haven, Conn.: Yale University Press, 2010).
14. Michael McDonald, "Voter Turnout," *United States Election Project*, www.electproject.org/home/voter-turnout/voter-turnout-data.
15. E. J. Dionne, *Why Americans Hate Politics* (New York: Simon & Schuster, 1991), 152.

16. American Political Science Association's Committee on Political Parties, "Toward a More Responsible Two-Party System," *American Political Science Review* XLIV (September 1950).
17. This is not new. Similar impulses have been observed in reactions against industrial modernization at the turn of the twentieth century. See Richard Hofstadter, *The Age of Reform: From Bryan to F.D.R.* (New York: Knopf, 1955).
18. Donald Critchlow, *The Conservative Ascendancy: How the Republican Right Rose to Power in Modern America* (Lawrence: University Press of Kansas, 2011); Bruce J. Schulman, *The Seventies: The Great Shift in American Culture, Society, and Politics* (New York: Free Press, 2001); and Stephen Skowronek, *The Politics Presidents Make: Leadership from John Adams to George Bush* (Cambridge: Harvard University Press, 1993).
19. Larry Bartels, "2016 Was an Ordinary Election, Not a Realignment," *Washington Post*, November 10, 2016, www.washingtonpost.com/news/monkey-cage/wp/2016/11/10/2016-was-an-ordinary-election-not-a-realignment/; and Sam Wang, "The Incredibly Stable 2016 Campaign," *Princeton Election Consortium*, September 29, 2016, election.princeton.edu/2016/09/29/the-incredibly-stable-2016-campaign/.
20. Shanto Iyengar and Sean Westwood, "Fear and Loathing across Party Lines: New Evidence on Group Polarization," *American Journal of Political Science*, 59 (July 2015): 690–707.
21. Nate Silver, "2016 Election Forecast," *FiveThirtyEight*, projects.fivethirtyeight.com/2016-election-forecast/.
22. Calculations based on all major-party voters in each of the four regions. The South includes Alabama, Arkansas, Florida, Georgia, Louisiana, Mississippi, North Carolina, South Carolina, Texas, Virginia, Kentucky, Oklahoma, Tennessee, and West Virginia. West includes Iowa, Kansas, Minnesota, Missouri, Nebraska, North Dakota, South Dakota, Arizona, Colorado, Idaho, Montana, Nevada, New Mexico, Utah, and Wyoming. Pacific Coast includes California, Oregon, and Washington. North includes Connecticut, Delaware, Illinois, Indiana, Maine, Maryland, Massachusetts, Michigan, New Hampshire, New Jersey, New York, Ohio, Pennsylvania, Rhode Island, Vermont, and Wisconsin. Alaska and Hawaii, which were added to the Union after World War II and which regularly vote Republican and Democratic, respectively, are not included in the analysis.
23. Nicole Mellow, *The State of Disunion: Regional Sources of Modern American Partisanship* (Baltimore, Md.: Johns Hopkins University Press, 2008).
24. The phrase "emerging Republican majority" was coined by Republican strategist Kevin Phillips, *The Emerging Republican Majority* (New Rochelle, N.Y.: Arlington House, 1969).
25. Mellow, *The State of Disunion*, ch. 3.
26. Remarks at Techport Australia, November 15, 2012, www.state.gov/secretary/20092013clinton/rm/2012/11/200565.htm.
27. Democratic primary debate, October 13, 2015, Las Vegas, Nevada. Quoted in Lauren Carroll, "What Hillary Clinton Really Said about the TPP and the 'Gold Standard.'" *PolitiFact*, October 13, 2015, www.politifact.com/truth-o-meter/statements/2015/oct/13/hillary-clinton/what-hillary-clinton-really-said-about-tpp-and-gol/.
28. Remarks by Granholm at Williams College, Williamstown, MA, November 10, 2016.
29. Eric Bradner and Deirdre Walsh, "Democrats Reject Obama on Trade," *CNN*, June 13, 2015, www.cnn.com/2015/06/12/politics/white-house-tpp-trade-deal-congress/.
30. Neoliberalism and globalization refer to different, though not unrelated, phenomena. *Globalization* is the movement of goods, capital, and people across national boundaries, and it was the buzzword of the 1990s. *Neoliberalism*, which has become the concept du jour in the academy, is concerned with limiting government's role in the economy through efforts to promote privatization, deregulation, and free market solutions more generally, and includes the aims of globalization.

31. Bartels, "2016 Was an Ordinary Election"; Martin Gilens, *Affluence and Influence: Economic Inequality and Political Power in America* (Princeton, N.J.: Princeton University Press, 2012).
32. Comments made at the LGBT for Hillary Gala in New York City on September 9, 2016. "Transcript: Clinton's Full Remarks as She Called Half of Trump Supporters 'Deplorables'," *Los Angeles Times*, September 10, 2016, www.latimes.com/nation/politics/trailguide/la-na-trailguide-updates-transcript-clinton-s-full-remarks-as-1473549076-htmlstory.html.
33. Eduardo Bonilla-Silva, *Racism without Racists* (Lanham, Md.: Rowman & Littlefield, 2014).
34. John B. Judis and Ruy Teixeira, *The Emerging Democratic Majority* (New York: Scribner, 2002).
35. "Full Text: Donald Trump Announces a Presidential Bid," *Washington Post*, June 16, 2015, www.washingtonpost.com/news/post-politics/wp/2015/06/16/full-text-donald-trump-announces-a-presidential-bid/.
36. Donald J. Trump Statement on Preventing Muslim Immigration. Press release from the Trump campaign on December 7, 2015, www.donaldjtrump.com/press-releases/donald-j.-trump-statement-on-preventing-muslim-immigration.
37. Ashley Parker, Nick Corasaniti, and Erica Berenstein, "Voices from Donald Trump's Rallies, Uncensored," *New York Times*, August 3, 2016, www.nytimes.com/2016/08/04/us/politics/donald-trump-supporters.html; also see Peter Holley, "Top Nazi Leader: Trump Will Be a 'Real Opportunity' for White Nationalists," *Washington Post*, August 7, 2016, www.washingtonpost.com/news/post-nation/wp/2016/08/07/top-nazi-leader-trump-will-be-a-real-opportunity-for-white-nationalists/.
38. John Higham, *Strangers in the Land: Patterns of American Nativism, 1860–1925* (New Brunswick, N.J.: Rutgers University Press, 1955).
39. Rogers Smith, *Civic Ideals: Conflicting Visions of Citizenship in U.S. History* (New Haven, Conn.: Yale University Press, 1999); Jeffrey Tulis and Nicole Mellow, *Legacies of Losing in American Politics* (Chicago: University of Chicago Press, 2017).
40. For how both of these traditions emerged from Progressive politics of the early twentieth century, see Nicole Mellow, "The Democratic Fit: Party Reform and the Eugenics Tool," in *The Progressives' Century*, eds. Bruce Ackerman, Stephen Skowronek, and Stephen Engel (New Haven, Conn.: Yale University Press, 2016).
41. A November 9, 2016, article in *Vox* by Zach Beauchamp, "Donald Trump's Victory Is Part of a Global White Backlash," summarizes and links to a variety of social science research on this topic, www.vox.com/world/2016/11/9/13572174/president-elect-donald-trump-2016-victory-racism-xenophobia.
42. Samuel Huntington, *Who Are We?: Challenges to America's National Identity* (New York: Simon & Schuster, 2005).
43. The debate between Latino Decisions and Edison over the accuracy of their respective findings centers on methodology. See "Lies, Damn Lies, and Exit Polls," *Latino Decisions*, November 10, 2016, www.latinodecisions.com/blog/2016/11/10/lies-damn-lies-and-exit-polls/.
44. John B. Judis and Ruy Teixeira, *The Emerging Democratic Majority* (New York: Scribner, 2002).
45. In addition to Judis and Teixeira's discussion of "ideopolises," see Richard Florida, *The Rise of the Creative Class: And How It's Transforming Work, Leisure, Community, and Everyday Life* (New York: Basic Books, 2002); Robert Reich, "What Is a Nation?" *Political Science Quarterly* 106 (1991): 193–209.

5

The Media

Covering Donald Trump

Marjorie Randon Hershey

Early media coverage of the 2016 presidential campaign portrayed it as a freak show. That was not surprising. There was the video showing a candidate who fired a machine gun in order to cook the bacon he had wrapped around its barrel. Another candidate was briefly attacked by a bald eagle while filming a campaign ad. There was the candidate whose private cell phone number was given out by a rival and who responded by setting fire to his flip phone. And then, of course, came the candidate—a major-party nominee for president—with the aerodynamically implausible hair style and the vulgar language.

The "Whoa, is this weird, or what?" tone of the media coverage started with the 2015–2016 Republican primary race. And it drew huge audiences for media outlets. Coverage of the Iowa caucuses on the three biggest cable networks (Fox News, CNN, and MSNBC) broke their own records for viewership of the Iowa event, drawing more than ten million viewers in prime time. Each of the Republican primary debates drew even more.[1]

The American presidency is an office with awesome responsibilities. Its occupant serves as commander-in-chief of the military. The president is the primary agenda-setter for Congress as well as the executive branch. He or she commands a great deal of media coverage domestically and around the world. So why did so much of the campaign news zero in on bizarre campaign events and Donald Trump's hair?

Media Norms and Voters' Needs

The media perform a vital public service in a democracy by keeping members of the public informed about what their government is doing. But performing that public service isn't their primary job. Most media—broadcast and cable TV and radio stations, newspapers, and most Internet sites—are privately owned enterprises. They must make a profit to survive. That requires getting and holding an audience. The media outlet then sells access to that audience to prospective sponsors, advertisers, or patrons, who in turn provide the funds needed to produce the outlet's content. Other media outlets, whether run by nonprofits or other groups or individuals, also want to reach as many people as possible, even if profit is not their goal. The result is that the editor of the *Los Angeles Times* must deal with the same challenge as the editor of the *Politico* website and even the producer of a *Survivor* episode: instead of waking up each morning asking, "How can I serve my First Amendment function today by informing the public about the nature of governance and politics?" he or she is more likely to think, "If I don't get enough readership or viewership for my newspaper or program or blog today, then my job is at risk."

The dramatic transition experienced by the media universe since the 1980s has heightened the media's need for audiences. Rapid recent changes in media technology have added tens of thousands of alternatives to the menu of media sources, from online newspapers to blogs, social media, and text messaging. In the process, these changes have undercut print journalism and increased the competition among all media outlets to survive and make a profit.[2] How, then, do news media meet this basic need for an audience amid the merciless competition for readers and viewers? No medium has the time or space to tell us everything that's happening, and even if it could, most of us wouldn't be interested in reading or watching it all. Any medium has to select the information it presents.

To survive, then, media people try to learn what their prospective audience wants to see covered in the news. They develop a definition of "news" based primarily not on the democratic citizen's need to know but on the media's need to gain an audience. (That is, they do so if they want to withstand the competition until the next fiscal year.) These norms, or operating rules, as to what they will define as news then determine the types of information they select to present. By looking for material matching that definition of news, media shape what we can learn from them about politics, government, and candidates.

What are these norms? Media analysts know that most people are more interested in drama, movement, and conflict than in stasis and calm. This is true even if the drama and conflict have relatively little bearing on people's real needs. Television "reality shows" win much bigger audiences than do analyses of the American economy, even though the economy shapes Americans' lives much more than knowing who got voted off the island. More people respond to information about change than to stories about continuity, even if their daily lives are structured by the continuity—the fundamental forces present day after day—rather than by the short-term change. In choosing which news to watch (or whether to watch any news), most people attend to news that's immediate and novel rather than older information, whether or not the immediate news item has any real value to the viewer. Most people respond more readily to pictures of individuals, especially to pictures of faces, than to words. That's why most news stories about economic downturns lead with a description of someone who lost his or her job, not with information that applies more generally.[3]

For most media, then, detailed discussions of the most vital and complex issues of governance are a one-way ticket to ratings hell. Observers may deplore the name-calling, the calculated outrage, and the incendiary language used at many political rallies and meetings. But events lacking drama and conflict are a non-starter in attracting coverage. As one commentator described a Republican presidential candidate debate in March 2016 that had been more civil and calm than earlier such debates: "The civility may be a good thing for voters, but it's really boring television."[4]

How did the need for audiences affect coverage of the 2016 presidential race? One effect was perfectly clear: Republican presidential candidate Donald Trump was a ratings machine. He drew journalists' and bloggers' attention with approximately the same effectiveness as the "ding" of a new text message. That probably affected voters' choices as to who should become president of the United States.

Covering Donald Trump

It started even before he declared his candidacy. Coverage of the presidential race during the "invisible primary" of 2015 was dominated by journalists' fascination with Trump—not because he was the most qualified candidate to emerge in the history of the republic, but because he was a constant generator of audiences for newscasts, blogs, and social media. His demographic profile wasn't unique for a presidential candidate; he was an older white male who had built a substantial set of inherited real estate holdings into an apparently large fortune at least in part by shady business practices. His ambition was more apparent than his partisanship or his commitment to specific issues. Trump had taken some liberal stands in the 1990s, including describing himself as pro-choice on abortion, and he contributed to several Democratic candidates. But after brief flirtations with running for president and governor of New York as early as 1988, Trump set out to reshape his public image during Barack Obama's first term as president. He stepped forward to lead the far-right "birther" movement of people who claimed that Obama was a Muslim born in Kenya who had ascended to the presidency through conspiracy and fraud. He promoted the view that Obama was not an American even in the face of Obama's Hawaii birth certificate. And then, Trump confirmed rumors by declaring his candidacy for president in 2015.

From the day of his announcement, Trump focused on generating drama and conflict to capture media attention. In his announcement speech, stressing his opposition to illegal immigration, he called undocumented Mexican immigrants "rapists" and "criminals." This startling overgeneralization guaranteed more than just one day's headlines. His eleven-year experience as the star of a network reality show (*The Apprentice*) taught him that such an insult would lead opposing groups to react with outrage to the slur, after which he could react with outrage to their outrage, and a one-day story would last a week. He treated his Republican rivals with colorful—and thus very heavily covered—contempt. In nationally televised debates, Trump referred to his main opponents, Senators Marco Rubio and

Ted Cruz, as "Little Marco" and "Lyin' Ted." At other times, his language was less restrained; he called various candidates "stupid," "losers," "unstable," "a basket case," and "unhinged."[5] In the general election campaign, he referred to his Democratic opponent as "the devil" with "tremendous hate in her heart" who would be sent to jail if Trump won the election.[6]

Trump added to the news-making drama with continuing attacks on the party whose nomination he was seeking—not a common practice in nomination campaigns. He flaunted his opposition to undocumented (and, implicitly, nonwhite) immigrants in the face of worried party leaders. The Republican Party's official response to its loss in the 2012 presidential race had been that in a nation where whites were projected to become a demographic minority by 2050, the party must make special efforts to appeal to Latino Americans or risk long-term failure.[7] By trashing undocumented Mexican immigrants (and, by extension, Mexican and other Latino Americans), Trump thumbed his nose at the party establishment—although one liberal analyst countered that Trump was simply "saying loudly, unambiguously, and repeatedly the ugly things that other Republican politicians try to camouflage in innuendo, focus-group-tested euphemisms, and consultantspeak."[8]

Not many days passed when Trump did not say something dramatic, conflict-filled, and thus "newsworthy." He later admitted that when speaking to large crowds, he would keep his eye on the television cameras' red lights, to make sure they were covering him live. If they weren't, he would say whatever it took to get them turned on again.[9] After a short period in which he maintained a calmer mode of speech, Trump came out with back-to-back statements that it was actually Hillary Clinton who had started the birther movement against Obama (an inaccurate claim) and that her Secret Service agents should disarm and "let's see what happens to her." He had previously suggested that only "Second Amendment people" (presumably, people with guns) could stop Clinton from appointing liberal Supreme Court judges, statements perilously close to inciting violence.

Trump also frequently made unscheduled call-ins to cable talk shows and Sunday morning news programs, and these programs' hosts, able to spot a headline-maker, took the calls. On the few occasions when his coverage paused, Trump restarted it using social media. With ten million followers on Twitter and nine million on Facebook by late 2015, Trump became his own social media outlet, which attracted more than three times as many readers as the *New York Times*. He refined his messages on sites such as Reddit according to the responses they received, which came in record numbers.[10] His extensive use of Twitter—he tweeted out more than five thousand times between June 2015 and mid-January 2016 and generated tens of millions of responses—was packed with insults. Among his most frequent targets were reporters, describing political journalists as "among the most dishonest people that I've ever met," and calling more than one individual reporter a "sleaze."[11] Trump often charged at rallies that the media were out to get him by publishing lies about him and intentionally "covering for" Clinton. Increasingly, the candidate even encouraged his boisterous crowds to threaten reporters present at these rallies.

It is fascinating, then, that media people, the target of so many of these insults, were anxious to cover them. As *FiveThirtyEight*'s Nate Silver wrote, "Trump has been able to disrupt the news pretty much any time he wants, whether by being newsworthy, offensive, salacious or entertaining. The media has almost always played along."[12]

Why? Because the coverage served the media outlets as well as Trump. As *New York Times* media columnist Jim Rutenberg pointed out, "There is always a mutually beneficial relationship between candidates and news organizations during presidential years. But in my lifetime it's never seemed so singularly focused on a single candidacy."[13] Rutenberg's *Times* and other "legacy" media were struggling against the twenty-four-hour Internet news cycle, and featuring Trump provided them with more content than they could ever use—content that attracted audiences, increased ratings, and brought in money from advertisers. Trump described it this way: "I go on one of these shows and the ratings double, they triple. . . . And that gives you power."[14]

The result was profoundly unbalanced coverage of the presidential candidates. Consider this example: On the night of March 8, 2016, several highly newsworthy events occurred. Trump narrowly won the Michigan primary. Hillary Clinton came surprisingly close to being beaten by Bernie Sanders in that primary. The latter was probably the more surprising result. Yet CNN, Fox, and MSNBC chose to ignore Clinton's contest in order to cover Trump without interruption for a full forty-five minutes, even though much of his speech was devoted to touting the virtues of the steaks and vodka produced by his companies. One commentator described the speech as an "infomercial" for Trump products. Even so, Trump's steaks carried "a higher news [read: ratings] value" in winning audiences than did Clinton's narrow victory.[15]

Between the announcement of his candidacy in June and the Iowa caucuses, it was not unusual for Trump to receive more than 60 percent of all mentions of the Republican presidential candidates on domestic national TV news programs, while the other sixteen Republican candidates divided the remaining 40 percent (see Figure 5.1).[16] Even on the day of the Iowa caucuses, when other candidates were campaigning heavily, Trump still attracted 50 percent of all mentions of Republican candidates. Fox News gave him more than twice as much free airtime as any other candidate from May to December 2015.[17] In fact, Nate Silver showed that out of all the important news stories on any topic that dominated the Internet from the announcement of his candidacy until March 2016, ranging from bombings and earthquakes to assorted other disasters, 36 percent of all such lead stories referred to Trump. As Silver noted, it is impossible to overstate the singularity and importance of this media emphasis.[18] Another data analysis showed that through mid-September 2016, eight major newspapers and websites carried twice as many headlines about Trump as about Clinton—a remarkable disparity.[19]

MediaQuant, which measures the "free" (or "earned") media coverage of each presidential candidate and computes a dollar value based on advertising rates, reported that in January and February of the 2016 primary season, when Trump was establishing himself as the Republican front-runner, he

Figure 5.1 Television News Mentions of Donald Trump as a Percentage of All Republican Presidential Candidates' Coverage, June 16, 2015–February 5, 2016

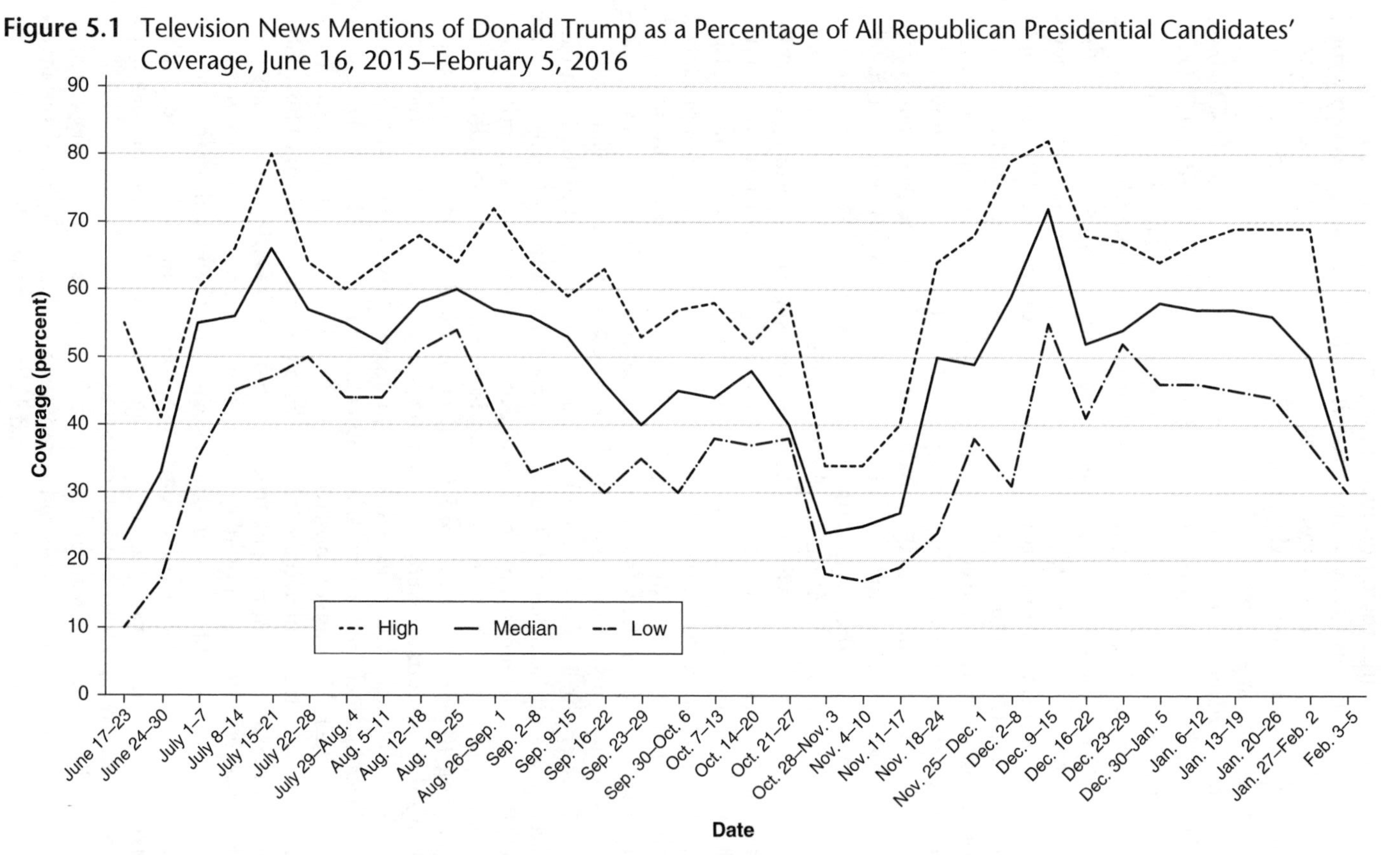

Source: Data calculated from 2016 Campaign Television Tracker, television.gdeltproject.org/cgi-bin/iatv_campaign2016/iatv_campaign2016?

received the equivalent of $1.9 *billion* in free media coverage, compared to $313 million for his main rival, Ted Cruz, and $204 million and $38 million for Marco Rubio and John Kasich, respectively. Trump outpaced his nearest rival, then, by a magnitude of more than six. In comparison, Hillary Clinton's free media amounted to about $746 million worth of coverage, about twice that of Bernie Sanders's $321 million.[20] In short, "Trump got one-third to one-half of the coverage—depending on the medium—and the remaining candidates split the rest."[21] Trump didn't start running media ads until January 2016, but his free media coverage kept his face and name in the public eye until that time.

The wildly disproportionate media focus on Trump was itself a frequent news story. A March 2016 Pew Research Center survey found that 75 percent of voters—including one-third of Trump supporters—said news organizations had given too much coverage to Trump, compared with no more than 40 percent who said that about any other candidate.[22] Much of his free media coverage was negative in tone; columnists used terms such as "bombastic," "demagogue," and "narcissist" frequently. Former Republican presidential candidate Mitt Romney called Trump "a phony, a fraud. . . . He's playing members of the American public for suckers."[23] But this didn't seem to hurt Trump's standing, because his supporters—middle-aged and older white males in particular, many of whom feared that they were losing societal dominance as a consequence of demographic change—were contemptuous of the mainstream media (and of the Republican party leadership as well). This inoculated them against media criticism of their candidate and may have even increased his appeal.

Some journalists defended their obsession with Trump. A few argued that his views were largely unknown prior to the campaign, whereas Hillary Clinton had been covered extensively for decades. Others claimed that Trump's candidacy was "extraordinary and precedent-shattering" and therefore warranted extraordinary levels of coverage. "If you have a nominee who expresses warmth toward one of our most mischievous and menacing adversaries [Russia], a nominee who shatters all the norms about how our leaders treat families whose sons died for our country, a nominee proposing to rethink the alliances that have guided our foreign policy for 60 years, that demands coverage—copious coverage and aggressive coverage," wrote the *New York Times*'s senior editor for politics."[24]

The problem was that the constraints of limited media space and time—even on the Internet, where space is not limited but most viewers' attention spans are—ensured that exceptional attention to one candidate precluded similar attention to his or her opponents. In addition, the heavy media focus on Trump's most recent outrageous statement meant that Trump was able to set the agenda for his own coverage. Media investigations into the myriad scandals with which Trump, his businesses, and his foundation were involved tended not to receive much coverage until fairly late in the campaign, when "Trump Shocker"–style stories had become old news and most prospective voters had already made up their minds about the candidates.

Thus, one of the several possible explanations for Trump's success in the 2016 presidential race is a media explanation. Effective candidates realize that media norms determine what media decide to cover and learn how to conform to those norms. Trump, as a pitchman and an entertainer, had lengthy experience attracting coverage. Political scientist John Sides demonstrated the very close relationship between Trump's share of the coverage in social media during the summer and fall of 2015 and his poll numbers during that time (see Figure 5.2). Note that increases in media coverage tended to *precede* Trump's rises in the polls. At least among voters already inclined toward his views,[25] this pattern suggests that media coverage could have been the cause rather than the effect of Trump's success in the nomination contest. Because this media attention came at the expense of his party rivals, it hampered their ability to break through as the main Trump alternative. And along with the powerful force of party identification in motivating people to support any candidate of their party, regardless of his or her qualifications, Trump's dominance of political news probably helped keep him competitive in the general election.

Trump's ability to dominate media coverage of the presidential campaign—indeed, to dominate the news more broadly in 2015 and 2016—suggests that the media's need for audiences, especially in this time of significant media transition, and the norms of coverage that have developed to meet that need, cast a long shadow over American election campaigns. When media outlets have limited resources and audiences have limited attention spans, one candidate's ability to soak up all the oxygen in the room can disproportionately affect who wins and, therefore, who governs.

Figure 5.2 Trump's Share of News Coverage and National Polling Numbers, May–September 2015

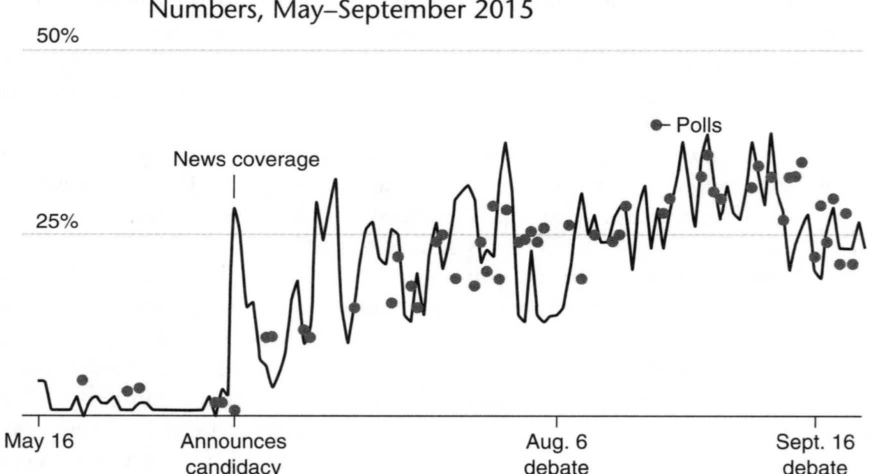

Source: Graph was generously shared by John Sides, based on data from Crimson Hexagon. See John Sides, "Why Is Donald Trump Declining in the Polls?" *Washington Post*, September 29, 2015, www.washingtonpost.com/blogs/monkey-cage/wp/2015/09/29/why-is-donald-trump-declining-in-the-polls-the-media-strike-again/.

Note: "News coverage" is Trump's percentage of the coverage received by him and twelve other candidates for the Republican presidential nomination (excluding only candidates Gilmore, Graham, Jindal, and Pataki).

Covering False Equivalences

Journalists are frequently accused of slanting the news. Although there isn't much evidence to support the charge that the mainstream media have a partisan slant,[26] even the accusation of bias is worrisome enough to affect the norms of reporting because it could reduce the audience for mainstream media outlets. To counter these accusations, the mainstream and broadcast media have traditionally followed the norm of "two-handed journalism" in reporting anything that could be viewed as controversial. To maintain the loyalty of a politically diverse audience, network news programs and newspapers typically follow a statement that suggests a particular point of view with a quote from another source reflecting the other side of the issue—the "other hand."

That makes sense on matters of opinion, such as whether Facebook should have a "dislike" button or whether same-sex marriage should be legal. It is much less reasonable on matters of fact: few reporters would feel the need to locate an opposing source on the question of whether Congress exists. The problem is that in the current climate of partisan and ideological polarization, what constitutes "facts" has become more open to partisan controversy than it might have been fifty years ago. Add to this that the two major parties' ideological stances have moved away from the center at differing rates. In what is called "asymmetric polarization," the voting behavior of Republican members of Congress has moved further toward the "right" than have Democratic members of Congress to the "left." And a larger proportion of Republican identifiers now call themselves "very conservative" than the percentage of Democrats who call themselves "very liberal."[27]

Bloggers and opinion journalists do not need to be troubled by this asymmetric polarization. Because they usually appeal to a niche audience that already knows their leanings, they can offer one view only or call out one side as more extreme than the other without worrying about losing readers. But what about broadcast journalists or reporters for mainstream newspapers? If a candidate takes an extreme stand, then to remain "fair," the reporter must locate a partisan on the other side. If that "other hand" takes a more moderate position, then the reporter faces a dilemma: either present both the extreme position and the moderate position as equivalent—and thus imply that the extreme view is just as normal and acceptable—or be accused of biased reporting. Similarly, if a candidate states an outright lie in a speech, how does the journalist cover the speech while avoiding accusations of bias? He or she could simply report the lie without comment, which makes the journalist complicit in its spread. Or he or she could find another source to refute the lie. In the latter case, readers and viewers are presented with both a lie and a rejection of it, with no way to tell which is accurate.

To report a lie and its rebuttal as being two reasonable alternatives is an instance of "false equivalence": presenting two things as equivalent when they are not. The mainstream media's need to maintain an audience makes it understandable that they would typically avoid judging the truth of a candidate's claim, because that would alienate the lying candidate's supporters. Instead, the journalist would find a source to provide the "other hand," and then present both claims as equally plausible. This may be especially appealing when the journalist is not sufficiently expert to know when a candidate is lying. It solves the journalist's problem of filing a balanced story about an unbalanced event. But it doesn't solve the reader's problem, which is how to determine where the truth lies. In fact, it may lead many readers and viewers to conclude that all candidates are equally inclined to mislead and, therefore, to revert to their own partisan preference in judging candidates.[28]

During much of the primary campaign, most mainstream journalists seemed bound by the "two-handed" norm to report the candidates' claims, whether accurate or not, as factual and equivalent. As the campaign wore on, however, fact-checking organizations reported an alarming number of misstatements by Donald Trump. The nonpartisan fact-checking site PolitiFact found that of all the candidates' claims they had tested, only 15 percent of Trump's statements were either true or mostly true, and 54 percent were either false or warranted the extreme rating "pants on fire"—in other words, not just inaccurate but also ridiculous. In comparison, PolitiFact rated 50 percent of Clinton's statements true or mostly true, and 13 percent false or "pants on fire." Trump repeated his false claims frequently, even after they were disproven. For instance, he stated falsely that he "was totally against the war in Iraq," that "veterans, in many cases, are being treated worse than illegal immigrants," and that Clinton "wants to raise taxes on African-American-owned businesses to as much as 50 percent more than they're paying now"—in just a two-week period. He did so even after it had become apparent that his claims were being double-checked.[29]

As late as one month before election day, two-handed journalism was alive and well. Trump was caught on tape boasting about assaulting women. He quickly responded that he had been fibbing. He claimed that Bill Clinton had done much worse and lied about it, that Hillary Clinton had attacked the women who reported her husband's assaults, and that the Clintons' behavior was more reprehensible than Trump's words. Trump then created a media event by bringing four of Bill Clinton's accusers into the second presidential debate as his guests. In doing so, Trump gave journalists an "other hand" in the form of a different compelling story. But it was a story that equated the behavior of one candidate with the actions of the other candidate's spouse—in other words, a false equivalence.

Bloggers judged Trump's statements in light of their personal preferences. But mainstream media outlets, by repeating Trump's false statements on a daily basis, risked normalizing them—making them appear to be true by simple repetition. Some mainstream journalists began to respond to this exceptional challenge by putting Trump's statements in context, even in articles that were not labeled as "news analysis." For instance, a *USA Today* story reported a Trump claim that Hillary Clinton was the one who started the birther rumors against Obama in 2008 and then added, "*but there is no factual basis for that claim.*"[30] Note that the reporter did not cite a Democratic source as the "other hand"; instead, he presented the factual context without attribution. Some TV journalists followed suit. Rather than letting Trump spinners repeat or try to sanitize his incorrect statements, by October interviewers had begun to question or make fun of these efforts. This was a risky step; it opened these media to charges that they were unfairly criticizing Trump and therefore, by implication, helping Hillary Clinton.

The challenge deepened when Trump made statements that questioned or even threatened democratic norms. After dropping in the polls in mid-summer, he claimed that the system was rigged against him, that if he lost, the media's unfair lies about him would be to blame, and that therefore he might not accept the results of the presidential election unless he won. Even many journalists who had corrected several of Trump's specific lies apparently regarded it as a bridge too far to call him out directly on these antidemocratic claims, at least in the news columns.

Another challenge for reporters were the cases in which Trump insinuated a false claim but did not state it precisely enough to permit fact-checking. For instance, after an American of Afghan parentage killed forty-nine people in a gay nightclub in Orlando, Florida, Trump implied that Obama was somehow complicit in the attack: "A lot of people think maybe [Obama] doesn't want to know about it. I happen to think that he just doesn't know what he's doing, but there are many people that think maybe he doesn't want to get it. He doesn't want to see what's really happening. And that could be."[31] Here was the reporters' dilemma: should they make Trump's implication explicit and write that he had accused Obama of possibly sympathizing with the gunman, or let his implication remain unchallenged?

Some venerable media outlets such as the *New York Times* and the *Washington Post* spelled out and criticized Trump's insinuations in their news columns, without attributing the criticism to an "other hand." So did many partisan news sites. But this was precarious new territory for most mainstream journalists, who clung tightly to their two-handed norm. In general, if Trump lied frequently or if there was evidence of unethical business dealings in his background, then the need for two-handed coverage led mainstream reporters to look for elements of Clinton's story that could be seen as equivalently bad. For example, analyses of the Clinton Foundation, and claims that Hillary Clinton met with foundation donors when she was secretary of state (with the unproven insinuation that donors were granted favors from the government), received massive coverage, whereas the smaller Trump Foundation's connections with Russia and Iran got much less play. Trump's insistence that his financial holdings would not be placed in a blind trust if he were elected, but rather would be managed by his children—and the possible conflicts of interest this posed—did not become a major news story until after he was elected.

As we will see, the outcome was that Clinton's coverage on "character" issues was at least as negative as Trump's. Although PolitiFact had found few of her statements to be false, Clinton was often portrayed as corrupt and deceptive. Columnist Gail Collins put it clearly: "What we have here is a candidate for president of the United States who makes stuff up all the time, but is either incapable of realizing that he's telling a lie, or constitutionally unable to take blame for being untruthful. Yet, according to the polls, Hillary Clinton's biggest problem is that the public thinks she's dishonest. Amazing."[32] It wasn't that the mainstream media were biased against Clinton. It's that the institutional needs of the media led reporters to seek whatever information would maintain the exciting story of a competitive election fought by two comparable, equivalent candidates.

Covering Hillary Clinton

For journalists, Clinton's candidacy posed another set of challenges. She was, as Bill Clinton memorably argued in his 1992 presidential campaign, "two for the price of one." This time, however, that meant both a precedent-breaker and a very old story. Although Hillary Clinton had been a familiar face in American politics for a quarter-century, as the wife of a two-term president and then a U.S. senator from New York and secretary of state, she was also the first woman in American history to win a major party's presidential nomination. Americans became accustomed to "firsts" among presidential candidates with respect to religion (Mitt Romney, a Mormon) and race (Barack Obama) in the 2000s. But it is unquestionably newsworthy when someone becomes the first member of a group comprising 51 percent of the population to be chosen as a presidential nominee in almost 230 years. Clinton, then, was both something old and something new.

Research on gender and campaigns shows that running for office "as a woman" (and, of course, it's difficult for the "first" of any group to run as anything other than emblematic of that group) has led to mixed results. Elected offices (especially executive positions, such as governor and president) are typically associated in voters' minds with masculine traits: leadership, strength, command. To win, it's been assumed, women candidates would have to exhibit these traits. Yet in 1992, when congressional scandals left many Americans disgusted with politics and inclined to vote for an outsider, women House and Senate candidates did very well. Unprecedented numbers of women won legislative seats by stressing that women were not politics-as-usual and that stereotypically gendered female traits such as morality and caring could bring in new voters and campaign donors.[33]

In 2016 the question for the media was, would Clinton's coverage emphasize the new—her historic breakthrough as a woman presidential candidate—or the old—her decades-long record of political involvement and that of her husband, the former president? Bill and Hillary Clinton's time in the public spotlight have coincided with a quarter-century of party and ideological polarization not seen in the United States since the 1890s. The return of overtly partisan mass media in the form of Fox News occurred during Bill Clinton's presidency. And President Clinton had provided ample fuel for the fires that surrounded his presidential years: a background in

Arkansas politics, where favor-trading was not just accepted but expected; a series of extramarital affairs that, although not unknown in presidential history, had rarely been publicized nationally during previous presidents' terms of office; and efforts to hide these facts that led him to lie under oath during the Republican-dominated Congress's effort to impeach him.

Although recent research finds that media coverage does not treat women U.S. House candidates differently from men candidates,[34] this may not be true of presidential campaigns. Even though the intense polarization of American politics means that partisanship influences people's votes more than a candidate's gender does, the much greater media coverage of the unique office of president might make gender bias more apparent. Clinton's 2008 run for the Democratic presidential nomination elicited a great deal of discussion of gender bias.[35] But because there have not been other women major-party presidential nominees, and because Clinton's public record is long, well known, and marked by controversies unrelated to her gender, it is hard to be sure whether the nature of her media coverage reflected her role as the first woman nominee or the challenges arising from her long and ambivalent relationship with journalists.

In her campaigns for the Democratic presidential nomination in 2008 and 2016, Clinton tried to deal with her role as the "first woman" by straddling both sides of the gender issue. She referred to her record, especially as secretary of state, to demonstrate that she had the masculine qualities typically associated with presidents: leadership skills, toughness, and persistence. Yet she also referred to issues involving children's needs, gender inequality in pay and health care, and the importance of breaking the "glass ceiling" in 2008 and 2016 by electing a woman president. Clinton presented herself as sufficiently masculine to take on the presidency but, at the same time, sufficiently female to bring new values to the office.

Media coverage of Clinton in 2016 seemed to reject both efforts. She was frequently described as "remote," "programmed," and "cold," adjectives suggesting that she failed to measure up to the traditional feminine qualities of warmth and responsiveness. Journalists quoted speakers who objected to Clinton "yelling" in her speeches. As one writer put it, "When Bernie [Sanders, Clinton's primary opponent] yells, it shows his dedication to the cause. When she yells, it's interpreted in a very different way: She's yelling at you."[36] So Clinton's media coverage didn't give her much credit for the unique values that a woman could bring to the presidency. Images of Clinton as aggressive and highly dispassionate, which might have been seen as positives in a male candidate, were often regarded as bitchy and off-putting in a woman.

Even on the day when Clinton won the number of delegates needed to sew up the Democratic nomination, ostensibly a time when readers might expect a lot of coverage of women's achievements in political history, the role of gender in elections, and the possible effects of this historic event on women's willingness to run for office in larger numbers, Trump got almost as much coverage for the unusual step of delivering a prepared speech calmly and without vulgarity or racial attacks. On this day, Trump, who had dominated the news so frequently by making shocking statements, made the news by sounding normal.

On the flip side, media coverage of Clinton's long record in public life generally focused not on her preparation and leadership but rather on the history of Clinton "scandals," many of them brought to public attention by frequent Republican-led investigations. Several of Clinton's actions offered ample material for this coverage. Her use of a private email server for her correspondence as secretary of state became a continuing story when a House Republican committee chair was able to subpoena tens of thousands of Clinton's emails and make them public. The disputed administration response to an attack on the American diplomatic compound in Benghazi, Libya, while Clinton served as secretary of state fit neatly into a narrative framed by conservative critics that Clinton and her husband were too lax in their dealings with the nation's enemies and too quick to cover up their mistakes. In sum, during the nominating season, although Clinton received twice as much media coverage as her main Democratic opponent, much of her "advantage" in coverage was devoted to stories about these investigations and the perceptions of dishonesty and distrust that attended them.

Clinton's online coverage (including social media) was more negative than Trump's during much of the nominating season. A study of more than 150,000 stories showed that about 41 percent of Clinton's coverage was negative in tone, compared with 36 percent of Trump's (and about 35 percent of Sanders's).[37] A Harvard study of broadcast news and newspapers reported that during 2015, a full 84 percent of Clinton's coverage was negative in tone, compared with 42 percent of Trump's and only 17 percent of Sanders's. This study found that "in 11 of the 12 months, her 'bad news' outpaced her 'good news,' usually by a wide margin, contributing to the increase in her unfavorable poll ratings in 2015."[38] Only after Clinton performed much more effectively in the first presidential debate with Trump did media coverage of Clinton become much more positive than negative, at least for the first few days after the debate.[39]

Although both parties' nominees had backgrounds that could be mined for stories about corruption and deception, Clinton's background was more fully mined. Data confirm that the familiar story line of "Clinton scandals" shaped her coverage, not the new story of the first woman presidential nominee or, in fact, any other aspect of her candidacy. In an August 2015 poll, Gallup asked respondents what they remember reading or hearing about the various presidential candidates.[40] About Hillary Clinton, then the Democratic front-runner, the word "email" dominated respondents' recollections—and not just among Republicans. The references to Clinton were overwhelmingly unfavorable; the only terms that came close to rivaling "email" in frequency were "scandal" and "Benghazi." Among the 750 adults familiar enough with Clinton to offer an opinion of her, the term "email" was mentioned 329 times, compared with only four mentions of "economy" and seven of "gun control." Clinton's policy emphases, then, were barely noticeable to respondents. The Gallup report of the poll concluded, in an impressive understatement, that "Clinton has not been able to control the messaging about her and her candidacy."

It appears, then, that media coverage heavily characterized Clinton as dishonest and corrupt, perhaps to counterbalance the risk some journalists were taking in publicizing Trump's bigoted remarks and frequent lies during the campaign. For a more granular look at this question, I analyzed media coverage during the weeks when each candidate became his or her party's presumptive nominee (see Figures 5.3 and 5.4). The analysis focused on two very different types of media outlets—the *New York Times* and Twitter—to learn whether their coverage characterized the candidates differently. The *Times*, a leading "legacy" medium with a substantial (1.4 million) national circulation, is read frequently by decision-makers who skew middle-aged and older. Twitter is a social medium carrying a lot of political content, with a much larger and younger audience than the *Times*. All *New York Times* articles, opinion pieces, and letters to the editor mentioning either candidate were coded during the weeks of May 2–8 (when Trump won a majority of Republican convention delegates) and June 6–12 (when Clinton's pledged delegate count reached a majority). These items varied greatly in length, from letters of a hundred words to articles of a few thousand words. Tweets, in contrast, can be no more than 140 characters in length, although they can be accompanied by photos, charts, or other visuals and linked to articles in other media that may be much longer than those carried by the *Times*. Of the more than 500 million tweets sent each day, these figures analyze the first 700 tweets per day mentioning either candidate in each of these two weeks.

Perhaps the most interesting finding from Figures 5.3 and 5.4 is that with a few important exceptions, these two quite different media outlets did not differ greatly in the degree to which they covered particular characteristics of the campaign environment and, to a lesser extent, of the candidates. The *tone* of their coverage differed, of course; an erudite, well-researched *Times* column can give a different impression from the tweet "Crooked Hillary Lies Again," even though the two may make essentially the same point about the same topic, and even though the tweet may occasionally link to the newspaper column. But especially in their portrayal of the campaign environment, Twitter and the *Times* stressed similar topics to similar degrees. For instance, they were within 6 percentage points of one another with respect to the extent to which their coverage mentioned issues, media bias, the candidates' professional qualifications, and the endorsements (and non-endorsements) they received.

Both outlets also presented clearly distinct portraits of the two candidates: Clinton was the liar and Trump was the bigot. It should not be surprising that Clinton's image as a crook was especially strong on Twitter,

Figure 5.3 Mentions of Candidates' Characteristics in *New York Times* and Twitter, 2016

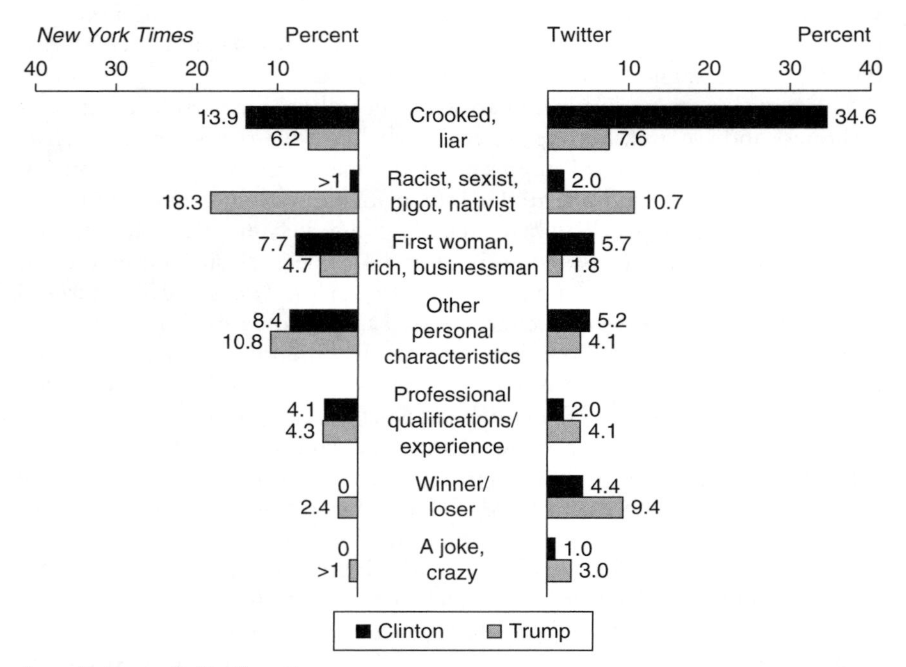

Source: Data compiled by the author.

Note: Bars show the percentage of all mentions in the *Times* coverage or in the tweets referring to the characteristic listed. The bars representing mentions of Clinton on Twitter can be added to those in Figure 5.4 (plus 8 percent unclassifiable mentions) to reach 100 percent. The same is true of Clinton's *Times* mentions (24 percent of which were unclassifiable), Trump's Twitter mentions (16 percent unclassifiable), and Trump's *Times* mentions (17 percent unclassifiable).

comprising more than one in three mentions of her candidacy and outpacing Trump on this characteristic by about five to one. Twitter tends to attract more negative and freewheeling posts, even compared with other social media.[41] The *Times* coverage gave Clinton a two-to-one "advantage" in references to lies and corruption, though this characterization appeared in only about 14 percent of her mentions. Interestingly, however, while Trump was portrayed as a racist, sexist, bigot, nativist, or xenophobe much more in both outlets than Clinton was, it was the staid *New York Times* that devoted almost 20 percent of its mentions of Trump to discussions of his bigotry, compared with only about 11 percent of the tweets.

Neither media outlet devoted much attention to Clinton's historic achievement as the first woman major-party presidential nominee. The *Times* took the lead here, with about 8 percent of its mentions of Clinton, and Twitter followed with just under 6 percent. Perhaps by the time Clinton locked up the Democratic nomination, the path-breaking nature of her victory was not nearly as interesting to audiences as was the image of "Crooked

Hillary," tarred by scandal. Trump, whose record of false statements had been well established by the time of these events, was mentioned as being a liar or corrupt in less than 8 percent of the coverage on either medium.

Another notable feature of the coverage in both the *Times* and the tweets is that mentions of both candidates' professional qualifications and experience never rose above 5 percent, even at the moment when both were becoming their parties' standard-bearers. References in this category mentioned the candidates' knowledge, fitness for the office, and previous experience. Other relevant criteria for the presidency, including the candidates' likely choices for vice president, mentions of their connections with Wall Street and the wealthiest Americans, and their association with change or with the "establishment," registered at no more than 1 or 2 percent of all mentions.

Overall, personal characteristics constituted about 40 percent of the mentions of both candidates. Aspects of the campaign environment got almost equal attention in both media (see Figure 5.4). Clinton's personal qualities dominated her mentions on Twitter, whereas the campaign environment got somewhat more attention in her coverage in the *Times*. Trump's portrayal was the reverse in both media: more environmental mentions on Twitter, more personal references in the *Times*.[42] Most frequently mentioned aspects of the campaign environment in both outlets involved internal party conflict (with Trump more frequently mentioned) and issues and policies (in which Clinton dominated). One clear difference between the mainstream coverage and the tweets was that coverage in the *Times* stressed the two candidates' support from various social-demographic groups much more than did coverage in Twitter.

Figure 5.4 Mentions of the Campaign Environment in *New York Times* and Twitter, 2016

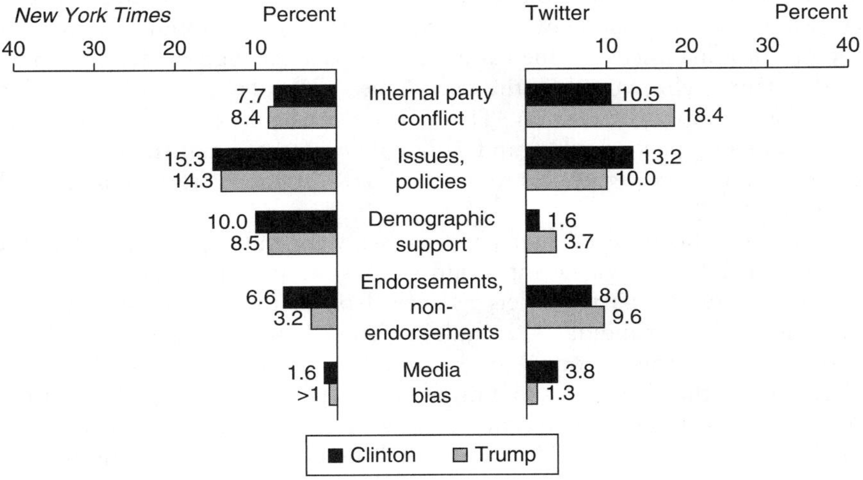

Percent	*New York Times* Clinton	*New York Times* Trump	Twitter Clinton	Twitter Trump
Internal party conflict	7.7	8.4	10.5	18.4
Issues, policies	15.3	14.3	13.2	10.0
Demographic support	10.0	8.5	1.6	3.7
Endorsements, non-endorsements	6.6	3.2	8.0	9.6
Media bias	1.6	>1	3.8	1.3

Source: Data compiled by the author.

The overwhelming majority of articles about Trump's victory made little or no mention of Clinton, whereas a large proportion of the Clinton articles discussed Trump—perhaps because he had already reached "presumptive" status, but also perhaps because he was the better lure for audiences. Why does this matter? Because the wide gap between women and men in willingness to run for office can be affected. If young women, in particular, hear less about women candidates or feel that women running for office are subjected to gender bias, it will be more difficult to close the gap with male candidates.

The similarities in the topics covered by both the *Times* and the tweets suggest that the norms governing what is news and deserves coverage do not vary as much as might be expected between the legacy media and self-produced social network news. *Times* editors and tweeters write about the same topics and to about the same extent. Some observers might argue that both outlets are reflecting the same reality with respect to public events. Others might suggest that writers in both outlets instead are responding to the same incentives—namely, to keep an audience by relying on a shared understanding of what readers and viewers want to see, and with reference to one another's output.

In Search of the Parties' "Establishment"

A lot of campaign coverage referred to the preferences and power of the party "establishment." Many younger voters, too, are convinced that there is a cadre of national party leaders, even political "bosses," who exercise behind-the-scenes control over what happens in campaigns. In a much more precise and less conspiratorial sense, a number of political scientists have argued that a network of party leaders, think tanks, and allied interest groups and media figures run the parties' nomination processes. These establishmentarians, the theory goes, communicate during the pre-primary phase of the campaign, in part through media coverage, to determine who would be the party's best candidate, before the voters have begun paying attention. Then, using media to communicate their endorsements, party leaders and policy demanders signal their choice to party activists, who support that candidate in the state primaries and caucuses.[43]

Voters who believed that party bosses were pulling the strings got a surprise in 2016. After Trump's mid-2015 announcement speech, he was largely ignored by party leaders as they debated the relative strengths of other Republican candidates, including former Florida governor Jeb Bush, Wisconsin governor Scott Walker, and Florida senator Marco Rubio. Throughout the summer and fall of 2015, party leaders and reporters pointed to Trump's most recent outrageous claim and predicted his dramatic collapse. Even after Trump had led the polls in the Republican race for eight months, media coverage reported almost no Trump endorsements by prominent Republicans. And yet, Bush, Walker, and others who had received those endorsements were no longer in the race because they weren't winning primaries and caucuses.

If party "bosses" rule, then how can we explain this puzzling outcome? Perhaps the large number—seventeen—of Republican presidential hopefuls kept any single establishment-preferred contender from breaking out of the pack. Given Trump's exceptionally high unfavorable ratings even among many Republicans, a one-on-one contest might well have produced different results. Another possible explanation is that the party establishment didn't take Trump seriously enough and then tried too late to settle on an acceptable alternative. Or maybe the party's leaders didn't have the power to persuade voters determined to thumb their nose at anything regarded as an establishment, including their own party. As Fred Malek, finance chair of the Republican Governors Association put it, "there's no single leader and no single institution that can bring a diverse group called the Republican Party together, behind a single candidate. It just doesn't exist."[44]

One response to the Trump phenomenon, then, was to raise questions about the strength of the party establishment in American politics. If some media outlets were part of the Republican establishment, then why did they give such overwhelming coverage to the party leaders' least favored candidate? The image of a party establishment that calls the shots, and against which grassroots party identifiers can rebel, is driven at least in part by the media's institutional need for an audience. Covering a group of individual personalities exercising power is simply more of an audience draw than is the reality of a diffuse, fairly decentralized, highly permeable party system. But if there really were a party establishment that determined election outcomes, as the coverage often suggested, then Donald Trump would not be the president of the United States.

How Well Does Media Campaign Coverage Provide What Citizens Need?

Examining the effects of media needs and norms raises an important question: How well or badly do the various parts of the media universe help viewers and readers to function effectively as democratic citizens? Did media coverage of the 2016 campaign help voters make informed choices about who will run the executive branch? Or did it feed voters a steady diet of sideshows and spectacle while the nation's major challenges went unexamined? And if President Trump continues to be as loose with the truth as Candidate Trump was—for example, in his claim that he won by a landslide, when in reality he lost the popular vote by nearly three million—how can the media respond?

The outsized focus on Donald Trump was not the media's finest hour. The near-constant stream of Trump eruptions, ranging from mockery of disabled reporters to shady business dealings to outright lies told with complete conviction, led to a campaign with less policy substance than Americans have witnessed in some time. Journalists didn't set out to hide the candidates' policy positions or to purposefully prevent voters from finding out what they'd need to know to hold a powerful government accountable. Journalists simply did their jobs: they chose among the various streams of information available to them as the norms of their institution instructed them. They met their institutional needs by working to attract as many viewers and readers as possible, and that led them to turn their lenses on Trump.

In particular, the media's institutional needs led journalists to frame Trump's often-dangerous and demeaning campaign rhetoric as wacky or startling rather than as threats to the preservation of a democracy. When an experienced reality TV star runs a controversial and often shocking campaign, it is difficult for media people to pull their eyes away from the clickbait long enough to focus on Hillary Clinton's Senate record or Marco Rubio's background in the Florida state legislature. The power of false equivalence tended to normalize Trump's deceptive statements and to encourage an outsized focus on Clinton's emails, so that even the reports of emailed Democratic bickering reminded voters of the charge that she was corrupt and untrustworthy. Certainly the media play an important job in investigating scandal and corruption, and they gorged on it in 2016. But when the candidates' office-holding experience and leadership background is confined to 4 percent of the coverage in both of two very different media outlets, then the clickbait has hijacked the coverage.

Granted, communications by definition require audiences, and most audiences prefer entertaining spectacles rather than dense policy analyses. The fault is as much ours as theirs. In fact, the media's audience-driven model seems very democratic. The United States is, after all, a system based on public consent. If voters prefer flamboyant characters to policy details, one could argue, it isn't the media's job to make us "eat our vegetables." And it is entirely understandable that broadcast and mainstream media would rely on two-handed journalism, even to the extent of creating false equivalences, as a means of defending themselves (and protecting their ratings) against accusations that they are biased toward one candidate.

But the challenge is that the need for any individual media outlet to win and hold an audience will always conflict with the need in a democratic society for voters to be well informed about their candidates, including the dull ones. Social media have expanded candidates' and others' ability to get their agendas heard by a wider audience. A single blogger may occasionally break a story about an issue that might not otherwise be heard. But even social media and blogs face institutional incentives to focus on the clickworthy rather than the underlying, not-very-entertaining structures and forces that constrain our lives.

In the 2016 campaign, media outlets' need for an audience also gave rise to an apparently big increase in the number of fake news sites. Material from some of these sites, no matter how obviously false it was, got shared or retweeted frequently on social media by people whose strong political attachments exceeded their willingness to check the facts. Some observers have argued that Facebook and Twitter should weed out content providers whose posts are demonstrably untrue. But that raises difficult questions about how to distinguish fake news from satiric sites, and about whether social media has the obligation to maintain freedom of speech, even if the speech in question is odious.

These challenges will continue throughout the Trump administration and beyond. As president, Trump probably will keep stirring the pot with constant drama in the form of impulsive tweets, shoot-from-the-hip charges, and claims with no apparent connection to known facts. The need for media outlets to keep an audience will encourage a focus on these dramatic events, even if the drama turns out to be manufactured or fake. The benefits of "balanced coverage" will lead journalists to create false equivalences and to be vulnerable to skilled manipulators. Yet in the end, we can't count on democracies to maintain themselves. There must be some means to solve the collective choice problem: the ability for the media as a whole to protect democratic values while specific media outlets meet their individual needs to turn a profit.

Notes

1. John Koblin, "Iowa Caucus Coverage Draws Large Crowds on Cable," *New York Times*, February 2, 2016, mobile.nytimes.com/2016/02/03/business/media/iowa-caucus-coverage-draws-large-crowds-on-cable.html.
2. Amy Mitchell and Jesse Holcomb, "The State of the Media 2016," Pew Research Center, June 15, 2016, www.journalism.org/2016/06/15/state-of-the-news-media-2016. See also Markus Prior, *Post-Broadcast Democracy* (Cambridge: Cambridge University Press, 2007).
3. See Doris A. Graber and Johanna L. Dunaway, *Mass Media and American Politics*, 9th ed. (Washington, D.C.: CQ Press, 2014), chs. 4 and 5; and Diana C. Mutz, *In-Your-Face Politics* (Princeton, N.J.: Princeton University Press, 2015).
4. Harry Enten, FiveThirtyEight.com blog on the March 10, 2016, Republican presidential debate.
5. Ben Jacobs and Alan Yuhas, "Donald Trump Threatens Ted Cruz with Lawsuit over Presidential Eligibility," *The Guardian*, February 15, 2016, www.theguardian.com/us-news/2016/feb/15/donald-trump-threatens-third-party-independent-run-us-presidential-election-2016.
6. See, for example, David Fahrenthold and Katie Zezima, "A Dark Debate," *Washington Post*, October 9, 2016, www.washingtonpost.com/politics/trump-remains-defiant-ahead-of-debate-as-surrogates-grapple-with-tape-fallout/2016/10/09/9a95a09a-8e28-11e6-9c85-ac42097b8cc0_story.html.
7. Republican National Committee, "Growth and Opportunity Project," 2013, growthopp.gop.com/RNC_Growth_Opportunity_Book_2013.pdf, 12–17.
8. Frank Rich, "Donald Trump Is Saving Our Democracy," *New York Magazine*, September 21, 2015, nymag.com/daily/intelligencer/2015/09/frank-rich-in-praise-of-donald-trump.html.
9. Philip Rucker and Marc Fisher, "Here's What President-Elect Donald Trump Has Been Doing after the Election," *Washington Post*, November 23, 2016, A1.

10. Pew Research Center, "Election 2016: Campaigns as a Direct Source of News," July 18, 2016, www.journalism.org/2016/07/18/election-2016-campaigns-as-a-direct-source-of-news.
11. Paul Waldman, "Trump Declares War on the Press," *Washington Post*, May 31, 2016, www.washingtonpost.com/blogs/plum-line/wp/2016/05/31/donald-trump-declares-war-on-the-press/.
12. Nate Silver, "How Trump Hacked the Media," *FiveThirtyEight,* March 30, 2016, fivethirtyeight.com/features/how-donald-trump-hacked-the-media/.
13. Jim Rutenberg, "The Mutual Dependence of Trump and the News Media," *New York Times*, March 21, 2016, B1.
14. Ibid.
15. Hadas Gold, "Trump Infomercial Captivates Networks," *Politico,* March 9, 2016, www.politico.com/story/2016/03/donald-trump-infomercial-220471.
16. Kalev Leetaru, "Here's What the Rest of the World Is Saying about Donald Trump," *Washington Post,* December 18, 2015, www.washingtonpost.com/news/monkey-cage/wp/2015/12/18/heres-what-the-rest-of-the-world-is-saying-about-donald-trump/.
17. Jill Colvin, "Trump: Relying on the Media, but Trying to Control Its Free Coverage," *Hoosier Times*, December 27, 2015, E3. Data are from the liberal group Media Matters.
18. Silver, "How Trump Hacked the Media."
19. See John Sides, "Is the Media Biased toward Clinton or Trump?" *Washington Post*, September 20, 2016, www.washingtonpost.com/news/monkey-cage/wp/2016/09/20/is-the-media-biased-toward-clinton-or-trump-heres-some-actual-hard-data/.
20. These calculations are reported by Nicholas Confessore and Karen Yourish, "Measuring Trump's Big Advantage in Free Media," *New York Times*, March 17, 2016, A3. MediaQuant weights its measure according to how many people are likely to see each specific source (print, broadcast, and online, including social media).
21. John Sides and Kalev Leetaru, "A Deep Dive into the News Media's Role in the Rise of Donald J. Trump," *Washington Post*, June 24, 2016, www.washingtonpost.com/news/monkey-cage/wp/2016/06/24/a-deep-dive-into-the-news-medias-role-in-the-rise-of-donald-j-trump/.
22. Pew Research Center, "Campaign Exposes Fissures over Issues, Values and How Life Has Changed in the U.S.," March 31, 2016, www.people-press.org/2016/03/31/campaign-exposes-fissures-over-issues-values-and-how-life-has-changed-in-the-u-s/. Pew data from October 17, 2016, showed that a third of Trump supporters were still saying their candidate got too much media coverage.
23. Romney's statement from Ed O'Keefe, "Mitt Romney Slams 'Phony' Trump," *Washington Post*, March 4, 2016.
24. Carolyn Ryan, quoted in Jim Rutenberg, "The Challenge Trump Poses to Objectivity," *New York Times*, August 8, 2016, A1.
25. Sides and Leetaru, "A Deep Dive into the News Media's Role in the Rise of Donald J. Trump." See also Kevin Reuning and Nick Dietrich, "Media, Public Interest, and Support in Primary Elections," May 16, 2016, unpublished paper at papers.ssrn.com/sol3/papers.cfm?abstract_id=2709208.
26. See, for example, Paul Allen Beck, Russell J. Dalton, Steven Greene, and Robert Huckfeldt, "The Social Calculus of Voting," *American Political Science Review* 96 (March 2002): 57–73.
27. See Marjorie Randon Hershey, *Party Politics in America*, 17th ed. (New York: Routledge, 2017), ch. 15.

28. See Justin Buchler, "When Covering Elections, Journalists Face a Debilitating Dilemma," *The Conversation*, April 5, 2016, theconversation.com.
29. *PolitiFact*, "All Statements Involving Donald Trump," www.politifact.com/personalities/donald-trump/statements/.
30. David Jackson, "Trump Changes His Tune, Says Obama Born in U.S.," *USA Today*, September 17, 2016, 1. Italics added.
31. Quoted in Lauren Carroll, "In Context: Did Donald Trump Suggest Barack Obama Has Terrorist Sympathies?" *PolitiFact*, June 15, 2016, www.politifact.com/truth-o-meter/article/2016/jun/15/context-did-donald-trump-suggest-barack-obama-has-/.
32. Gail Collins, "Trump Makes His Birther Lie Worse," *New York Times*, September 16, 2016, A17.
33. See Corrinne McConnaughy, "Do Gendered Comments Help or Hurt Hillary Clinton?" *Monkey Cage, Washington Post,* March 17, 2016.
34. See Danny Hayes and Jennifer L. Lawless, "A Non-gendered Lens?" *Perspectives on Politics* 13 (March 2015): 95–118. See also these authors' *Women on the Run* (New York: Cambridge University Press, 2016).
35. See Susan J. Carroll, "Reflecting on Gender and Hillary Clinton's Presidential Campaign," *Politics & Gender* 5 (2009): 1–20; Jennifer L. Lawless, "Sexism and Gender Bias in Election 2008," *Politics & Gender* 5 (2009): 70–80.
36. Quoted in Dana Milbank, "The Sexist Double Standards Hurting Hillary Clinton," *Washington Post*, February 13, 2016, www.washingtonpost.com/opinions/the-sexist-double-standards-hurting-hillary-clinton/2016/02/12/fb551e38-d195-11e5-abc9-ea152f0b9561_story.html.
37. Data from Gary King's Crimson Hexagon research, reported in Jeff Stein, "Study: Hillary Clinton, Not Donald Trump, Gets the Most Negative Media Coverage," *Vox*, April 15, 2016, www.vox.com/2016/4/15/11410160/hillary-clinton-media-bernie-sanders.
38. Thomas E. Patterson, "Pre-primary News Coverage of the 2016 Presidential Race," June 13, 2016, shorensteincenter.org/pre-primary-news-coverage-2016-trump-clinton-sanders/.
39. Data from The Data Face cited in John Sides, "After the Debate, Trump Is Still Dominating News Coverage," *Washington Post*, October 1, 2016, www.washingtonpost.com/news/monkey-cage/wp/2016/09/30/after-the-debate-trump-is-still-dominating-news-coverage-but-clinton-is-getting-the-good-press/.
40. Lydia Saad and Frank Newport, "'Email' Defines Clinton; 'Immigration' Defines Trump," *Gallup*, September 16, 2015, www.gallup.com/poll/185486/email-defines-clinton-immigration-defines-trump.aspx.
41. On the use of social media for political information, see Maeve Duggan and Aaron Smith, "The Political Environment on Social Media," Pew Research Center, October 25, 2016, http://assets.pewresearch.org/wp-content/uploads/sites/14/2016/10/24160747/PI_2016.10.25_Politics-and-Social-Media_FINAL.pdf.
42. For Clinton, 41.2 percent of her mentions in the *Times* were of the campaign environment, as were 37.1 percent on Twitter. Her personal qualities were the subject of 35.1 percent of the *Times* mentions and fully 54.9 percent on Twitter. For Trump, these figures were 35.4 percent, 43 percent, 47.7 percent, and 40.7 percent, respectively. The remaining mentions were scattered across a variety of less populated categories.
43. Marty Cohen, David Karol, Hans Noel, and John Zaller, *The Party Decides* (Chicago: University of Chicago Press, 2008).
44. Quoted in Alexander Burns, Maggie Haberman, and Jonathan Martin, "Inside the Republican Party's Desperate Mission to Stop Donald Trump," *New York Times*, February 28, 2016, A1.

6

Campaign Finance

Where Big Money Mattered and Where It Didn't

Marian Currinder

Speaking at the March 10, 2016, Republican presidential primary debate, Donald Trump sought to distinguish himself from the competition by claiming that he could not be bought: "I'm self-funding my campaign. Nobody is going to be taking care of me. I don't want anybody's money."[1] Trump's independence from big donors was a central message of his campaign, at least during the primaries. It was a staple of his stump speeches and a major selling point for many of his supporters.

Upon securing his party's nomination, Trump changed his tune. He personally invested about $56 million into his campaign, but he also received help from thousands of individual donors, and more than ten super PACs.[2] In the final week of the election, these PACs spent more than $46.2 million on Trump's behalf.[3] One of these committees, the Great America PAC, began repurposing itself after the election to promote President Trump's agenda from outside the White House. Ed Rollins, senior strategist for the PAC, said that having an external operation helps keep supporters engaged after the campaign ends. The PAC is also a good tool for putting pressure on members of Congress who might try to stymie Trump's agenda, according to Rollins.[4]

Although Trump's evolution from a professed self-funding billionaire to a candidate soliciting funds from other wealthy people is fascinating, his resounding victory over traditional big money is the most important campaign finance story of the 2016 elections. Trump raised less than half of what Democratic presidential nominee Hillary Clinton raised. The outside groups supporting Clinton spent more than three times as much as the outside groups supporting Trump, and his campaign ran a small fraction of the television ads that her campaign ran. His celebrity status (as well as his ongoing stream of outrageous comments) bought him a lot of free coverage. But Clinton was hardly an unknown candidate, and she had her own share of highly publicized controversies.

How did Trump do it? As many observers of the 2016 presidential campaign have noted, where the money came from mattered a lot more than how much was raised. This was the case in both the primary and general elections. The candidates who lasted the longest—Trump, Clinton, Ted Cruz, and Bernie Sanders—won the support of "robust small-donor bases."[5] Raising $1 million in increments of $200 buys a candidate the support (and likely the votes) of 5,000 individuals. Raising $1 million from a single, wealthy donor may buy a candidate the ability to reach potential voters, but many fewer people feel that they have invested in the campaign.

"The top-line numbers don't tell the whole story," said Sheila Krumholz, executive director of the Center for Responsive Politics. "When you look deeper into their finances we start to see a narrative emerge."[6] That narrative is about connecting with voters.

Although big spending didn't pay off in the presidential contest, it did in congressional races. Ninety-six percent of Senate races and 94 percent of House races were won by the biggest spender. Strong support from small donors seemed to matter less in congressional races. Of the fifty candidates who received most of their funds from small donors, twenty-eight won. And despite Trump's victory, voters generally don't support congressional candidates who primarily fund their own campaigns. Of the nine self-funders vying for Senate seats, none won. Only six of the twenty-seven House candidates who self-funded won.[7]

This chapter examines campaign spending in the 2016 presidential and congressional races. While candidates fought over who would do more to change the broken campaign finance system, donors forked over approximately $7 billion in campaign money. About one-quarter of those donations came from outside groups. These spenders, mostly super PACs, kicked in 73 percent more in 2016 than they did during the 2012 campaign. Spending by presidential candidates increased by about 10 percent compared to four years earlier, while spending by House and Senate candidates decreased by 16 percent and 25 percent, respectively. Even though congressional candidate spending was down, overall spending on congressional races was up by about $245 million. Trump's nontraditional candidacy and campaign freed up big money to be donated and spent down the ballot, where it made a much greater difference than in the presidential race.[8]

The Supreme Court Continues to Empower Wealthy Donors

Understanding the outsized role that wealthy contributors played in the 2016 elections requires a quick review of recent Supreme Court decisions related to campaign finance.

The Supreme Court's *Citizens United* decision in 2010 laid the groundwork for record-breaking spending in the 2012 presidential race. The decision allowed corporations and unions to legally spend unlimited amounts of money on behalf of candidates, as long as they did not coordinate with the candidates' own campaigns. The Court, in other words, extended to corporations and unions the same right to unlimited independent spending that individuals enjoy.

Shortly after *Citizens United*, the U.S. Court of Appeals for the District of Columbia issued a decision that paved the way for a new player in the campaign finance game. In *SpeechNow.org v. Federal Election Commission*, the Court ruled that contributions to PACs that only make independent expenditures cannot be limited. These committees, known as super PACs, can accept unlimited contributions from individuals, corporations, and unions, and then use that money to advocate on behalf of candidates they support and against candidates they oppose. Super PACs were big players in the 2012 campaign and even bigger players in the 2016 campaign. In 2012, 1,310 super PACs spent approximately $609.4 million; in 2016, 2,398 super PACs spent over $1.1 billion.[9]

The Supreme Court has issued one major campaign finance decision since *Citizens United*. In 2014, *McCutcheon v. Federal Election Commission* eliminated the total limit on how much individuals can give to candidate campaigns, PACs, and party committees. In 2012, the limit for all donations was $123,200; in 2016, no such cap existed (see Table 6.1). Taken together, *Citizens United* and *McCutcheon* empowered wealthy donors to flood the system with unlimited amounts of money.

In 2016, at least 1,174 people contributed more than the 2012 limit of $123,200; the average total contribution for those donors who broke the old limit was $281,568. When independent spending by individuals—which was never limited by law, even before *McCutcheon*—is factored in, many of these wealthy donors shelled out millions.[10] In fact, at least one hundred donors gave $1 million or more during the 2016 election cycle. Hedge fund manager Tom Steyer topped the list of Democratic mega-donors, giving over $67 million to support his party's candidates. And, as was the case in 2012, Las Vegas hotel magnate Sheldon Adelson was the biggest Republican donor in 2016, doling out over $47 million.[11]

The Early Race for the White House

Wealthy contributors in 2016 quickly adjusted to the new legal landscape and spent millions on direct contributions and outside expenditures. For most of these spenders, the investment did not pay off—at least not in the form of a winning candidate.

The story of who the money came from mattering more than how much was raised is rooted in the 2016 presidential primaries. Among the seventeen Republican contenders, former Florida governor Jeb Bush attracted the most outside financial support by far. He was, however, unable to attract the support—and votes—of small donors and left the race on February 20, 2016. On the Democratic side, Sen. Bernie Sanders of Vermont attracted less than $1 million in outside support but built a vast and enthusiastic network of small donors that kept him in the race much longer than initially

Table 6.1 Contribution Limits for 2015–2016

	To Each Candidate or Candidate Committee per Election	*To Each PAC*[a]	*To State, District, or Local Party Committee per Calendar Year*	*To National Party Committee per Calendar Year*	*Additional National Party Committee Accounts*[b]
Individual may give	$2,700*	$5,000	$10,000 (combined limit)	$33,400* per year	$100,200* per account per year
Authorized campaign committee may give	$2,000	$5,000	No limit	No limit	
PAC (multicandidate) may give	$5,000	$5,000	$5,000 (combined limit)	$15,000 per year	$45,000 per account per year
PAC (not multicandidate) may give	$2,700	$5,000	$10,000 (combined limit)	$33,400* per year	$100,200* per account per year
State, district, or local party committee may give	$5,000	$5,000	No limit	No limit	
National party committee may give	$5,000[c]	$5,000	No limit	No limit	

Source: Compiled by the author.

* Indexed for inflation in odd numbered years.

[a] *PAC* here refers to a committee that makes contributions to other federal political committees. Independent-expenditure-only political committees (sometimes called super PACs) may accept unlimited contributions, including from corporations and labor organizations.

[b] The limits in this column apply to a national party committee's accounts for (1) the presidential nominating convention, (2) election recounts and contests and other legal proceedings, and (3) national party headquarters buildings. A party's national committee, Senate campaign committee, and House campaign committee are each considered separate national party committees with separate limits. Only a national party committee, not the parties' national congressional campaign committees, may have an account for the presidential nominating convention.

[c] Additionally, a national party committee and its senatorial campaign committee may contribute up to $46,800 combined per campaign to each Senate candidate.

anticipated. Sanders ended his candidacy on July 12, after racking up wins in an impressive twenty-two states.

The Republican Field

Of the seventeen Republicans who officially sought their party's presidential nomination in 2016, five did not make it to the February 1 Iowa caucus. Rick Perry, Scott Walker, Bobby Jindal, Lindsey Graham, and George Pataki left the race in 2015. Despite their longshot chances, these candidates still managed to attract the support of some big donors. Wisconsin governor Scott Walker, for example, was an early favorite of billionaire industrialists Charles G. and David H. Koch. Joe Ricketts, the billionaire founder of TD Ameritrade, also gave big to Walker. During his short-lived campaign, Walker raised a total of about $8.5 million and received about $25 million in outside support. His inability to catch fire with the voters and his September 21, 2015, departure from the race sent an early signal that big donors do not always pick big winners.

Three more candidates for the Republican nomination—Mike Huckabee, Rick Santorum, and Rand Paul—left the race shortly after the Iowa caucus. Carly Fiorina, Chris Christie, and Jim Gilmore quit after performing poorly in the February 9 New Hampshire primary. By February 12, the field had thinned considerably and only six candidates remained.

One of the six, Jeb Bush had been by many accounts the early favorite to win the Republican nomination. Bush entered the race on June 15, 2015, amid speculation that he would raise more money than any other Republican campaign in modern history.[12] The speculation was accurate: Bush kicked off his campaign with more financial backing than the rest of the Republican field combined.[13] Several donors, including "an insurance mogul, a coal baron, several oil kings, and hedge-fund honchos," each contributed at least $1 million to Bush's campaign. More than 250 others gave him between $100,000 and $1 million, and another 650 or so gave between $25,000 and $100,000.[14]

Most of these big contributions went to Right to Rise, a super PAC backing Bush's run for the White House. Prior to officially declaring his candidacy, Bush devoted several months to raising tens of millions of dollars for the super PAC. Because it was an all but sure thing that he would run, his fundraising for Right to Rise was heavily criticized for flouting the rules that prohibit coordination between candidates and the super PACs that support them. About one month before he officially declared himself a candidate, Bush accidentally admitted in an interview with a reporter that he was running. As soon as he realized what he had said, he walked back the remark and qualified it with an awkward ". . . if I run."[15] The Federal Election Commission (FEC), the agency responsible for enforcing federal campaign finance laws, failed to take action against Bush and Right to Rise.

Despite Bush's entering the race with far more money than his competitors, his campaign would soon prove that money isn't everything. Right to Rise blew through almost $120 million in less than one year and failed to move the needle for Bush. The super PAC spent $84 million on positive advertisements, designed to reintroduce Bush to voters; $94,100 hosting dinners and events at private clubs; $15,800 on valet parking; $8.3 million on staff; $88,387 on candidate branding; $10 million on consultants; $48,544 on trips to Las Vegas; and $4,837 on pizza.[16] Yet Bush won not a single primary or caucus.

In retrospect, it is easy to say that the warning signs predicting Bush's failure were there from the beginning. The field was very crowded, and Bush was a weak front-runner from the start. He entered the race with more endorsements than the other Republican challengers, but most of his endorsements were not from high-level party officials. Voters were not excited by his candidacy, perhaps because they were ready for change. As the son of one president and the brother of another, Bush had credentials that were no match for the unsettled political atmosphere.[17]

Perhaps the most telling factor in Bush's failure to launch was his inability to raise large amounts of money for his actual campaign committee. Right to Rise appealed to the wealthy donors who wanted to give more than the $2,700 they could legally give to Bush's campaign committee. Prior to declaring his candidacy, Bush focused his efforts on raising millions for the super PAC rather than on building a strong network of smaller donors to his own campaign. As a result, Bush directly controlled much less money and lacked broad donor (and voter) support. Outside money can certainly help swing a race, but a campaign needs a solid base of people who feel personally invested in the candidate in order to succeed.[18]

After Bush's February 20, 2016, departure from the race, five Republican candidates remained. Retired pediatric neurosurgeon Ben Carson and Florida senator Marco Rubio were the next to go. They closed out their candidacies a few weeks after Bush ended his.

Carson entered the race with high favorability ratings among Republicans but soon discovered that there is a difference between being liked and attracting votes. His supporters liked him enough to contribute $63.3 million to his campaign and $18.7 million to outside groups supporting his candidacy—impressive numbers for a political novice. In fact, among the Republican candidates, only Ted Cruz raised more for his campaign committee.

Carson's strong support from small donors buoyed his candidacy and kept him in the "final five" until March 4, 2016, when he officially exited the race. When he left the political stage, his strong favorability ratings were still intact but his campaign organization was in financial disarray. In the two months after ending his campaign, Carson spent almost $1 million, mostly on political strategy consultants. Strangely, none of these payments were for services performed earlier in the campaign. Indeed, some of the recipients made more after the campaign was over than they did when Carson's candidacy was still in play.[19]

Carson's heavy spending on consultants and fundraising rather than advertising and grassroots organization had drawn criticism earlier in the campaign. In an interview with CNN, Carson acknowledged that "mistakes were made" and that he "probably had the wrong team in place, people who had different objectives" than he did. As one article aptly put it, "Ben Carson ran for president, and his consultants won."[20]

Marco Rubio was the only candidate who came close to raising as much outside money as Jeb Bush, his one-time mentor in Florida politics. In addition to attracting $110 million from outside groups, Rubio raised $52 million for his campaign committee. When Rubio entered the race on April 13, 2015, he was considered the first, real contender on the Republican side. He had support among the GOP establishment, Tea Party–aligned voters, and social conservatives. And like Ben Carson, Rubio scored high on the likeability scale. But despite these credentials, Rubio was unable to establish a broad base of support and left the race on March 15, 2016.

Part of Rubio's inability to build a strong base can be attributed to his lack of direct outreach to voters. He did not have much of a ground network, and voters did not feel particularly connected to him. About 27 percent of Rubio's campaign money came from small donors, many of whom resided in Florida. Strong "home team" support is important but doesn't necessarily translate into strong "away team" support in other states.

Most of the outside money supporting Rubio came from one super PAC, the Conservative Solutions PAC. The PAC was bolstered by a 501(c)(4) social welfare organization called the Conservative Solutions Project. Named for the section of the tax code that governs them, 501(c)(4) organizations are prohibited from spending more than half of their funds for political purposes and are attractive to donors who wish to remain anonymous because the law does not require these groups to disclose their funders. As a requirement of their tax status, 501(c)(4)s must be set up to benefit the broader public.

The Conservative Solutions Project formed within weeks of Rubio's declaring his candidacy, and of the $13.8 million the organization raised immediately, $13.5 million came from a single, anonymous donor. About 90 percent of the money raised by the Conservative Solutions Project went to consultants and firms tied to the Rubio campaign. The Conservative Solutions Project and the Conservative Solutions PAC shared staff, a building, and vendors—all raising questions about whether the group was formed to benefit the broader public or solely to support Rubio. The organization has yet to report any of its spending to the FEC and so far has faced no sanctions.[21]

As was the case with Jeb Bush, Marco Rubio attracted mega-donors but was unable to turn strong financial support from a few into votes from the many. With Rubio out, three candidates remained: Ted Cruz, John Kasich, and Donald Trump.

Texas senator Ted Cruz entered the race on March 23, 2015, and was immediately considered too extreme and too disliked to win. As a first-term senator, he had alienated his Republican colleagues with incendiary comments and tactics, and quickly earned a reputation as a self-promoter.

Cruz kicked off his campaign with low favorability ratings from the voters and no endorsements from the party establishment. His base in Washington didn't seem to extend much beyond conservative rabble-rousers in the House of Representatives. But Cruz somehow managed to turn this negative into a positive and remained in the race longer than fifteen of the seventeen Republican candidates. He raised far more money—$90 million—for his campaign committee than any of his challengers, and attracted an impressive $53.5 million in outside support. Small donors, who made up about 40 percent of Cruz's fundraising base, are more likely to vote for the candidates to whom they contribute.[22]

In addition to corralling small donors to support his cause, Cruz also attracted mega-donors who filled the coffers of several super PACs backing his candidacy. Eight outside groups raised more than $52 million on behalf of Cruz, and just six donors accounted for 79 percent of all the money raised by four of these groups. The multi–super PAC strategy set Cruz apart from his opponents, most of whom had the backing of one, major super PAC. Strategists for the Cruz campaign assigned different wealthy donors to different super PACs, and each of these super PACs was given a distinct responsibility within the campaign. Some focused on advertising, while others focused on outreach or digital strategies or polling.[23] In the end, Cruz proved a more viable candidate than expected.

Ohio governor John Kasich was the last Republican candidate to leave the race, departing one day after Cruz and clearing the way for Donald Trump's nomination. Kasich ran as a moderate, though his record was actually more that of a conservative. He raised approximately as much money as Scott Walker did, yet his campaign lasted about seven months longer than Walker's. Kasich raised more money for his campaign committee (almost $19 million) than twelve of his competitors, while his outside support put him in the middle of the pack. And middle of the pack is essentially where Kasich stayed, trying to appeal to mainstream Republican voters who mostly didn't bite. Big donors didn't bite either, and Kasich couldn't compete with the media-magnet that was Donald Trump.[24]

The Democratic Field

Sen. Bernie Sander's impressive and enduring run for the White House made it easy to forget that three other Democrats also challenged Hillary Clinton for the party's nomination: Martin O'Malley, the former two-term governor of Maryland; Lincoln Chafee, a Republican-turned-independent-turned-Democrat; and former senator Jim Webb of Virginia.[25] Webb struggled to attract donors and ended his campaign on October 20, 2015, after raising just under $777,000 for his campaign committee. Chafee ended his longshot campaign on October 23 after raising just $418,136—90 percent of which came from his own pocket. O'Malley fared much better, raising about $5.7 million for his campaign committee, but dropped out after a dismal performance in the February 1 Iowa caucus.

O'Malley was the only candidate seeking a major-party nomination for president to take public financing in the 2016 election. With public funding comes spending limits, which is why most candidates today reject it: they can raise and spend a lot more on their own. In 2008, Barack Obama became the first major-party nominee to reject general election matching funds and the spending limits that come with them. His decision was trend setting. Although taking public financing used to be a sign of broad-based candidate strength, today it signals an inability to raise big money.[26]

By February 2, 2016, the race for the Democratic nomination was between Hillary Clinton and Bernie Sanders. Clinton entered the race as the party's presumptive nominee, but Sanders shook up the so-called money primary and radically changed the way future presidential candidates will approach fundraising.[27]

Sanders raised a striking $228.2 million for his campaign committee, mostly from small donors. The average contribution to his campaign was about $27 and only 5 percent of his contributions came from donors who maxed-out at $2,700. Sanders turned the $27 average contribution to his campaign into a rallying cry for his army of small donors. His supporters would regularly shout out the dollar amount at his rallies as a way of distinguishing their candidate from "big-money" candidates, especially Clinton. Only 2 percent of Sanders's overall contributions came from donors affiliated with Wall Street.[28] And he received less than $1 million in outside support.

Sanders' approach to fundraising was reminiscent of Obama's in 2008. He built a movement of devoted supporters to whom he could repeatedly return for small donations. By doing so, Sanders kept them engaged, even invested in his campaign. Sanders supporter Emily Condit, for example, reported that she contributed to Sanders on three separate occasions, giving $5 each time. Donors without a job (either unemployed or retired) gave more to Sanders than any other category of donor; indeed, about 29 percent of his total contributions came from individuals outside of the workforce.[29]

In all, Sanders received more than 7.6 million contributions from more than 2.4 million people. Ninety-four percent of his donations were raised online at a clip of 19,740 donations per day. For a campaign to generate broad-based and ongoing enthusiasm is challenging and requires a sophisticated netroots strategy. Sanders supporters, who were, on average, twenty-seven years old, were passionate about their candidate and were also tapped in to Twitter, Facebook, Reddit, and a host of other online platforms to share their enthusiasm. Social media, as Sanders demonstrated, can be an incredibly powerful tool for both fundraising and voter mobilization.[30]

Table 6.2 Overall Spending by Presidential Primary Candidates

Candidate (Party)	*Outside Support*	*Campaign Funds*
Jeb Bush (R)	$121,733,869	$34,088,583
Ben Carson (R)	$18,698,473	$63,336,171
Lincoln Chafee (D)	$0	$418,136
Chris Christie (R)	$23,746,147	$8,433,750
Ted Cruz (R)	$53,479,471	$89,528,776
Carly Fiorina (R)	$14,627,477	$11,974,161
Jim Gilmore (R)	$407,173	$391,436
Lindsey Graham (R)	$5,015,904	$5,858,698
Mike Huckabee (R)	$6,030,777	$4,335,904
Bobby Jindal (R)	$4,517,207	$1,442,464
John Kasich (R)	$15,507,064	$18,897,737
Martin O'Malley (D)	$1,165,608	$5,706,888
George Pataki (R)	$1,547,674	$28,485
Rand Paul (R)	$11,600,497	$12,149,234
Rick Perry (R)	$15,242,021	$1,427,133
Marco Rubio (R)	$110,168,551	$52,331,502
Bernie Sanders (D)	$922,901	$228,171,330
Rick Santorum (R)	$764,072	$1,765,798
Scott Walker (R)	$25,006,621	$8,515,722
Jim Webb (D)	$27,117	$776,828

Source: Center for Responsive Politics.

On July 12, 2016, Sanders appeared side-by-side with Hillary Clinton, acknowledged that she had won the Democratic nominating process, and endorsed her candidacy. However, he stopped short of officially dropping out of the race and reminded the crowd that "we have begun a political revolution . . . and that revolution continues."[31] About one month later, Sanders launched Our Revolution, a 501(c)(4) organization dedicated to supporting and electing candidates who share his ideals.

Table 6.2 summarizes overall spending by the presidential primary candidates.

The General Election

Donald Trump's victory marked the first time since 1996 that the president-elect raised less money than his opponent. Trump, in fact, raised remarkably less than Hillary Clinton—half as much in campaign money and $162 million less in outside money (see Table 6.3). He played an

Table 6.3 Overall Spending in the 2016 Presidential General Election

	Clinton	*Trump*
Candidates	$435,367,811	$231,546,996
Party committees	$262,210,294	$244,425,987
Outside groups	$263,658,413	$101,633,308
Total	**$961,236,518**	**$577,606,291**

Source: Center for Responsive Politics.

"unconventional and disorganized money game" throughout the campaign and did not even begin actively fundraising until five months before election day (he sent his first fundraising email in mid-June 2016). Trump coasted through the primaries, benefiting from heaps of free media coverage. He also kicked in $56 million of his own money—far short of the $100 million he promised to spend, but hardly small change.

Hillary Clinton's fundraising operation, by contrast, was a "well-oiled machine," made up of more than one thousand big-money bundlers, an extensive network of outside groups, and a massive joint fundraising venture with the Democratic Party. She had 815 paid campaign staffers, while Trump topped out at about 168.[32]

Small Donors and Big Donors

Donald Trump was far less reliant on big donors than was Hillary Clinton, but he also had the luxury of almost nonstop free media, as well as his own wealth. Clinton received 54 percent ($266 million) of her funding from donors giving $200 or more, while Trump received just 15 percent ($38 million) of his overall funds from these donors (see Figure 6.1). Small donations—less than $200—made up 27 percent of Trump's overall funds and just 18 percent of Clinton's.

Because he waited so long to start raising funds, Trump's support from small donors came later in the campaign. He relied heavily on social media, using techniques such as staging Facebook Live events to look like actual news programs. Two such events were held during his final debate with Clinton, raising $9 million from more than 150,000 people.[33] As the race entered the final stretch, Trump repeatedly went back to his loyal supporters, sending emails and text messages asking them to contribute. He promised to triple-match any donation of $75 or more. His efforts paid off: small donors were responsible for $35 million of the $61 million he raised in October 2016.[34] Many of Trump's small donors gave by purchasing merchandise from his website. He sold countless "Make America Great Again" hats, as well as "Hillary for Prison" buttons.

Hillary Clinton was far more reliant than Trump on big donors and went after them early in the campaign. Even before she officially announced

Figure 6.1 Small Donors versus Large Donors in the Presidential Race, 2012–2016

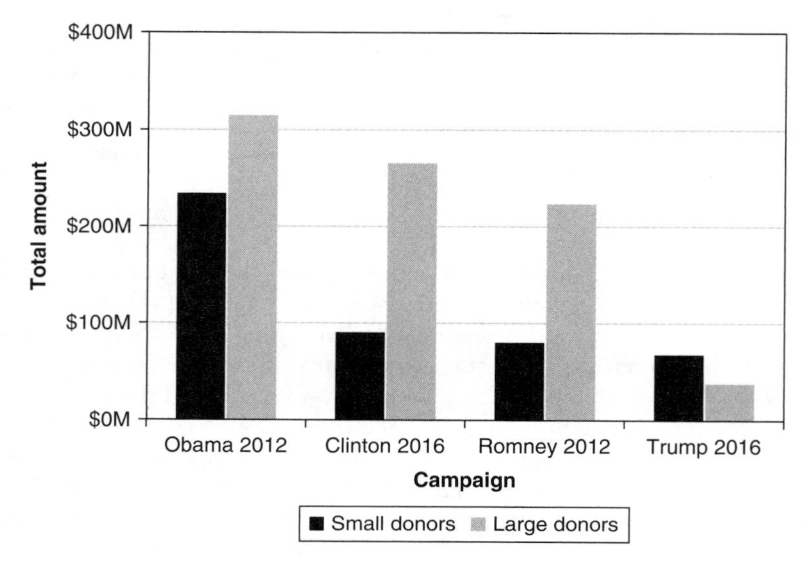

Source: Center for Responsive Politics.

her bid for the White House, Clinton was worried about money. Reports detailing the phenomenal amounts of money that Jeb Bush was raising for his campaign made Clinton anxious and pushed her to raise her fundraising game. She ramped up her appeals to wealthy donors and decided to ignore some of the restrictions that President Obama had imposed on his fundraising team, such as allowing lobbyists to bundle checks and permitting some of those registered to represent foreign government to raise money as well.

Clinton's efforts paid off, at least from a financial perspective. By the end of September 2016, she and her allies had brought in $1.14 billion. More than a fifth of that money was donated by just one hundred wealthy individuals and labor unions. In fact, the top five donors to her campaign contributed one out every $17 for her run: hedge fund manager Donald Sussman ($20.6 million); Chicago venture capitalist J. B. Pritzker and his wife, M. K. ($16.7 million); Univision chairman Haim Saban and his wife, Cheryl ($11.9 million); hedge fund titan George Soros ($9.9 million); and SlimFast founder S. Daniel Abraham ($9.7 million).[35]

Ironically, Clinton mega-donor Donald Sussman claimed that his top policy priority was campaign finance reform. "It's very odd to be giving millions when your objective is to actually get the money out of politics," Sussman said. "I am a very strong supporter of publicly financed campaigns, and I think the only way to accomplish that is to get someone like Secretary

Clinton, who is committed to cleaning up the unfortunate disaster created by the activist court in *Citizens United*."[36]

Despite making his independence from wealthy contributors a centerpiece of his campaign, Trump ultimately pursued some of the mega-donors he previously had derided. After labeling his Republican opponents "puppets" of Las Vegas hotel magnate Sheldon Adelson, Trump cozied up to Adelson after winning his party's nomination. Adelson and his wife, Miriam, gave more than $11 million to super PACs and the Republican Party to support Trump. The family of hedge fund manager Robert Mercer gave Trump $3.4 million—a lot of money, but much less than the $13.5 million they gave to Ted Cruz during the primaries.

The 2016 election saw a huge increase in the number of mega-donors who gave $500,000 or more to super PACs. Overall contributions from these donors topped $1 billion and constituted about 15 percent of the total cost of the 2016 elections for president and Congress. Among these donors were ninety billionaires whose super PAC contributions totaled $562 million—more than half of the overall total donated to super PACs. During the 2012 campaign, these donors gave about $444 million. The surge in super PAC spending in 2016 suggests that the wealthiest donors are ever more willing to spend millions of dollars exploiting loose campaign finance laws to benefit their favored candidates.[37]

For all of the focus on small donors in 2016, the amount of money these donors give has actually made up a shrinking portion of total individual contributions over the past two decades (see Figure 6.2). The Internet

Figure 6.2 Percentage of Individual Contributions in Presidential Election Cycles (2016 Dollars)

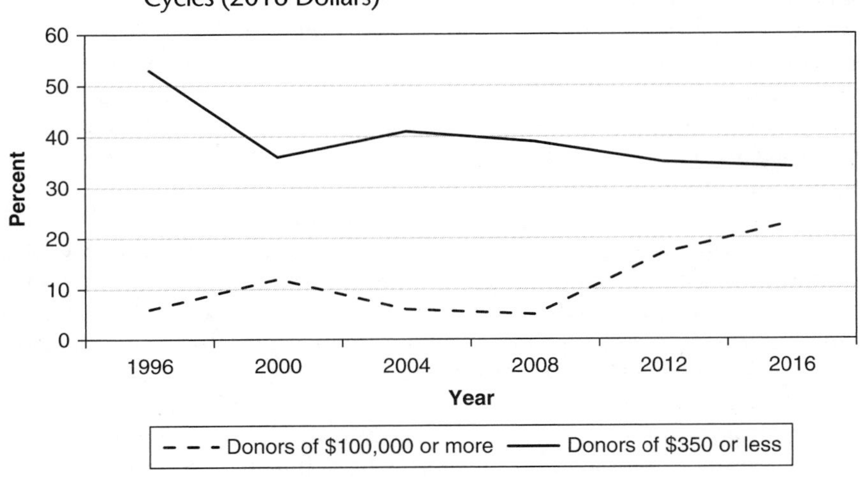

Source: Data from *The Atlantic*.

and social media have allowed candidates to connect with donors like never before; at the same time, changes in campaign finance law have increased the ability of the wealthy to give like never before. Most candidates running for Congress do not have access to the free media coverage that presidential candidates attract and will raise money where they can most easily find it. And that means going to big donors first.[38]

Nonetheless, one of the most valuable properties coming out of the 2016 election is Trump's fundraising list. All of the Trump campaign's small donor data will be merged with the Republican Party's list, which spans years and contains detailed information about party supporters. The consolidated list will be a boon for Republican candidates for all offices because many of Trump's supporters were first-time donors. The party's challenge will be keeping these donors engaged and in the fold.[39]

Outside Spending

The 2016 campaign began with all eyes focused on Right to Rise, the pro–Jeb Bush super PAC that spent a formidable $86 million during the primaries to promote Bush's failed candidacy. As the campaign drew to an end, Priorities USA Action, the largest of several super PACs supporting Hillary Clinton, officially broke Right to Rise's record, making well over $100 million in independent expenditures. Most of that spending went toward funding attacks against Donald Trump. Priorities USA Action accounted for a remarkable 76 percent of all outside money spent on Clinton's behalf during the campaign.[40]

Trump's late entry into the campaign finance game meant that his campaign had to scramble to deflect the onslaught of spending against him. Uncertainty even existed about which super PACs Trump had sanctioned, so donors were confused about which groups they should give to and which they should avoid. Keep in mind that Trump had sworn off all super PACs earlier in the campaign, claiming that he was beholden to no one but himself. By mid-October 2016, outside groups had spent about $178 million opposing him and $84 million supporting him. Groups opposing Clinton, by contrast, spent only $50 million and groups supporting her spent $37 million.[41]

Spending in 2016 marked a complete turnaround from the 2012 campaign, when groups supporting Republican presidential nominee Mitt Romney drastically outspent groups supporting President Barack Obama. Some of the biggest Republican outside funders in 2012, notably Republican operative Karl Rove's American Crossroads, chose to sit out the 2016 election or to invest in congressional races.

Hillary Clinton's campaign dominated the 2016 outside spending game. Groups supporting her outspent groups supporting Trump by a two-to-one margin. A number of groups formed specifically to support Clinton's run for the White House, but three dominated.

Priorities USA Action was the election's spending goliath by far. The group took in about $176 million and made about $117 million in independent expenditures on Clinton's behalf. Priorities USA's biggest donors include Donald Sussman, who gave nearly $21 million to the group, George Soros, and Fred Eychaner. Sussman gave more than any other individual contributor in 2016 to support Clinton's run.

The mega-contributions to Priorities USA Action allowed the group to undertake $6 million in last-minute spending in nine television markets in three states, including Wisconsin. This marked the first time the group had spent money in Wisconsin, a decision that likely came back to haunt it after Clinton lost the state in a surprise upset. The group's ads attacked Trump, attempting to use his most offensive and provocative public comments against him.[42]

Another outside group, Correct the Record, raised about $9.5 million but made no independent expenditures because it openly coordinated with the Clinton campaign. Super PACs are forbidden from coordinating with the candidate campaigns they support. In this case, the group took advantage of the FEC's "internet exemption," which exempts content posted for free online from the rules banning coordination. Correct the Record invested in pushing back against anti-Clinton content on social media. Although the group admitted it was spending money on Clinton's behalf, it argued that what it was doing did not constitute "coordinated communications."[43]

A third group, American Bridge 21st Century, raised just over $19 million but reported only $143,186 in independent expenditures. That money was spent on anti-Trump videos and mailings. The group mostly devotes itself to opposition research against Republican candidates.

Although Priorities USA Action, Correct the Record, and American Bridge 21st Century were Clinton's main sources of outside support, she benefited from spending by several other groups as well. United We Can, a super PAC affiliated with the Service Employees International Union (SEIU), spent $8 million opposing Trump and $3.8 million supporting Clinton; Women Vote! spent $4.4 million opposing Trump and $4.2 million supporting Clinton; Planned Parenthood Votes spent $2.7 million opposing Trump and $2.5 million supporting Clinton; and NextGen Climate Action Committee, run by billionaire environmentalist Tom Steyer, spent $4.6 million opposing Trump.[44]

Chaotic is probably the best way to describe the outside groups supporting Donald Trump—especially when compared to Clinton's highly structured organization. When a super PAC named Make America Great Again popped up during the primaries to support Trump, the candidate moved to shut it down—even though it had already raised $1.7 million. Eventually, several pro-Trump super PACs set up shop during the general election, but it remained unclear whether Trump actually approved any of them. This confusion hindered their fundraising efforts.

Rebuilding America Now raised a lot of late money on Trump's behalf, bringing in about $18 million between July and September 2016. Former World Wrestling Entertainment executive Linda McMahon donated $6 million to the super PAC. After calling Trump's comments about women "deplorable," McMahon nonetheless described Trump as an "incredibly loyal, loyal friend." Rebuilding America Now raised just over $20 million and spent about $17 million in independent expenditures.[45]

Great America PAC raised about $16 million, $14.5 million of which was spent on ads promoting Trump as well as on ads promoting the super PAC itself. The group raised a lot of money from limited liability companies (LLCs), which do not have to disclose their donors. Great America PAC came under fire when *The Telegraph* reported that it had solicited foreign contributions, telling undercover reporters posing as consultants that they could funnel money through a company run by the PAC's director and through two different 501(c)(4) organizations. A complaint was filed with the FEC, but so far the agency has not taken action.[46] After candidate Trump won the election, Great America PAC refashioned itself into an organization dedicated to supporting President Trump's political and policy agenda.

Other super PACs working on Trump's behalf raised and spent much less. The Committee to Restore America's Greatness, for example, raised just $585,318 and made only $16,000 in independent expenditures. The group, which is run by former Richard Nixon adviser and Trump confidant Roger Stone, managed to spend $554,456 of the money it raised, mostly on consulting and legal fees. American Horizons, a super PAC run by Ian Hawes, a twenty-five-year-old Maryland man with no ties to Trump, also engaged in questionable spending. The group raised about $1.1 million by telling donors that their money would be spent to elect Trump. But only $12,000 of that amount was spent on Trump's behalf and the rest went to a consulting company owned by Hawes.[47]

Trump's candidacy attracted a handful of other super PACs, but their overall spending on Trump's behalf was fairly minimal. His candidacy also attracted the support of one of the most powerful membership associations in the United States, the National Rifle Association (NRA). Although the NRA is not a super PAC, it spent $10.4 million on ads supporting Trump and $18.3 million on ads opposing Clinton.[48] Like other 501(c)(6) membership associations that engage in political spending, the NRA does not have to reveal its donors' names.

Organized labor spent more on the 2016 election than ever before, donating more than $132 million to super PACs and spending an additional $35 million to influence voters. The AFL-CIO contributed $14.6 million to pro-Clinton super PACs, the National Education Association donated $18.1 million, and the SEIU gave $19 million. But despite this massive spending, Clinton underperformed with union members. Her support from union households in the election was reportedly 10 percentage points below President Obama's support in 2012.[49]

Dark Money

Outside spenders that do not have to disclose their donors (so-called dark money groups) spent almost $181 million in the 2016 election, much less than the $308 million these groups spent in 2012. The drop in spending reflected a lack of enthusiasm for Donald Trump among conservative dark money groups, such as American Crossroads GPS. Although some liberal dark money groups have begun spending more, conservative groups have traditionally dominated this realm of campaign finance, accounting for 76 percent of total dark money spending in 2016.[50]

Most dark money spending focused on congressional races, but Trump did benefit from late spending by the 45Committee—a group linked to Chicago Cubs owner Todd Ricketts. The 45Committee spent $20 million on anti-Clinton ads in October 2016. Trump also benefited from $30 million in spending by the U.S. Chamber of Commerce, some of which was anti-Clinton.[51] The Chamber does not have to disclose its donors.

Sixty days before the election—on September 9, 2016—the FEC's reporting window opened, meaning that any group that spent money on ads mentioning candidates had to report that spending to the agency. Before September 9, only ads that explicitly called for the election or defeat of a candidate had to be reported. The reporting requirement triggered a sharp drop-off in dark money spending and a simultaneous uptick in super PAC spending. By not spending money during the FEC's reporting window, 501(c)(4) groups get around creating a written record of their engagement in political activity; in other words, avoiding the reporting window is another way for these groups to keep their spending in the dark.[52] If a 501 (c)(4) group is found to be primarily political in operation, it can lose its (c)(4) status and, with that, its ability to keep its donors secret. Because many super PACs have affiliated (c)(4) groups, spending can be coordinated in a mutually beneficial way.

Another way for political spenders to keep their identities hidden (at least temporarily) is to not register until after the FEC's final preelection reporting deadline passes. Nearly thirty super PACs registered after October 20, the final preelection reporting date in 2016. This meant that these groups could raise and spend unlimited amounts of money before election day without having to disclose their donors until thirty days after the election.[53]

Just as dark money groups can hide where their money comes from, candidates can mask where their money goes. Trump, for example, routed much of his campaign spending through consulting firms. This allowed him to avoid reporting who, exactly, he was paying and what he was paying them for. For example, the Trump campaign paid Giles-Parscale, a consulting firm, $56 million over a period of six months to run his digital operation. Although the firm then spent that money hiring hundreds of people, creating ads, and making ad buys, the Trump campaign did not have to itemize any of these expenses—it just had to report $56 million in consulting fees.

The Clinton campaign used the same technique, routing $55 million through Bully Pulpit Interactive, a digital consulting firm. This strategy allows candidates to essentially outsource their campaigns and avoid public scrutiny into how their campaigns are spending millions of dollars.[54]

The Race to the Finish Line

In the final two months of the campaign, Hillary Clinton swamped Donald Trump in ad buys. During the month of September, her campaign inundated the airwaves to the tune of $66 million. This was twice what her campaign spent on media buys in August and nearly triple the $23 million that Trump spent on ads in September.[55] Trump also spent $5 million on voter data in September—a huge increase over the $250,000 his campaign spent on data in August.[56]

Clinton spent more than $95 million overall during the month of September, while Trump reported spending a total of $70 million. Clinton began October with $59 million in cash on hand, compared with Trump's $35 million on hand.[57] Heading into the final week of the campaign, the candidates were expected to spend $44 million between them, fighting it out over the airwaves. Both campaigns focused their final spending in Florida, Ohio, and Pennsylvania. Clinton also did some last-minute spending in Virginia, New Mexico, Colorado, Michigan, and Wisconsin.[58]

In the end, massive amounts of money did not save Clinton's candidacy. Even as she relied heavily on a "big money strategy," Clinton also promised to "fight hard to end the stranglehold that the wealthy and special interests have on so much of our government." She condemned the "secret, unaccountable money in politics," while benefiting from pro-Clinton super PACs that spent millions in untraceable dollars.[59] Her vow to dismantle the very system of which she took profuse advantage was but one paradox in a campaign of many.

Donald Trump's definition of "self-funding" was another conundrum. The early money that he poured into his campaign was in the form of loans, not donations. Theoretically, this means that they have to be paid back unless the lender (himself) forgives them. And a good chunk of the money that his campaign spent during the primaries went to companies controlled by Trump, including millions for flights on his own planes and helicopter, and payments to his bodyguard and his head of security at the Trump Organization. Reconciling Trump's popular promise to totally self-fund his campaign with his decision to raise millions from small donors and multimillionaires is difficult in principle but clearly worked in practice.[60]

Congressional Races

Donald Trump's "loss" in the outside money game was an indisputable gain for congressional Republicans. Although spending massive amounts of money did not pay off in the presidential race, congressional candidates who outspent their challengers won at a higher rate than in recent elections: 94 percent of Senate races and 96 percent of House races were won by the biggest spender. The ranks of successful congressional candidates who spent less than their challengers include only three senators and twenty-six House members.[61]

Senate Republicans faced the unenviable task of defending twenty-four Senate seats, compared to just ten held by Democrats. Vulnerable as they were, Senate Republicans and their outside supporters rose to the challenge and, in the end, maintained a fifty-two-seat majority, losing just two seats. The Democrats gained 6 seats in the House, but Republicans held the majority, securing 241 seats.

Although some of the 2012 campaign's biggest outside spenders on the Republican side chose to sit out the 2016 presidential election, several invested heavily in congressional races—particularly on the Senate side. Indeed, spending by House candidates' own campaigns was down 16 percent and spending by Senate candidates' campaigns was down 25 percent in 2016, compared to 2012. But overall spending in congressional races reached an all-time high of about $4.3 billion.[62] This record-setting total spending was largely thanks to outside groups that spent upwards of $490 million (see Figure 6.3).

Figure 6.3 Outside Spending in Senate Races, 2010–2016

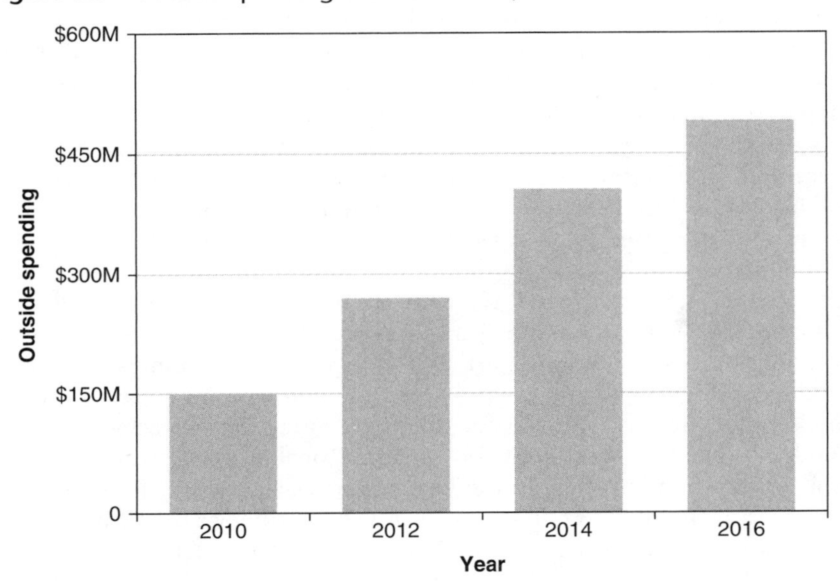

Source: Center for Responsive Politics.

The Koch brothers and their extensive network of conservative funders did not invest in Donald Trump's candidacy, but invested heavily—about $250 million—in congressional races. They spent $10 million helping Pennsylvania senator Pat Toomey beat back a strong challenge from Democrat Katie McGinty and $1 million helping to save Wisconsin senator Ron Johnson from losing his seat to former Democratic senator Russ Feingold. Toomey and Johnson were considered two of the weakest Republican incumbents on the 2016 ballot.[63]

Senate Republicans also benefited heavily from a huge last-minute fundraising push by two outside groups connected to Senate majority leader Mitch McConnell. The Senate Leadership Fund, a super PAC, and its affiliated 501(c)(4) nonprofit, One Nation, spent $165 million—$25 million of which was raised within a six-day span, just before election day. McConnell "sent up a flare" near the end of the campaign, personally reaching out to a network of Republican donors to warn them that the party's control of the Senate was at risk.[64] The effort worked, as the money these groups spent played a decisive role in a number of Senate races.

The battle for control of the Senate came down to tight races in Indiana, Missouri, Nevada, New Hampshire, North Carolina, and Pennsylvania. Despite heavy outside spending by liberal groups, Democrats won only two of them: Catherine Cortez Masto won in Nevada and Maggie Hassan won in New Hampshire. The Senate Majority PAC, a super PAC connected to Senate Democratic leader Harry Reid, spent close to $80 million on behalf of Senate Democrats. And Majority Forward, a liberal nonprofit, threw in just over $10 million to support Democratic candidates.

As was the case in the presidential election, dark money nonprofits like One Nation and Majority Forward dramatically reduced their spending once they ran up against the FEC's September 9 reporting deadline, stepping aside to let their affiliated super PACs pick up the slack. This strategy allows nonprofits that engage in political activity to avoid potential IRS scrutiny.[65] Republicans won seven of the eight Senate races that received the most dark money. More than $80 million in untraceable money was spent on Senate races, and conservative groups accounted for 68 percent of that amount.

Single-candidate super PACs that are not linked to the political parties also emerged as major players in several Senate races. Granite State Solutions, a super PAC supporting Democratic New Hampshire senate candidate Maggie Hassan, spent $21 million and was the biggest spending single-candidate group outside of the presidential race. Fighting for Ohio Fund, a super PAC backing Ohio senator Rob Portman, spent $9.3 million to keep him in office. In the Pennsylvania Senate race, Prosperity for Pennsylvania spent $3.6 million on Senator Pat Toomey's behalf while New American Jobs Fund spent $5.8 million trying to defeat Toomey.[66] And the Reform America Fund, backed by wealthy Wisconsinite Diane Hendricks, spent $5.4 million to support Republican senator Ron Johnson.

The Missouri Senate race saw outside spending skyrocket to record levels in the state. October FEC spending reports showed that outside groups had already spent $23.4 million to support either Republican senator Roy Blunt or his Democratic challenger, Jason Kander. In the 2012 Missouri Senate race, when Democrat incumbent Claire McCaskill defeated Republican challenger Todd Akin, outside groups spent a total of $13.7 million. In 2016, at least ten outside groups backed Blunt and at least seven supported Kander.[67]

Spending in the North Carolina Senate race that pitted Republican senator Richard Burr against Democratic challenger Deborah Ross soared to at least $81 million, with the candidates spending only $23 million of that amount. The remaining $48 million came from outside groups, most of them from outside the state.[68]

Nothing, however, topped the Pennsylvania Senate race, which was the most expensive of all in 2016 (see Table 6.4). Preliminary spending totals in the race topped $165 million—$27.81 for each of the nearly six million votes cast in the state.[69] The Toomey campaign spent $27.8 million (or $9.63 for each of the 2.89 million votes he won), and the McGinty campaign spent $12.7 million (or $4.53 for each of the 2.79 million votes she received).[70] The remaining $125 million was spent in the form of outside money.

Because Republicans in the House did not face as severe a challenge to their majority as their Senate colleagues, outside spending in House races was not as pronounced (see Table 6.5). Still, the main outside groups affiliated with the parties—House Majority PAC on the Democratic side and Congressional Leadership Fund on the Republican side—spent $53 million and $39 million, respectively. The House Majority PAC took advantage of Trump's various controversies throughout the campaign to raise millions. By convincing donors that Trump was going to drag down the entire

Table 6.4 Most Expensive Senate Races, 2016

Rank	*Race*	*Candidate*	*Outside Spending*	*Total*
1	Pennsylvania Senate	$40,516,131	$121,769,778	$169,285,909
2	New Hampshire Senate	$30,063,341	$88,907,150	$118,970,491
3	Nevada Senate	$21,201,476	$91,452,237	$112,653,713
4	Ohio Senate	$30,924,453	$52,386,891	$83,311,344
5	Florida Senate	$30,002,035	$49,299,526	$79,301,561
6	North Carolina Senate	$19,206,056	$59,979,258	$79,185,314
7	Missouri Senate	$21,853,617	$45,302,702	$67,156,319
8	Indiana Senate	$19,981,337	$45,336,975	$65,318,312
9	Wisconsin Senate	$35,144,671	$28,305,749	$63,450,420
10	Illinois Senate	$25,405,056	$4,962,629	$30,367,685

Source: Center for Responsive Politics.

Table 6.5 Most Expensive House Races, 2016

Rank	*Race*	*Candidate*	*Outside Spending*	*Total*
1	Minnesota District 8	$4,872,823	$15,778,187	$20,651,010
2	Virginia District 10	$5,861,489	$14,618,676	$20,480,165
3	Pennsylvania District 8	$3,672,763	$15,616,403	$19,289,166
4	Nevada District 3	$2,595,008	$15,821,916	$18,416,924
5	Colorado District 6	$5,051,922	$12,965,671	$18,017,593
6	Florida District 18	$7,226,778	$10,276,484	$17,503,262
7	Florida District 26	$4,044,160	$13,191,556	$17,235,716
8	Illinois District 10	$8,618,198	$8,352,229	$16,970,427
9	Maine District 2	$5,178,447	$10,068,301	$15,246,748
10	Nevada District 4	$3,442,770	$11,618,021	$15,060,791

Source: Center for Responsive Politics.

Republican ticket with him, the PAC played on fears of the longshot possibility of House Democrats regaining majority control.

The biggest single-candidate super PAC in House races supported Republican Amie Hoeber to the tune of $3.2 million—$2.1 million of which came from Hoeber's husband, Mark Epstein. Hoeber was unsuccessful in her attempt to unseat Maryland Democrat John Delaney.[71]

The Democratic Congressional Campaign Committee (DCCC), the fundraising committee for House Democrats, spent $157 million trying to link vulnerable House Republicans to Donald Trump. Taking advantage of an FEC loophole that allows candidates to split the cost of ads with their parties as long as the ads use generic references to "Democrats" or "Republicans," the DCCC was able to pump millions into a number of competitive races. For example, the DCCC and Illinois representative Brad Schneider combined forces to run more than $3.2 million worth of ads in Schneider's district.[72]

The DCCC also invested $4.8 million on behalf of Steve Santarsiero, who ran in Pennsylvania's 8th congressional district and lost. Meanwhile, the National Republican Congressional Committee, the DCCC's Republican counterpart in the House, spent a total of $121 million defending Republican incumbents. The committee invested big in several races, including spending $5.9 million trying (and failing) to hold Nevada's 4th congressional district.[73]

In the 2016 election, victorious Senate candidates spent an average of $10.4 million and successful House candidates spent an average of $1.3 million.[74] The House average was on par with the 2014 election, but the Senate average represented an increase of about $1.8 million. Factoring in outside spending nearly doubled the average cost of winning a Senate seat in 2016 to $19.4 million—almost $3 million more than in 2014. The overall share of outside spending in Senate races has gone from 22 percent in 2012, to 37 percent in 2014, to 47 percent in 2016. Outside spending in House races continues to be less of a factor than it is in Senate races, accounting for about 14 percent of overall spending in 2016. This figure is on par with outside spending in the 2012 and 2014 House races.[75]

Conclusion

The role of money in the 2016 elections defies neat synopsis. In the presidential election, the candidate who was predicted to handily win outraised her unconventional opponent by more than double. And yet she lost. The opposite was true in congressional races: most Senate and House seats went to the highest spender, typically the incumbent. In fact, Senate and House incumbents saw their highest reelection rates in years. Ninety percent of Senate incumbents won, as did 97 percent of House incumbents.

Small donors figured prominently in the presidential race, with both Donald Trump and Bernie Sanders demonstrating that robust small donor support is as meaningful—if not more meaningful—than big-money support. Where the money comes from matters as much as how much is raised. This certainly was the case in the election for president, but it may have been less important in congressional contests, in which candidates do not need to appeal to voters beyond their districts or states.

Yet as important as the "power of small donors" narrative is, it is ultimately overshadowed by the ability and willingness of wealthy individuals to flood the system. The Supreme Court's *Citizens United* and *McCutcheon* decisions legalized unbridled campaign spending. As a result, candidates are more dependent on wealthy donors who can max out their campaign contributions *and* write million-dollar checks to the super PACs supporting their candidacies. This was especially evident in 2016's Senate races, where outside groups were responsible for almost half of the money spent on Senate campaigns. The amount of outside money spent in federal races has been trending upward for years and, in the absence of a legislative or legal intervention, will continue in that direction.

Where does this leave the average citizen? The 2016 presidential election showed that forces beyond the candidates' control sometimes prevail. That Trump and his supporters raised and spent much less money than Clinton sends a powerful message to the many cynics who believe that money is all that matters. Ultimately, winning the most electoral votes is all that matters, and Trump succeeded in that task without the financial backing and organization that most analysts thought necessary. But none of this negates the fact that our campaign finance laws at least give wealthy donors the option to inject millions into elections if they so choose. This systemic reality will continue to dominate the financing of future elections.

Notes

1. "Transcript of Republican Debate in Miami, Full Text," *CNN*, March 15, 2016, www.cnn.com/2016/03/10/politics/republican-debate-transcript-full-text/index.html.
2. Center for Responsive Politics, "Donald Trump," www.opensecrets.org/pres16/candidate.php?id=N00023864.
3. Russ Choma, "Millions of Dollars Pouring in for Trump at Last Minute," *Mother Jones*, November 7, 2016, www.motherjones.com/politics/2016/11/last-seven-days-money.
4. Matea Gold, "Pro-Trump Super PAC Aims to Serve as New President's Main Outside Ally—Even against Republicans, If Necessary," *Washington Post*, November 11, 2016, www.washingtonpost.com/news/post-politics/wp/2016/11/11/pro-trump-super-pac-aims-to-serve-as-new-presidents-main-outside-ally-even-against-republicans-if-necessary/.
5. Matea Gold, "How the Stampede for Big Money Enabled Donald Trump's Rise," *Washington Post*, November 8, 2016.
6. Ashley Balcerzak, "Where the Money Came from, Not How Much, Mattered in the Presidential Race," Center for Responsive Politics, November 9, 2016, www.opensecrets.org/news/2016/11/where-the-money-came-from-not-how-much-mattered-in-the-presidential-race/.
7. Ibid. Self-funded candidates include those who spent at least $500,000 of their own money on their campaigns.
8. Ashley Balcerzak, "UPDATE: Federal Elections to Cost Just under $7 Billion, CRP Forecasts," Center for Responsive Politics, November 2, 2016, www.opensecrets.org/news/2016/11/update-federal-elections-to-cost-just-under-7-billion-crp-forecasts/.
9. Center for Responsive Politics, "Outside Spending by Super PACs," www.opensecrets.org/outsidespending/summ.php?cycle=2016&chrt=V&disp=O&type=S.
10. Jack Noland, "In First Post-McCutcheon Presidential Election, More Big Donors, Giving More," Center for Responsive Politics, November 10, 2016, www.opensecrets.org/news/2016/11/in-first-post-mccutcheon-presidential-election-more-big-donors-giving-more/.
11. Center for Responsive Politics, "Top Individual Contributors: All Federal Contributions," www.opensecrets.org/overview/topindivs.php.
12. Matea Gold and Tom Hamburger, "Super PAC Backing Jeb Bush Unlikely to Hit $100 Million by End of June," *Washington Post*, June 9, 2015, www.washingtonpost.com/politics/super-pac-backing-jeb-bush-unlikely-to-hit-100-million-by-end-of-june/2015/06/09/f5f0d5a2-0ef1-11e5-a0dc-2b6f404ff5cf_story.html.
13. Nicholas Confessore and Sarah Cohen, "How Jeb Bush Spent $130 Million Running for President with Nothing to Show for It," *New York Times*, February 22, 2016, www.nytimes.com/2016/02/23/us/politics/jeb-bush-campaign.html?_r=1.
14. Rick Newman, "These Donors Lost the Most Money on Jeb Bush," *Yahoo Finance*, February 22, 2016, finance.yahoo.com/news/these-donors-lost-a-ton-of-money-on-jeb-bush-180816776.html.
15. Jose A. DelReal, "Why Jeb Bush Was an Official 2016 Candidate for Just Three Seconds on Wednesday," *Washington Post*, May 13, 2016, www.washingtonpost.com/news/post-politics/wp/2015/05/13/why-jeb-bush-was-an-official-2016-candidate-for-just-three-seconds-wednesday/.
16. Confessore and Cohen, "How Jeb Bush Spent $130 Million Running for President with Nothing to Show for It."

17. Harry Enten, "Jeb Bush's Path to Defeat Began a Year Ago," *FiveThirtyEight*, February 20, 2016, fivethirtyeight.com/features/jeb-bushs-path-to-defeat-began-a-year-ago/.
18. Alec Goodwin, "Jeb's Magnificent Super PAC: An Autopsy," Center for Responsive Politics, June 30, 2016, www.opensecrets.org/news/2016/06/jebs-magnificent-super-pac-an-autopsy/.
19. Alec Goodwin, "Failed Carson Campaign Spent Heavily in April and May, Routed Funds to Former Staffers," Center for Responsive Politics, June 24, 2016, www.opensecrets.org/news/2016/06/failed-carson-campaign-spent-heavily-in-april-and-may-routed-funds-to-former-staffers/.
20. Julie Bycowicz and Chad Day, "Carson Spent Heavily on Consultants, Lightly on Campaigning," *Associated Press*, March 4, 2016, elections.ap.org/content/carson-spent-heavily-consultants-lightly-campaigning.
21. Robert Maguire and Anna Massoglia, "New Tax Forms Show Strong Ties between pro-Rubio Group and Campaign," Center for Responsive Politics, May 24, 2016, www.opensecrets.org/news/2016/05/new-tax-forms-rubio-dark-money-legacy-even-darker/.
22. Will Tucker, "Big Money—If Not the GOP Establishment—Has Been with Ted Cruz from the Start," Center for Responsive Politics, March 25, 2016, www.opensecrets.org/news/2016/03/big-money-if-not-the-gop-establishment-has-been-with-ted-cruz-from-the-start/.
23. Ibid.
24. Harry Enten, "The Long, Weird Kasich Campaign Gives In to Reality," *Five ThirtyEight*, May 4, 2016, fivethirtyeight.com/features/the-long-weird-kasich-campaign-gives-in-to-reality/.
25. Harvard University professor Lawrence Lessig ran briefly on a campaign finance reform platform but failed to attract strong support. He raised about $1.2 million for his campaign, all from individual donors.
26. Libby Watson, "Why Did Only 1 Presidential Candidate Take Public Financing?" *Sunlight Foundation*, January 27, 2016, sunlightfoundation.com/2016/01/27/why-did-only-1-presidential-candidate-take-public-financing/.
27. Ned Resnikoff, "How Bernie Sanders Changed Democratic Fundraising, Beating Hillary Clinton's Total," *International Business Times*, June 8, 2016, www.ibtimes.com/how-bernie-sanders-changed-democratic-fundraising-beating-hillary-clintons-total-2379240.
28. Seema Mehta, "Who Gives Money to Bernie Sanders?" *Los Angeles Times*, June 3, 2016, www.latimes.com/projects/la-na-pol-sanders-donors/.
29. Mehta, "Who Gives Money to Bernie Sanders?"
30. Resnikoff, "How Bernie Sanders Changed Democratic Fundraising, Beating Hillary Clinton's Total."
31. Clare Foran, "The End of a Political Revolution," *The Atlantic*, July 12, 2016, www.theatlantic.com/politics/archive/2016/07/sanders-endorses-clinton/486122/.
32. Balcerzak, "Where the Money Came from, Not How Much, Mattered in the Presidential Race," and Matea Gold and Anu Narayanswamy, "Donald Trump's Campaign Spending More Than Doubled in September. Here's Where the Money Went," *Washington Post*, October 20, 2016, www.washingtonpost.com/news/post-politics/wp/2016/10/20/donald-trumps-campaign-spending-more-than-doubled-in-september-heres-where-the-money-went/.
33. Fredreka Schouten, "Energized Donors Push Team Clinton Near $1 Billion Mark," *USA Today*, October 21, 2016, www.usatoday.com/story/news/politics/elections/2016/2016/10/20/energized-donors-push-team-clinton-near-1-billion-mark/92479306/.

34. Matea Gold and Anu Narayanswamy, "Trump Leans on Small Donors as Wealthy Givers Pull Back," *Washington Post*, October 28, 2016, www.washingtonpost.com/politics/trump-leans-on-small-donors-as-wealthy-givers-pull-back/2016/10/28/87ba7e64-9d1e-11e6-9980-50913d68eacb_story.html.
35. Matea Gold and Anu Narayanswamy, "How Mega-Donors Helped Raise $1 Billion for Hillary Clinton," *Washington Post,* October 24, 2016, www.washingtonpost.com/politics/how-mega-donors-helped-raise-1-billion-for-hillary-clinton/2016/10/22/a92a0ee2-9603-11e6-bb29-bf2701dbe0a3_story.html.
36. Ibid.
37. Paul Blumenthal, "Super PAC Mega-Donors Expand Election Influence with Record $1 Billion in Contributions," *Huffington Post*, November 1, 2016, www.huffingtonpost.com/entry/super-pac-donors_us_5817b30be4b0390e69d21648.
38. Ian Vandewalker and Lawrence Norden, "Small Donors Still Aren't as Important as Wealthy Ones," *The Atlantic*, October 18, 2016, www.theatlantic.com/politics/archive/2016/10/campaign-finance-fundraising-citizens-united/504425/.
39. Ben Kamisar and Jonathan Swan, "Trump Small-Donor Army a Double-Edged Sword for GOP," *The Hill*, October 26, 2016, thehill.com/homenews/campaign/302772-trump-small-donor-army-a-double-edged-sword-for-gop.
40. Soo Rin Kim, "Mine, All Mine: Single Candidate Super PACs, Creeping Down-Ballot," Center for Responsive Politics, November 10, 2016, www.opensecrets.org/news/2016/11/mine-all-mine-single-candidate-super-pacs-creeping-down-ballot/.
41. Melissa Yeager, "A Democratic Outside Group Finally Outspent Jeb Bush's Big-Money Super PAC," *Sunlight Foundation*, October 20, 2016, sunlightfoundation.com/2016/10/20/a-democratic-outside-group-finally-outspent-jeb-bushs-big-money-super-pac/.
42. Nicholas Confessore, "'Super PAC' Bolsters Ads to Aid Clinton in 3 Battleground States," *New York Times*, October 31, 2016, www.nytimes.com/2016/11/01/us/politics/priorities-usa-advertising-hillary-clinton.html.
43. Libby Watson, "The Final Stretch: The Big-Spending Super PACs behind Hillary Clinton," *Sunlight Foundation*, November 1, 2016, sunlightfoundation.com/2016/11/01/the-final-stretch-the-big-spending-super-pacs-behind-hillary-clinton/.
44. Ibid.
45. Libby Watson, "The Final Stretch: The Chaotic Super PACs Supporting Donald Trump," *Sunlight Foundation*, November 1, 2016, sunlightfoundation.com/2016/11/01/the-final-stretch-the-chaotic-super-pacs-supporting-donald-trump/.
46. Ibid.
47. Ibid.
48. Ibid.
49. Carrie Levine, "Clinton Got Union Money, but Trump Won Many Workers' Hearts and Minds," Center for Public Integrity, November 18, 2016, www.publicintegrity.org/2016/11/18/20480/clinton-got-union-money-trump-won-many-workers-hearts-and-minds.
50. Robert Maguire, "$1.4 Billion and Counting in Spending by Super PACs, Dark Money Groups," Center for Responsive Politics, November 9, 2016, www.opensecrets.org/news/2016/11/1-4-billion-and-counting-in-spending-by-super-pacs-dark-money-groups/.
51. Ibid.

52. Ashley Balcerzak, "Dark Money Ads Plunged When Reporting Requirement Kicked In," Center for Responsive Politics, October 19, 2016, www.opensecrets.org/news/2016/10/dark-money-ads-plunged-when-reporting-requirement-kicked-in/.
53. Ashley Balcerzak, "PACs Pop Up Just in Time to Avoid Reporting Donors," Center for Responsive Politics, November 7, 2016, www.opensecrets.org/news/2016/11/pacs-pop-up-just-in-time-to-avoid-reporting-donors/.
54. Shane Goldmacher, "How Politicians Hide Their Spending from the Public," *Politico*, November 2, 2016, www.politico.com/story/2016/11/how-politicians-hide-their-spending-from-the-public-230609.
55. Matea Gold and Any Narayanswamy, "Hillary Clinton Spent $66 Million Just to Air Ads in September," *Washington Post*, October 20, 2016, www.washingtonpost.com/news/post-politics/wp/2016/10/20/hillary-clinton-spent-66-million-just-to-air-ads-in-september/.
56. Matea Gold and Anu Narayanswamy, "Donald Trump's Campaign Spending More Than Doubled in September. Here's Where the Money Went."
57. Nicholas Confessore, "Trump and Clinton Both Accelerated Spending in September," *New York Times*, October 20, 2016, www.nytimes.com/2016/10/21/us/politics/campaign-fundraising-money.html.
58. Theodore Schleifer and Gregory Wallace, "The $44 Million Closing Arguments Begin," *CNN*, November 1, 2016, www.cnn.com/2016/11/01/politics/donald-trump-hillary-clinton-advertising/.
59. Carrie Levine, Michael Beckel, and Dave Levinthal, "Donald Trump Dismantles Hillary Clinton's Big Money Machine," *Time*, November 9, 2016, time.com/4563949/donald-trump-hillary-clinton-money-machine-election/.
60. David A. Graham, "The Lie of Trump's 'Self-Funding' Campaign," *The Atlantic*, May 13, 2016, www.theatlantic.com/politics/archive/2016/05/trumps-self-funding-lie/482691/.
61. Ashley Balcerzak, "Where the Money Came from, Not How Much, Mattered in the Presidential Race."
62. Ashley Balcerzak, "UPDATE: Federal Elections to Cost Just Under $7 Billion, CRP Forecasts."
63. Andy Kroll, "Trump Might Be a Dream Come True for Megarich Campaign Donors," *Mother Jones* (January/February 2017), www.motherjones.com/politics/2016/11/donald-trump-dark-money-election.
64. Mary Troyan and Fredreka Schouten, "Mitch McConnell's Late Fundraising 'Flare' Raised Millions for Senate Races," *USA Today*, November 10, 2016, www.usatoday.com/story/news/politics/2016/11/10/mitch-mcconnells-late-fundraising-flare-raised-millions-senate-races/93607956/.
65. Llewellyn Hinkes-Jones, "Super PAC Spending Replaces Dark Money as Election Nears," *Bloomberg BNA*, October 17, 2016, www.bna.com/super-pac-spending-n57982078708/.
66. Kim, "Mine, All Mine: Single Candidate Super PACs, Creeping Down-Ballot."
67. Steve Kraske and Dave Helling, "Outside Spending Rockets in Missouri Senate Race, Setting Apparent Record with Two Weeks to Go," *Kansas City Star*, October 21, 2016, www.kansascity.com/news/local/news-columns-blogs/the-buzz/article109750872.html.
68. Greg Gordon, "A Huge Amount of Money Is Pouring into the NC Race That Could Decide the Senate," *McClatchy DC*, November 4, 2016, www.mcclatchydc.com/news/politics-government/election/article112455312.html.
69. These numbers will shift slightly once final spending figures and vote tallies are available.

70. Laura Olson, "How Much Did Pennsylvania's U.S. Senate Race Cost?" *The Morning Call*, November 17, 2016, www.mcall.com/news/local/elections/mc-pa-senate-toomey-mcginty-cost-20161117-story.html.
71. Kim, "Mine, All mine: Single Candidate Super PACs, Creeping Down-Ballot."
72. Scott Bland, "Dems Use Loophole to Pump Millions into Fight for the House," *Politico*, October 18, 2016, www.politico.com/story/2016/10/democrats-house-campaign-money-229957.
73. Soo Rin Kim, "Parties Pull Out the Stops with 'Outside' Spending," Center for Responsive Politics, November 10, 2016, www.opensecrets.org/news/2016/11/parties-pull-out-the-stops-with-outside-spending/.
74. These figures reflect reports filed with the FEC through October 19, 2016; the averages will increase once all final spending is reported.
75. Soo Rin Kim, "The Price of Winning Just Got Higher, Especially in the Senate," Center for Responsive Politics, November 9, 2016, www.opensecrets.org/news/2016/11/the-price-of-winning-just-got-higher-especially-in-the-senate/.

7

Congress

Nationalized, Polarized, and Partisan

Gary C. Jacobson

Over the past several decades, American voters' political attitudes, social values, demography, residency choices, and even beliefs about reality have grown increasingly divided along party lines.[1] Deepening partisan divisions have inspired high levels of party-line voting and low levels of ticket splitting, resulting in thoroughly nationalized, president- and party-centered congressional elections.[2] The question going into the 2016 elections was whether this configuration would persist. The answer was an emphatic yes: All of the major trends were sustained and in some respects strengthened. In the end, the vast majority of partisans remained loyal to their candidates in both the presidential and congressional elections. Despite the deep divisions within the Democratic and Republican Parties exposed by the presidential nominating contests, the congressional results were indistinguishable from what one would expect in any close election between a generic Republican and a generic Democratic presidential candidate.

In a year when the presidential contest was nasty, brutal, and long, with the winner, Donald Trump, riding in on a wave of anger at government and demand for change in Washington, the congressional elections produced, by historical standards, very little change indeed (see Table 7.1). Only seven House incumbents lost in the November general elections (five others were defeated in primaries, three of them victims of redistricting[3]), and only twelve seats changed hands from one party to the other, both results near post–World War II lows.[4] Two incumbent senators lost, and theirs were the only Senate seats that changed party hands, again nearly the lowest turnover on record.[5] Widespread disgust with politicians in Washington did not preclude the pattern of congressional election results we would expect if voters were basically content with their elected leaders.

It was not obvious before the election that party loyalty and the status quo would prevail in voting for the president and Congress. Trump's rise to the top of the Republican field in the face of nearly unanimous opposition from established GOP leaders, donors, and pundits, and the continuing refusal of many prominent Republicans to rally to his side after his nomination, exposed deep fissures within the party. Hillary Clinton's unanticipated difficulty in fending off Bernie Sanders's challenge to her nomination revealed tensions

Table 7.1 Membership Changes in the House and Senate 2010–2016

	Republicans	*Democrats*	*Independents*
House of Representatives			
Elected in 2014	247	188	
Elected in 2016	241	194	
Incumbents reelected	213	168	
Incumbents defeated	6	1	
Open seats retained	25	17[a]	
Open seats lost	3	2	
Senate			
After the 2014 election	54	44	2[b]
After the 2016 election	52	46	2[b]
Incumbents reelected	20	7	
Incumbents defeated	2	0	
Open seats retained	2	3	
Open seats lost	0	0	

Source: Compiled by the author.

[a] Includes CA-17, where Democrat Ro Khanna defeated incumbent Democrat Mike Honda.

[b] The independents caucus with the Democrats.

within the Democrats' traditional center-left coalition as well. The public did not warm to either nominee. Trump was by far the least popular candidate ever to win a major-party nomination, let alone the presidency. His net favorability rating (the percentage with a favorable opinion of him minus the percentage unfavorable) began in deep negative territory and remained there throughout the general election campaign; it averaged –29 points in October–November polls. Had it not been for Trump, Clinton would have set the record, with a net favorability averaging –11 points over the same period. Both candidates were unusually unpopular within their own parties. For comparison, Figure 7.1 displays data on favorability of the candidates in 2012 and 2016 (for the October–November period), broken down by party. Trump's favorable ratings were 20 points below Mitt Romney's among Republicans, while his unfavorable ratings were 22 points higher. The equivalent figures for Barack Obama, compared to Clinton, were 13 points and 12 points, respectively.

Offsetting any temptation disaffected partisans may have had to cross party lines, however, was their even more negative view of the other party's candidate. Not only did an average of 91 percent of Republican and Democratic voters express unfavorable opinion of the other party's candidate, but for both candidates about 80 percent chose the "very unfavorable" option; the comparable figures for Obama and Romney had been 54 percent and

Figure 7.1 Partisan Opinions of the Candidates, 2012 and 2016

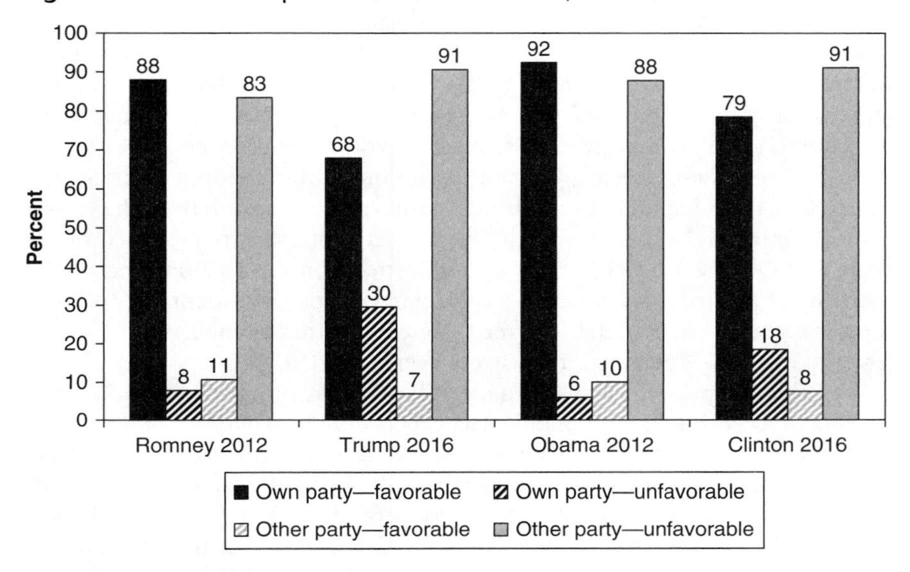

Sources: 2012 data from Gallup, CBS News/*New York Times*, CNN, and Pew surveys; 2016 data from Gallup, YouGov, CBS News/*New York Times*, ABC News/*Washington Post*, and Fox News surveys.

48 percent, respectively. Regarding the top of the ticket, then, divisions within the parties were overshadowed by even wider divisions between them.[6]

One reason so many Republican leaders and pundits had opposed Trump was their fear that his unpopularity would lead to a landslide defeat that would cost them the Senate and perhaps even the House.[7] Vocal elite opposition continued after he became the nominee, but it was confined largely to Republicans who did not have to face the electorate. Those on the ballot with Trump had a tougher choice because they needed the votes of his enthusiastic white working-class supporters but risked losing support from more upscale Republicans and independents, particularly women, if they embraced his candidacy too closely. In the end, however, they largely closed ranks and did not suffer for it. Trump won the electoral if not the popular vote despite his negatives and, if anything, helped rather than hurt down-ballot Republicans in an election that was as partisan, nationalized, and president-centered as it had been in 2012.

The House Elections

Republicans lost only six seats in the 2016 House elections, an outcome that counts as a clear victory because they were defending the 247 seats they had won in 2014, which was their highest total since the 1920s. The GOP ended up with only one seat fewer than they had won in their historic sweep in

2010. Their structural advantage in the distribution of voters across House districts[8]—exemplified by the fact that, despite losing the national popular tally by five million votes in 2012, Mitt Romney had won pluralities in 226 districts, compared to Obama's 209—would have protected their majority against anything less than an enormous pro-Democratic tsunami, and of course none materialized. Democratic voters tend to be concentrated in cities and therefore are distributed among congressional districts less efficiently than are their Republican counterparts. Remarkably, the results in 2016 mirrored almost perfectly the district partisanship measured by the vote for Obama in 2012. Before the election, only thirty-one seats—7.1 percent of the total—were held by the party whose presidential candidate had lost the district in 2012. After the election, that number was down to twenty-three (5.3 percent), the lowest ever recorded.

Table 7.2 presents a more nuanced look at the link between House and presidential voting by dividing districts according to whether Obama's vote was at least 2 points above (Democratic districts) or 2 points below (Republican districts) his national major-party vote share of 51.96 percent or fell somewhere in between (the balanced districts). By this definition, only nine districts were won by the "wrong" party in 2016, down from sixteen before the election. Of the twelve seats that changed parties, eight were won by the party with a favorable partisan balance, and only one by a candidate facing an unfavorable balance; the other three changes were in balanced districts. Figure 7.2 shows that victories that go against the partisan grain have become exceedingly rare in the 2010s and now account for only about 2 percent of House seats.[9] The figure also shows that the decline in numbers has hurt the Democrats much more than the Republicans. Consistent party-line voting in the electorate magnifies the advantage Republicans enjoy from the more efficient distribution of their loyal voters across districts.[10]

The persistence of an extraordinarily strong relationship between district partisanship (as proxied by the 2012 presidential vote) and House voting in 2016 is also evident in aggregate voting data. The correlation

Table 7.2 District Partisanship and House Election Results, 2016

District Partisanship	*Won by Democrat*	*Won by Republican*	*Number of Districts*
Democratic (> 2 points)	178 (+5)	6 (–5)	184
Republican (> 2 points)	3 (–2)	221 (+2)	224
Balanced	13 (+3)	14 (–3)	27
Total	194 (+6)	241 (–6)	435

Source: Compiled by the author.

Note: District partisanship is measured by the 2012 presidential vote. Democratic districts are those in which the major-party vote for Obama was at least 2 percentage points above his national share; Republican districts are those in which Obama's vote was at least 2 points below that share; and those falling in between were the balanced districts. The Obama vote has been updated in districts that were redrawn between 2012 and 2016 under court order. The change from the preelection distribution is shown in parentheses.

Figure 7.2 House Candidates Winning against the Partisan Grain, 1952–2016

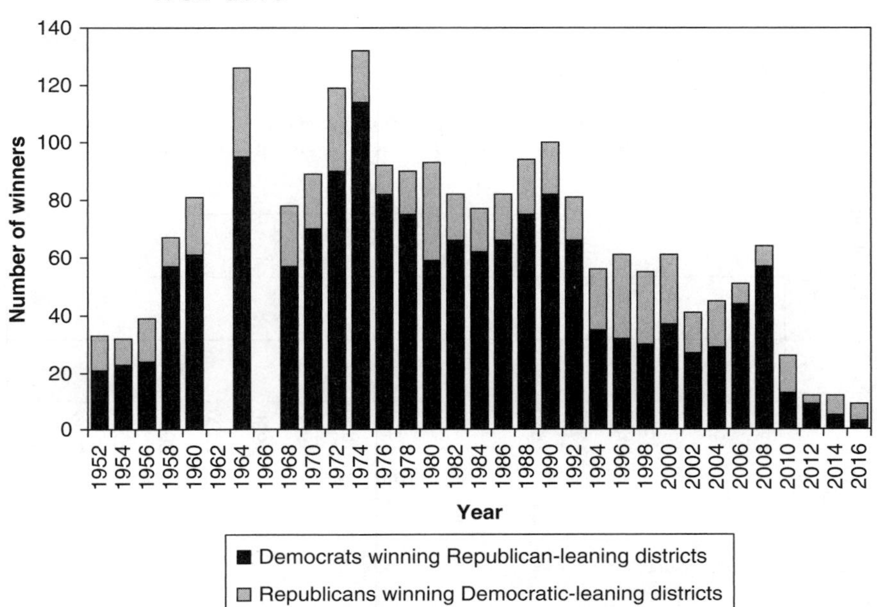

Source: Compiled by the author.

Note: Leaning districts are defined as those in which the district-level presidential vote was at least two percentage points higher than the national average for that party for that year's election or, for midterms, the previous presidential election.

between the district-level vote share of each party's House and presidential candidates has grown substantially during the twenty-first century (see Table 7.3 and Figure 7.3). The correlation reached a record high of .95 in 2012 and remained at .95 (using the 2012 presidential vote) in 2016. A simple logit model estimating the effect of district partisanship on which party wins each House seat now predicts the actual result with about 95 percent accuracy.[11] Moreover, as district partisanship has become such a dominant force, the value of incumbency, measured in the share of the vote won by reelection-seeking members, has dropped to levels last seen in the 1950s.[12] House incumbents were very successful in 2016, winning 98 percent of their general election contests. This was not, however, because they were incumbents, but because they ran in districts that favored their party. Only eleven (3 percent) had to defend seats that favored the rival party; four of them lost, accounting for a majority of incumbent defeats. District partisanship was also the key to success for candidates running for forty-seven seats that were open in 2016. Only one open-seat candidate took a district that favored the other party by the measure used here; 94 percent of the winners took districts won by their party's presidential candidate in 2012.

Figure 7.3 Correlations between the Presidential and Congressional Vote at the State and District Levels, 1952–2016

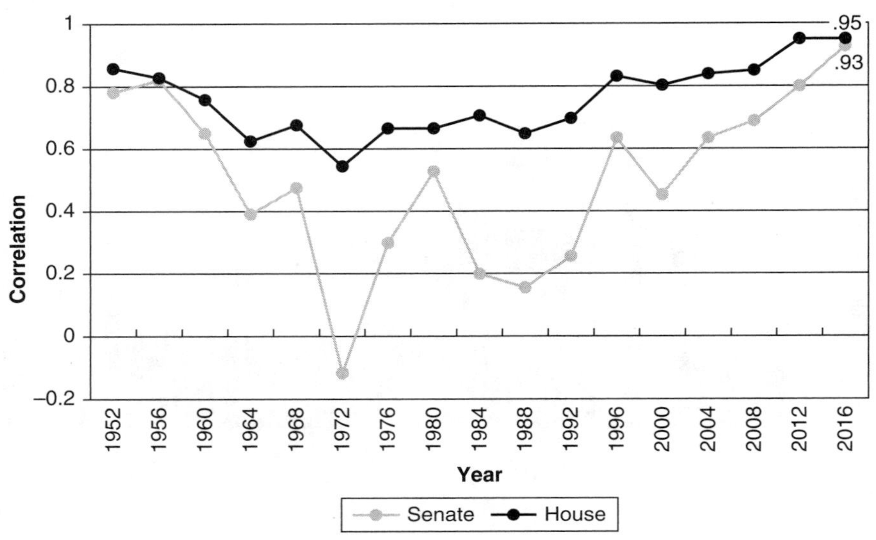

Source: Compiled by the author.

Table 7.3 The District-level Presidential Vote and House Results, 2000–2016

House Election Year	*Presidential Vote Year*	*House/President Vote Correlation*	*Percent Winners Correctly Predicted*	*Value of Incumbency*
2000	2000	.80	80.4	8.6
2002	2000	.81	86.2	8.5
2004	2004	.84	86.4	6.8
2006	2004	.84	83.5	6.5
2008	2008	.85	80.7	7.1
2010	2008	.92	91.3	4.8
2012	2012	.95	94.0	2.5
2014	2012	.94	94.3	3.7
2016	2012	.95	94.7	2.4

Source: Compiled by the author.

Note: Complete 2016 presidential vote data are not yet available.

Survey data also point to electoral coherence nearly as strong in 2016 as in 2012, when the presidential candidacies were far more typical. National exit poll data found that the high levels of partisan loyalty and low levels of ticket splitting evident in recent years largely persisted in 2016 (see Table 7.4). Democrats were a bit less loyal to Clinton than they had been to Obama (they voted 92–7 for him, compared to 89–9 for her) and Republicans were also a bit less loyal to Trump (90–7 compared to 93–6 for Romney). But by historic standards, these were still high levels of party loyalty. Party-line voting was even more prevalent in the House races (93–6 when both parties are combined), and the level of ticket splitting that can be estimated from exit poll data remained very low, about 6.8 percent, compared to 6.5 percent in 2012.

Table 7.4 also shows that demography shaped House voting in almost exactly the same way it shaped presidential voting. The differing vote margins produced by differences in gender and marital status, race, age cohort, and religion were about the same for all offices. Only one difference was greater than 4 percentage points (6 points for Asians between Trump and the Republican

Table 7.4 The Electoral Coalitions of Presidential and House Candidates, 2016

	Percent Voting for			
	Hillary Clinton	*House Democrat*	*Donald Trump*	*House Republican*
Party identification				
Democrat (37)	89	92	9	5
Republican (33)	7	7	90	94
Independent (30)	42	46	48	49
Demographics				
Men (48)	41	44	53	54
Women (52)	54	54	42	44
Married (30)	49	49	47	49
Unmarried (22)	62	64	33	35
White (70)	37	39	58	59
Black (12)	88	89	8	10
Hispanic/Latino (11)	65	67	29	32
Asian (4)	65	64	29	35
18–29 (19)	55	57	37	41
30–44 (25)	50	53	42	45
45–64 (40)	44	45	53	54
65 or over (16)	45	46	53	52
White, Born-Again Christian				
Yes (26)	16	15	81	83
No (74)	59	61	35	37

(Continued)

Table 7.4 (Continued)

	Percent Voting for			
	Hillary Clinton	*House Democrat*	*Donald Trump*	*House Republican*
Opinion of Obama				
Approve (54)	84	84	10	15
Disapprove (45)	7	9	90	89
Opinion of Clinton				
Favorable (43)	95	92	3	7
Unfavorable (54)	11	15	82	82
Opinion of Trump				
Favorable (38)	4	8	95	90
Unfavorable (61)	77	76	15	23

Source: 2016 national exit poll data, reported at www.foxnews.com/politics/elections/2016/exit-polls (accessed November 11, 2016).

Note: The percentage of respondents in each category is in parentheses.

House candidate); and the average absolute difference was only 1.9 points, with a standard deviation of 1.3 points. People with favorable opinions of their own party's presidential candidate were very unlikely to vote for a House candidate of the other party, but those with unfavorable opinions were more likely to vote for their party's House candidate than for its presidential candidate. Significant shares of voters with unfavorable opinions of Clinton and Trump nonetheless voted for them (11 percent and 15 percent, respectively).

The extreme nationalization of the 2016 House elections is also evident in Figure 7.4, which displays the standard deviations of the House vote swing from one party to the other from the prior election in districts with stable boundaries for elections since 1946.[13] The smaller the standard deviation, the more uniform the swing across districts, and thus the more nationalized the election. The 2016 swing was clearly the most uniform in any presidential election year in the entire postwar period, with a standard deviation (4.5 points) less than half the size of its average for the 1970s and 1980s. It is matched in the postwar era only by the 2014 midterm election.

In sum, the highly unorthodox and disruptive Trump candidacy, and all of the intraparty conflict it provoked at the elite level, did nothing to alter the basic—and very strong—link between House and presidential voting that has emerged over the past several decades. Despite having considerable reservations about their nominee, Republican voters did not desert Trump or Republican House candidates in significant numbers. Nor did the Democrats' lack of enthusiasm for Clinton inspire them to vote for Trump or House Republicans. Consistent with other manifestations of the strong feelings accompanying partisan polarization that have been driving ordinary Republicans and Democrats farther and farther apart from each other, a deep antipathy toward the other party and its presidential candidate strongly discouraged defection.[14]

Figure 7.4 The Nationalization of U.S. House Elections, 1946–2016

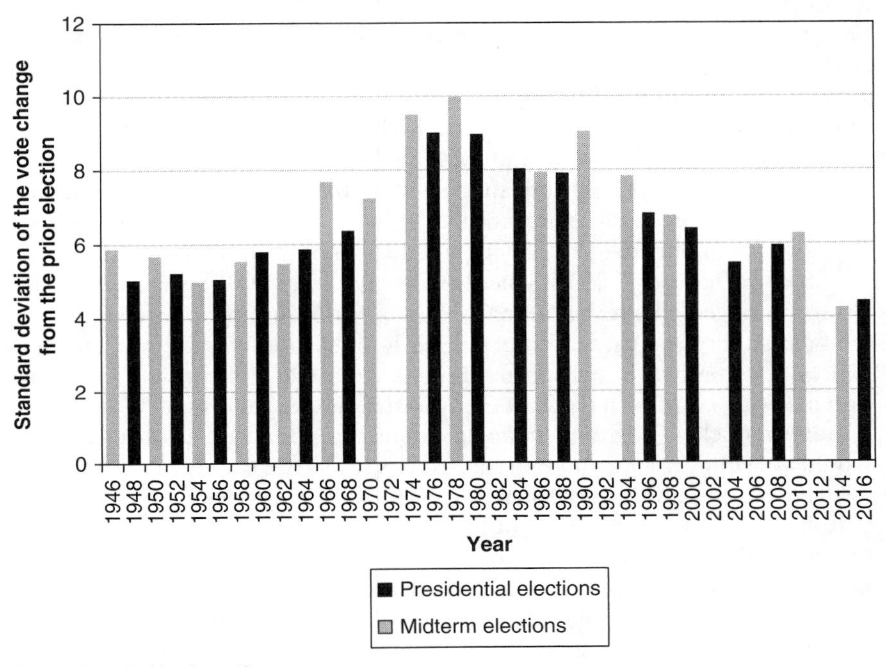

Source: Compiled by the author.

The Senate

The Trump candidacy loomed large over the Senate races in 2016. Democratic leaders hoped, and Republican leaders feared, that Trump's high negatives would enable Democrats to regain the Senate majority they had lost in 2014. Their prospects were brightened by the fact that twenty-four Republican but only ten Democratic seats were at stake. Seven of the Republican seats were in states won by Obama in 2012, and six of them were listed in the Cook Political Report's March 2016 ratings as being at risk: four toss-up and three only leaning Republican.[15] Two Democratic seats were also deemed competitive (one toss-up, one leaning Democratic). Thus, even with only a modest wind at their backs, the Democrats appeared to have a good shot at gaining the four additional seats they would need to control the Senate, assuming they also won the White House with a vice president who could break ties. The wind never materialized, the Democrats lost the White House, and Republicans maintained a 52–48 Senate majority after the election.

Polling data showing that large majorities of voters held negative views of Trump put Republican Senate candidates in competitive states in a bind. For example, *Economist*/YouGov polls taken at approximately weekly intervals during the last three months of the campaign regularly asked respondents about Trump's character and qualifications. In response, an average of 59 percent said he was not qualified; 57 percent said he did not have the right temperament; 58 percent deemed him dishonest; 58 percent said he was dangerous; 56 percent, crazy; and 52 percent, racist.[16] What Republican Senate candidates (and most other observers) could not easily anticipate was that, for many voters, such views did not keep them from voting for Trump. On average in these surveys, Clinton led Trump by only about 4 points. Among Trump supporters in these surveys, 15 percent considered him a racist, 13 percent said he was crazy, and only 81 percent deemed him qualified—yet they intended to vote for him anyway.

Before October 7, 2016, when a videotape from 2005 surfaced in which Trump bragged about his sexual exploits, including groping assaults on women, twenty-eight of the thirty-three Republican Senate candidates had expressed some level of support for Trump, although with considerable variation in enthusiasm, with the least enthusiastic saying they would "vote for the Republican ticket." Of the remaining candidates, three had already said they would not support him, and two refused to say.[17] After the tape became news, virtually all Republican candidates condemned his behavior, but only nine withdrew their support. Three of the nine reverted to backing Trump when the blowback from Trump supporters protesting their apostasy became too intense to resist, eloquent testimony to the cross-pressures Trump's candidacy had put them under.[18] The final patterns of Republican support for Trump clearly reflected strategic sensitivities. Only five of the eleven Republican candidates (45.4 percent) in contests the Cook Report classified as competitive (toss-up or leaning to a party) said they would vote for him, compared to twelve of fourteen candidates (85.7 percent) in safely red states; the difference was statistically significant ($\chi^2 = 4.59$, $p = .032$). The same pattern holds if analysis is confined to the twenty-two Republican incumbents. Eleven of thirteen (84.6 percent) in safely Republican states eventually supported Trump, compared to four of nine (44.4 percent) in other states; the difference is again statistically significant ($\chi^2 = 3.96$, $p = .047$). Of the eight Republicans running in safe Democratic states where their already-slim prospects freed them to reveal their sincere preferences, five supported Trump (62.5 percent).

In the end, every Republican incumbent who voted for Trump won, while the two who did not support him lost. One of them, Mark Kirk of Illinois, was already in serious electoral trouble and would have lost with or without Trump. But the other, Kelly Ayotte of New Hampshire, was certainly hurt by his candidacy. Already facing a stiff challenge in a state leaning blue, she deserted Trump (whom she had earlier called a "role model") after the videotape surfaced, saying she would write in Republican vice presidential nominee Mike Pence. More important than her vacillation or apostasy, however, was that Clinton won the state. In fact, for the first time in history, *every Senate contest was won by the party that won the state's electoral votes*. The uniqueness of this result is clear from Figure 7.5. In elections since 1952, the highest previous level of consistency in elections for these offices was 82 percent, in 2012. The upward trend was already there, but the jump to 100 percent in 2016 is still remarkable.

The close relationship between the Republican share of major-party votes for president and senator in 2016 is displayed in Figure 7.6. Notice that the coincidence of voting for both offices tended to be especially close in the tightest contests clustered at the center of the graph. In Nevada, Colorado, New Hampshire, Pennsylvania, Wisconsin, and North Carolina, the difference between Republican presidential and Senate vote share was no more than 1 percentage point. Only one close Senate race did not coincide with a close presidential race (Missouri), and only one close presidential race did not coincide with a close Senate race (Florida). Thus Trump's unexpected victories in Wisconsin and Pennsylvania almost certainly helped Republicans retain control of the Senate, as did his victory in North Carolina, another swing state, while his losses in Nevada and New Hampshire probably reduced the size of the GOP majority in that chamber.[19]

The vote shares of Trump and Republican Senate candidates depicted in Figure 7.6 are correlated at .93, which is the highest such correlation since at least 1952 (see Figure 7.3). In 2016, Senate elections nearly matched the House elections in this regard. By all of these measures, then, the 2016 Senate elections were, like the House elections, thoroughly nationalized, party- and president-centered affairs.

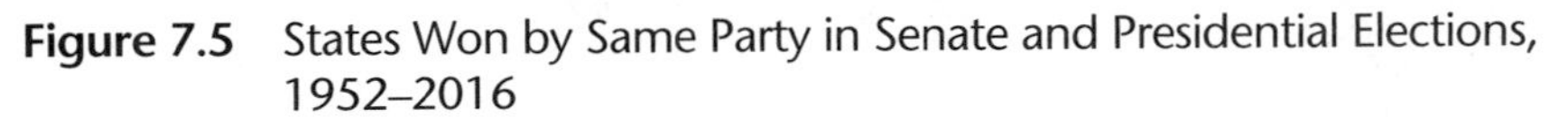

Figure 7.5 States Won by Same Party in Senate and Presidential Elections, 1952–2016

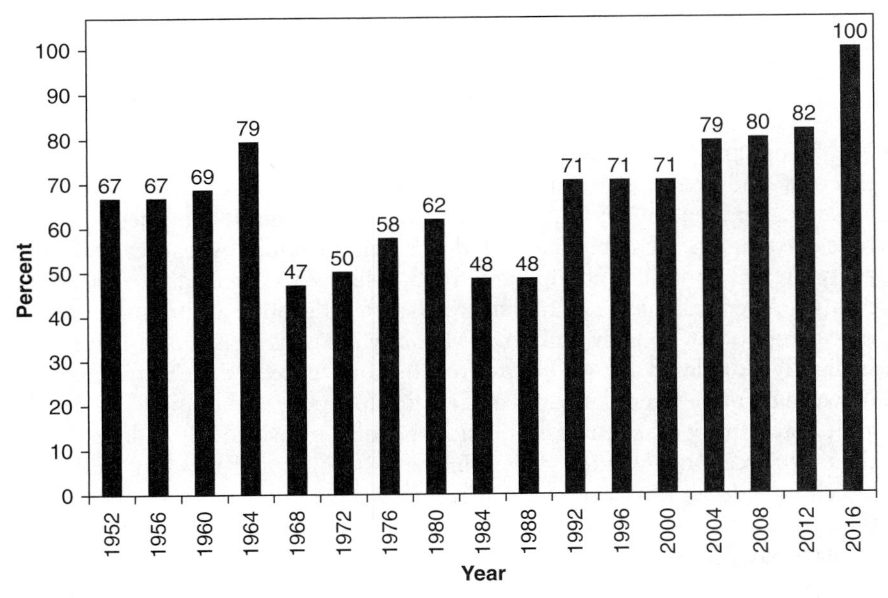

Source: Compiled by the author.

Figure 7.6 The Vote for President and Senator, 2016

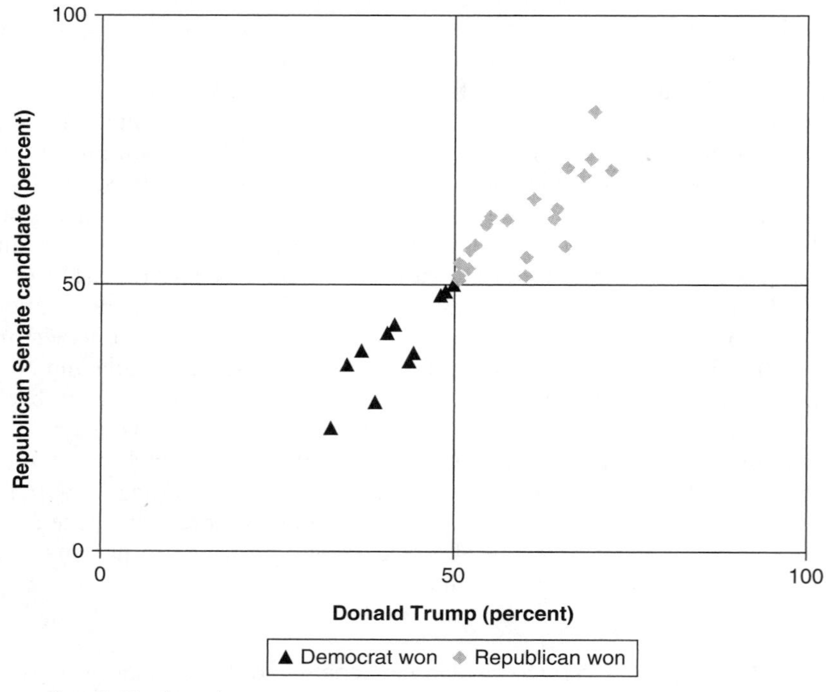

Source: Compiled by the author.

Money in the 2016 Congressional Elections

The House and Senate election results that conformed so closely to local partisanship and presidential voting in 2016 were the most expensive House and Senate campaigns on record, with well over one billion dollars spent on contests for seats in each chamber.[20] Independent spending by parties and nonparty groups continued its upward trend, rising 25 percent above the 2014 totals.[21] A remarkable $116 million was spent independently to influence the race between Pat Toomey and Katie McGinty in Pennsylvania (see Table 7.5). In lightly populated New Hampshire, the total exceeded $68 million, and between them the candidates and outside groups spent a whopping $95 per eligible voter. In six other contests, outside spending exceeded $40 million. More than 70 percent of the money spent in the first nine states listed in Table 7.5, which include all of the most competitive races, came from outsiders rather than the candidates' campaigns. This is now the norm; in states thought to be in play, party and allied groups invest heavily in pursuit or defense of Senate majorities, usually outspending the candidates by a substantial margin.[22] As Table 7.5 shows, their involvement drops dramatically when the outcome is not considered to be in doubt.

Table 7.5 Senate Election Results and Campaign Money, 2016 ($1,000s)

				Independent Spending			
State	*Candidate*	*% Vote*	*Candidate Receipts*	*Party*	*Non-Party*	*$ Per Voter*	*% Outside*
Pennsylvania	*Pat Toomey* (R)	48.8	20,176	21,529	33,219	7.7	73.1
	Katie McGinty (D)	47.3	14,130	30,015	32,130	7.8	81.5
Nevada	Joe Heck (R)	44.7	11,178	24,633	22,641	29.7	80.9
	Catherine Cortez Masto (D)	47.1	16,362	17,539	22,545	28.6	71.0
New Hampshire	*Kelly Ayotte* (R)	47.8	15,472	6,940	20,972	41.7	64.3
	Maggie Hassan (D)	48.0	15,526	20,866	19,661	53.8	72.3
North Carolina	*Richard Burr* (R)	51.1	11,670	15,910	12,873	5.5	71.2
	Deborah Ross (D)	45.4	10,902	14,858	13,041	5.3	71.9
Ohio	*Rob Portman* (R)	58.0	19,295	3,645	29,656	6.0	63.3
	Ted Strickland (D)	37.2	10,902	9,563	6,747	3.1	59.9
Missouri	*Roy Blunt* (R)	49.2	11,001	15,144	7,592	7.5	67.4
	Jason Kander (D)	46.4	10,745	8,459	12,456	7.0	66.1
Indiana	Todd Young (R)	52.1	9,111	14,871	10,424	7.1	73.5
	Evan Bayh (D)	42.4	3,472	12,728	4,365	4.2	83.1
Florida	*Marco Rubio* (R)	52.0	2,204	16,999	13,155	2.2	93.2
	Patrick Murphy (D)	44.3	14,539	2,679	7,212	1.7	40.5
Wisconsin	*Ron Johnson* (R)	50.2	16,165	3,108	12,083	7.3	48.4
	Russ Feingold (D)	46.8	21,677	4,668	5,009	7.3	30.9
Colorado	Darryl Glenn (R)	44.3	3,628	0	2,411	1.5	39.9
	Michael Bennet (D)	50.0	14,929	0	1,109	4.0	6.9

(Continued)

Table 7.5 (Continued)

				Independent Spending			
State	*Candidate*	*% Vote*	*Candidate Receipts*	*Party*	*Non-Party*	*$ Per Voter*	*% Outside*
Louisiana	John Kennedy (R)	60.7	2,758	0	298	0.9	9.8
	Foster Campbell (D)	39.3	1,735	0	3,048	1.4	63.7
Illinois	*Mark Kirk* (R)	39.8	8,273	0	2,107	1.2	20.3
	Tammy Duckworth (D)	54.9	15,084	0	126	1.7	0.8
Arizona	*John McCain* (R)	53.7	11,315	0	1,762	2.8	13.5
	Ann Kirkpatrick (D)	40.8	8,483	0	36	1.8	0.4
Georgia	*Johnny Isakson* (R)	54.8	8,110	0	1,588	1.4	16.4
	Jim Barksdale (D)	41.0	4,912	0	4	0.7	0.1
California	Kamala Harris (D)	61.6	14,446	0	1,467	0.6	9.2
	Loretta Sanchez (D)	38.4	4,477	0	0	0.2	0.0
Kentucky	*Rand Paul* (R)	57.3	3,372	0	648	1.2	16.1
	Jim Gray (D)	42.7	5,420	0	338	1.8	5.9
Iowa	*Chuck Grassley* (R)	60.1	8,624	0	363	0.2	2.0
	Patty Judge (D)	35.7	2,076	0	33	0.9	1.6
Maryland	Kathy Szeliga (R)	35.7	1,479	0	302	0.4	17.0
	Chris Van Hollen (D)	60.9	11,468	0	0	2.7	0.0
Arkansas	*John Boozman* (R)	59.8	3,998	0	195	2.0	4.7
	Conner Eldridge (D)	36.2	1,865	0	0	0.9	0.0
Alaska	*Lisa Murkowski* (R)	44.4	4,153	0	147	8.3	3.4
	Ray Metcalfe (D)	11.6	17	0	0	0.0	0.0
Washington	Chris Vance (R)	41.0	428	0	113	0.1	20.9
	Patty Murray (D)	59.0	9,810	0	33	1.9	0.3

New York	Wendy Long (R)	25.7	632	0	43	0.0	6.4
	Chuck Schumer (D)	67.0	17,182	0	100	1.3	0.6
South Carolina	*Tim Scott* (R)	60.6	5,943	0	122	1.6	2.0
	Thomas Dixon (D)	36.9	37	0	0	0.0	0.0
Utah	*Mike Lee* (R)	68.2	3,779	0	78	1.9	0.0
	Misty Snow (D)	27.1	51	0	0	0.0	0.0
Oklahoma	*James Lankford* (R)	67.7	2,804	0	0	1.0	0.0
	Mike Workman (D)	24.6	0	0	0	0.0	0.0
Kansas	*Jerry Moran* (R)	62.2	4,350	0	.5	2.1	0.0
	Patrick Wiesner (D)	32.2	35	0	0	0.0	0.0
Alabama	*Richard Shelby* (R)	64.0	3,383	0	0	0.9	0.0
	Ron Crumpton (D)	35.9	33	0	0	0.0	0.0
Connecticut	Dan Carter (R)	34.6	365	0	0	0.1	0.0
	Richard Blumenthal (D)	63.2	7,155	0	0	2.8	0.0
Hawaii	*John Carroll* (R)	21.2	54	0	0	0.1	0.0
	Brian Schatz (D)	70.1	3,677	0	0	3.6	0.0
Idaho	*Mike Crapo* (R)	66.1	4,076	0	0	3.5	0.0
	Jerry Sturgill (D)	27.7	728	0	0	0.6	0.0
North Dakota	*John Hoeven* (R)	78.5	2,864	0	0	4.9	0.0
	Eliot Glassheim (D)	17.0	21	0	0	0.0	0.0
Oregon	Mark Callahan (R)	33.4	32	0	0	0.0	0.0
	Ron Wyden (D)	56.6	8,336	0	0	2.8	0.0
South Dakota	*John Thune* (R)	71.8	5,010	0	0	7.9	0.0
	Jay Williams (D)	28.2	0	0	0	0.0	0.0
Vermont	Scott Milne (R)	32.3	113	0	0	0.2	0.0
	Patrick Leahy (D)	60.0	3,855	0	0	7.8	0.0

Source: Campaign Finance Institute, "Independent Spending Dominated the Closest Senate and House Races in 2016," www.cfinst.org/Press/PReleases/16-11-10/independent_spending_dominated_the_closest_senate_and_house_races_in_2016.aspx.

Note: Incumbents are italicized.

Both sides also spent lavishly in competitive House contests, with independent spending also exceeding candidate spending in these races. Detailed data on House campaign finances are not yet available, but the summary data are clear (see Figure 7.7). Preliminary spending totals indicate that the average candidate in a close race (that is, one where the winner received 55 percent or less of the major-party vote) was supported by about $5 million, with winners having a bit more than losers. About 56 percent of the money spent in these races was not under the candidate's control; more than half was spent independently by the parties, which have now assumed a dominant role in mounting competitive House campaigns. Winners in marginally competitive districts (winner with between 55.1 and 60 percent of the vote) raised substantial amounts themselves but received less outside help, and the large majority who were completely safe received almost none. Most of these latter candidates were of course incumbents, and some of the money they raised was passed on to other candidates or party committees, because safe incumbents are now expected to help their party's needier candidates.[23]

Did all of this extravagance matter? The election results make clear that the huge sums expended by outside groups in 2016 did nothing to disrupt basic state or district partisan inclinations or to separate Senate and presidential voting. Indeed, their activities may have heightened party regularity.

Figure 7.7 Competition and Money in the House Elections, 2016

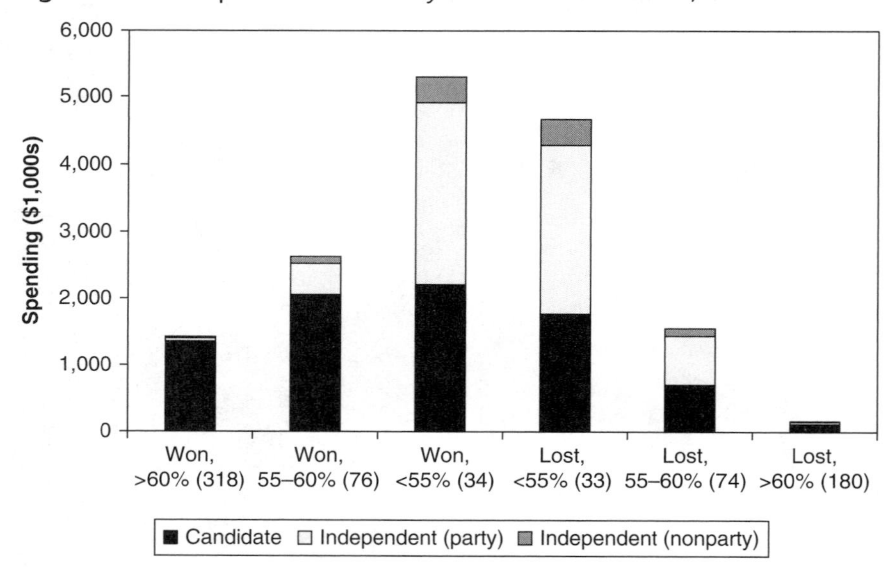

Source: Campaign Finance Institute, "Independent Spending Dominated the Closest Senate and House Races in 2016," www.cfinst.org/Press/PReleases/16-11-10/independent_spending_dominated_the_closest_senate_and_house_races_in_2016.aspx.

Note: Number of cases is in parentheses.

According to the state exit polls, both Senate candidates in the tightest and most expensive races inspired higher than average levels of party loyalty, exceeding 90 percent.[24] In most of the very close contests (Pennsylvania, Nevada, North Carolina, and Wisconsin), the candidates had virtually equal financial support. Democrat Maggie Hassan enjoyed a modest financial advantage in New Hampshire, but total spending on both sides far exceeded what was needed for maximum saturation, so this could scarcely have mattered. This is now typical: Both sides spend so much in competitive Senate races that the balance of resources hardly matters; both sides have more than ample resources for making their case and mobilizing their supporters. The same is true of virtually all potentially competitive House elections. None of this implies that the campaigns are irrelevant, however. Although the outcomes are largely predictable based on the fundamentals of local partisanship and short-term national trends, campaigns are still necessary to provide voters with the information and motivation that brings these fundamentals to bear on their decisions.[25] Because unilateral financial disarmament would be fatal in a competitive contest, it never happens. Rather, competitive candidates and their "independent" allies engage in ever more expensive arms races as each side tries to keep the other from gaining an advantage.

The 115th Congress (2017–2018)

The 2016 elections may have reinforced the congressional status quo, but Donald Trump's ascension to the presidency changes its dynamics radically for the 115th Congress. After Barack Obama took office in 2009, congressional Republicans focused their energies exclusively on opposing his proposals, notably on health care reform and financial regulation. After taking control of the House in 2010, they tried to undo these reforms while blocking any further initiatives. The consequence was gridlock broken only when action was unavoidable, such as on the annual budget, or when Obama issued executive orders that bypassed Congress. The partisan acrimony and stalemate that ensued brought Congress's standing with the public to an all-time low. Since the beginning of the 112th Congress in 2011, an average 78 percent of Americans have disapproved of Congress's performance, with only 16 percent approving.[26] Disaffection with Congress has been thoroughly bipartisan, with each side blaming the other party for the government's inability to act. With a Republican in the White House, blame can no longer be shared. Republicans now assume full responsibility for governing the country. How successfully they can transition from obstruction, which is easy, to governing, which is anything but, is an open question.

The elections did nothing to dampen the forces that have contributed to party polarization, which reached record levels in the 113th and 114th Congresses.[27] The incoming party contingents represent an equally divergent set of districts. As Figure 7.8 shows, the average 26-percentage-point difference in the underlying partisanship of the districts won by Republicans and Democrats in 2016 (as measured by the 2012 presidential vote) matches the previous highs reached in 2012 and 2014.[28] Party differences in electoral bases are strongly related to party differences in presidential support and roll call voting, which means that the House will be at least as polarized along party lines in the 115th Congress as in its recent predecessors.[29] In particular, the electoral constituencies of the House Democrats—those constituents who actually voted for them—contain very few Republicans or Trump supporters and thus provide little electoral incentive for them to cooperate with the president or the congressional Republicans. A postelection *Economist/YouGov* survey found that among the slight majority of voters who preferred Clinton to Trump, 94 percent viewed Trump unfavorably, 85 percent, very unfavorably. If the Republican House majority remains unified, this will not matter, but items in Trump's agenda that challenge conservative Republican orthodoxies—a huge new federal investment in infrastructure, perhaps—may need Democratic votes to advance.

States tend to be more diverse politically and less lopsided in their partisanship than House districts, so the gap between the parties' electoral

Figure 7.8 The Polarization of U.S. House Districts, 1952–2016

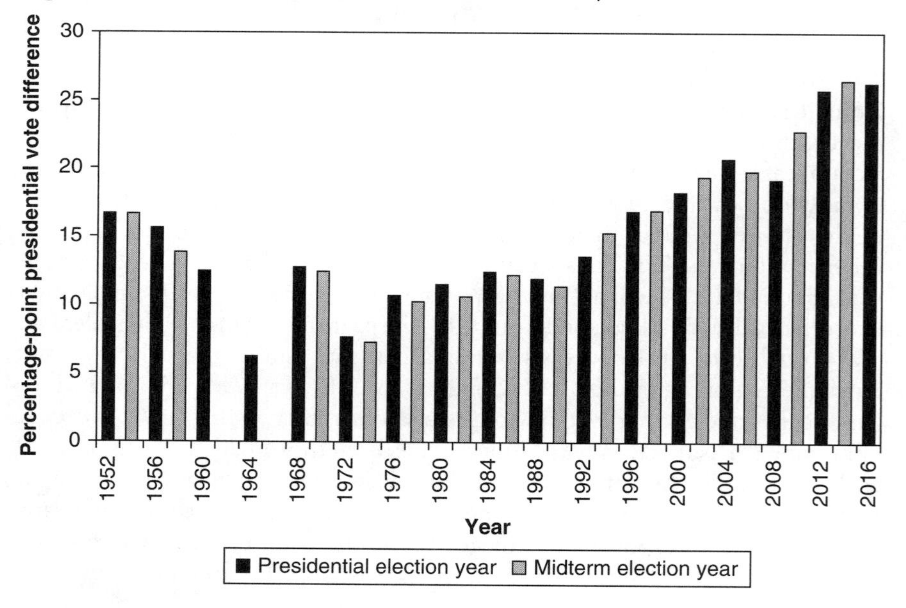

Source: Compiled by author.

Note: Entries are the percentage-point differences in the average presidential vote between districts won by Democrats and districts won by Republicans; data for 1962 and 1966 are unavailable because of redistricting; entries for midterm elections are calculated from the previous presidential election; data for 2016 are based on Obama's vote in 2012.

constituencies is always narrower in the Senate than in the House. But the gap nonetheless reached a record high of 19 percentage points in 2016 (see Figure 7.9). The number of senators representing states won by their party's candidate in the most recent presidential election reached another postwar high after the 2016 elections and now stands at eighty-six, up from eighty-four after 2014 and seventy-nine after 2012. Forty-nine of the fifty-two Republican senators are from states won by Trump. So are eleven of the forty-eight Democrats, but seven of them represent states where Trump's margin was narrow, putting them under little pressure to support him. Indeed, in light of the intense dislike of Trump expressed by their Democratic electoral constituents, most Senate Democrats will have every reason to use the filibuster as enthusiastically as Republicans did when they were in the minority. It remains to be seen whether the filibuster will survive the fierce conflicts that can be expected if Trump and his Senate allies attempt to implement the more divisive components of his agenda—such as building a wall on the Mexican border, gutting Obamacare, conferring huge tax cuts on corporations and wealthy individuals, and abandoning steps to slow global warming.

Figure 7.9 The Polarization of State Constituencies, 1952–2016

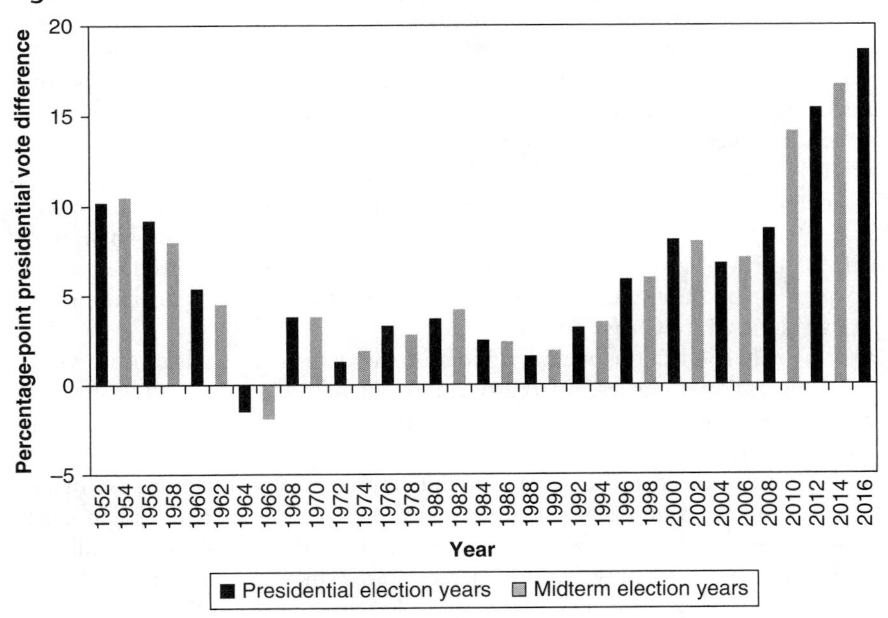

Source: Compiled by author.

Note: Entries are the percentage-point differences in the average presidential vote between states won by Democrats and states won by Republicans in the Senate elections; entries for midterm election years are calculated from the presidential election two years earlier.

The polarized 115th Congress represents a thoroughly polarized public. Partisan divisions in the electorate along the lines of race and ethnicity, age, education, gender, region, religiosity, and social values continued to grow wider in 2016. (Table 7.4 offers some evidence for those divisions.) Urban-rural differences also increased noticeably.[30] Marisa Abrajano and Zoltan Hajnal have recently argued that as America has become more diverse racially and ethnically, whites have responded by becoming more conservative and Republican whereas racial and ethnic minorities have remained disproportionately liberal and Democratic. By their evidence, racial and ethnic differences are now more potent drivers of political division than any other demographic differences.[31] In 2016 Trump's welcoming of white nationalists and hard-line anti-Muslim and anti-immigrant voices into his coalition and administration immediately provoked a backlash and street protests by people who saw his victory and its implications as dire threats to them and their communities. In a Gallup poll taken immediately after the election, a record low of only 10 percent of partisans on the losing side expressed a favorable opinion of the president-elect. In contrast, Trump's favorability ratings among Republicans shot up after he won, creating a notably larger postelection partisan gap in favorability than for any of his three most recent predecessors.[32] Trump's presidency promises to be highly polarizing from day one.

The demographics of the congressional parties mirror some of the demographic divisions between ordinary Democrats and Republicans (see Table 7.6). The House Republicans in the 115th Congress are 91 percent male, 96 percent white, and 99 percent Christian; none admits to being other than heterosexual. Altogether, 86 percent are (presumably) straight white Christian men. House Democrats, in contrast, are 32 percent female, 43 percent minority, and 14 percent other than Christian; six are openly gay. Overall, only 31 percent are straight white Christian men. Senate party differences are similar except for the larger proportion of white Democrats; 85 percent of Republican senators, compared to 56 percent of Democrats, are straight white Christian men.

The 2016 elections actually widened the demographic distance between the congressional parties. Of the twenty-eight new House Republicans, only two are women and only one is not a Christian; twenty-five (89 percent) are white Christian men. Of the twenty-six new House Democrats, five are women and seventeen (65 percent) have nonwhite ethnic origins, including six blacks, five Hispanics, four Asians (with Vietnamese, Japanese, and Indian backgrounds represented), a Native American, and the Congress's first member of Dominican heritage; only four (15 percent) are white Christian men. The two new Republican senators (Todd Young of Indiana and John Kennedy of Louisiana) are white Christian men; the five new Democratic senators include only one white man (Chris Van Hollen, of Maryland), along with a white woman (Maggie Hassan of New Hampshire), a Latina (Catherine Cortez Masto of Nevada), an Asian American woman (Tammy Duckworth of Illinois), and a

Table 7.6 Demographics of the 115th Congress

	House of Representatives				*Senate*			
	Republicans		*Democrats*		*Republicans*		*Democrats*	
	N	%	N	%	N	%	N	%
Total	241		194		52		48	
Men	220	91.3	132	68.0	47	90.3	32	66.7
Women	21	8.7	62	32.0	5	9.7	16	33.3
Whites	230	95.4	110	56.7	49	94.2	42	87.5
Nonwhites	11	4.6	84	43.3	3	5.8	6	12.5
Blacks	2	0.8	44	22.7	1	1.9	2	4.2
Hispanics	7	2.9	27	13.9	2	3.8	2	4.2
Asians			12	6.2			2	4.2
Other	2	0.8	1	0.5				
Christian	239	99.2	166	85.6	52	100.0	36	75.0
Other	2	0.8	28	14.4			12	25.0
LGBT (lesbian, gay, bisexual, or transgender)			6	3.1			1	2.1
Straight White Christian Men	208	86.3	61	31.4	44	84.6	27	56.3
Other	33	13.7	133	68.6	8	15.4	21	43.7

Source: Compiled by the author.

woman with a mixed minority ethnic heritage (Kamala Harris of California, who is Afro-Caribbean and Indian). Thus the Democratic parties in both chambers grew more diverse after 2016, while the election reinforced the Republicans' white Christian male homogeneity. Republicans succeeded in 2016 by effectively mobilizing their overwhelmingly white voter base, but it remains questionable how long they can thrive as a nearly all-white party in the face of long-term demographic changes that will continue to shrink the white share of the population.[33]

The electoral and demographic underpinnings of the 115th Congress portend a Congress at least as fiercely polarized as the one it replaces. The difference is that a unified Republican government is now in place. If Republicans stick together, they can override any Democratic opposition; polarization will no longer breed gridlock. But Democrats are now free to indulge in responsibility-free opposition of the kind enjoyed so fully by Republicans during the Obama years, while Republicans will bear the full credit or blame for Congress's performance. Their fates, for better or worse, will be in the unpredictable hands of Donald Trump because the nationalization of electoral politics has made it exceedingly difficult for the president's partisans in Congress to escape his shadow.[34] The Republicans' formidable structural advantages—in Senate as well as House elections[35]—will be hard for Democrats to overcome, but the 2006 and 2008 elections showed what is possible when enough voters become fed up with a Republican president. Trump's victory in 2016 was a necessary, if by no means sufficient, condition for a Democratic takeover of Congress in 2018 or 2020. What happens will depend on whether the changes in domestic and foreign policy that Trump and the congressional Republicans actually deliver, and the national and international conditions that follow, turn out to be what voters want.

Notes

1. Alan I. Abramowitz, "The New American Electorate: Partisan, Sorted, and Polarized," in James A. Thurber and Antoine Yoshinaka, eds., *American Gridlock: The Sources, Character, and Impact of Political Polarization* (New York: Cambridge University Press, 2015), 19–44.
2. Gary C. Jacobson, "It's Nothing Personal: The Decline of the Incumbency Advantage in U.S. House Elections," *Journal of Politics* 77 (July 2015): 861–873.
3. Court-ordered redistricting occurred in Florida, North Carolina, and Virginia between 2014 and 2016.
4. The record for the fewest incumbent defeats in House general elections is six (1986, 1988, 1998, and 2000); the postwar average is twenty-three. The only two postwar elections with less partisan turnover were 1988 (nine) and 1968 (eleven).
5. In 1990, only one Senate seat changed party hands; in every other postwar election, the number has exceeded two, with an average near seven.
6. Clinton and Trump were also both much less popular among independents than their predecessors in 2012; favorability averaged about 34 percent for Trump, 31 percent for Clinton, compared to about 50 percent for both candidates in 2012.
7. Ben Kamisar, "GOP Memo Says What to Do If Trump Is Nominee," *The Hill*, December 2, 2015; Michael Gerson, "Trump Declares War on America's Demography," *Washington Post*, August 13, 2015.
8. Gary C. Jacobson and Jamie L. Carson, *The Politics of Congressional Elections*, 9th ed. (New York: Rowman & Littlefield, 2016), 21–23.
9. The number of districts won against the grain in 2014, twelve, is lower than the sixteen mentioned in the text; the latter is different because the district-level presidential vote was recalculated for three states (North Carolina, Virginia, and Florida) following court-ordered redistricting.
10. Data on the district-level presidential vote in 2016 are not available as of this writing, but the picture is unlikely to change appreciably when they can be analyzed.
11. Logit is a variation on ordinary least squares regression more suitable for dependent variables that take only two discrete values—win or lose, in this case.
12. The value of incumbency is estimated here by a modified version of the Gelman-King index, which substitutes the district-level presidential vote in the current or, for midterms, most recent presidential election for the lagged vote, allowing

years ending in "2" and districts redrawn between apportionment decades to be included. For details, see Jacobson, "It's Nothing Personal: The Decline of the Incumbency Advantage in U.S. House Elections." I also estimated the 2016 incumbency advantage using the original Gelman-King procedure, and the coefficient was virtually identical: 2.4 percent.

13. The swing is measured by the change in the Democrat's share of the major-party vote from the previous election in stable districts. From 1972 onward, years ending in "2" cannot be included because almost all of the districts were redrawn. In 1952 and 1962, a sufficient number of districts remained unchanged after reapportionment (184 and 155, respectively) to include in the analysis.
14. Shanto Iyengar and Sean J. Westwook, "Fear and Loathing across Party Lines: New Evidence on Group Polarization, *American Journal of Political Science* 59 (July 2015): 690–707; Alan I. Abramowitz, "Partisan Nation: The Rise of Affective Partisan Polarization in the American Electorate," paper presented at the State of the Parties Conference, University of Akron, Akron Ohio, November 7–8, 2013.
15. "2016 Senate Race Ratings for March 25, 2016," *Cook Political Report*, March 25, 2016, cookpolitical.com/senate/charts/race-ratings/9421.
16. Averages are from weekly *Economist*/YouGov polls taken between August and November 2016, available at today.yougov.com/publicopinion/archive/.
17. The three early nonsupporters were Mark Kirk of Illinois, Mike Lee of Utah, and Chris Vance of Washington. Kirk and Vance were running in very blue states, but Lee opposed Trump, not popular among Utah Republicans, because of Trump's character and ideology. Pat Toomey of Pennsylvania refused to say how he would vote until election day, when he admitted a vote for Trump. Mark Callahan, a challenger in Oregon, refused to say how he would vote until the end.
18. The six who withdrew their support permanently were Lisa Murkowski of Alaska, John McCain of Arizona, Joe Heck of Nevada, Kelly Ayotte of New Hampshire, Rob Portman of Ohio, and Scott Milne of Vermont. The vacillators were Darryl Glenn of Colorado, Mike Crapo of Idaho, and John Thune of South Dakota.
19. Senate data from California (two Democrats) and Alaska (a Libertarian and independent took 44 percent of the vote) are excluded from Figure 7.6 and from the correlation in Figure 7.3. The Utah presidential vote includes the vote for Evan McMullin in the Republican total for this analysis; McMullen won 21 percent of the vote as an alternative for Republicans who could not accept Trump. The results are insensitive to this choice (the correlation of .93 is unchanged).
20. Based on extrapolation of data through October 16 on candidate receipts and through election day on independent spending.
21. Campaign Finance Institute, "Independent Spending in Senate Races Over $500 Million," news release, November 4, 2016.
22. See, for example, Gary C. Jacobson, "Obama and Nationalized Electoral Politics in the 2014 Midterm," *Political Science Quarterly* 130 (Spring 2015): 13; Gary C. Jacobson, "Congress: Partisanship and Polarization," in *The Elections of 2012*, ed. Michael Nelson (Washington, D.C.: CQ Press, 2014): 157–159.
23. Jacobson and Carson, *The Politics of Congressional Elections*, 97–101.
24. State exit poll data may be found at www.foxnews.com/politics/elections/2016/exit-polls.
25. Gary C. Jacobson, "How Do Campaigns Matter?" *Annual Review of Political Science* 18 (2015): 31–47.

26. Calculated from 216 Gallup, CBS News/*New York Times*, NBC News/*Wall Street Journal*, ABC News/*Washington Post*, Fox News, CNN, and AP-Gfk surveys.
27. "House and Senate Means, 1879–2016 (as of October 2016)," *Voteview Blog*, November 18, 2016, voteviewblog.com.
28. The average major-party vote for Obama was 66.8 percent in districts won by Democrats and 40.6 percent in districts won by Republicans in 2016.
29. Gary C. Jacobson, "Partisan Polarization in Presidential Support: The Electoral Connection," *Congress and the Presidency* 30 (Spring 2003): 8–11.
30. Lazaro Gamio, "Urban and Rural Americans Are Becoming Increasingly Polarized," *Washington Post*, November 17, 2016, www.washingtonpost.com/graphics/politics/2016-election/urban-rural-vote-swing/.
31. Marisa Abrajano and Zoltan L. Hajnal, *White Backlash: Immigration, Race, and American Politics* (Princeton, N.J.: Princeton University Press, 2015).
32. Trump received 82 percent favorable ratings from Republicans, 10 percent from Democrats, a difference of 72 points; the comparable figures for Obama in 2008 were 35, 95, and 60, respectively; for George W. Bush in 2000, they were 93, 31, and 62; and for Bill Clinton in 1992, they were 25, 88, and 63. See Jeffrey M. Jones, "Trump's Favorability Up, but Trails Other Presidents-Elect," *Gallup*, November 17, 2016, www.gallup.com/poll/197576/trump-favorability-trails-presidents-elect.aspx?g_source=Politics&g_medium=newsfeed&g_campaign=tiles.
33. Gary C. Jacobson, "The Obama Legacy and the Future of Partisan Conflict: Demographic Change and Generational Imprinting," *Annals of the American Academy of Political and Social Science* 667 (September 2016): 72–91.
34. Gary C. Jacobson, "Obama and Nationalized Electoral Politics in the 2014 Midterm," 1–26.
35. Jacobson and Carson, *The Politics of Congressional Elections*, 283–284.

8

The Presidency

Donald Trump and the Question of Fitness

Paul J. Quirk

For the institution of the presidency, the central event of the 2016 elections was the election of a president, Donald Trump, who was widely criticized as "unfit" for the office. This judgment was shared not only by Democrats and by his rivals during the Republican nomination contest, but also by former Republican presidents and presidential candidates, Republican policy experts, officials of prior Republican administrations, leading conservative commentators, and nearly all significant daily newspapers. A winning coalition of voters—about 49 percent of the two-party national vote but a clear majority of the Electoral College—disagreed. What should we make of this situation? Were there compelling grounds for the critics' harsh judgment? Or is Trump just a different kind of president, a rough-around-the-edges outsider, but a bold leader underappreciated by Washington insiders? In effect, a massive disagreement exists between nearly half the voters and most members of the political elite—those who have made careers practicing or commenting on politics and government. Which side proves correct may have vast consequences for the country and the world.

Trump's victory and the events of the campaign also raise questions about the character of the electoral process and the electorate. Considering the overwhelming opposition to his candidacy by elites, and the critical coverage by most of the mainstream media, what was it about the electoral process that made his election possible? How can we explain the support for Trump by so many voters? The 2016 election is in the books, and the country will experience the consequences, positive or negative. But these questions about the causes of Trump's election have bearing on presidential elections in 2020 and beyond.

This chapter proceeds, first, by reviewing the principal thinking, by scholars and others, about the personal qualifications for the office of president—what we may call, focusing on the low end of the relevant range, the question of fitness. Because some of this thinking could reflect elitist or insider biases rather than real requirements of the office, we assess the nature of the evidence about these qualifications. Second, the chapter considers the evidence about Donald Trump's qualifications or fitness that was exhibited and discussed during the campaign. What are the grounds for believing that either Trump's alleged weaknesses or his distinctive skills are genuinely important for his performance as president? Third, regardless of these judgments, Trump's victory in both the nomination process and the general election, despite widespread challenges to his qualifications and fitness, requires explanation. Does the election of Trump indicate something new about the electoral process or the behavior of voters? Finally, because the pre-inaugural stage of the presidential transition provides preliminary evidence on Trump's actual conduct and performance as president, the chapter concludes by assessing that evidence.

In considering these inevitably controversial issues, the chapter tries to steer between, on the one hand, mere expression of the author's partisan, ideological, or professional biases and, on the other hand, what is called "false equivalence" or "false balance"—an automatic assumption that there are two, more or less equally valid sides to every political debate and, thus, that to be objective and fair, political commentary should offer roughly equal support for both parties, or all candidates, in all cases.[1] In the end, the chapter acknowledges that there is uncertainty and room for debate about the prospects for the Trump presidency. Nevertheless, it concludes that Trump is indeed a remote outlier at the low end of any conventional scale of presidential qualifications. At a minimum, the risks of his presidency are extraordinary.

The Presidential Difference: Elite Perspectives

Regardless of party, ideology, or positions on issues, a vital function of the presidential election is to select an individual who is—by virtue of personality, experience, skills, and other traits—reasonably suited to the office of president. In fact, the performance of the presidency and the U.S. national government depends on the person of the president to an exceptional degree, by comparison with the roles of individuals in other elective offices or policymaking institutions.[2] The president's individual characteristics are crucial for several reasons. The president does not have unilateral power over legislation; he or she needs the consent of Congress to enact a law. The president must persuade Congress, rather than counting on party discipline for support on legislation. In that respect, the country is buffered from a president's possibly idiosyncratic preferences or arbitrary decisions. However, compared with the prime minister in a parliamentary system, for example, the president has a massively more complex management task.[3] He appoints and must oversee the coordination of a few hundred relatively high-ranking political appointees in the White House and the executive branch, most of whom would be permanent civil servants in any other major democracy.[4] Because the United States has exceptionally active, far-flung political, military, and economic activities in the international arena, the president is responsible for a vast array of challenging decisions. If the president and his immediate subordinates make mistakes, neglect important issues, or lack effective coordination, they can cause serious harm.[5]

In considering the important attributes the president should have, scholars have stressed such qualities as the ability to bargain with and persuade other policymakers,[6] the ability to lead the public through effective communication,[7] the ability to manage arrangements for advice and implementation,[8] and the possession of a sound personality, free of significant personality defects.[9] In an influential effort to sum up what he calls "the presidential difference," Fred Greenstein identifies six broad factors to account for the individual effects: (1) public communication, which includes choosing powerful and persuasive rhetoric and actually delivering it effectively, (2) organizational capacity, especially for designing advisory systems and managing their operation, (3) political skill, in forming coalitions and building support, within the particular context of Washington, (4) vision, to identify and convey a compelling account of his policy goals, (5) cognitive style, such as to ensure a reasonably informed and sophisticated understanding of important issues, and (6) emotional intelligence, such that the president is neither hampered by ineffectiveness in his interpersonal relations nor driven to destructive behavior by his own inner demons.[10] In part, scholars of presidential leadership merely divide up the relevant attributes in different ways. But they also disagree on some points—for example, about whether a president needs extensive knowledge of government and policy, or can rely on delegation to subordinates.[11]

In some ways, the evidence for the effects of any of the relevant attributes is unavoidably problematic. Every president has a multitude of potentially relevant attributes and tendencies. The situations in which presidents act are complex and only partly under their control; and there are few presidents on which to test generalizations about the effects of their attributes and conduct. Greenstein's six factors each have many aspects. And there have been only thirteen presidents in the modern era (from the 1930s to the present), prior to Trump, to observe.[12] There are many more variables than presidents. Greenstein's approach is to review some well-documented personal attributes, in each of the six categories, for each president from Franklin D. Roosevelt to Barack Obama, and then to use narrative accounts of major episodes to identify the influence of those attributes on the outcomes.

Not everything that happens in a presidency turns on the distinctive personal attributes of the president. In fact, the best evidence is that presidents have little influence over Congress, except insofar as the members share the president's policy goals for their own partisan, ideological, or constituency reasons.[13] Similarly, presidents have little influence on public opinion.[14] When a president goes on a public campaign to build support for a policy, public support, on average, does not budge. A president's persuasive skills are less important than many people suppose.[15]

Some attributes are important mainly for peripheral aspects of the presidency. People hold up the president for young children to emulate. The president represents the entire country in ceremonial functions—from laying a wreath at the Tomb of the Unknown Soldier to awarding the Medal of Freedom to a national hero. A president cannot serve in such roles as effectively if he has demonstrated manifestly poor character—for example, as President Bill Clinton did when he was caught lying under oath about a sexual relationship with a White House intern.[16] To some people, it was an offense to the moral order that Clinton was permitted to remain president. Perhaps the failure to remove Clinton from office did in some small way compromise the effectiveness of moral instruction about marital fidelity, sexual exploitation, truth-telling, or the importance of moral behavior. Yet, apart from the enormous distraction of his impeachment and trial, the episode had little apparent effect on his performance in government roles.[17] (It did reduce the Republicans' willingness to deal with him, however.) A president's suitability as a role model or ceremonial figure, or ability to command personal respect, is presumably a significant, yet still secondary consideration regarding qualifications for office.

Greenstein's narratives, however, offer convincing evidence that some of each president's important successes and failures do result from their own actions and decisions, and do reflect their distinctive personal attributes. On the positive side, among many examples, George H. W. Bush's numerous strong interpersonal relationships helped him build the international coalition that stood firm against Iraq's invasion of Kuwait in the first Gulf War. On the negative side, Lyndon Johnson's willingness to domineer and intimidate his advisers bolstered his disastrous commitment to the Vietnam War. Richard Nixon's paranoid tendencies, insecurity, and aggression led to the Watergate scandal that ended his presidency. Bill Clinton's impulsive self-indulgence and risk-taking led to his impeachment and near-removal from office in the Monica Lewinsky scandal. George W. Bush's rigidity and lack of intellectual curiosity promoted an incautious, premature decision to launch the Iraq War.[18]

References to personality defects, inner demons, and self-destructive behavior may seem to overdo the element of psychological drama. In fact, however, issues of emotional strength and stability have apparently played central roles in major events in a good percentage of presidencies—including, among more recent ones, those of Lyndon Johnson, Richard Nixon, and Bill Clinton.[19] Another aspect of a president's psychological state—age-related cognitive decline—may have played an important role in the Iran-contra scandal that tarnished the last part of Ronald Reagan's presidency.

In view of the complexities of presidential leadership and the limitations of the evidence, scholars cannot claim much precision either in identifying the specific attributes that favor or disfavor competent, constructive performance or in estimating how much, or under what circumstances, they do so. The literature shows that presidents matter—that they perform well or poorly, make good decisions or bad ones, with major consequences.[20] Costly mistakes occur quite frequently. To a great extent, any conclusions about specific attributes owe their credibility to how well they match with common experience in other organizational or social contexts.[21] Directly relevant experience matters, which is why professional sports teams hire coaches who have played or coached the sport. Rigid defense of prior judgments is a common failure in any leadership position and is often costly. Intelligence, attention to detail, and flexibility are generally rewarded. And so on. Commentators cannot predict presidential success or failure based solely on a candidate's experience, skills, or personality; but their concerns about qualifications or fitness for the presidency are generally well grounded.

Elections and Fitness

In a democracy, the citizens, not scholars, commentators, or other elites, choose the leaders of government. But if scholars and commentators are correct about which personal attributes are desirable in a president, the voters' interests will be best served if they manage to elect qualified presidents.

Realistically, a democratic electoral process will be, at best, moderately selective for the suitable personal attributes. American presidential elections and voting behavior have a number of features that tend to weaken selection based on qualifications for the office—making the selection less reliable with respect to them. Some of the selection-weakening features are long-standing; others are of recent origin.

Voters' Criteria

Many voters pay a great deal of attention to the personal qualities of the candidates—probably more than pay attention to their policy proposals.[22] But the qualities that voters look for are often different from those that significantly affect presidential performance.

One sort of quality that many voters care about and candidates strive for is interpersonal warmth, accessibility, or likability.[23] In a 2008 debate in the Democratic nomination campaign, a moderator asked Hillary Clinton whether she was likable. Her opponent, Barack Obama, interjected, "Hillary, you're likable enough." Candidates make a major production of appearing at coffee shops in casual clothes and chatting amiably with the customers.

A second broad quality is personal morality—including virtues such as truthfulness, faithfulness, honesty, empathy, and generosity, among others. Candidates put their families on display, tell heart-warming stories about helping sick children, or pass out food packages at the site of a natural disaster. They show up at church, with a press entourage. Campaigns and the media give a great deal of attention to particular episodes that one side or the other portrays as relevant to these personal moral qualities. In 2012, Republican candidate Mitt Romney suffered criticism and ridicule for being reckless or cruel because he had once made a pet dog ride on top of the car on a family road trip. Democrat John Edwards was criticized for paying $200 for a haircut. The media generally give vast attention to evidence that remotely suggests financial wrong-doing or even ethically marginal conflicts of interest.

These concerns are not entirely irrational. People may realize that they will see the president in diverse settings, from State of the Union addresses to Easter egg hunts on the White House lawn, hundreds of times during a four-year term. Life is a bit more agreeable if you like and respect a president whom you are forced to see almost daily. But these attributes generally have little bearing on presidential performance. In the movie *Sleeper*, the Woody Allen character says that when Richard Nixon was president, they counted the silverware every time he left the White House. But petty financial dishonesty is not actually a pressing concern with respect to presidents. Nor is the president's comfort and skill in interacting with ordinary citizens. Nor is a strict policy of truth-telling in all matters even an appropriate expectation.[24] A cold, formal, conceited snob with lax financial ethics and some skill in dissembling could lead the country wisely and effectively.

Another preference of ordinary citizens is actually perverse, from the standpoint of presidential qualifications: Many voters evidently prefer an "outsider" to a candidate who has held elected or appointed office in Washington, or even in a major state capital.[25] Candidates such as Ben Carson, a retired pediatric neurosurgeon who sought the Republican nomination with no prior political or government experience, claim outsider status as a major selling point. Candidates argue about who is the most pure outsider. Outsider candidates have been competitive at times in the polls—not only Carson and businesswoman Carly Fiorina in the 2016 Republican nomination campaign, but also Herman Cain (owner of a chain of carry-out pizza restaurants) in the 2012 Republican race. In view of the complexities of the policymaking process, a candidate with no prior experience in how government works is a risky choice.

In these discussions, debate often centers on contested interpretations of single episodes or situations, resulting in judgments that are likely to overlook the bulk of the evidence about the candidate's life and career. Was Romney in fact mean to the dog? Did Barack Obama go to church services presided over by a minister who was hostile to white people? The campaign debate sometimes resembles the media coverage of a criminal case, in which establishing exactly what a suspect did or did not do on a particular occasion is the essence of the matter. But to the extent that a personal quality actually matters, only general or repetitive patterns of behavior are usually important for predicting future performance.

In sum, voters are highly concerned about presidential candidates' personal attributes—and what are often called "character issues." But most of their attention focuses on matters that have little or no diagnostic value for predicting presidential performance.

Campaign Information

An American presidential campaign bombards the voters with virtually daily, prominent news coverage for at least a full year, with less intense coverage for most of the previous year. However, as scholars have shown in research spanning many elections, the quality of the information that voters receive is in many ways unsatisfactory.[26] Most of the criticism concerns the shallow treatment, in campaign debate and the media, of policy issues and the candidates' positions. But apart from the limited range of so-called character issues, discussed earlier, the same shallowness pertains to the skills, experience, and personal attributes of the candidates.

The central finding is that coverage is dominated by "horse-race" information—who is leading and why, what candidates' strategies are, and how events are helping or hurting their prospects. In a word, media coverage helps people figure out who will win, not who should be president. Coverage of policy issues is accordingly skimpy—amounting to only 10 percent of all news coverage, in one recent study.[27] This coverage reflects the fact that most readers and viewers decide on their preferred party or candidate early in the campaign. Their motivation for attending to news is to see how their candidate is doing. By catering to that audience, however, the media fail to provide in-depth information that might help undecided voters make an intelligent decision, or might change the minds of some early deciders.

Although media coverage of presidential campaigns pays lavish attention to "character issues," it rarely explores issues of fitness in relation to plausible requirements for satisfactory presidential performance. In 2000, the news media thoroughly scrutinized available records to assess rumors that George W. Bush had failed to show up for National Guard duty. It gave only minimal attention to his habit, as governor of Texas, of putting in short work days and avoiding lengthy discussions of issues, and to his lack of information about national and international policies. Media coverage that sought to inform voters about the candidate's qualifications would have discussed the implications that Bush's relaxed, hands-off approach would have for his presidency. A serious effort to explore qualifications would feature full discussion of a candidate's experience, skills, and personality, and all major aspects of the president's job.

The most intense exposure voters have to the candidates as individuals comes in televised presidential debates.[28] During the nomination process, the debates occur within each party and may have as many as ten participants on stage before the field is winnowed down. During the general election campaign, the debates will have one Democratic and one Republican participant, with a third-party candidate on rare occasions.[29] Presidential debates are notoriously poor at exploring the substantive merits of the candidates' positions and claims.[30] Among other reasons, the candidates simply pivot from difficult questions and deliver tangentially related prepared remarks, and there is generally no fact-checking by an authoritative source in real time. Even the next day's media coverage includes little independent assessment of broader, more complex claims (as opposed to simple facts).

With respect to personal qualities, debates certainly reveal some things about candidates—their degree of preparation, quickness on their feet, nervousness, and propensity to anger, among others. But once in office, presidents almost never debate anyone. Nor do they ever have to respond to a difficult question, or decide a complex issue, within seconds without help. Occasionally, candidates may reveal a notable lack of serious thinking in their policy positions, as when Texas governor Rick Perry could not remember the third cabinet department that he had proposed to eliminate. But usually candidates who have appeared uninformed in various campaign settings perform well enough in televised debates to bolster their credibility with the voters. Both Ronald Reagan in 1980 and George W. Bush in 2000 were thought to outperform the low expectations of commentators and thereby helped their campaigns.

One feature of media coverage of campaigns that sometimes diminishes the availability of helpful information for voters is the expectation of political balance on the part of mainstream news organizations.[31] Nothing guarantees that two opposing candidates do the same amount of misrepresentation of policy information; offer policies that are equally credible to independent experts; have equally relevant experience or equally sound personalities, and so on. Journalists have difficulty negotiating the resulting balancing act—avoiding assessments that merely reflect their own partisan or ideological views, and yet avoiding false equivalence, which ignores real and important differences to maintain the appearance of fairness.[32]

In one area of fitness or qualifications for the presidency, the flow of potentially relevant information is constrained by an official rule of the American Psychiatric Association—the so-called *Goldwater Rule*—which bars psychiatrists from making public statements about the psychological condition of political candidates.[33] Adopted after an embarrassing 1964 episode in which numerous psychiatrists commented for a magazine article—adversely, contradictorily (citing numerous, completely distinct personality disorders), and clearly inaccurately—on the personality of 1964 Republican presidential candidate Barry Goldwater, the rule declares it unethical to pronounce on the mental health of a public figure without having examined him or her and obtained the individual's consent for such comment. The effect of the Goldwater rule is that the psychiatric profession is silent, even individually, on the psychological soundness of presidential candidates. The rule is arguably better suited to protecting the psychiatry profession from controversy than to providing informed advice to the public.

Primary Elections

The challenges for voters of sizing up candidates as potential presidents are more important and difficult because the major American political parties choose their candidates for the office through a long series of primary elections and open caucuses in each state, with ordinary voters doing the choosing. This nomination process resulted, in part unexpectedly, from reforms calling for greater participation by ordinary voters that the Democratic Party adopted prior to the 1972 election.[34] To avoid possible challenges to their delegates, state Democratic parties established primaries and caucuses, and state Republican parties essentially imitated the Democrats to avoid a competitive disadvantage. From the beginning, the primary-based nomination process has had serious critics, with some of the concerns centering on its ability to select well-qualified candidates for president.[35]

Three main concerns have emerged about the primary-based nomination process. First, ordinary voters lack awareness of the leadership skills and working relationships of potential presidential candidates. As political scientist Nelson Polsby wrote early in the party reform era, primary voters are not in a position to identify the natural leaders of their party.[36] They are not familiar with the potential candidates' experience, skills, and personal attributes relevant for the presidency. Second, primary voters are more ideologically extreme than the electorate as a whole.[37] Third, primary elections present voters with choices among several candidates, not just two major-party candidates, as in the general election. A candidate can win early primary elections with a modest share of the vote—say, a 25–30 percent share, with six or seven candidates in the race—and then ride the resulting momentum to victory when the field narrows in the later primaries. This strategic situation can benefit an extreme candidate, since there often will be fewer competitors at the extremes. It can also benefit a candidate whose support is intense, but narrow, with widespread opposition, for whatever reason. Such a candidate is not penalized for being strongly opposed by most voters.

As Polsby warned, primary elections appear to pose considerable risk that a party's nominee will lack relevant experience and skills, be ideologically extreme, or have poor relationships with other leaders. Such a candidate presumably would be more likely to lose the general election, costing the party the chance to govern. But he or she could also end up as president, imposing an unqualified or extreme chief executive on the country.

Selections: Nominees and Contenders

The proof of these concerns is of course in the candidates. However, assessing the evidence has not been straightforward. Presidential elections generate small numbers of candidates—one for each party every four years, including an incumbent president almost every second election. From 1972 to 2012, the two parties, taken together, nominated only fourteen individuals for president who were not already sitting presidents. At the same time, of course, other changes were also occurring in the political system, potentially obscuring the effects of the primaries.

Moreover, one widely read book claimed, on the basis of sketchy evidence, that by the 2000s party insiders had recaptured control of party nominations.[38] Nominations were decided through an "invisible primary" in which candidates competed for endorsements and campaign contributions, with the winner ultimately dominating the actual primaries. The argument implied that Polsby's concerns about the nominations were exaggerated or misplaced.

Nevertheless, there is evidence for the reality of Polsby's concerns. In the first election under the new primary-based nomination process, in 1972, the Democrats nominated George McGovern, the most liberal member of the Senate. He ran a left-liberal campaign and was buried in the election by the incumbent Republican president, Richard Nixon. In 1976, the Democrats nominated the relatively inexperienced and often naïve Jimmy Carter, who defeated a Watergate-weakened Republican ticket, and then went on to an error-prone and generally unsuccessful presidency. In 1980, the Republican primaries produced a victory for Ronald Reagan—who was at the time far to the right of the mainstream of even the Republican Party. Despite two terms as governor of California, Reagan was notable for misinformation about policy. After defeating the somewhat hapless reelection effort of Carter, Reagan conducted a highly controversial, polarizing presidency. Contrary to what Polsby might have expected in such a case, Reagan ended his presidency generally popular and a conservative icon, with lasting effects on American politics.

In contrast, the five nonincumbent nominees from 1984 to 1996 (Democrats Walter Mondale, Michael Dukakis, and Bill Clinton; and Republicans George H. W. Bush and Bob Dole) were all experienced, informed politicians in the ideological mainstream of their parties. In 2000, however, Republican nominee George W. Bush had been a successful governor of Texas; but he was known for short working hours and a hands-off approach and was notably uninformed about national issues. In effect, Bush had even less substantive experience than his brief political résumé indicated.

In 2012, another kind of evidence emerged, mainly on the Republican side—namely, candidates who were notably inexperienced, ideologically extreme, or both, and who, although not ultimately successful in winning the nomination, appeared highly competitive at some stage of the process. In both 2012 and 2016, very large fields emerged of experienced, talented, candidates in the ideological mainstream of the Republican Party. But they did not dominate the contests. In 2012, Michele Bachmann, a junior House member notorious for flamboyant, wildly uninformed, far-right pronouncements, led the polling in the important Iowa Republican caucuses at an early stage. Herman Cain, who had no prior political experience or national reputation, led the national Republican primary polls for a month in fall 2011. Ron Paul, a House member from Texas with by far the most conservative voting record in the House—he voted *no* on routine appropriations bills that otherwise passed unanimously—outlasted most other members of the large Republican field, other than the winner Mitt Romney, as did Rick Santorum, among the most conservative senators on social issues. In 2016, Ben Carson, a Christian conservative pediatric neurosurgeon with no prior political experience, briefly led the large Republican field in national polls.

The Democrats offer only one similar case, though a notable one: In the 2016 Democratic nomination campaign, Sen. Bernie Sanders of Vermont ran a strong second to early front-runner Hillary Clinton—despite being the most liberal member of the Senate.

Taking all the above considerations together—voters' criteria, the quality of campaign information, and the primary-based nomination process—nominating campaigns in recent years have appeared quite open to candidates with extreme ideological positions, severely limited relevant experience, and minimal knowledge of government or policy. The most extreme candidates nominated have been the Democrat McGovern and the Republican Reagan. The least experienced have been the Democrat Carter and the Republican George W. Bush. The least knowledgeable about, or even interested in, policy issues and governmental processes have been Reagan and Bush. Some of those who had substantial support for a period—Paul, Bachmann, Cain, Carson, and Sanders—were even more pronounced cases of inexperience or ideological extremity. But of these, only the ideologically extreme Sanders was highly competitive.

Donald Trump and Qualifications for the Presidency

The nomination and election to the presidency of Donald Trump was a major surprise. In numerous ways, his experience, dispositions, and other attributes appeared to make him essentially ineligible for serious consideration.

Trump's Democratic opponent, Hillary Clinton, was, if anything, exceptionally qualified. She had some serious political liabilities, including an enduring distaste for her from a sizable group of voters, and she had made at least one major mistake in her time in government—using a private email server to handle official communications while she was secretary of state. In his report to Congress on the FBI's investigation, Director James Comey concluded that although there was no clear evidence that Clinton or her staff had intended to violate laws, they had been "extremely careless in their handling of very sensitive, highly classified information." Comey also made clear that some of Clinton's public claims and explanations about the practice had been false, although he did not accuse her of perjury. However, a newspaper investigation pointed out that similar practices had been commonplace in Washington at around the same time, including on the part of recent Republican secretaries of state.[39] With respect to qualifications for the presidency, the central fact about the email scandal was that it was not part of any more general pattern—carelessness about security, management failure, illegality, or whatever. The intense Republican criticism of Clinton's conduct in the email scandal rarely or never linked it to any other episode in Clinton's career.

Congressional Republicans spent about $7 million in several investigations of Clinton's role in the failure to provide adequate security for an American diplomatic compound in Benghazi, Libya, where four Americans were killed by rioting Islamic radicals. But decisions about how many guards to post at such a location were handled well below the level of a secretary of state, and the investigations came up empty of wrong-doing on Clinton's part.

Republicans and conservatives naturally had many objections to Clinton's candidacy—mainly on policy or ideological grounds. But from the standpoint of an informed, politically neutral conception of qualifications for the presidency, she was, if anything, superior. She had been a major adviser in her husband Bill Clinton's White House; an effective senator from New York; and a respected, accomplished secretary of state. Clinton was highly knowledgeable about national issues; took positions that reflected the center-left mainstream of her party; and had well developed proposals on a wide range of subjects. She was criticized on various grounds, often with considerable validity—too secretive, too calculating, too eager to build her personal wealth, and too insensitive to potential conflicts of interest. Some people undoubtedly objected, on the basis of sexist stereotypes, to the idea of a female president. But Clinton had no glaring weaknesses from the standpoint of, for example, Greenstein's six factors: no problematic emotional or cognitive tendencies—in short, no attribute that nonpartisan commentators cited as a serious risk of a Clinton presidency.

Over the course of his eighteen-month campaign for the presidency, Trump demonstrated far more numerous and serious deficiencies in relation to standard conceptions of qualifications for the presidency than any competitive candidate ever before. To be sure, he had important valuable qualities. He was a highly successful real estate developer and television and entertainment producer, as well as a popular TV performer. Although always a polarizing figure—disapproved by the majority of people—Trump had an exceptional ability to attract attention and support from a sizable segment of the public. He identified some genuine and arguably overlooked concerns and communicated effectively to many people. Using common words, simple sentences, and frequent repetition, he was especially effective with less educated voters.

Trump's negative traits were numerous and readily identified, although in some cases their relevance to his potential performance as president was debatable. Among reasonably neutral or independent commentators, and many Republican leaders, it was widely accepted that Trump exhibited each of the following traits:

1. He made false statements with extreme frequency. The various politically neutral fact-checking websites that rate the veracity of statements by politicians agreed that Trump's frequency of clearly false statements was "off the charts" by comparison to any other presidential candidate in the 2016 race or in the roughly two prior decades of such fact-checking. The falsehoods ranged from minor to important (for example, a claim that many economists supported his tax plan), and from plausible to bizarre

(for example, a claim that Barack Obama had "created ISIS"). They included denials of his own previous statements that were immediately available on video. Some observers wondered whether Trump lived in a fantasy world. His supporters often acknowledged his rampant falsehoods, saying that they "take Trump seriously, but not literally."

2. He issued a stream of crude insults against his opponents and others who criticized or offended him. The "Upshot" blog of the *New York Times* maintained a list of more than two hundred people, places, institutions, and other entities that Trump had insulted on Twitter during his campaign. The center-right news magazine *The Economist*, in a cover story, charged Trump with "the debasing of American politics."

3. He ran his businesses and financial affairs in ways that encouraged or allowed illegal or unethical conduct for his financial benefit. The sales practices and instructional methods used by Trump University led to a class-action lawsuit alleging fraud; the suit was eventually settled, awarding the plaintiffs sizable amounts of compensation. Thousands of lawsuits were filed against Trump's hotels and other properties, often brought by small businesses that had not been paid for their services. Trump's foundation admitted that it had used donors' contributions, illegally, to benefit Trump.

On at least one point, some of the criticism of Trump's business practices was unwarranted. Democratic critics alleged, and Trump eventually admitted, that he had paid little or no federal income tax for an eighteen-year period over which he was able to distribute a nearly $1 billion one-year loss to reduce his annual obligation. Clinton and the media pounced on the admission. But Trump insisted, correctly, that normal business practice expects people to use all means within the law to reduce their tax obligations. On the other hand, Democratic and media critics were on strong grounds in complaining that Trump's refusal to release his tax returns, unprecedented in recent decades, pointed to a wide range of possible unethical or unsavory conduct.

4. He allegedly had a history of aggressive sexual conduct toward women, which in some cases had reached the level of criminal sexual assault. Undeniably, he had claimed to engage in such conduct. In the infamous *Access Hollywood* outtakes leak, Trump bragged about kissing women or grabbing their genitals without their permission—explaining that you can get away with such conduct "when you're a star." In the aftermath of the tape's release, nine women came forward with public allegations that Trump had groped or forced himself on them. (They did not claim actual or attempted rape.) None of the allegations of harassment or assault concerned recent events and none were proved. Trump claimed that the bragging was mere "locker-room talk" and that all of the women's complaints were fabricated. In some of the cases, however, the women had told others of the

assaults at the time they occurred, describing some of the same methods that Trump bragged about—making Trump's blanket denial hard to credit.

5. He was prone to statements and practices that amounted to, or at least approached, racial and religious bigotry. According to some reports, Trump had ordered or condoned exclusion of African Americans from renting in his apartment buildings and from holding certain jobs in his casinos. During the campaign, he retweeted inflammatory material from avowed white supremacists and resisted demands that he reject their support. But some of the Democrats' accusations against Trump were dubious. For example, he was called racist for claiming that, because he planned to build a wall on the Mexican border, a Mexican-American judge could not handle the Trump University fraud trial fairly. His claim was widely disparaged. But as for racism, Mexicans are not a race and there was no evidence of what Trump would have said about a Canadian judge if he had planned a wall on the Canadian border.

A forgiving supporter could argue that none of these attributes or tendencies would actually matter to Trump's performance as president: He would stop offering the constant falsehoods or people would learn to ignore them. He would tone down the insults, at least when they might affect important relationships. He would have no occasion for business fraud or nonpayment of debts. He would be too closely watched to assault any women or to discriminate against minority group members directly; and in any case, he would not promote policies that tolerated sexual assault or racial discrimination. For each of the preceding items, in other words, one could take the position, "Yes, that was regrettable, but not relevant." This response would lean heavily on the hope that Trump would change his behavior when he became president, or that his personal proclivities would not affect his policy decisions or official acts.

Trump, however, also had other attributes and tendencies, widely recognized by observers, with more direct bearing on presidential performance:

6. He entirely lacked experience in government, public service, the military, or public affairs. He was the only candidate with no such experience to win a party presidential nomination since 1940, and only the second in American history.

7. He was extremely uninformed about issues. In meetings with newspaper editorial boards, he left them dismayed by his lack of familiarity with the major issues facing the country. Relatedly, he had a very short attention span for receiving information. The ghostwriter who actually wrote most of Trump's book, *The Art of the Deal*, said that Trump was unable or unwilling to focus on the book for more than a few minutes at a time. Trump largely declined to prepare for the presidential debates, which polls and analysts agreed he lost badly.

8. His policy positions were casual, lacking serious deliberation, and often, by broad consensus among relevant experts, unworkable or dangerous. He promised to cut back the U.S. commitment to NATO, to withdraw military protection from Japan and Korea (suggesting that they acquire nuclear weapons to defend themselves), to demand drastic changes in trade relationships (tearing up existing agreements with China, in particular), to cut taxes massively while rejecting cuts in middle-class entitlement programs, to punish companies that moved plants outside the country, and to remove several million undocumented immigrants. He promised to build a wall on the Mexican border and require Mexico to pay for it. All of these positions, and others, were derided by relevant experts as impossible or destructive.

9. He made numerous promises and threats that indicated ignorance of, or lack of concern about, provisions of the Constitution. He threatened to punish news organizations, such as the *New York Times*, that had criticized him. He promised to resume torture in antiterrorism investigations. He explained that he would force the military to carry out orders that violated international human rights laws—such as killing family members of terrorists. He called for religious discrimination on a massive scale—prohibiting any Muslim from entering the country, and building a registry of all Muslims already living in the country. He cited the internment of Japanese Americans during World War II—pronounced by Republican president Gerald Ford "a national mistake . . . [which] shall never again be repeated"—as a supporting precedent for this measure. He called for jailing protesters who burned the American flag, a protected form of expression under long-settled constitutional doctrine.

In a more general way, Trump sometimes ignored, rejected, or did not understand fundamental values of the constitutional system. He proclaimed that "only I" can solve the country's problems, language characteristic of authoritarian rule, rather than a representative democracy with three independent branches of government. He threatened that he would prosecute and jail Hillary Clinton in the email matter, even though the FBI had found that her conduct did not warrant prosecution. He publicly encouraged a foreign power, Russia, to interfere with the election by publishing Democrats' private communications.

10. Most important, in the end, he exhibited a consistent set of highly problematic personality traits, which fit broadly under the rubric of "narcissistic personality." Abiding by the Goldwater rule, many psychiatrists withheld opinions. But a few psychiatrists and numerous psychologists and other mental health professionals weighed in with a verdict of narcissism that was widely shared. Psychologist Sam Vaknin listed nine criteria for narcissism and observed that Trump clearly exhibited each one. As a reporter summarized the statement,

> A narcissist feels grandiose and self-important, and often exaggerates to the point of lying [about] his or her accomplishments and skills. A narcissist is obsessed with fantasies of "unlimited success, fame, fearsome power or omnipotence." The narcissist is convinced that he or she is special and, because of that, should be treated as a high-status person. A narcissist requires "excessive admiration" and feels entitled, demanding special and often unreasonable treatment. A narcissist is "interpersonally exploitative," using others to achieve his or her own goals, and is also devoid of empathy. A narcissist is also envious of others and will seek to hurt or destroy people, and, lastly, a narcissist "behaves arrogantly and haughtily," and "rages when frustrated, contradicted, or confronted by people he or she considers inferior to him or her and unworthy."[40]

Trump manifested three kinds of narcissistic behavior. First, he made outlandish claims of power, knowledge, skill, and success: "I know more about ISIS than the generals." Referring to the country's various problems, "I alone can fix it." The grandiosity of such claims would have embarrassed someone with a well-balanced personality. Second, as noted earlier, he made radically unconventional policy pronouncements, with minimal consultation or deliberation, and without specific plans or explanations. (A typical elaboration: "It will be so great. Believe me.") He either had supreme confidence in his own off-the-cuff judgments, or he felt entitled to say whatever came to mind and abandon it later.

Third, Trump responded to criticism or opposition with unconcealed, long-lasting, and often destructive anger, often losing sight of his own best interests in his efforts to exact punishment. Among many examples, he attacked the reporters at his rallies as "totally corrupt"; he barred reporters for major newspapers from receiving press credentials to cover his campaign; and he went on tirades lasting several days—attacking debate moderator and Fox News commentator Megyn Kelly; the parents of a Muslim American soldier killed in Iraq, Khizr and Ghazala Khan, who had severely criticized Trump at the Democratic National Convention; and a former winner of Trump's Miss Universe pageant who complained that Trump had treated her abusively for gaining weight.

Two major magazines, the *Atlantic* and *Vanity Fair*, consulted qualified professionals and found essentially complete agreement that Trump had very strong and well-defined narcissistic traits.[41] Harvard psychologist Howard Gardner, when asked for a summary assessment of Trump's personality, said "remarkably narcissistic." Clinical psychologist George Simon said that Trump was "so classic" that he was collecting video clips of him to illustrate narcissism in workshops, sparing him the task of hiring actors and writing vignettes for them to perform.

Trump's angry responses seemed at times to be out of control. At the very least they went far beyond the limits of generally accepted conduct and were widely considered self-destructive. Because he often carried on his vendettas in a late-night stream of tweets, there was discussion that his campaign aides might try to take away his phone.

This second group of traits—inexperience, lack of information, reckless policy pronouncements, disregard for the Constitution, and pervasive narcissism—have definite and alarming, if not dire, implications for Trump's performance as president. Casual decisions on major issues, angry response to criticism, defiant self-assertion, and uncalculating retribution: The possibilities for calamitous failure are unlimited.

None of Trump's problematic attributes was a matter of partisanship, ideology, or group interest. And they led to a rejection of his candidacy, on grounds of unfitness, by an unprecedented range of Republican or conservative public figures, commentators, and publications. These included all five of the living former Republican presidential nominees (although Bob Dole and, under reelection pressure, John McCain recanted); the three leading conservative magazines (the *National Review*, the *Weekly Standard*, and *Commentary*); prominent conservative columnists George Will, David Brooks, Ross Douthat, and Erick Erickson (editor of the "Red State" blog); fifty Republican foreign policy experts who signed an open letter;[42] and many other Republican officials. Republican members of Congress, afraid of punishment from the Trump supporters among their constituents, mostly declared that they would vote for Trump in the general election and then avoided talking about him or defending his conduct.[43] When asked about Trump's latest violation of traditional norms, they often simply refused to comment. In one indication of the Republican confusion, a poll showed that almost 70 percent of Republican congressional staff members either planned to vote for a different presidential candidate than their boss or did not know which candidate their boss planned to vote for.[44] Near the end of the campaign, Trump had been endorsed by only one significant newspaper, the *Las Vegas Review-Journal*, owned by the billionaire Republican donor Sheldon Adelson. Numerous Republican newspapers withheld their endorsement from the Republican nominee, in some cases endorsing Clinton. *USA Today*, which had never before made an endorsement in a presidential election, pronounced Trump unfit and urged readers to vote for Clinton.

The Voters and Trump's Fitness

Although Trump lost the national popular vote, he came within two percentage points of Clinton's vote share and won the election in the Electoral College. In the immediate aftermath of his upset victory, a great deal of attention focused on why the poll-based forecasts had been wrong.[45] But that was not the major puzzle. At the beginning of the election year, the so-called "fundamentals"—the economy, Obama's approval ratings, and the eight-year Democratic occupancy of the White House—predicted a close election.[46] In the late spring and early summer, both the polls and the perceived greater weaknesses of Trump as a candidate made Clinton the betting favorite. If, at that time, a sophisticated observer of American elections knew what was coming in the summer and fall for the two campaigns—on the one hand, the FBI's mixed-message clearing of Clinton of any criminal charges in the email scandal, and on the other hand, Trump's multiple apparent political calamities (the poorly received Republican convention; the prolonged feuds with the Kahn family and the former Miss Universe; defeats in the three televised presidential debates; investigative reports showing financial improprieties, benefiting Trump, in the operations of the Trump Foundation; intelligence reports of Russian intervention on Trump's behalf; and, above all, the revelation of Trump's bragging about groping and kissing women without permission, corroborated by complaints of alleged victims)—that observer would have predicted a massive victory for Clinton. Considering all of this—enough bad news to sink several candidacies in previous elections—the real puzzle is what accounts for Trump's victory. The psychologist Howard Gardner, after his comment on Trump's personality in fall 2015, had added, "For me, the compelling question is the psychological state of his supporters. They are unable or unwilling to make a connection between the challenges faced by any president and the knowledge and behavior of Donald Trump."[47] A year later, the question pertained to almost half of the voters.

This chapter is not the place for a detailed interpretation of the campaign. We can, however, point out that there are two quite different issues about voters. First, why did as many as 30–40 percent of Republican primary voters (roughly 15–20 percent of the entire electorate) overlook Trump's deficiencies as a candidate and potential president when several other, well-qualified Republicans were available to vote for? Second, why did 46 percent of the national electorate overlook those deficiencies (and the series of failures, scandals, and embarrassments in the summer and fall), when the only alternative capable of winning was a normal or above-average, moderate-liberal Democratic candidate, Hillary Clinton?[48] In effect, there are two different phenomena to explain: on the one hand, *enthusiasm* for Trump, in the presence of Republican alternatives; and on the other hand, *tolerance* of Trump, in the absence of such alternatives.

Various observers, drawing on a wide range of evidence, have pointed to a number of sources of Trump enthusiasm. These include white racial resentment and disaffection with the country's increasing racial and ethnic diversity; white working-class economic anxiety, with associated beliefs about adverse effects of trade and immigration; populist rejection of big-city, coastal elites, especially among the less educated and rural white population; a rejection of "political correctness" and left-wing identity politics; and attraction to the idea of an authoritarian strongman.[49] These explanations are not necessarily in conflict and in some cases are closely related. The correct account might combine several of these influences.

Notably, such influences are all consistent with identity-based, emotional, or "gut-level" responses, as opposed to informed, deliberated, or rational ones.[50] Indeed, political scientists have long exaggerated the rationality and competence of ordinary citizens.[51] In identity-based responses, a certain group (say, less educated, rural whites) may support a candidate because he proclaims their virtue, gives voice to their resentments, or sounds like they do. Group members may not do much deliberating about the consequences of that candidate becoming president. They use voting to affirm their identity. Such identity-based, emotional responses make sense of the fact that Trump appealed successfully to working-class whites, even though his policies offered few benefits for working-class people, and far more for the wealthy.[52] These uncalculating emotional responses also make sense of Trump enthusiasts' lack of concern about his fitness for the office.

The main source of the much broader, general-election Trump tolerance is less mysterious. It was mostly a Republican vote. The electorate has become increasingly polarized on partisan lines, and voters of each party are increasingly consistent in supporting their party's presidential nominee.[53] In research on public opinion about public policy, scholars have debated whether partisan citizens rationally process substantive information about issues or merely react on the basis of what their party's leaders are saying.

In the 2016 election, Trump's candidacy, with his glaring weaknesses and issues of fitness, cast light on a related question: Do partisan citizens process substantive information about the candidates? Indeed, do they even process party-labeled cues and information about their party's nominee? Specifically, the election demonstrated what happens when large numbers of Republican legislators, former administration officials, policy experts, financial contributors, intellectuals, and newspapers reject, or at least distance themselves from, the Republican nominee. In the event, roughly 90 percent of Republican party identifiers voted for Trump—about the same rate of party loyalty as the Democratic candidate enjoyed—suggesting that Trump's personal deficiencies, and the rejection or grudging support of his candidacy by a broad spectrum of Republican elites, had virtually no effect on Republican voters.

Despite the differences between the candidates, Clinton's voters were probably roughly similar to Trump's in their propensity for identity-based emotional responses and party loyalty. To be sure, the Democratic ticket had a historically unprecedented absolute advantage with better educated voters.[54] This may suggest that informed, deliberated vote decisions played a larger role in her support than it did in Trump's. But Clinton's campaign also relied heavily on identity-based appeals, directed primarily toward women and African Americans.[55] In general, the nature of voting behavior is not dramatically different between the two parties.

Scholars will be analyzing the sources of support for Trump for a number of years. If the lesson of the 2016 election is that voters have become more prone to identity-based and emotional responses, especially in the primaries; more prone to strict party loyalty in general elections; and less deliberative or responsive to substantive information about issues and candidates, then future presidential elections may bring even more divisive or authoritarian departures from American political norms.

The Transition and Prospects

Although a president-elect does not take office until the inauguration on January 20, his activities from election day until then—the so-called transition period—lay the foundation for his presidency and provide insights into its character. The transition is a difficult challenge for the president-elect because he needs to select numerous high-level administration officials; get up to speed on pressing issues, especially in foreign policy; and make plans for major policy initiatives.[56]

In his transition, Trump and his advisers had distinctive circumstances to deal with. First, the Republicans had solid majority control of both the House and the Senate. Because the party has moved steadily to the right in recent years, Congress will likely have a more cohesive ideological majority than any previous Congress in fifty years. If Trump were a regular Republican, he would be in a position to implement a sweeping agenda of conservative policy change.[57] Second, however, Trump's positions on several major issues during the campaign—among them, trade, taxes, Social Security, infrastructure, and spending—were out of step with established Republican doctrine.[58] He thus faced challenges in developing an effective collaboration with the Republican Congress. Finally, the campaign had left the country even more severely divided than it had been in recent times. Trump's positions and rhetoric had been notably divisive, and protests of his election—a new genre of protest in American politics—occurred in a number of cities. Whether he recognized it or not, Trump had an interest in subduing the division.

In some cases, Trump's transition decisions were predictable and appropriate. That his skilled campaign manager and sometimes personal handler Kellyanne Conway became White House counselor made sense. But the same kinds of deficiencies in deliberation, management, and personal conduct that Trump exhibited in the campaign showed up in several ways in the transition.

Although some of his early appointments received wide approval, others appeared ill considered. In his first announcements, Trump named Reince Priebus, the current chair of the Republican National Committee, to be White House chief of staff; and Steve Bannon, an adviser to Trump's campaign and editor of the "alt-right" *Breitbart News* website, to be his leading White House political strategist. Although Priebus had no direct experience in government, he had been Trump's main bridge to mainstream Republicans, and they applauded his appointment. But Bannon had been the instigator of some of Trump's most extreme positions and divisive rhetoric, and had savaged Speaker of the House Paul Ryan for his occasional willingness to cooperate with Democrats. Bannon was a target of media criticism for *Breitbart*'s pandering to racist and anti-Semitic elements of the alt-right. Pairing Priebus and Bannon in top White House positions appeared to set up pitched battles over the tone and direction of Trump's presidency.

Trump evidently chose key appointees for their emphatic agreement with his hardline views on Islam and China. For the post of National Security Adviser, he named Michael T. Flynn, a retired general who had been dismissed by President Obama as director of the Defense Intelligence Agency. Flynn tweeted that "fear of Muslims is RATIONAL" and was a promoter of various conspiracy theories—for example, that Democrats had imposed Islamic sharia law in parts of Florida.[59] After Flynn's appointment was announced, numerous permanent staff at the National Security Council, not wanting to serve under him, reportedly planned to leave the agency. Similarly, Trump named Peter Navarro, an economist known as a "strident critic of China," to head a new White House office to coordinate trade and industrial policy.[60] Although one would not expect a president to appoint opponents of his policies, Flynn and Navarro could be expected to push Trump even further outside the mainstream of informed opinion on these issues. In fact, however, Flynn's reckless conduct led to his forced resignation within the first month of Trump's presidency. He had secretly and illegally negotiated with Russian officials prior to the inauguration and later lied about it to Vice President Pence, who had then put his own reputation on the line in defending Flynn publicly about the matter. Trump asked for Flynn's resignation, explaining that the deceit had undermined the administration's ability to trust him.

Trump's finger-pointing at Flynn would not be the last word on the episode. The Flynn revelations raised questions about what Trump had known and when he had known it. Many doubted that Flynn would have negotiated with the Russians without Trump's approval, potentially implicating the president in the illegal activity. The affair also coincided with leaked intelligence reports that Trump aides had been in frequent contact with Russian operatives during the campaign. By mid-February, it appeared that impending investigations of Trump's and his aides' relations with Russia could pose a significant threat to his presidency.[61]

Trump's selections were short on relevant policy expertise. Most notably, apart from Navarro, none of his economic advisers had credentials as economists. Trump named Ben Carson as secretary of Housing and Urban Development, despite Carson's admission that he had no knowledge of the department's work. In a bizarre twist, Trump appointed a handful of billionaires and several other extremely wealthy individuals to cabinet posts (collectively, his cabinet selections had more than fifty times the net worth of George W. Bush's first cabinet), resulting in protests from Senate leaders who were responsible for confirming them.[62] After promising to end the corrupt influence of Wall Street, Trump appointed a raft of Wall Street executives to high posts. Trump supporter Newt Gingrich remarked that having promised to "drain the swamp" of corporate lobbyists, Trump was now "knee-deep in alligators."

Observers described Trump's management style during the transition as "chaotic."[63] To some degree, the weaknesses of his appointments may also have reflected his shortage of contacts, support, and even acceptance among Republican elites. Trump's cabinet selections appear likely to produce some problems even if they surmount difficulties with Senate confirmation: a greater-than-normal frequency of scandals, administrative failures, or major policy mistakes.

At the same time, Trump was encountering opposition to some of his central policy positions from the most important Republicans in Congress. Senate majority leader Mitch McConnell criticized Trump's tax-cut, Social Security, Medicare, and infrastructure proposals on the grounds that they would substantially increase the already excessive long-term federal deficit. Several prominent Republicans criticized Trump's notions of penalizing companies that moved jobs abroad by imposing tariffs on their imports—a superficially appealing strategy that they felt would start a trade war. Meanwhile, some of Trump's proposals and promises appeared likely to sink under their own weight, including the giant wall on the Mexican border and deportation of millions of undocumented immigrants, the notion of bringing back manufacturing jobs (in an age when manufacturing is increasingly automated), and the promise to restore production and use of coal. Republicans in Congress were developing their own plans for tax reform, Medicare, and other issues. Partly as a result of his casual policy decisions at earlier stages, Trump was in danger of losing control of the agenda even before he took office.

Third, apart from such problems with appointments and plans, Trump was doing actual, immediate harm to his presidency and the country's interests through self-absorbed, uninformed, or reckless conduct in several areas. He announced his intention to reside much of the time in his apartment in New York, rather than moving full-time to the White House. This was an insistence on privileged treatment that would prove awkward for a great deal of presidential business. In a similar way, he refused to divest himself of his business holdings and transfer his wealth to a blind trust. He made clear that he would take advantage of the absence of any conflict-of-interest legislation that formally applies to the president. Instead of divesting, he promised that his son-in-law would run his businesses and would not "do any deals" during his presidency. He also said that he would remain executive producer of the *Celebrity Apprentice* television program. Trump thus ignored the obvious objection—that political and business leaders in the United States and around the world, interested in decisions by the U.S. government, would be able to reward or punish the president through his hotels, casinos, and other financial interests. Critics pointed out the possibilities for massive corruption.[64]

Perhaps because he was caught unprepared, Trump accepted a congratulatory phone call from the president of Taiwan—a serious breach of protocol under diplomatic agreements between the United States and China. (In effect, the United States protects Taiwan's independence while maintaining the fiction that Taiwan is a renegade province of China.) When China issued a major protest, Trump did not respond graciously; he rejected the complaint, criticized China, and questioned the formal one-China policy that has helped stabilize relations between the United States and China for thirty-five years. In all likelihood, Trump was unaware of the long-standing agreement with China. Such lack of knowledge should not have been surprising. Trump had declined to receive the daily briefings from the CIA that all presidents and presidents-elect have received since the early 1960s. He had also refused to confer with the State Department about his conversations with foreign leaders.

In mid-December, the intelligence community issued an official, extraordinary finding: that Russia had intervened in the presidential campaign by hacking into the email servers of multiple political groups, both Democratic and Republican, and selectively leaking the Democrats' private emails. In addition, Russia had conducted the operation with the explicit intent to help Trump win the election, and the effort was directed by Russian president Vladimir Putin. The report indicated a high degree of confidence in these findings. Because none of the leaked information had been highly damaging to the Clinton campaign, there was no implication that the Russian interference had changed the outcome of the election. Nevertheless, the report was a major embarrassment for Trump—reinforcing criticism that he had close ties with an unfriendly and historically hostile foreign power.

In statements that were without precedent, Trump publicly rejected the intelligence findings and belittled the capabilities of the intelligence community. Other Republicans, alarmed by Trump's conduct, acknowledged that such statements were a serious matter. They would hurt the morale of the intelligence community, discourage candor in its future findings, and display confusion to the nation's enemies.

In late December, about a month before the beginning of his presidency, Trump had other things on his mind. He tweeted a response to a negative review of the restaurant in the Trump Tower, disparaging the magazine and its editor. "Has anyone looked at the really poor numbers of @VanityFair Magazine. Way down, big trouble, dead! Graydon Carter, no talent, will be out!"

Yet within days and without warning, he suddenly tweeted what, if taken seriously, would be a momentous change in national security policy—his intention to "greatly strengthen and expand" the American nuclear weapons capability. Later, he explained that the additional capability might be needed for conflict in Europe—a more-or-less direct threat to Russia. Evidently a response to a remark that the Russian president had made in a speech earlier in the day, the announcement not only would provoke Russia but also appeared to reverse more than four decades of efforts by presidents of both parties to achieve negotiated arms reduction and promote nuclear nonproliferation.[65] His off-the-cuff declarations will undoubtedly discourage Russia's and other countries' cooperation with those efforts, if Trump does not indeed abandon them—making the world, by most qualified accounts, more dangerous.

In short, the transition bore out the concerns about Trump's experience, skills, and personality that had emerged, for anyone paying attention, during the campaign—if anything, confirming them earlier and more convincingly than Trump's many critics would have expected. For liberals, there was some compensation in the evidence of careless or ill-advised decisions and self-absorption: They might reduce the magnitude of conservative policy change that Trump could achieve. At least they would harm the reputation of the Republican Party. For Americans of any persuasion and for the world, they also implied real dangers.

Notes

1. David T. Z. Mindich, *Just the Facts: How "Objectivity" Came to Define American Journalism* (New York University Press, 1998); Brian Montopoli, "Falling Over Backward Seeking Balance," *Columbia Journalism Review*, October 14, 2004. For a contrary statement by the public editor of the *New York Times*, see Liz Spayd, "The Truth about 'False Balance,'" September 10, 2016, www.nytimes.com/2016/09/11/public-editor/the-truth-about-false-balance.html.
2. Michael Nelson, ed., *The Presidency and the Political System*, 10th ed. (Washington, D.C.: CQ Press, 2013); Ludger Helms, *Presidents, Prime Ministers and Chancellors: Executive Leadership in Western Democracies* (London: Palgrave Macmillan, 2005).
3. James G. Benze Jr., "Presidential Management: The Importance of Presidential Skills," *Presidential Studies Quarterly* 11 (Fall 1981): 470–478; James P. Pfiffner, *The Managerial Presidency,* 2nd ed. (College Station: Texas A & M University Press, 1999).
4. David E. Lewis, *The Politics of Presidential Appointments: Political Control and Bureaucratic Performance* (Princeton, N.J.: Princeton University Press, 2008).
5. John P. Burke and Fred I. Greenstein, *How Presidents Test Reality: Decisions on Vietnam, 1954 and 1965* (New York: Russell Sage Foundation, 1991); Bob Woodward, *Plan of Attack: The Definitive Account of the Decision to Invade Iraq* (New York: Simon & Schuster, 2004); John P. Burke, *Honest Broker? The National Security Adviser and Presidential Decision Making* (College Station: Texas A & M University Press, 2009).
6. Richard Neustadt, *Presidential Power and the Modern Presidents: The Politics of Leadership from Roosevelt to Reagan* (New York: Macmillan, 1990); and Barbara Kellerman, *The Political Presidency: Practice of Leadership* (New York: Oxford University Press, 1984). Several sentences in this paragraph also appear in Bruce Nesmith and Paul J. Quirk, "The Presidency: No Exit from Deadlock," in Michael Nelson, ed., *The Elections of 2012* (Washington, D.C.: CQ Press, 2013), ch. 8.
7. Samuel Kernell, *Going Public: New Strategies of Presidential Leadership*, 3rd ed. (Washington, D.C.: CQ Press, 1997).

8. Pfiffner, *The Managerial Presidency*, 2nd ed.
9. James David Barber, *The Presidential Character: Predicting Performance in the White House*, 4th ed. (Englewood Cliffs, N.J.: Prentice Hall, 1992).
10. Fred I. Greenstein, *The Presidential Difference: Leadership Style from FDR to George W. Bush* (Princeton, N.J.: Princeton University Press, 2004).
11. Paul J. Quirk, "Presidential Competence," in *The Presidency and the Political System,* 9th ed., ed. Michael Nelson (Washington, D.C.: CQ Press, 2010), 108–141.
12. There are analytic advantages to confining attention, in the study of presidential leadership, to the post–New Deal period of active government, expansive presidential roles, and American leadership of the Western world.
13. George C. Edwards III, *At the Margins: Presidential Leadership of Congress* (New Haven, Conn.: Yale University Press, 1990); for a somewhat more expansive view of the president's leverage, see Matthew Beckmann, *Pushing the Agenda: Presidential Leadership in US Lawmaking, 1953–2004* (New York: Cambridge University Press, 2010).
14. George C. Edwards III, *On Deaf Ears: The Limits of the Bully Pulpit* (New Haven, Conn.: Yale University Press, 2006); and Brandice Canes-Wrone, *Who Leads Whom? Presidents, Policy, and the Public* (Chicago: University of Chicago Press, 2005).
15. George C. Edwards III, *Predicting the Presidency: The Potential of Persuasive Leadership* (Princeton, N.J.: Princeton University Press, 2016).
16. Ken Gormley, *The Death of American Virtue:* Clinton v. Starr (New York: Crown, 2010).
17. Michael Nelson, Barbara A. Perry, and Russell Riley, eds., *42: Inside the Presidency of Bill Clinton* (Ithaca, N.Y.: Cornell University Press, 2016).
18. Fred I. Greenstein, *The Presidential Difference: Leadership Style from FDR to Barack Obama* (Princeton, N.J.: Princeton University Press, 2012).
19. Greenstein, *The Presidential Difference*, chs. 6, 7, 12.
20. John P. Burke, Fred I. Greenstein, Larry Berman, and Richard H. Immerman, *How Presidents Test Reality: Decision on Vietnam, 1954 and 1965* (New York: Russell Sage Foundation, 1989); Burke, *Honest Broker?*; and Bob Woodward, *Plan of Attack* (New York: Simon & Schuster, 2004).
21. Paul C. Nutt, *Why Decisions Fail: Avoiding the Blunders That Lead to Debacles* (San Francisco: Berrett-Koehler Publishers, 2002); and Max H. Bazerman, *Judgement in Managerial Decision Making* (New York: Wiley, 2002).
22. Amanda Bittner, *Platform or Personality? The Role of Party Leaders in Elections* (Oxford, U.K.: Oxford University Press, 2011); Harold D. Clarke, Allan Kornberg, Thomas J. Sccotto, Jason Reifler, David Sanders, Marianne C. Stewart, and Paul Whiteley, "Yes We Can! Valence Politics and Electoral Choice in America, 2008," *Electoral Studies* 30 (September 2011): 450–461; and Lynn Vavreck, "Why This Election Was Not about Issues," *New York Times*, November 23, 2016, www.nytimes.com/2016/11/23/upshot/this-election-was-not-about-the-issues-blame-the-candidates.html.
23. Clarke et al., "Yes We Can!"
24. Jonathan Rauch, "Why Hillary Needs to Be Two-Faced," *New York Times,* October 22, 2016, www.nytimes.com/2016/10/23/opinion/campaign-stops/why-hillary-clinton-needs-to-be-two-faced.html.
25. Ariel Edwards-Levy, "Republicans Support Outsider Presidential Candidates over the Establishment, Polls Show," *Huffington Post*, September 9, 2015, www.huffingtonpost.com/entry/political-outsiders-are-leading-the-republican-field_us_55e4bb21e4b0b7a96339f0a9.
26. Thomas E. Patterson, "News Coverage of the 2016 General Election: How the Press Failed the Voters," *Shorenstein Center on Media, Politics, and Public*

Policy (December 7, 2016), shorensteincenter.org/news-coverage-2016-general-election/; Thomas E. Patterson, *Informing the News: The Need for Knowledge-Based Journalism* (New York: Vintage Books, 2013).
27. Patterson, "News Coverage of the 2016 General Election."
28. William L. Benoit, Mitchell S. McKinney, and R. Lance Hollbert, "Beyond Learning and Persona: Extending the Scope of Presidential Debate Effects," *Communication Monographs* 68 (September 2001): 259–273; Robert V. Friedenberg, "Patterns and Trends in National Political Debates: 1960–1992," in *Rhetorical Studies of National Political Debates, 1960–1992*, ed. Robert V. Friedenberg (Westport, Conn.: Praeger, 1994) ; and Kathleen Hall Jamieson, "Television, Presidential Campaigns, and Debates," in *Presidential Debates: 1988 and Beyond* ed. Joel L. Swerdlow (Washington, D.C.: Congressional Quarterly, 1987).
29. There could be more than three candidates who qualify (on the basis of current poll support) for participation in the general election debates. The requirement has been 10 percent support in current polls. But no more than one minor-party or independent candidate has ever had such support in the era of televised debates.
30. William L. Benoit, Mitchell S. McKinney, and R. Lance Hollbert, "Beyond Learning and Persona: Extending the Scope of Presidential Debate Effects," *Communication Monographs* 68 (September 2001): 259–273.
31. See footnote 1.
32. Paul Krugman, "Hillary Clinton Gets Gored," *New York Times*, September 5, 2016, www.nytimes.com/2016/09/05/opinion/hillary-clinton-gets-gored.html; Liz Spayd, "The Truth about 'False Balance,'" *New York Times*, September 10, 2016, www.nytimes.com/2016/09/11/public-editor/the-truth-about-false-balance.html; and Jonathan Chait, "New York Times Public Editor Liz Spayd Writes Disastrous Defense of False Equivalence," *New York*, September 12, 2016, nymag.com/daily/intelligencer/2016/09/times-writes-disastrous-defense-of-false-equivalence.html.
33. Benedict Carey, "The Psychiatric Question: Is It Fair to Analyze Donald Trump from Afar?" *New York Times*, August 15, 2016, www.nytimes.com/2016/08/16/health/analyzing-donald-trump-psychology.html.
34. Byron E. Shafer, *The Quiet Revolution: The Struggle for the Democratic Party and the Shaping of Post-Reform Politics* (New York: Russell Sage Foundation, 1983)
35. Nelson W. Polsby, *Consequences of Party Reform* (Oxford, U.K.: Oxford University Press, 1983).
36. Ibid.
37. David W. Brady, Hahrie Han, and Jeremy C. Pope, "Primary Elections and Candidate Ideology: Out of Step with the Primary Electorate," *Legislative Studies Quarterly* 32 (February 2007): 79–105; Seth J. Hill, "Institution of Nomination and the Policy Ideology of Primary Electorates," *Quarterly Journal of Political Science* 10 (December 2015): 461–487; Stephen A. Jessee, "Voter Ideology and Candidate Positioning in the 2008 Presidential Election," *American Politics Research* 38 (March 2010): 195–210.
38. Marty Cohen, David Karol, Hans Noel, and John Zaller, *The Party Decides: Presidential Nominations before and after Reform* (Chicago: University of Chicago Press, 2008).
39. Rosalind S. Helderman and Tom Hamburger, "State Dept. Inspector General Report Sharply Criticizes Clinton's Email Practices," *Washington Post*, May 25, 2016, www.washingtonpost.com/politics/state-dept-inspector-general-report-sharply-criticizes-clintons-email-practices/2016/05/25/fc6f8ebc-2275-11e6-aa84-42391ba52c91_story.html.

40. Samantha Kilgore, "Malignant and Psychopathic" Donald Trump? Expert Studies 600 Hours of Trump Footage," *Inquisitr*, March 9, 2016, www.inquisitr.com/2870145/malignant-and-psychopathic-donald-trump-expert-studies-600-hours-of-trump-footage/.
41. Henry Alford, "Is Donald Trump Actually a Narcissist? Therapists Weigh In!" *Vanity Fair*, November 11, 2015, www.vanityfair.com/news/2015/11/donald-trump-narcissism-therapists; and Dan P. McAdams, "The Mind of Donald Trump," *Atlantic* (June 2016), www.theatlantic.com/magazine/archive/2016/06/the-mind-of-donald-trump/480771/. There was not necessarily a consensus view on whether Trump's narcissism reached the level of a personality disorder.
42. David E. Sanger and Maggie Habermann, "50 G.O.P. Officials Warn Donald Trump Would Put Nation's Security 'at Risk,'" *New York Times*, August 8, 2016, www.nytimes.com/2016/08/09/us/politics/national-security-gop-donald-trump.html.
43. "Mr. Ryan, Your Views on Donald Trump? Next Question Please," *New York Times*, mobile.nytimes.com/2016/09/24/us/politics/ryan-trump.html.
44. Alex Gangitano, "Nearly Half of GOP Staffers Aren't Voting Same Way as Their Boss," *Roll Call*, November 2, 2016, www.rollcall.com/news/hoh/nearly-half-gop-staffers-arent-voting-way-boss?utm_name=newsletters&utm_source=rollcallheadlines&utm_medium=email.
45. One of the leading forecasters—Nate Silver and the *FiveThirtyEight* website—estimated Trump's chances of winning the election higher than the others did, at 29 percent. But all of the forecasters predicted a Clinton victory, with probabilities ranging from 71 percent to 98 percent.
46. Andrew Prokop, "Few Predicted Trump Had a Good Shot of Winning. But Political Science Models Did," *Vox*, November 9, 2016, www.vox.com/2016/11/9/13571872/why-donald-trump-won.
47. Alford, "Is Donald Trump Really a Narcissist?"
48. After the election, there were, as always with a defeated presidential candidate, many criticisms of Clinton's campaign. By conventional reckoning, none of them rose (or sunk) to the level of Trump's series of summer disasters, or raised serious questions about Clinton's fitness for office. See the present volume, Chapter 3.
49. "How Deplorable Are Trump Supporters," *Economist*, September 13, 2016, www.economist.com/blogs/graphicdetail/2016/09/daily-chart-8?fsrc=scn/tw/te/bl/ed/; Eduardo Porter, "Where Were Trump's Votes? Where the Jobs Weren't," *New York Times*, December 13, 2016, www.nytimes.com/2016/12/13/business/economy/jobs-economy-voters.html; Katherine J. Cramer, "For Years I've Been Watching Anti-Elite Fury Build in Wisconsin. Then Came Trump." *Vox*, November 16, 2016, www.vox.com/the-big-idea/2016/11/16/13645116/rural-resentment-elites-trump; George F. Will, "Higher Education Is Awash with Hysteria," *Washington Post*, November 18, 2016, www.washingtonpost.com/opinions/higher-education-is-awash-with-hysteria-that-might-have-helped-elect-trump/2016/11/18/a589b14e-ace6-11e6-977a-1030f822fc35_story.html; and Amanda Taub, "The Rise of American Authoritarianism: A Niche Group of Political Scientists May Have Uncovered What Is Driving Trump's Ascent. What They Found Has Implications That Go Beyond 2016," *Vox*, March 1, 2016, www.vox.com/2016/3/1/11127424/trump-authoritarianism.
50. Gabriel S. Lenz, *Follow the Leader? How Voters Respond to Politicians' Policies and Performance* (Chicago: University of Chicago Press, 2012); Joan C. Williams, "What So Many People Don't Get about the U.S. Working Class," *Harvard Business Review*, November 10, 2016, hbr.org/2016/11/what-so-many-people-dont-get-about-the-u-s-working-class.

51. James A. Kuklinski and Paul J. Quirk, "Reconsidering the Rational Public: Cognition, Heuristics, and Mass Opinion," in Arthur Lupia, Mathew D. McCubbins, and Samuel L. Popkin, eds., *The Elements of Reason* (New York: Cambridge University Press, 2000), ch. 8.
52. Paul Krugman, "Seduced and Betrayed by Trump," *New York Times*, December 2, 2016, www.nytimes.com/2016/12/02/opinion/seduced-and-betrayed-by-donald-trump.html; and Ben Casselman, "Trump's Proposals Won't Help the White Working Class or the Urban Poor," *FiveThirtyEight*, November 15, 2016, fivethirtyeight.com/features/trumps-proposals-wont-help-the-white-working-class-or-the-urban-poor/.
53. Amber Phillips, "Is Split-Ticket Voting Officially Dead," *Washington Post*, November 17, 2016, www.washingtonpost.com/news/the-fix/wp/2016/11/17/is-split-ticket-voting-officially-dead/.
54. Nate Silver, "Education, Not Income, Predicted Who Would Vote Trump," *FiveThirtyEight*, November 22, 2016, fivethirtyeight.com/features/education-not-income-predicted-who-would-vote-for-trump/.
55. Mark Lilla, "The End of Identity Liberalism," *New York Times*, November 18, 2016, www.nytimes.com/2016/11/20/opinion/sunday/the-end-of-identity-liberalism.html.
56. James P. Pfiffner, *The Strategic Presidency: Hitting the Ground Running* (Lawrence: University Press of Kansas, 1996); John P. Burke, *Presidential Transitions: From Politics to Practice* (Boulder, Colo.: Lynne Rienner, 2000); and John P. Burke, "Lessons from Past Presidential Transitions," *Presidential Studies Quarterly* 31 (March 2001): 5–24.
57. Edwards, *At the Margins: Presidential Leadership of Congress*.
58. Andrew C. McCarthy, "Trump's Populist Contradictions," *National Review*, April 27, 2016, www.nationalreview.com/corner/434673/trumps-populist-contradictions; and Jennifer Rubin, "Republican Contradictions Abound in the Age of Trump," *Washington Post*, December 19, 2016, www.washingtonpost.com/blogs/right-turn/wp/2016/12/19/republican-contradictions-abound-in-the-age-of-trump/.
59. Matthew Rosza, "Michael Flynn's Conspiracy-Minded Son, Who Tweeted about 'Pizzagate' Theory, Used to Be on Donald Trump's Transition Team," *Salon*, December 6, 2016, www.salon.com/2016/12/06/michael-flynns-conspiracy-minded-son-who-tweeted-about-the-pizzagate-theory-is-on-donald-trumps-transition-team/.
60. Binyamin Applebaum, "Trump Taps Peter Navarro, Vocal Critic of China, for New Trade Post," *New York Times*, December 21, 2016, www.nytimes.com/2016/12/21/us/politics/peter-navarro-carl-icahn-trump-china-trade.html.
61. Karen DeYoung, Abby Phillip, and Jenna Johnson, "Flynn Departure Erupts into a Full-Blown Crisis for the Trump White House," *Washington Post*, February 14, 2017, www.washingtonpost.com/politics/flynn-departure-erupts-into-a-full-blown-crisis-for-the-trump-white-house/2017/02/14/c1f3cb90-2db-11e6-8d72-263470bf0401_story.html?utm_term=.4018fa7b6933&wpisrc=nl_most-draw5&wpmm=1.
62. Rupert Neate, "Donald Trump Faces Senate Backlash over 'Cabinet of Billionaires,'" *Guardian,* December 18, 2016, www.theguardian.com/us-news/2016/dec/18/donald-trump-senate-backlash-cabinet-of-billionaires.
63. Josh Voorhees, "Trump's Transition Operation Is Just as Chaotic as His Campaign," *Slate*, November 15, 2016, www.slate.com/blogs/the_slatest/2016/11/15/donald_trump_s_transition_team_is_stuck_in_transition.html.
64. Norman L. Eisen, Richard Painter, and Laurence H. Tribe, "The Emoluments Clause, Its Text, Meaning, and Application to Donald J. Trump," *Governance Studies at Brookings*, December 16, 2016, www.brookings.edu/wp-content/uploads/2016/12/gs_121616_emoluments-clause1.pdf.
65. Hans M. Kristensen and Robert S. Norris, "Status of World Nuclear Forces," *Federation of American Scientists*, fas.org/issues/nuclear-weapons/status-world-nuclear-forces/.

9

The Meaning of the 2016 Election

The President as Minority Leader

Andrew Rudalevige

The "Time for Change" model constructed by political scientist Alan Abramowitz uses just three variables to predict the outcome of presidential elections: the second-quarter annualized change in gross domestic product (GDP), the incumbent president's job approval rating, and a dummy variable penalizing an incumbent party seeking a third (or more) term. President Barack Obama's approval rating as the summer of 2016 began hovered around the 50 percent mark. U.S. GDP increased 1.4 percent from March to June, after a tiny 0.8 percent rise in the previous quarter.

These were not terrible numbers. But they were not so robust as to give the Democratic nominee seeking to succeed Obama a contextual wind at her back—at least not one forceful enough to sweep aside voters' general reluctance to continue one party in power. Indeed, the Time for Change model, despite its own author's discomfort with its conclusion, predicted a narrow Republican win.[1]

Another approach that averaged together a variety of econometric election forecast models predicted a narrow popular vote win for the Democratic presidential nominee.[2] And still other political science forecasts grounded in the "fundamentals" of economic performance and incumbent approval came to similar conclusions: that the election was a toss-up.

And so it proved. The models were right, even if most of the pundits were wrong. Donald Trump wound up with just over three hundred votes in the electoral college, a comfortable majority that disguised extraordinarily slim margins in a handful of key states. Meanwhile, Democratic nominee Hillary Clinton won the national popular vote by just over 2 percentage points. Down-ballot incumbents were the big winners around the country: Democrats netted just a handful of additional House seats as 97 percent of incumbents were duly reelected. Republicans also lost only two Senate seats in a year when Democrats confidently expected to win four or more and regain a majority in that chamber. Just one incumbent governor lost, and barely.

So 2016 was a strange sort of "change" election. In important ways not much changed. As political scientist Larry Bartels concluded, "An extraordinary campaign has produced a remarkably ordinary election outcome, primarily reflecting partisan patterns familiar from previous election cycles."[3] As noted, the House and Senate remained quite stable, with Republican majorities continuing in both chambers. And even at the presidential level, we should be cautious of basing sweeping punditry on very thin margins. If just forty thousand (of 6.6 million) Trump voters across Michigan, Wisconsin, and Pennsylvania had cast their vote the other way, or if Democratic turnout in a handful of urban areas had matched 2012 levels, or perhaps even if FBI director James Comey had timed or worded his missives to Congress differently, Hillary Clinton would have taken the oath of office in January 2017.

Yet the wider meaning of the election surely lies in the underlying chaos uneasily tucked beneath that smooth statistical surface. It lies in the apolitical backstory of the president-elect, in the toxic and frequently fact-free nature of much of the campaign's discourse, and in the public's deep discontent with the Democratic standard-bearer. More systematically it lies in the fact that, despite the complete triumph of partisanship to which the 2016 election bore witness, America's polarizing polity no longer has a majority party.

This in turn leaves the U.S. presidency returning to its structural roots—not as "tribune of the people," but as a particularly powerful sort of minority leader. That will make the task of uniting a deeply divided nation all the more challenging in the years to come.

Time for a Change?

As political science *éminence grise* David Mayhew has observed, presidential elections without an incumbent on the ballot show a very different pattern from those with a president running for reelection. In the latter case, close to 70 percent of elections have kept in power the party already in power. But open-seat elections show a close-to-even split. There have been twenty-four such elections since 1796, including 2016: In eleven of them, the party in office held the presidency, whereas in thirteen, the out-party triumphed.[4] The switch of parties after eight years has been the most common outcome since 1952, when Dwight D. Eisenhower succeeded the twenty years of Democratic leadership provided by Franklin D. Roosevelt and Harry Truman. Eisenhower's eight years were followed by eight Democratic years under John F. Kennedy and Lyndon B. Johnson; eight Republican years under Richard Nixon and Gerald Ford were next. Ronald Reagan defeated Jimmy Carter after one term, and George H. W. Bush, riding on Reagan's coattails, became the first sitting vice president to win the top job since 1836. But in 1992, Democrat Bill Clinton restored normal service. His eight years in office were followed by eight of Republican George W. Bush's, and then eight of Democrat Barack Obama's. The 2016 Trump victory, seen as part of this sort of regular cycle, is not surprising.

Likewise, political science models relying on the "fundamentals" predicted a very close election—a "coin toss."[5] When the popular vote forecasts compiled in the October issue of the journal *PS: Political Science and Politics* are averaged together, the result is an expected 50.7 percent of the two-party vote for Hillary Clinton. Her actual share of the two-party vote? 51.1 percent.[6] Those models that did not include poll data—focusing instead on the state of the economy and approval ratings for the incumbent president (and thus, by proxy, his party)—tended to suggest an overall Republican advantage. After all, Democrats faced a fifty–fifty public split on President Obama's performance generally, and on the sluggish, if consistent, nature of the economic recovery during his tenure. Certainly the stock market had risen dramatically and payrolls had grown by several million jobs since both cratered in 2008 and 2009. But the former helped those with the wherewithal to hold invested assets for the long term, whereas the latter seemed to boost low-wage service far more than long-term security. An old anecdote took on new life: Told about all the jobs created by the current regime, a worker replied, "I know. I have three of them."[7] That the Federal Reserve Bank's prime lending rate stood at a paltry 0.50 percent on election day testified to the fragility of the wider economy.

In arguing for the primacy of these systematic factors in forecasting election results, quantitatively minded political scientists have long been in conflict with journalists and cable television pundits. The latter see the ebb and flow of newsworthy events during the campaign season as determining the outcome. Their stock in trade is "game changers"—*The Gamble*, a book by political scientists John Sides and Lynn Vavreck, points out that nearly seventy events during the 2012 campaign were described in the media that way.[8] But, Sides and Vavreck argue, the "game" was heavily constrained by the hand dealt to each candidate by the preexisting fundamentals. Candidates worked within contours defined well before the official campaign began; although poll numbers bounced around in the short-term news cycle—with each debate performance or well-publicized gaffe—they tended to remain steady in the long term. Campaign efforts themselves might matter, especially when it came to mobilizing sympathetic voters. But because both candidates spent enormous amounts of money with equally strategic skill, the net result in favor of one or the other was likely to be minor.

For most of the year, it seemed that 2016 would present an unintentional natural experiment testing this hypothesis. Clinton, by conventional standards, ran a competent campaign, flush with cash, consultants, and local volunteers armed with the latest technology devoted to getting out the vote. Trump, by contrast, had a skeletal campaign organization. He relied on a fervid social media presence and a series of interviews and live rallies that received near-blanket coverage on cable news outlets (although his spending, and that of anti-Clinton Super PACs, wound up totaling more than $320 million). Clinton opened nearly 500 field offices nationwide, compared to just over 200 for Trump, with impressive numerical advantages in key swing states like Florida (68 for Clinton, 29 for Trump), Ohio (69 to 22), and North Carolina (38 to 11).[9]

Yet Clinton would lose all those states. Her get-out-the-vote efforts fell short, too, in other key states, such as Michigan, Wisconsin, and Pennsylvania. In the end, she polled fewer votes than Barack Obama in 2012. Trump, meanwhile, exceeded Mitt Romney's vote total. That meant that overall turnout between 2012 and 2016 increased somewhat—but there were important differences in *who* turned out. Republicans did; Democrats did not. Having an expensive, "professional" campaign infrastructure did not seem to help Clinton solve that problem.

Why? It's possible that Clinton's infrastructure was simply used poorly—that turnout was substituted for outreach, that the Brooklyn headquarters staff was blinded by its own assumptions about its advantages. That's probably part of the story.[10] But we also need to move from forecasting, to explaining. For that, we might do worse than to turn to the factors working with and within those fundamentals: the issues, the candidates—and the gold standard of voter choice, party affiliation.

Partisanship: A Strong Drug[11]

In October 2016, surveys suggested that support for third parties was running far higher than in prior election years, and that Republicans, especially, were likely to defect from their ticket. Donald Trump, after all, was an odd standard-bearer for a party previously dedicated to free trade, a strong presence abroad, the rule of law, and family values. In October, only about 81 percent of Republican women and 84 percent of Republican men said they planned to vote for Trump—and that figure was on the high end of the polling results.[12] The responses marked a dramatic drop from recent elections, in which 90–95 percent of partisans stuck with their party's nominee. "Trump May Depress Republican Turnout, Spelling Disaster for the GOP," warned election guru Nate Silver.[13] Certainly losing one in five GOP women would have been fatal to Trump's chances of victory.

But in the end, Gary Johnson and Jill Stein, the Libertarian and Green Party nominees, totaled less than 5 percent of the vote combined.[14] Republican voters stuck with Trump (as Democrats did with Clinton). Exit polls suggested that nine in ten Republicans of both sexes did indeed vote Republican.[15] Across the board, past partisan patterns repeated themselves.

This was particularly notable in at least two demographic groups, given the identities and conduct of the candidates. First, many observers had forecast a record gender gap, given the combination of the first major-party female nominee and an opponent with a history of making crude comments about women. "A historically overwhelming share of women say they will vote for the Democrat, Hillary Clinton," wrote Harry Enten on the *FiveThirtyEight.com* website in mid-October.[16]

The gender gap did grow—but only because more male voters supported Trump than had voted for Romney. Surprisingly, the Democrats' edge among female voters remained largely static. Clinton had a 12 percentage point advantage among female voters, but Obama's had been 11 points in 2012. That needle did not move.

Nor, despite Trump's attacks on immigrants generally and Mexican Americans specifically throughout the campaign, did his share of the Latino vote drop dramatically from that of previous Republican candidates. Exit polls suggested that Trump's share of the Latino vote was basically the same as 2008 GOP nominee John McCain's and actually rose from 2012 nominee Mitt Romney's (from 27 percent to 29 percent). Clinton, by contrast, won just 65 percent of the Latino vote, compared to 71 percent for Obama in 2012. The Trump vote was just under the one-third of the Latino population that identifies with the GOP. Although some scholars found the exit polls methodologically problematic, it was difficult to argue that Republican-leaning Latinos had deserted the party en masse.

The same could be said for almost every demographic group—white voters (among whom Trump led by 21 percentage points, compared to 20 for Romney), older voters (Trump won by 8 points, compared to 12 for Romney), and even voters under age thirty, who gave Obama a 24-point edge in 2012 but who broke by just 18 points for Clinton. The religious (those who say they attend church weekly or more) and especially white evangelical Christians also voted for Trump in similar numbers to Romney. In the end, 81 percent of "born-again" voters favored the decidedly secular Trump (compared to 78 percent for Romney).

In short, partisan affiliation turned out to be an excellent predictor. Thus the best forecaster of the polarized 2016 vote in any given state turned out to be the polarized 2012 vote in that same state.[17] Party loyalty extended down the ballot, too. Despite loud worries that Trump would drag down Republicans running for Congress, very few voters split their tickets. In House races, this might be explained in part by the huge advantages of incumbency, buttressed by creative partisan gerrymandering. Yet the Senate results, fought over more competitive terrain, revealed a historical first. Not a single state chose a senator of a different party from the person who won the state's presidential vote. That was the first time this had ever happened in the hundred years since U.S. senators began to be elected by the people rather than state legislatures.

Issues and Candidates in a Post-Fact World

Partisanship is indeed a strong drug. Even so, why did Republican voters "come home" so reliably, after a campaign season spent telling pollsters of their doubts about Donald Trump? Trump was hardly a consensus choice for the nomination. His small but devoted faction of primary voters helped Trump stand out in a huge field: With seventeen competing candidates of varying quality, a quarter or less of the vote was enough to win early victories and traverse a nominating schedule the Republican National Committee had tweaked to help consolidate the party behind the front-runner. They had certainly not expected that front-runner to be a man with little history with the party and less commitment to its governing ideology.

The Republican National Convention in Cleveland was marked by party disunity—the Republican governor of Ohio, along with four of the last five GOP nominees for president, refused even to attend—capped by Sen. Ted Cruz's prime-time speech that failed to endorse the nominee and told listeners to "vote your conscience."[18] After all this, how could Republican Latinos and Republican women ultimately ignore Trump's bullying jibes, or military voters his treatment of the Khan family, or religious voters their doubts about his commitment to Christian tenets? (How could Cruz, for that matter, eventually decide that Trump suited his conscience just fine?)

One way to answer the question is to flip it around—it was never likely that partisans were going to forsake their party's candidate, even if they had qualms. This is not simply a matter of "shy" voters unwilling to tell questioners about their fealty to an imperfect candidate. It reflects, rather, a fundamental fact: Partisan polarization is a real, and still growing, factor in American politics.[19] Thus, for any party identifier, the other party's positions are increasingly distant.

Worse still may be the way personal attitudes toward that other party have evolved. "It's one of the few regrets of my presidency that the rancor and suspicion between the parties has gotten worse instead of better," Obama said in his 2016 State of the Union address.[20]

Indeed, one recent study shows that although people's feelings about their own party have remained steady, their assessment of the opposition party has grown increasingly dire. Political scientists Marc Hetherington and Thomas Rudolph found that the average ratings Republicans gave to "atheists" and "illegal immigrants" in 2012 were significantly more positive than their ratings for the Democratic Party.[21] In 2016, far more GOP voters approved of Russian strongman Vladimir Putin's performance than of Barack Obama's.[22] Hetherington put it bluntly: "[W]e hate our political opponents now."[23]

That was made easier in 2016 by the confluence of at least three reinforcing factors. One was the combination of major-party nominees—each was, perhaps, the only candidate who could have lost to the other. A second was the alignment of the economic issues that took prominence in the campaign—consistent with the "fundamentals," but underlying them—and which favored Trump. And the third circles back to the nature of polarization, this time transferred to the media and especially to the global explosion of social media. In short, the campaigns took place in what seemed to be parallel universes—where facts were very much in the eye of the beholder, received from a bespoke blend of news and "news" sources that catered to one's preexisting beliefs.

"I'm a Christian, and I shouldn't hate, but it's awfully close." So said one otherwise-genial senior citizen to a reporter for the *Toronto Star*.[24] The reporter, seeking to explore Hillary Clinton's consistently high unfavorable ratings after three decades of public service, was shocked by the virulent hatred for her that he encountered in Walmart parking lots in the Virginia exurbs, far away from Trump rallies. "'Unfavorably' doesn't begin to describe the intensity of the antipathy," he wrote. His respondents called Clinton deceitful, dishonest, incompetent, selfish, and corrupt. They could recite ("immediately, though often inaccurately") numerous controversies dating from before Bill Clinton's presidency.[25] Those impressions had only hardened as a result of the lengthy investigation into possible security breaches related to Clinton's use of a private email server while secretary of state, the multiple congressional efforts to find her responsible for the 2012 deaths of American diplomats in Benghazi, Libya, and the charges of "pay to play" connections between the State Department and the Clinton Foundation. That none of these matters had ever yielded grounds for criminal indictment or even direct culpability made little difference. Her perceived (and, it must be said, often quite real) lack of forthrightness in explaining such matters only dug her hole deeper. "She's as dirty as the day is long. It's so obvious," one interviewee concluded.[26]

Clinton tried to laugh this off: "I have created so many jobs in the conspiracy theory machine factory," she said in September 2016. There was something to that, even if her own instincts bolstered those employment figures. Certainly it was not hard to see some measure of sexism at work as well—mostly latent but also overt, not least in the epithets routinely used to abuse Clinton. ("Slut" and "bitch" are two of those that could be quoted by the *Toronto Star*.) To her supporters, this was obviously unfair, a bizarre exercise in double standards. Unlike Bill Clinton, Trump faced no outrage over his calculated avoidance of military service during the Vietnam War. Unlike Hillary Clinton, he faced no outrage over his lack of transparency—he was the first candidate in forty years not to publicly release his tax returns[27]—or the fiscal chicanery of his own charitable foundation. She was excoriated for her (only) husband's marital meanderings, but Trump (married three times) could brag about how as "a star" he could get away with sexual assault. She was tagged as "Crooked Hillary," but he was the one whose career was marked by allegations of fraud and propelled politically by the outright lie of "birtherism." A *Politico* study tracking both candidates' rhetoric for five days found that "Trump has built a cottage industry around stretching the truth," averaging "about one falsehood every three minutes and 15 seconds" that he spoke.[28]

Thus, Clinton's supporters argued incessantly, how could anyone treat the two as equivalent? How could anyone rationally conclude that she was somehow *worse*?

Yet if the dislike of Clinton was not always rational, it was visceral. It was very real. And it was exactly the calculation many Trump voters made in justifying their ultimate support. "They're like, 'Trump is a bigot,'" one evangelical voter told the *Washington Post*. "He is! But Hillary is 10 times worse."[29] The Canadian reporter found the same effect. "Trump is not great. Trump is all we have," said one voter. Another said that whatever Trump's failings, "it's like good versus evil."[30]

These polarized emotions showed up in the exit polling. Only 38 percent of voters approved of Trump, and just 43 percent of Clinton. Similarly, 63 percent said Trump was not honest or trustworthy—but 61 percent said the same of Clinton. It was not that all voters hated *both* candidates—in fact less than 20 percent of the electorate did. But this "pox on both your houses" camp broke heavily for Trump, 49 percent to 29 percent (the rest went for third-party candidates or blanked their ballots). Trump won the votes of a relatively impressive 15 percent of those who disapproved of him. He won 20 percent of the large majority of voters who said he did not have the right temperament to be president. He won 21 percent of those who said he was dishonest. And he won an astounding 18 percent—nearly one in five—of those who said flatly that he was *unqualified* to be president.

Further, despite a Clinton resume that on paper made her the most accomplished presidential candidate since George H. W. Bush—detailing a lifetime aimed at doing just that—close to half the country thought she was not qualified to be president either.[31]

Leading Democrats, starting with President Obama, downplayed these concerns in their effort to clear the field for Clinton's nomination. Although hindsight is 20/20, it seems that one lesson of the process is a reminder that the duty of a political party is to nominate a candidate who can win an election. The glass ceiling was a real and disturbing issue. But so, for Clinton, was her vote ceiling.

"Where the middle class gets crushed." The focus on the candidates' character dominated the framing of the campaign—the loudest argument for each was the apocalyptic awfulness of the other. One postelection study showed that more than 75 percent of Clinton's television ads were attacks on Trump's personality and temperament. Only 9 percent were about jobs or the economy.[32] Indeed, the first positive advertisement on the list of the TV spots aired most often by the Clinton campaign came in at number seven—and it aired fewer than one-tenth as many times as the six negative ads above it.[33]

There was a positive case to be made about economic growth—as noted earlier, this was at least a fifty–fifty proposition—but Clinton did not consistently make it. She offered no broad narrative telling that story. As the *Washington Post*'s David Maraniss noted, there was instead a rich irony in the long trajectory of the Clinton family from its deep understanding of rural Arkansans in the 1980s to its embrace of and by the coastal elites by the 2010s.[34]

Trump, by contrast, had nothing if not narrative. And Clinton's tactics allowed his interpretation of "the worst so-called recovery since the Great Depression" in which "the hard times never seem to end"[35] to take hold, at least among those most nervous about the effects of globalization and immigration. About one-third of Trump's ads talked about the economy, still a low number historically but much higher than Clinton's.[36] And the single advertisement he aired most—"Two Americas: Economy"—contrasted a bleak high-tax, big-government wasteland under Hillary Clinton ("where the middle class gets crushed") with a Trump future in which "small businesses thrive," there are "millions of new jobs," "wages go up," and "the American dream [is] achievable." Trump's second most-aired ad was simply entitled "Change."[37]

These broad-stroke promises to reopen shuttered coal mines and steel mills, to stop the outsourcing of local employment to lower cost foreign climes, to garner only the positive aspects of global trade while avoiding all its disruptions—in short, to "win"—found a substantial audience disgusted with past governmental performance and ready to believe. One postelection analysis found a massive economic divide between counties Clinton won and those carried by Trump. The fewer than 500 Clinton counties generated 64 percent of American economic activity in 2015. Trump won more than 2,600 counties, which together made up the remaining 36 percent of GDP.[38] In short, it was not just partisan feeling that was polarized and geographically specific, but the economy, too.[39]

The key divide in the electorate was not exactly left–right, since Trump talked about preserving entitlements like Social Security, ripping up trade treaties and security alliances, massive infrastructure spending, and even (sometimes) the need for universal health care. These had hardly been core GOP talking points; nor were they in the 2016 party platform. A more accurate interpretation highlighted a division between those favoring an "open" society and economy, and those who felt harmed by it and thus clamored instead for something "closed."[40] "Make America Great Again"—Trump's slogan—implied a rose-colored past greatness, when foreign companies couldn't compete with American factories and "good" immigrants (that is, one's European grandparents) were the ones getting jobs in those factories to support their nuclear families and make life better for future generations.

Doubt about that future now permeated those in the electorate left behind by open borders. Indeed, the dimensions of the Trump vote were very much along the lines of the open–closed divide. Counties boasting the largest percentage of college graduates voted Republican nearly 30 percentage points less than those with the fewest; those with the largest losses in manufacturing jobs voted more heavily for Trump. White voters supported Trump across the board. But at the county level, one key driver seemed to be not the total number of racial minorities present—after all, local diversity strongly predicted the Clinton vote—but rather how that diversity had changed in recent years. The Trump vote increased as the percentage increase of Latino residents of a county rose, even or especially when it started at a very small base. The future that change foretold seemed to be prominent in their white neighbors' minds.[41]

Economic openness, then, was connected in many voters' minds to more cultural aspects of openness. Recent rapid-fire shifts in attitudes toward (and laws governing) civil rights, gender roles, and sexual identities were joyously liberating for some, but threatening for others. That divide in turn played into one very real issue at stake in 2016—control of the Supreme Court. Justice Antonin Scalia's unexpected death in February 2016 (and the Republican Senate's precedent-shattering refusal to fill the vacancy) had left a court divided down the middle on important questions. Trump dispensed with past pieties by openly declaring he would have a litmus test for Court nominees: namely, that they would vote to overturn *Roe v. Wade*. Pro-life and religious right voters consistently cited the damage to be wrought by a liberal, secular Supreme Court in justifying their return to the Republican fold.

Thus when the campaign did touch on issues, that terrain proved to be favorable to Trump's rhetorical instincts, and he took full advantage. Putting America first, without the exasperating need for compromise, sounded very good to those angered by decades of government decisions that seemed designed to help insiders and establishment elites. Being a political novice actually made Trump more credible, not less. Even though his personal history made him an implausible populist, he was able to claim that the special benefits he had derived from existing policies gave him special knowledge about how to fix them.

Ronald Reagan famously said that there are simple answers—but rarely easy ones. Trump's narrative promised instead both simple answers and easy solutions. He claimed too that he "alone" could provide them. Voters dubious about the present and nervous about the future were ready to believe he could.

"Facts don't do what I want them to," sang David Byrne and Talking Heads in 1980.[42] But in the 2016 campaign, facts were rather more malleable than that. For Hillary Clinton, another line from the same song was perhaps apropos: "Facts are useless in emergencies."

As noted earlier, Trump supporters who came to that position from a reflexive anti-Clinton stance hardly needed evidence to justify their choice. But any facts needed to support any view were readily available to them. The explosion of ideologically targeted information gave new depth to the phenomenon of "narrowcasting" long tracked, and bemoaned, by scholars of political communication.[43]

The rise of national broadcasting in the twentieth century, starting with radio and expanded by network television, had made possible a unifying political conversation grounded in widely held premises. Arguments were usually about policy options, rather than about the facts underlying those choices. This could be constraining, since the agenda was limited and dissenting views not always fully broached. The "mainstream media" that served as gatekeeper frustrated activists of all ideological stripes.

The rise of cable television and especially the Internet, though, provided near-infinite space for political debate (while allowing those with less interest in that debate to avoid it almost entirely). Social media brought billions of people around the world into networked contact. But it also undermined James Madison's defense against "the mischiefs of faction" in *Federalist* No. 10—in a large, federal republic with Facebook, gathering like-minded factions together across geographic space turned out to be rather easy. And social media's egalitarian nature stripped the credential-hungry gatekeepers of the past of their power: Anyone with a Twitter account was, on the face of it, as credible a source as anyone else. It was reassuring to seek out information that told you your instincts were correct, that your preferences were accurate, that anyone with any sense agreed with you. By 2016, the echo-chamber amplification of purely partisan viewpoints, misleading "clickbait" headlines, and straightforwardly false "news" items were the result. Indeed, the last of these were on an industrial scale, some originating from organized Russian efforts to cause mischief in the electoral process.[44]

In short, "facts" were a market rather than a magisterium—and the 2016 election had different meanings depending on which facts you chose to argue from. As a result, making a rational case for or against a given candidate or policy platform was far trickier. Meanwhile candidates (led by, but not solely, Trump) did their best to undermine the credibility of a "mainstream media" that was clearly "biased" and unfair.[45] Statistics—unemployment and crime rates, for instance—were subject to more than the usual mechanisms of manipulation. But even things clearly shown on tape or in print were made subject to doubt, including outright negation reminiscent of the editing of the past envisioned in the novel *1984*. Trump himself said many times that he had opposed the 2003 war in Iraq from the outset (he had not), while in the vice presidential debate Republican nominee Mike Pence confidently denied the existence of multiple claims that had, in truth, been made by his running mate. Pence's approach reduced his Democratic opponent, Tim Kaine, to querulous insistence. It was clear he didn't know how to respond. Neither did Clinton. Nor did the media.

On balance, the Clinton campaign was by far the more truthful, judged by its day-by-day rhetoric.[46] But it was preaching largely to its own choir—and the echo chamber deafened its supporters, too, convincing them that "no one could take the email imbroglio seriously," or that "people surely must realize her fundamental honesty," or that "no equivalence could be drawn" between the scale of the two campaigns' misdeeds. In the end, voters in neither camp heard anything with which they were unlikely to agree—nor anything that would convince them to change sides. Both personality and issues, dragged through this polarizing filter, turned out to reinforce rather than mitigate partisan views.

The President as Minority Leader

All this adds up to a rather disquieting disunity. A superficial glance at the election returns might suggest a new realignment under a resurgent Republican Party that, as of 2017, controlled all branches and levels of government. President Obama's personal popularity had failed to translate into any sort of lasting gains for his party; in fact, there were thirteen fewer Democratic governors and nearly one thousand fewer Democratic state legislators in office eight years after his triumphant first election.

Further, the scope of the Republican victory was so surprising as to energize a GOP policy agenda that had failed to gain veto-proof traction in the Obama years. As Trump said of the House Speaker and Senate majority leader, neither of whom had been outspoken fans of his campaign, "Paul Ryan right now loves me, Mitch McConnell loves me, it's amazing how winning can change things."[47]

True enough. But even before the ballots were counted, political scientists were betting on partisan overreach—and backlash—to come. The early part of the twenty-first century, Morris Fiorina wrote, was reminiscent of the "era of indecision" of the late nineteenth century, when parties were also ideologically homogenous, opposed, and "well-sorted."[48] From 1876 to 1892, only one presidential candidate received more than 50 percent of the national popular vote—and then lost the Electoral College—while party control of Congress fluctuated regularly.[49]

Now, as then, neither party commands a majority, Fiorina argued. (In 2012, in fact, Republicans won a solid House majority while failing to win a plurality of House votes nationally.) "Today's close party divide combined with today's ideologically well-sorted parties" leads to the pursuit of the policies favored by the party's base at the expense of those sought by the handful of unaffiliated voters who carom from party to party in search of satisfaction. One result is "majoritarian instability" and backlash.[50] Even Trump's supra-partisan populism, as we have seen, prevailed only because of lockstep party unity, which meant that it was unclear who owed what, to whom, for his victory. It is certainly hard to claim a presidential mandate while running nearly three million votes behind your opponent in the national popular vote.

On that score—having won just 46 percent of votes overall—Trump is by definition a minority president and, in contrast to George W. Bush in 2000, one without a month-long drama starring hanging chads and divided courts to distract from that result. Trump's patently false post-election claims to have actually won the popular vote "if you deduct the millions of people who voted illegally" only called more attention to the matter.[51]

The question is a broader one, though: Most presidents these days risk being not "tribunes of the people," as Andrew Jackson famously put it, but minority leaders.

To be sure, the presidency was designed not as a bastion of majority rule, but as a check on it. The power of the people's passions was expected to reside in the legislative branch, so powerfully that dividing that branch in half seemed prudent. The presidency would be needed to withstand the "impetuous vortex" of the Congress.[52] In the *Federalist Papers,* Alexander Hamilton denounced the idea of "the servile pliancy of the executive to a prevailing current, either in the community or in the legislature."[53]

More than two centuries later, however, managing the "public presidency" is a huge part of the job of chief executive. And if the president now speaks constantly to the voters—a shift that scholars argue is so important as to represent a "second constitution"[54]—to whom, and for whom, does he speak? Upon closer examination, we might doubt the president's status as a majoritarian leader.

The divergence in 2016 between the electoral and popular votes naturally reenergized the long-standing debate about the virtues of the undemocratic (but quite republican) Electoral College. But even in "normal" elections in which the leading vote-getter does become president, presidents tend to enter office with far less support than the conventional wisdom recalls. In 1980, an election widely remembered as a landslide, Ronald Reagan earned less than 51 percent of the national popular vote. In 1896, a year treated in the political science literature as a sweeping partisan realignment, William McKinley won a whopping 51.1 percent. And so on. The literature on presidential electoral mandates suggests that they are rare, perhaps even "a myth."[55] See, for example, Figure 9.1, which shows that in only thirty of the forty-nine elections from 1824 to 2016 did the winning candidate get even a majority of the popular vote. In just twenty-one of those elections did the new president get more than 52 percent. Less than a quarter of the time (twelve of forty-nine) did the winning candidate receive 55 percent or more of the popular vote.

Thus, most presidents are opposed by at least a substantial minority of the voting public even at the outset of their terms—and presumably some proportion of the large nonvoting public as well. (Since Bill Clinton got 49.2 percent of the popular vote in 1996, for example, with about 50 percent turnout, only a quarter of the adult public could be said to have registered affirmative support for his candidacy.) Certainly Hillary Clinton's turnout gap, compared to Obama's, haunted Democrats in 2016.

The Electoral College helps to paper over these divisions and make the country appear more unified than it is.[56] Memories of Reagan's 1980 landslide are predicated on his stunning tally of 489 electoral votes, 91 percent of the total, not his 50.8 percent of the popular vote. Bill Clinton received 43 percent of the popular vote in 1992, yet nearly 70 percent of the Electoral College vote.

But public opinion data tend to reflect or even lag the vote returns, at least after the proverbial "honeymoon" period presidents typically enjoy. Obama briefly had a 68 percent job approval rating upon his first

Figure 9.1 Popular Vote Share by Winning Presidential Candidates, 1824–2016

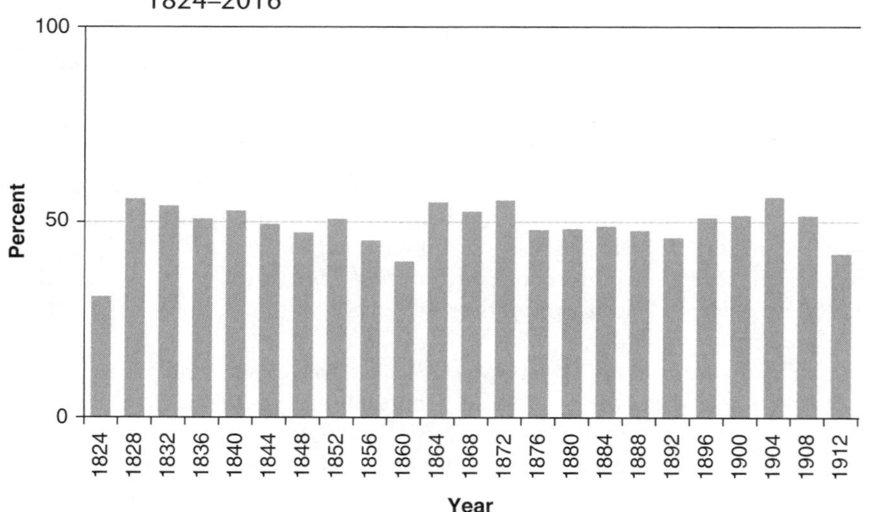

Source: Data from *Dave Leip's Atlas of U.S. Presidential Elections*, uselectionatlas.org.

inauguration in January 2009—but as of late December 2016, average public approval for his entire tenure stood at just 48 percent.[57] George W. Bush's immense jump in job approval on September 12, 2001—from 51 percent to 90 percent—reflected both events and his performance, but in retrospect was clearly anomalous; that 90 percent figure dropped off sharply over time, and his second term approval averaged just 36.5 percent.

Scholars have suggested different rationales for the very consistent trend of increasing disapproval of presidents.[58] What is going on in the nation, and the world, certainly makes up part of the explanation. Additionally, though, as presidents make decisions in office, they necessarily create policy winners and losers. Losers tend to be unhappy. The aggregation of angry minorities eventually forms a majority, or close to it. And so every president from Lyndon B. Johnson through Barack Obama saw their approval drop below 40 percent at some point—four of them (Nixon, Carter, and both Bushes) below 30 percent. Average approval over the past fifty-plus years (that is, since Lyndon B. Johnson's 1965 inauguration) is barely 51 percent.

Thus, contemporary presidents can realistically expect to have at best only half of the public behind them during their term. And even this figure disguises deep division, since presidential approval in recent years has become highly polarized. George W. Bush famously claimed to be a "uniter, not a divider," but the gap between Republican and Democratic voters in judging Bush was often more than 70 percentage points. Political scientist Gary Jacobson found that Bush provoked "the widest partisan divisions among ordinary Americans regarding any . . . president since the advent of

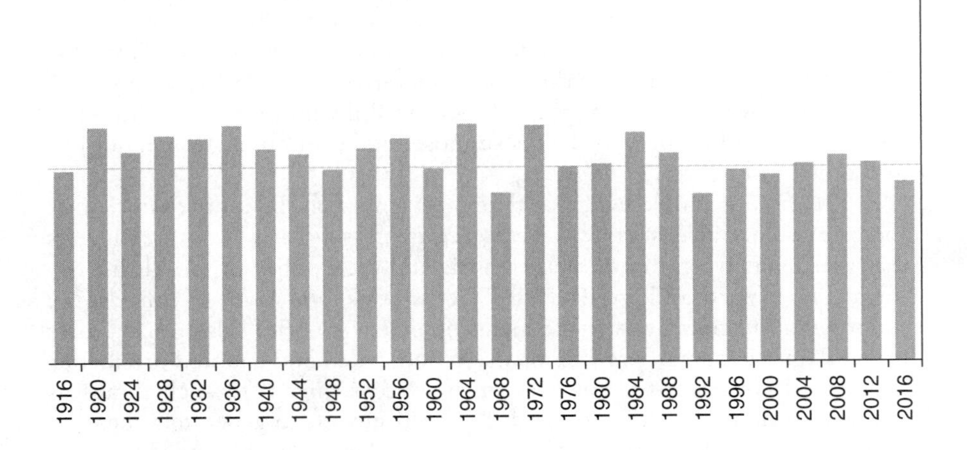

scientific survey research on such questions more than sixty years ago."[59] Or at least the widest divisions until Barack Obama took office. Obama likewise hoped to transcend red states and blue states in favor of the United States, but Jacobson discovered the same pattern of polarized approval, though of course one that flipped the party labels at each pole.[60] A year into Obama's administration, 82 percent of Democrats approved of his job performance, but only 18 percent of Republicans shared that sentiment. And even as Obama's overall ratings trickled upward as his second term wound down, the partisan gap only grew: On election day 2016, 91 percent of Democrats approved of the president, but only 11 percent of Republicans did the same.

Trump's challenge is perhaps even greater, given the relentlessly negative tone of his campaign and the scope of the conspiring forces he claimed had organized against him—"banking institutions, the judiciary, media conglomerates, voting security experts, Democratic tricksters, scientific polling and also perhaps military leaders."[61] As his presidency began, his approval rating was at a historically low 45 percent.[62]

Still, when Trump claimed victory in the predawn hours of November 9, he struck a statesmanlike, conciliatory tone: "It's time for America to bind the wounds of division. . . . To all Republicans and Democrats and independents across this nation, I say it is time for us to come together as one united people. . . . I pledge to every citizen of our land that I will be president for all Americans, and this is so important to me. For those who have chosen not to support me in the past, of which there were a few people [laughter], I'm reaching out to you for your guidance and your help so that we can work together and unify our great country."[63]

In offering these words, Trump echoed the rhetoric of his immediate predecessor—who on election night 2008 promised those Americans whose vote he had not won that "I hear your voices, I need your help, and I will be your President too"—as well as of presidents throughout history.[64] "We are all Republicans, we are all Federalists," Thomas Jefferson proclaimed in 1801.[65] "The President is the direct representative of the American people," Andrew Jackson told Congress in 1834.[66] As Bill Clinton put it in an interview late in 2000, "the president is supposed to be a unifying force, not just in rhetoric but in fact."[67]

Yet there is ample evidence that presidents may be unifiers in neither rhetoric nor fact, at least in recent years. A growing scholarly literature suggests that presidents weight both their rhetoric and their policy proposals heavily toward their partisan base. B. Dan Wood's book *The Myth of Presidential Representation* gives away that conclusion in its very title.[68] Using sixty years of the *Public Papers of the Presidents*, Wood coded and counted presidents' liberal and conservative sentences in nine areas, linked to such things as military spending, health care, and the environment, to generate a measure of presidential policy attitudes. He found that these converge very little with measures of the "national mood" that others have calculated concerning the same policy arenas for the same time frame. Instead, presidents' utterances typically reflect their partisan constituency. Rather than change their positions to accommodate the political center, presidents try to persuade people near the center to adopt their own presidential preferences.[69] In this, they tend to be unsuccessful—as George Edwards has found, presidential persuasion works mostly when the president's missives fit existing public opinion. Otherwise, Oval Office rhetoric largely falls "on deaf ears."[70]

Other studies using different data find roughly similar sorts of presidential targeting. Matthew Eshbaugh-Soha and Brandon Rottinghaus conclude that presidents' policy proposals are more heavily weighted toward their partisan base than toward the center of public opinion by about a five-to-four margin, and that this ratio increases as polarization does. That is, as approval from presidential co-partisans rises, so does the likelihood of presidents increasing their partisan position-taking.[71] This conclusion is congruent with a recent study of mandate rhetoric that finds both an increase in its use since 1969 and also a key shift in its content. Since Nixon, "the emphasis is less on 'the people' than on distinctions between the candidates and the campaign promises made by the winner."[72] That is, mandate claims are increasingly used instrumentally, to support particular policies supported by the president's co-partisans. Those promised policies may not be supported by a wide majority (or any majority at all).

Empirical evidence that "follows the money" also supports this insight. A wave of recent research has shown that presidents use their authority over federal grants and budgeting to target geographic areas most useful to their political allies. Studies show that "presidential pork" is widespread, that a "particularistic president" targets discretionary federal funds and grants toward areas (even at the county level) providing political support, and that as presidential travel has increased, it has been to places that further the administration's immediate partisan concerns.[73]

Thus it would take a major effort by any new president to lay claim to the status of majority leader, and president-elect Trump's first wave of postelection tweets, campaign-style pep rallies, and proposed cabinet nominations did not suggest much commitment to that path. Precedent suggests instead that while claiming to be the people's tribune, the new president will define "the people" in a rather partisan manner. Put another way, common ground is visible only if presidents look for it—and despite their rhetoric, they rarely have such broad support that they have reason to do so.

Again, if this partisan presidency superficially reflects the anti-majoritarian roots of the presidential office, it does so in an era when broad public legitimacy is a crucial part of presidential power. The risk of the presidency following the track of the media from broadcast news to narrowcast subscription is troubling—but may well be a trend hardened by the results of the 2016 election. It may even be part of its lasting legacy.

Looking Back, and Ahead

E pluribus unum has always been a difficult motto for a diverse nation to live up to, and the 2016 election has put American fealty to it to the test. This came home to me on a beautiful fall day in late September, when I found myself in picturesque Spring Run, Pennsylvania, in search of gas. Spring Run, home to 568 registered voters, is four miles north of the Pennsylvania Turnpike, sixty miles (and an intervening mountain range) west of Harrisburg, and a million miles away from East Coast cosmopolitanism.

More than 85 percent of Spring Run's voters endorsed Donald Trump on election day, six weeks after my visit. One needed no skill in punditry to predict that outcome: When I went into the single building that served as general store, café, post office, and gas station, the décor was not institutional beige. Instead, in every booth of the restaurant and on every wall of the retail store was a Donald Trump sign. Between them hung homemade "Hillary for Jail" posters. And covering the ceiling was an enormous Confederate flag.

There is a plausible argument consistent with this chapter that party affiliation mattered so much (and Clinton inspired so little) that any GOP candidate would have won the 2016 election. Yet that flag was a common enough companion to Trump signs, even well north of the Mason-Dixon line, to make the case that it did in fact matter who was nominated. It is far harder to imagine Jeb Bush retweeting the views of white supremacists or turning to the head of the so-called alt-right news industry to run his campaign. That, in turn, spurned its own outrage and overreach. One distressing meaning of the 2016 election, in short, is that a disconcerting number of Americans hate each other, and the Clinton-Trump contest made it acceptable, even noble, to express that fact.

Yet the divides the campaign exposed were rarely along clear moral fault lines. Inequality is not simply a matter of race, but of class—in a nation that had long told itself it had only a universal middle class. There is inequality of geography. Inequality of opportunity. And it became clear that these dimensions have been correlated in ways that effectively discarded large swaths of the country. In a battle of the future versus the past, the past won.

That cannot be allowed to stand as the ultimate outcome, and the challenge for our leaders will be to bring those whom the system has left behind to a place where the future brings opportunity rather than fear. That requires building new coalitions rather than clinging to past clichés. Bending that curve will be hard for anyone. It would have been especially hard for whichever minority leader won the election of 2016, with one segment of the population wildly enthusiastic, one distrustful and resentful.

That returns us to the Time for Change model that proved so accurate in forecasting the election result. America rolled the dice in 2016—and the result is a high-stakes experiment in the making, producing the first president with no experience in government or governance, who ran on no clear ideological vision but on business acumen derived from widespread and less-than-transparent global corporate interests. It was change, for sure, albeit superimposed on a mass of incumbency and entrenched interests. Could it achieve change for the better? Disheartening campaigns of the past did indeed produce presidents who rose to the occasion, even to greatness.

Yet scholars of public administration have long proclaimed that "running government like a business" is a dubious proposition; the greatest student of the presidency, Richard Neustadt, likewise wrote that the "presidency is no place for amateurs."[74] As a divided America awaited the Trump administration, it hoped those maxims would be proven wrong. Still, one thing was certain. As George Washington informed his protégé in the hit musical of 2016, *Hamilton*: "Winning was easy, young man—governing's harder."

Notes

1. Alan Abramowitz, "Will Time for Change Mean Time for Trump?" *PS: Political Science and Politics* 49 (October 2016): 659–660.
2. "Econometric Models," *Pollyvote* blog, n.d., pollyvote.com/en/components/econometric-models/.
3. Larry Bartels, "2016 Was an Ordinary Election, Not a Realignment," *Washington Post*, "Monkey Cage" blog, November 10, 2016, www.washingtonpost.com/news/monkey-cage/wp/2016/11/10/2016-was-an-ordinary-election-not-a-realignment/.
4. David R. Mayhew, "The Meaning of the 2012 Election," in Michael Nelson, ed., *The Elections of 2012* (Washington, D.C.: Sage/CQ Press, 2013), 204–205. Mayhew excludes 1824, when there was no serious two-party competition, from this calculation. But one could plausibly see 1824 winner John Quincy Adams as a greater continuation of the current regime than his rival Andrew Jackson would have been—if so, that makes the count 13–12 rather than 13–11 in favor of the "out party" in such elections.
5. Bartels, "2016 Was an Ordinary Election, Not a Realignment."
6. As of December 28, 2016. For the forecasts, see James E. Campbell, ed., "Symposium: Forecasting the 2016 American National Elections," *PS: Political Science and Politics* 49 (October 2016): 649–690.

7. See, for example, Democratic pollster Celinda Lake's version, in James Hohmann, "Democrats Angry That Clinton Had No Economic Message," *Washington Post*, "The Daily 202" blog, link.washingtonpost.com/view/544d9b843b35d04a52943ddf4umeo.44pr/6caea881.
8. John Sides and Lynn Vavreck, *The Gamble: Choice and Chance in the 2012 Election* (Princeton, N.J.: Princeton University Press, 2013), 1; and see, as an exemplar of the journalistic genre, John Heilemann and Mark Halperin, *Game Change* (New York: HarperCollins, 2010).
9. Joshua Darr, "Where Clinton Is Setting Up Field Offices—and Trump Isn't," *FiveThirtyEight,* October 7, 2016, fivethirtyeight.com/features/trump-clinton-field-offices/.
10. Sam Stein, "Clinton Camp Mastered the Science of Politics, but Forgot the Art, Staffers Say," *Huffington Post*, November 21, 2016, www.huffingtonpost.com/entry/clinton-campaign-politics_us_5833866de4b030997bc10520; and Edward-Isaac Dovere, "How Clinton Lost Michigan—and Blew the Election," *Politico*, December 14, 2016, www.politico.com/story/2016/12/michigan-hillary-clinton-trump-232547.
11. Thanks to Brendan Nyhan of Dartmouth College for suggesting (a slightly different version of) this phrase.
12. From a Survey Monkey poll taken October 3–9; and see Nate Silver, "Election Update: Trump May Depress Republican Turnout, Spelling Disaster for the GOP," *FiveThirtyEight,* October 23, 2016, fivethirtyeight.com/features/election-update-trump-may-depress-republican-turnout-spelling-disaster-for-the-gop/, which places the Republican figure overall at just under 80 percent.
13. Silver, "Trump May Depress Republican Turnout."
14. Johnson received about 3.25 percent and Stein just 1 percent of the national vote. Other minor-party candidates and write-ins made up another 1.75 percent of the vote. It is probably worth noting, though, that in Michigan, Pennsylvania, and Wisconsin the left-leaning Stein's vote tally was larger in each state than the gap between Trump and Clinton.
15. All 2016 exit poll data cited here are from the surveys conducted by Edison Research for the National Election Pool. The results can be found on various media outlets, including at www.cnn.com/election/results/exit-polls. Data comparing 2016 to past elections are available in Alec Tyson and Shiva Maniam, "Behind Trump's Victory: Divisions by Race, Gender, Education," Pew Research Center, November 9, 2016, www.pewresearch.org/fact-tank/2016/11/09/behind-trumps-victory-divisions-by-race-gender-education/.
16. Harry Enten, "Men Are Treating 2016 as a 'Normal' Election; Women Aren't," *FiveThirtyEight,* October 17, 2016, fivethirtyeight.com/features/men-are-treating-2016-as-a-normal-election-women-arent/.
17. Utah was the only significant outlier here. The candidacy of Evan McMullin, a conservative Mormon with national security credentials, attracted 21.6 percent of the vote there (amounting to more than 40 percent of McMullin's national vote total).
18. Howard Kurtz, "Party Disunity? Cruz's 'Me' Moment Is the Latest Distraction at Trump's Convention," *Fox News.com*, July 21, 2016, www.foxnews.com/politics/2016/07/21/party-disunity-cruzs-me-moment-is-latest-distraction-at-trumps-convention.html.
19. See, for example, James E. Campbell, *Polarized: Making Sense of a Divided America* (Princeton, N.J.: Princeton University Press, 2016).
20. "Remarks of President Barack Obama—State of the Union Address, as Delivered," Office of the White House Press Secretary, January 13, 2016, www.whitehouse.gov/the-press-office/2016/01/12/remarks-president-barack-obama-%E2%80%93-prepared-delivery-state-union-address.

21. Marc J. Hetherington and Thomas J. Rudolph, *Why Washington Won't Work: Polarization, Political Trust, and the Governing Crisis* (Chicago: University of Chicago Press, 2015).
22. Dave Weigel, "GOP Voters Warm to Russia, Putin, Wikileaks, Poll Finds," *Washington Post*, December 14, 2016, www.washingtonpost.com/news/post-politics/wp/2016/12/14/gop-voters-warm-to-russia-putin-wikileaks-poll-finds/.
23. Marc J. Hetherington, "POLisci: Why Washington Won't Work," *Cook Political Report,* September 15, 2015, cookpolitical.com/story/8857.
24. Daniel Dale, "Hillary Clinton Faces Intense Animosity as She Approaches the White House," *Toronto Star*, October 30, 2016, www.thestar.com/news/world/2016/10/30/hillary-clinton-faces-intense-animosity-as-she-approaches-white-house.html.
25. Andrew Rudalevige, "The Broken Places," in Michael Nelson, Barbara Perry, and Russell Riley, eds., *42: Inside the Presidency of Bill Clinton* (Ithaca, N.Y.: Cornell University Press, 2016).
26. Dale, "Hillary Clinton Faces Intense Animosity as She Approaches the White House."
27. When one page of one return was leaked to the *New York Times*, revealing a $900 million loss that year, Trump shrugged off the implication of this for his business acumen and simply said that his ability to avoid paying taxes "makes me smart."
28. Kyle Cheney et al., "Donald Trump's Week of Misrepresentations, Exaggerations, and Half-Truths," *Politico,* September 25, 2016, www.politico.com/magazine/story/2016/09/2016-donald-trump-fact-check-week-214287.
29. Julie Zauzmer, "Hopeful and Relieved, Conservative White Evangelicals See Trump Win as Their Own," *Washington Post,* November 15, 2016, www.washingtonpost.com/news/acts-of-faith/wp/2016/11/15/hopeful-and-relieved-evangelicals-see-trumps-win-as-their-own/.
30. Dale, "Hillary Clinton."
31. Only 52 percent said she was qualified, 47 percent that she was not.
32. Lynn Vavreck, "Candidates Fed a Focus on Character over Policy," *New York Times,* November 25, 2016, A16.
33. The top six ads aired in aggregate 117,143 times, while number seven ("How To") was aired 11,642 times. Many thanks to Mike Franz for providing 2016 advertising data as compiled by the Wesleyan Media Project.
34. David Maraniss, "The Clintons Were Undone by the Middle American Voters They Once Knew So Well," *Washington Post,* November 9, 2016, www.washingtonpost.com/politics/the-clintons-were-undone-by-the-middle-american-voters-they-once-knew-so-well/2016/11/09/a6d1ae42-a6ad-11e6-8042-f4d111c862d1_story.html.
35. See, for example, the Trump campaign website, including the "Economy" section and the text of Trump's speech on jobs on September 15, 2016, www.donaldjtrump.com/press-releases/trump-delivers-speech-on-jobs-at-new-york-economic-club.
36. Vavreck, "Candidates Fed a Focus on Character over Policy."
37. Data from Wesleyan Media Project courtesy of Mike Franz.
38. Brookings Institution study summarized by Jim Tankersley, "Donald Trump Lost Most of the American Economy in This Election," *Washington Post,* "Wonkblog," November 22, 2016, www.washingtonpost.com/news/wonk/wp/2016/11/22/donald-trump-lost-most-of-the-american-economy-in-this-election/.
39. Of course, the two were not unrelated. The week before the election, only 16 percent of GOP voters said the economy was improving, and 81 percent that it was in decline. The week after, a 49- to 44-percent plurality of Republicans had decided the economy was in fact heading upwards. See Justin McCarthy and Jeffery Jones, "U.S. Economic Confidence Surges after Election," *Gallup*, November 15, 2016, www.gallup.com/poll/197474/economic-confidence-surges-election.aspx.

40. "The New Political Divide," *The Economist,* July 30, 2016, www.economist.com/news/leaders/21702750-farewell-left-versus-right-contest-matters-now-open-against-closed-new.
41. Loren Collingwood, "The County-by-County Data on Trump Voters Showed Why He Won," *Washington Post*, "Monkey Cage" blog, November 19, 2016, www.washingtonpost.com/news/monkey-cage/wp/2016/11/19/the-country-by-county-data-on-trump-voters-shows-why-he-won/; see also Clare Malone, "One Pennsylvania County Sees the Future, and Not Everyone Likes It," *FiveThirtyEight,* October 17, 2016, fivethirtyeight.com/features/one-pennsylvania-county-sees-the-future-and-not-everyone-likes-it/.
42. Talking Heads, "Crosseyed and Painless," from the album *Remain in Light.*
43. For example, Wilson Cary McWilliams, "The Meaning of the Election: Ownership and Citizenship in American Life," in Michael Nelson, ed., *The Elections of 2004* (Washington, D.C.: CQ Press, 2005), 192.
44. Craig Timberg, "Russian Propaganda Effort Helped Spread 'Fake News' during the Election, Experts Say," *Washington Post,* November 24, 2016, www.washingtonpost.com/business/economy/russian-propaganda-effort-helped-spread-fake-news-during-election-experts-say/2016/11/24/793903b6-8a40-4ca9-b712-716af66098fe_story.html.
45. Jim Rutenberg, "Fair Play in a Fact-Challenged Political Landscape," *New York Times,* July 3, 2016, www.nytimes.com/2016/07/04/business/media/fair-play-in-a-fact-challenged-political-landscape.html.
46. Cheney et al., "Donald Trump's Week"; and "The 2016 Election Factchecker," *Washington Post,* November 3, 2016, www.washingtonpost.com/graphics/politics/2016-election/fact-checker/.
47. "Donald Trump's *New York Times* Interview: Full Transcript," *New York Times,* November 23, 2016, www.nytimes.com/2016/11/23/us/politics/trump-new-york-times-interview-transcript.html.
48. Morris P. Fiorina, "Party Sorting and Democratic Politics," *Contemporary American Politics* No. 4 (Fall 2016), Hoover Institution, Stanford University.
49. It is of course rather hard to know who won what in the 1876 election, where a series of disputed electoral votes were assigned by strict party-line votes by a special commission, and charges of popular vote corruption were rampant.
50. Morris P. Fiorina, "The Temptation to Overreach," *Contemporary American Politics* No. 5 (Fall 2016), Hoover Institution, Stanford University.
51. Glenn Kessler, "Factchecker: Donald Trump's Bogus Claim That Millions of People Voted Illegally for Hillary Clinton," *Washington Post*, November 28, 2016, www.washingtonpost.com/news/fact-checker/wp/2016/11/27/trumps-bogus-claim-that-millions-of-people-voted-illegally-for-hillary-clinton/.
52. *Federalist* No. 48.
53. *Federalist* No. 71.
54. Jeffrey Tulis, *The Rhetorical Presidency* (Princeton, N.J.: Princeton University Press, 1987), 17–20, 128; and Tulis, "The Two Constitutional Presidencies," in Michael Nelson, ed., *The Presidency and the Political System*, 10th ed. (Washington, D.C.: Sage/CQ Press, 2014), 1–32.
55. See Lawrence J. Grossback, David A. M. Peterson, and James A. Stimson, *Mandate Politics* (New York: Cambridge University Press, 2006); and Robert Dahl, "The Myth of the Presidential Mandate," *Political Science Quarterly* 105 (Autumn 1990): 355–372.
56. Judith Best, "Presidential Selection: Complex Problems and Simple Solutions," *Political Science Quarterly* 119 (Spring 2004): 39–59.
57. The Gallup Organization has asked the same question ("Do you approve or disapprove of the job X is doing as president?") since the 1940s. See www.gallup.com/poll/124922/presidential-approval-center.aspx, the source for data in this section.

58. John Mueller, *War, Presidents, and Public Opinion* (New York: Wiley, 1973); Richard Brody, *Assessing the President* (Palo Alto, Calif.: Stanford University Press, 1991); Paul Brace and Barbara Hinckley, *Follow the Leader* (New York: Basic Books, 1992); Paul Gronke and Brian Newman, "FDR to Clinton, Mueller to?: A Field Essay on Presidential Approval," *Political Research Quarterly* 56 (2003): 501–512; and Diane Heith, "The Presidency and Public Opinion," in Lori Cox Han, ed., *New Directions in the American Presidency* (New York: Routledge, 2011).
59. Gary C. Jacobson, "George W. Bush, Polarization, and the War in Iraq," in Bert Rockman, Colin Campbell, and Andrew Rudalevige, eds., *The George W. Bush Legacy* (Washington, D.C.: CQ Press/Sage, 2008), 62.
60. Gary C. Jacobson, "Polarization, Public Opinion, and the Presidency: The Obama and Anti-Obama Coalitions," in Bert Rockman, Andrew Rudalevige, and Colin Campbell, eds., *The Obama Presidency: Appraisals and Prospects* (Washington, D.C.: CQ Press/Sage, 2012).
61. Jose DelReal and Sean Sullivan, "Facing Potential Loss, Trump Expands the List of Conspirators Plotting against Him," *Washington Post,* October 28, 2016, www.washingtonpost.com/politics/facing-potential-loss-trump-expands-the-list-of-conspirators-plotting-against-him/2016/10/27/7177c1ba-9ba8-11e6-9980-50913d68eacb_story.html.
62. Gallup poll conducted January 20–22, 2017, http://www.gallup.com/poll/202811/trump-sets-new-low-point-inaugural-approval-rating.aspx.
63. "Transcript: Donald Trump's Victory Speech," *New York Times,* November 9, 2016, www.nytimes.com/2016/11/10/us/politics/trump-speech-transcript.html.
64. Julia Azari, *Delivering the People's Message: The Changing Politics of the Presidential Mandate* (Ithaca, N.Y.: Cornell University Press, 2014), 154.
65. Jefferson's first inaugural address.
66. Jackson's "Protest" to the Senate, quoted in Sidney M. Milkis and Michael Nelson, *The American Presidency: Origins and Development*, 6th ed. (Washington, D.C.: Sage/CQ Press, 2012), 133.
67. Quoted in Michael Paterniti, "Bill Clinton: The Exit Interview," *Esquire* (December 2000), www.esquire.com/features/exit-interview-clinton-1200.
68. B. Dan Wood, *The Myth of Presidential Representation* (New York: Cambridge University Press, 2009).
69. Further, for a similar conclusion from very different empirical analysis, see James Druckman and Lawrence Jacobs, *Who Governs?: Presidents, Public Opinion, and Manipulation* (Chicago: University of Chicago Press, 2015).
70. George C. Edwards, III, *On Deaf Ears: The Limits of the Bully Pulpit* (New Haven, Conn.: Yale University Press, 2006); see also Brandice Canes-Wrone, *Who Leads Whom? Presidents, Policy, and the Public* (Chicago: University of Chicago Press, 2005).
71. Matthew Eshbaugh-Soha and Brandon Rottinghaus, "Presidential Position-Taking and the Puzzle of Representation," *Presidential Studies Quarterly* 43 (March 2013): 1–15; see also Jeffrey E. Cohen, *The President's Legislative Policy Agenda* (New York: Cambridge University Press, 2012).
72. Azari, *Delivering the People's Message*, 7.
73. John Hudak, *Presidential Pork: White House Influence over the Distribution of Federal Grants* (Washington, D.C.: Brookings Institution, 2014); Douglas Kriner and Andrew Reeves, *The Particularistic President* (New York: Cambridge University Press, 2015); and Brendan J. Doherty, *The Rise of the President's Permanent Campaign* (Lawrence: University Press of Kansas, 2012).
74. See, for example, James Q. Wilson, *Bureaucracy* (New York: Basic Books, 1989); and Richard E. Neustadt, *Presidential Power* (New York: Wiley, 1960), 180.